The Social Fabric

DAVID ZALEWSKI

THE SOCIAL FABRIC

American Life from 1607 to 1877

FOURTH EDITION

Editors

JOHN H. CARY   *Cleveland State University*

JULIUS WEINBERG   *Cleveland State University*

DAVID ZALEWSKI

LITTLE, BROWN AND COMPANY   *Boston   Toronto*

Library of Congress Cataloging in Publication Data
Main entry under title:

The Social fabric.

   Includes bibliographies.
   Contents: v. 1. American life from 1607 to 1877 —
v. 2. American life from the Civil War to the present.
   1. United States — Social conditions. I. Cary,
John H. (John Henry), 1926–   . II. Weinberg, Julius,
1922–   .
HN57.S623   1983   306′.0973   83–17563
ISBN 0–316–13072–9 (v. 1)
ISBN 0–316–13073–7 (v. 2)

Library of Congress Catalog Card Number 83–17563

ISBN 0-316-13072-9

9 8 7 6 5 4 3 2

ALP

Published simultaneously in Canada
by Little, Brown & Company (Canada) Limited

Printed in the United States of America

Cover illustration: Edward Hicks, "The Residence of David Twining," 1787, The
Abby Aldrich Rockefeller Folk Art Center, Williamsburg, Virginia

Dedicated with love to

Kathryn Ditter Cary

and to Sean, Paul, Kenneth, and Carolyn

DAVID ZALEWSKI

Preface

> I know histhry isn't thrue Hinnessy, because it ain't like what I see ivry day in Halsted Sthreet. If any wan comes along with a histhry iv Greece or Rome that'll show me th' people fightin', gettin' dhrunk, makin' love, gettin' married, owin' the grocery man an' bein' without hard-coal, I'll believe they was a Greece or Rome, but not befure.

The sentiment of Mr. Dooley, Finley Peter Dunne's comic Irish philosopher, expresses the attitude of many people toward history. Young Americans, especially, question the relevance of a history that deals only with politics, diplomacy, governments, and famous leaders, and ignores the daily life of average men and women. Two recent trends, however, are doing much to remedy this neglect. One is increased popular interest in the forgotten mass of men and women who tilled our fields, built our cities, and fought our wars, but who achieved no particular fame and left very little record of their lives and thought. The second development is the renewed concern of historians with social history.

This kind of history has more meaning for us, and touches our lives more directly, than any other aspect of our past. In an age seeking "relevance" nothing is more relevant than American social history. Each of us has direct experience, or an intimate awareness, of being part of a family, of falling in love and marrying, of poverty and pain, of suffering in war, of earning a living, of social oppression and reform. By understanding the social life of an earlier age, we can gain an understanding of ourselves and of others, in whatever time or place they lived.

This is an anthology of American social history for college history courses. It began with our belief that college students would find more meaning in the kind of history described by Mr. Dooley than in political, diplomatic, or constitutional history. This and the companion volume of *The Social Fabric,* which covers the period from 1865 to the present, touch upon marrying and making love, fighting and getting drunk, owing the grocer, and going without heat. Covering the time from the earliest settlement of America to Reconstruction, it contains descriptions of what it was like to cross the ocean in an immigrant ship and the Great Plains in a covered wagon, what marriage and the family were like in the seventeenth century and what sex was like in the nineteenth, what life was like for women workers in New England factories and for slaves on southern plantations, and how people behaved in a frontier revival meeting or in an austere Shaker community.

No single book can treat every aspect of our history, but these volumes examine American life in much of its diversity. There are essays on women as well as men, on Indians and blacks as well as whites, and on the poor and the oppressed as well as the rich and the powerful. The sectional, class, racial, and religious differences among our heterogeneous people have created serious strains that at times threatened to tear the nation apart. But with all their diversity, the American people have also shared many common attitudes and traditions that provided a common social fabric to bind them together.

We have selected the readings from some of the most interesting writing on the American past. We have prefaced each reading with an introductory note, explaining the relation of the subject to broader developments in American history of the period. Each selection is also accompanied by an illustration, which provides a visual commentary on the topic under consideration. The study guide that follows the selection will help you review the special aspects of the reading, and may suggest issues for class discussion. The bibliographical note will help you find further material, should you wish to read more on the topic.

The Fourth Edition

This new edition of *The Social Fabric* features very extensive changes in volume I, with nine new articles included. We have been assisted by the questionnaires, printed at the end of each volume, which many student readers have sent to the publisher, as well as the suggestions and criticisms of teachers who have used the book. One suggestion, from teachers who divide the American history course at 1877 rather than 1865, was to include the first selection of volume II, by Joel Williamson, as the last selection in volume I. We have done this, without dropping any of the twenty other topics treated.

Some readers felt that the selection on marriage in colonial Virginia was charming and informative; others suggested that we substitute a more recent work. In this edition, we have included a new selection by Lyle Koehler on women and children in seventeenth-century New England. We have omitted the essay on the New England town, and have strengthened the readings on the American Revolution by introducing a selection from Charles Royster's highly regarded study to complement Wallace Brown's popular essay on the Loyalists. There is also a new selection by Everett Dick on the Second Great Awakening that is a somewhat broader treatment of religion on the frontier than was presented in the third edition.

The section on the Age of Jackson has been retitled "The Age of Reform," and an article on the temperance crusade by Mark Lender and James Martin has been added. In place of an article on crime and law enforcement in the nineteenth century, we have introduced a selection from Michael Feldberg's book on crowds and riots in Jacksonian America. The graphic article on the Donner Party, which many students liked, has been replaced by a selection from John D. Unruh's recent revisionist study of the western migration that is more representative of the experiences of most migrants. A number of teachers felt that the antislavery crusade should be covered in this volume; we have included a selection from Robert Abzug's recent biography of Theodore Dwight Weld. The selection that concluded the third edition of volume I was a description of the life of Johnny Reb and Billy Yank during the American Civil War. Fond as we were of this selection, we agreed with those readers who suggested that it romanticized that great national conflict, and we have substituted a very different article by one of the most distinguished American historians, Allan Nevins.

The response of students and teachers in both four-year colleges and community colleges to this anthology has been most gratifying. A number of teachers who used the earlier editions of *The Social Fabric* in introductory courses have indicated that these volumes rank with the most successful supplementary materials they have ever used. We hope that the revisions in the fourth edition make them even more useful in American history courses.

J.C.
J.W.

Contents

V WESTERN EXPANSION AND CIVIL WAR

The Social Fabric

1 COLONIAL AMERICANS

All Americans are descended from ancestors who came to the western hemisphere from other parts of the world in what was to be the largest migration of people in recorded history. For some 15,000 years, the land we know as the United States was inhabited by Indian peoples who had crossed from northern Asia to Alaska and made their way across both American continents. When Jamestown, Virginia was founded in 1607, the Indian population of North America may have numbered 500,000 to 1,500,000 people, thinly scattered in tribes from the warlike Iroquois hunters of the Northeast to the pueblo dwellers of the Southwest.

During the next two centuries, one tribe after another encountered invaders from England and other European countries who brought very different social values, technological developments, agricultural traditions, governmental institutions, and diseases with them. The Europeans also brought hundreds of thousands of African slaves to the New World, and the encounter of these three peoples makes up much of the sometimes tragic and occasionally brutal history of early America. People of English descent comprised half of the population of newcomers by the end of the eighteenth century, and the colonies had been under the English government. Thus, English influences were naturally predominant in shaping colonial institutions and social life. However, Africans and continental Europeans comprised the other half of the population, and their language, religion, and social attitudes modified English institutions and contributed significantly to the rich variety of American society.

The first article in this section depicts the life and culture of the Seneca Indians in the eighteenth century, by which time all of the eastern Indian tribes had suffered serious consequences from the European invasion of their lands. The selection describes the power of women in Seneca society, the way in which parents raised their children, and their attitudes toward crime, war, and other social questions. The second reading treats the conditions of slavery in Virginia, the complex relationship that existed between master and slave, and the ways in which slaves rebelled at their enslavement. It would seem that Europeans of the seventeenth and eighteenth centuries had some peculiar ideas about their own superiority and the inferiority of other peoples to be able to self-righteously dispossess the Indians from their homelands and to enslave millions of Africans. The third essay may provide some indirect evidence of this sort of thinking, for it concerns the New England male's assumption of his own superiority and the divine law of women's submissiveness. Of course, conflict in colonial America was not always between different ethnic or racial groups. The last reading describes the conflict within New England society that we know as the Salem witchcraft trials. In this affair, once again, some members of society were so confident of the rightness of their views that they accused hundreds of people of witchcraft and put twenty men and women to death to clear New England of the Devil.

3

*Bertoli's 1796 portrait of Cornplanter (Ki-on-twog-ky) reflects
European influence on the clothing and weapons of the Seneca.*

1

ANTHONY F. C. WALLACE

Indian Life and Culture

In order to understand the history of the United States, we must look to two remote cultures — the European world in the fifteenth century, on the eve of the discovery of the Western Hemisphere, and the ancient Indian culture that existed on this side of the Atlantic. The red man has lived on this continent for about 20,000 years and has been in contact with Europeans and Africans for nearly five hundred years. Yet most Americans know little about Indian life and culture. The movie image of a treacherous savage and the trinket purchased at a souvenir shop have left the real character of the Indian as invisible to the white majority as that of the black man has been for more than three hundred years.

Oliver La Farge has suggested that the Indian has always been unknown to more recently arrived fellow countrymen, because of a number of myths that whites found it convenient to believe. The earliest of these myths — picturing the Indian as a noble, uncorrupted child of nature — survived in distant Europe longer than it did in the British colonies. Here, as settlers pushed inland and came into conflict with the Indian over land, the more convenient myth of the brutal, treacherous savage supplanted it. Eventually, as industrialized America pushed the Indian tribes onto reservations, a third myth, that of a drunken, irresponsible dependent, became popular.

Anthropologists and historians have been devoting serious attention to the American Indian since Lewis Henry Morgan published a path-breaking study of the Iroquois in 1851. Yet, much of the writing has necessarily been based on a record left by whites, has dealt mostly with Indian-white relations, and leaves one wondering what Indian life looked like from the inside. In fact, Indian life was somewhat different in different historical periods, and it varied considerably from the warlike tribes of the Northeast to the buffalo hunters of the Plains and the pueblo peoples of the Southwest.

Anthony F. C. Wallace is one of the leading students of the Iroquois. His book, *The Death and Rebirth of the Seneca,* is a remarkable study of the devastating effects of European influences on this Iroquois tribe and of the attempt of the prophet Handsome Lake to renew the spirit of his people. The following selection is a general introduction to the Seneca in the eighteenth century. Wallace describes their farming, hunting, warfare, marriage, and training of children, and thus conveys a sense of the fierce independence and loyalty of these earliest Americans.

. . . The traditional Iroquois dwelling unit was called a longhouse. It was a dark, noisy, smoke-filled family barracks; a rectangular, gable-roofed structure anywhere from fifty to seventy-five feet in length, constructed of sheets of elm bark lashed on stout poles, housing up to fifty or sixty people. The roof was slotted (sometimes with a sliding panel for rainy days) to let out some of the smoke that eddied about the ceiling. There was only one entrance, sometimes fitted with a wooden or bark door on wooden hinges, and sometimes merely curtained by a bearskin robe. Entering, one gazed in the half-light down a long, broad corridor or alleyway, in the center of which, every twelve or fifteen feet, smoldered a small fire. On opposite sides of each fire, facing one another, were double-decker bunks, six feet wide and about twelve feet long. An entire family — mother, father, children, and various other relatives — might occupy one or two of these compartments. They slept on soft furs in the lower bunks. Guns, masks, moccasins, clothing, cosmetic paint, wampum, knives, hatchet, food, and the rest of a Seneca family's paraphernalia were slung on the walls and on the upper bunk. Kettles, braided corn, and other suspendable items hung from the joists, which also supported pots over the fire. Each family had about as much room for permanent quarters as might be needed for all of them to lie down and sleep, cook their meals, and stow their gear. Privacy was not easily secured because other families lived in the longhouse; people were always coming and going, and the fires glowed all night. In cold or wet weather or when the snow lay two or three feet deep outside, doors and roof vents had to be closed, and the longhouses became intolerably stuffy — acrid with smoke and the reeking odors of leftover food and sweating flesh. Eyes burned and throats choked. But the people were nonetheless tolerably warm, dry, and (so it is said) cheerful.

The inhabitants of a longhouse were usually kinfolk. A multifamily longhouse was, theoretically, the residence of a maternal lineage: an old woman and her female descendants, together with unmarried sons, and the husbands and children of her married daughters. The totem animal of the clan to which the lineage belonged — Deer, Bear, Wolf, Snipe, or whatever it might be — was carved above the door and painted red. In this way directions were easier to give, and the stranger knew where to seek hospitality or aid. But often — especially in the middle of the eighteenth century — individual families chose to live by themselves in smaller cabins, only eighteen by twenty feet or so in size, with just one fire. As time went on, the old longhouses disintegrated and were abandoned, and by the middle of the century the Iroquois were making their houses of logs.

Around and among the houses lay the cornfields. Corn was a main food. Dried and pounded into meal and then boiled into a hot mush, baked into dumplings, or cooked in whole kernels together with beans and squash and pieces of meat in the thick soups that always hung in kettles over the fires, it kept the people fed. In season, meats, fresh fruits, herb teas, fried grasshoppers, and other delicacies added spice and flavor to the diet. But the Iroquois were a cornfed people. They consumed corn when it was fresh and stored it underground for the lean winter months. The Seneca nation alone raised as much as a million bushels of corn each year; the cornfields around a large village might stretch for miles, and even scattered clearings in the woods were cultivated. Squash, beans, and tobacco were raised in quantity, too. Domesticated animals were few, even after the middle of the century: some pigs, a few chickens, not many horses or cattle. The responsibility for carrying on this extensive agricultural establishment rested almost entirely on the women. Armed with crude wooden hoes and digging-sticks, they swarmed over the fields in gay, chattering work bees, proceeding from field to field to hoe, to plant, to weed, and to harvest. An individual woman might, if she wished, "own" a patch of corn, or an apple or peach orchard, but there was little reason for insisting on private tenure: the work was more happily done communally, and in the absence of a regular market, a surplus was of little personal advantage, especially if the winter were hard and other families needed corn. In such circumstances hoarding led only to hard feelings and strained relations as well as the possibility of future difficulty in getting corn for oneself and one's family. All land was national land; an individual could occupy and use a portion of it and maintain as much privacy in the tenure as he wished, but this usufruct title reverted to the nation when the land was abandoned. There was little reason to bother about individual ownership of real estate anyway: there was plenty of land. Economic security for both men and women lay in a proper recognition of one's obligation to family, clan, community, and nation, and in efficient and cooperative performance on team activities, such as working bees, war parties, and diplomatic missions.

If the clearing with its cornfields bounded the world of women, the forest was the realm of men. Most of the men hunted extensively, not only for deer, elk, and small game to use for food and clothing and miscellaneous household items, but for beaver, mink, and otter, the prime trade furs. Pelts were the gold of the woods. With them a man could buy guns, powder, lead, knives, hatchets, axes, needles and awls, scissors, kettles, traps, cloth, ready-made shirts, blankets, paint (for cosmetic purposes), and various notions: steel springs to pluck out disfiguring beard, scalp, and body hair; silver bracelets and armbands and tubes for coiling hair; rings to hang from nose and ears; mirrors; tinkling bells. Sometimes a tipsy hunter would give away his peltries for a keg of rum, treat his friends to a debauch, and wake up with a scolding wife and hungry children calling him a fool; another might, with equal improvidence, invest in a violin, or a horse, or a gaudy military uniform. But by and large, the products of the commercial hunt — generally conducted in the winter and often hundreds of miles from the home village, in the Ohio country or down the Susquehanna River — were exchanged for a limited range of European consumer goods, which had become, after five generations of contact with beaver-hungry French, Dutch, and English traders, economic necessities. Many of these goods were, indeed, designed to Indian specifications and manufactured solely for the Indian trade. An Iroquois man dressed in a linen breechcloth and calico shirt, with a woolen blanket over his shoulders, bedaubed with trade paint and adorned with trade armbands and earrings, carrying a steel knife, a steel hatchet, a clay pipe, and a rifled gun felt himself in no wise contaminated nor less an Indian than his stone-equipped great-great-grandfather. Iroquois culture had reached out and incorporated these things that Iroquois Indians wanted while at the same time Iroquois warriors chased off European missionaries, battled European soldiers to a standstill, and made obscene gestures when anyone suggested that they should emulate white society (made up, according to their information and experience, of slaves, cheating lawyers with pen and paper and ink, verbose politicians, hypocritical Christians, stingy tavern keepers, and thieving peddlers).

Behavior was governed not by published laws enforced by police, courts, and jails, but by oral tradition supported by a sense of duty, a fear of gossip, and a dread of retaliatory witchcraft. Theft, vandalism, armed robbery, were almost unknown. Public opinion, gently exercised, was sufficient to deter most persons from property crimes, for public opinion went straight to the heart of the matter: the *weakness* of the criminal. A young warrior steals someone else's cow — probably captured during a raid on a white settlement — and slaughters it to feed his hungry family. He does this at a time when other men are out fighting. No prosecution follows, no investigation, no sentence: the unhappy man is nonetheless severely punished, for the nickname "Cow-killer" is pinned to him, and he must drag it rattling behind him wherever he goes. People call him a coward behind his back and snicker when they tell white men, in his presence, a story of an unnamed Indian who killed cows when he should have been killing men. Such a curse was not generalized to the point of ostracism, however. The celebrated Red Jacket, about whom the "Cow-killer" story was told, vindicated his courage in later wars, became the principal spokesman for his nation, and was widely respected and revered. But he never lost the nickname.

Disputes between people rarely developed over property. Marital difficulties centering around infidelity, lack of support, or personal incompatibility were settled by mutual agreement. Commonly, in case of difficulty, the man left and the woman, with her children, remained with her mother. A few couples remained together for a lifetime; most had several marriages; a few changed mates almost with the season. Men might come to blows during drunken arguments over real or fancied slights to their masculine honor, over politics, or over the alleged mistreatment of their kinfolk. Such quarrels led at times to killings or to accusations of witchcraft. A murder (or its equivalent, the practice of witchcraft) was something to be settled by the victim's kinfolk; if they wished, they might kill the murderer or suspected witch without fear of retaliation from his family (provided that family agreed on his guilt). But usually a known killer would come to his senses, admit himself wrong, repent, and offer retribution in goods or services to the mourning family, who unless exceptionally embittered by an unprovoked and brutal killing were then expected to accept the blood money and end the matter.

Drunkenness was perhaps the most serious social problem. Two Moravian missionaries who visited the Iroquois country in 1750 had the misfortune to reach the Seneca towns at the end of June, when the men were just returning from Oswego, where they had sold their winter's furs, and were beginning to celebrate the start of summer leisure. Hard liquor was dissolving winter's inhibitions and regrets. At Canandaigua, the missionaries, who were guests at the house of a prominent warrior, had just explained the friendly nature of their errand when the rum arrived. "All the town was in a state of intoxication, and frequently rushed into our hut in this condition," complained the white men. "There was every reason to think that fighting might ensue, as there were many warriors among those who were perfectly mad with drink." After a sleepless night the missionaries traveled on, reaching the outskirts of Geneseo on the second of July. "The village," said the observers in surprise, "consisted of 40 or more large huts, and lies in a beautiful and pleasant region. A fine large plain, several miles in length and breadth, stretches out behind the village." But the kegs of rum had anticipated them. "When we caught sight of the town we heard a great noise of shouting and quarreling, from which we could infer that many of the inhabitants were intoxicated, and that we might expect to have an uncomfortable time. On entering the town we saw many drunken Indians, who looked mad with drink. . . ."

Alas, poor Christians! They had to hide in a stuffy garret, without food or water. David, their devoted Indian convert and servant, stole out toward evening with a kettle to fetch his masters some water and was seen. "A troop of drunken women came rushing madly toward him. Some of them were naked, and others nearly so. In order to drive them away he was obliged to use his fists, and deal blows to the right and left. He climbed up a ladder, but when he had scarcely reached the top they seized it and tore it from under his feet." David barely managed to escape "in safety" from these playful Amazons. The missionaries decided not to wait the two days until the liquor ran out to meet the chiefs in council; they bent their prayers to an early departure. They finally managed to escape at dawn by jumping down from an opening in the gable and tiptoeing away. "The Lord watched over us in such a manner that all the drunken savages were in their huts, not a creature to be seen. Even the dogs, numbering nearly 100 in the whole village, were all quiet, wonderful to relate, and not a sound was heard. A dense fog covered the town, so that we could not see 20 steps before us. A squaw stood at the door of the last hut, but she was sober and returned our greeting quietly."

But such drunken debauches were only occasional rents in a fabric of polite social behavior. Other missionaries were more favorably impressed than the Moravians. The Seneca, said a Quaker scribe, "appear to be naturally as well calculated for social and rational enjoyment, as any people. They frequently visit each other in their houses, and spend much of their time in friendly intercourse. They are also mild and hospitable, not only among themselves, but to strangers, and good natured in the extreme, except when their natures are perverted by the inflammatory influence of spirituous liquors. In their social interviews, as well as public councils, they are careful not to interrupt one another in conversation, and generally make short speeches. This truly laudable mark of good manners, enables them to transact all their public business with decorum and regularity, and more strongly impresses on their mind and memory, the result of their deliberations."

During the seventeenth and eighteenth centuries Iroquois men earned a reputation among the French and English colonists for being the most astute diplomatically and most dangerous militarily of all the Indians of the Northeast. Yet at the same time the Iroquois were famous for the "matriarchal" nature of their economic and social institutions. After the colonial era came to an end with the victory of the United States in the Revolutionary War, the traditional diplomatic and military role of the Iroquois men was sharply limited by the circumstances of reservation life. Simultaneously, the "matriarchal" character of certain of their economic, kinship, and political institutions was drastically diminished. These changes were codified by the prophet Handsome Lake. As we shall see later in more detail, the changes in kinship behavior that he recommended, and which to a considerable degree were carried out by his followers, amounted to a shift in dominance from the mother-daughter relationship to that of the husband-wife. Handsome Lake's reforms thus were a sentence of doom upon the traditional quasi-matriarchal system of the Iroquois.

The Iroquois were described as matriarchal because of the important role women played in the formal political organization. The men were responsible for hunting, for warfare, and for diplomacy, all of which kept them away from their households for long periods of time, and all of which were essential to the survival of Iroquois society. An expedition of any kind was apt to take months or even years, for the fifteen thousand or so Iroquois in the seventeenth and eighteenth centuries ranged over an area of about a million square miles. It is not an exaggeration to say that the full-time business of an Iroquois man was travel, in order to hunt, trade, fight, and talk in council. But the women stayed at home. Thus, an Iroquois village might be regarded as a collection of strings, hundreds of years old, of successive generations of women, always domiciled in their longhouses near their cornfields in a clearing while their sons and husbands traveled in the forest on supportive errands of hunting and trapping, of trade, of war, and of diplomacy.

The women exercised political power in three main circumstances. First, whenever one of the forty-nine chiefs of the great intertribal League of the Iroquois died, the senior women of his lineage nominated his successor. Second, when tribal or village decisions had to be made, both men and women attended a kind of town meeting, and while men were the chiefs and normally did the public speaking, the women caucused behind the scenes and lobbied with the spokesmen. Third, a woman was entitled to demand publicly that a murdered kinsman or kinswoman be replaced by a captive from a non-Iroquois tribe, and her male relatives, particularly lineage kinsmen, were morally obligated to go out in a war party to secure captives, whom the bereaved woman might either adopt or consign to torture and death. Adoption was so frequent during the bloody centuries of the beaver wars and the colonial wars that some Iroquois villages were preponderantly composed of formally adopted war captives. In sum, Iroquois women were entitled formally to select chiefs, to participate in consensual politics, and to start wars.

Thus the Iroquois during the two centuries of the colonial period were a population divided, in effect, into two parts: sedentary females and nomadic males. The men were frequently absent in small or large groups for prolonged periods of time on hunting, trading, war, and diplomatic expeditions, simultaneously protecting the women from foreign attack and producing a cash crop of skins, furs, and scalps, which they exchanged for hardware and dry goods. These activities, peripheral in a geographical sense, were central to the economic and political welfare of the Six Nations. The preoccupation of Iroquois men with these tasks and the pride they took in their successful pursuit cannot be overestimated. But the system depended on a complementary role for women. They had to be economically self-sufficient through horticulture during the prolonged absences of men, and they maintained genealogical and political continuity in a matrilineal system in which the primary kin relationship (not necessarily the primary social relationship) was the one between mother and daughter.

Such a quasi-matriarchy, of course, had a certain validity in a situation where the division of labor between the sexes required that men be geographically peripheral to the households that they helped to support and did defend. Given the technological, economic, and military circumstances of the time, such an arrangement was a practical one. But it did have an incidental consequence: It made the relationship between husband and wife an extremely precarious one. Under these conditions it was convenient for the marital system to be based on virtually free sexual choice, the mutual satisfaction of spouses, and easy separation. Couples chose one another for personal reasons; free choice was limited, in effect, only by the prohibition of intraclan marriage. Marriages were apt to fray when a husband traveled too far, too frequently, for too long. On his return, drunken quarreling, spiteful gossip, parental irresponsibility, and flagrant infidelity might lead rapidly to the end of the relationship. The husband, away from the household for long periods of time, was apt in his travels to establish a liaison with a woman whose husband was also away. The wife, temporarily abandoned, might for the sake of comfort and economic convenience take up with a locally available man. Since such relationships were, in effect, in the interest of everyone in the longhouse, they readily tended to become recognized marriages. The emotional complications introduced by these serial marriages were supposed to be resolved peacefully by the people concerned. The traveling husband who returned to find his wife living with someone else might try to recover her; if she preferred to remain with her new husband, however, he was not entitled to punish her or her new lover, but instead was encouraged to find another wife among the unmarried girls or wives with currently absent husbands.

The basic ideal of manhood was that of "the good hunter." Such a man was self-disciplined, autonomous, responsible. He was a patient and efficient huntsman, a generous provider to his family and nation, and a loyal and thoughtful friend and clansman. He was also a stern and ruthless warrior in avenging any injury done to those under his care. And he was always stoical and indifferent to privation, pain, and even death. Special prominence could be achieved by those who, while adequate in all respects, were outstanding in one or another dimension of this ideal. The patient and thoughtful man with a skin "seven thumbs thick" (to make him indifferent to spiteful gossip, barbed wit, and social pressures generally) might become a sachem or a "distinguished name" — a "Pine Tree" chief. An eloquent man with a good memory and indestructible poise might be a council speaker and represent clan, nation, even the confederacy in far-flung diplomatic ventures. And the stern and ruthless warrior (always fighting, at least according to the theory, to avenge the death or insult of a blood relative or publicly avowed friend) might become a noted war-captain or an official war-chief. The war-captain ideal, open as it was to all youths, irrespective of clan and lineage or of special intellectual qualifications, was perhaps the most emulated.

In the seventeenth century an Onondaga war-captain named Aharihon bore the reputation of being the greatest warrior of the country. He realized the ideal of autonomous responsibility to virtually pathological perfection. Let us note what is told of Aharihon in the *Jesuit Relations.*

Aharihon was a man of dignified appearance and imposing carriage, grave, polished in manner, and self-contained. His brother had been killed about 1654 in the wars with the Erie, a tribe westward of the Iroquois. As clansman and close relative, he was entitled — indeed obligated — either to avenge his brother's death by killing some Erie people or by adopting a war captive to take his place. Aharihon within a few years captured or had presented to him for adoption forty men. Each of them he burned to death over a slow fire, because, as he said, "he did not believe that there was any one worthy to occupy his [brother's] place." Father Lalemant was present when another young man, newly captured, was given to Aharihon as a substitute for the deceased brother. Aharihon let the young man believe that he was adopted and need have no further fear, and "presented to him four dogs, upon which to hold his feast of adoption. In the middle of the feast, while he was rejoicing and singing to entertain the guests, Aharihon arose, and told the company that this man too must die in atonement for his brother's death. The poor lad was astounded at this, and turned toward the door to make his escape, but was stopped by two men who had orders to burn him. On the fourteenth of February, in the evening, they began with his feet, intending to roast him, at a slow fire, as far up as the waist, during the greater part of the night. After midnight, they were to let him rally his strength and sleep a little until daybreak, when they were to finish this fatal tragedy. In his torture, the poor man made the whole village resound with his cries and groans. He shed great tears, contrary to the usual custom, the victim commonly glorying to be burned limb by limb, and opening his lips only to sing; but, as this one had not expected death, he wept and cried in a way that touched even these Barbarians. One of Aharihon's relatives was so moved with pity, that he advised ending the sufferer's torments by plunging a knife into his breast — which would have been a deed of mercy, had the stab been mortal. However, they were induced to continue the burning without interruption, so that before day he ended both his sufferings and his life." Aharihon's career of death continued without interruption, and by 1663 he was able to boast that he had killed sixty men with his own hand and had burned fully eighty men over slow fire. He kept count by tattooing a mark on his thigh for each successive victim. He was known then as the Captain General of the Iroquois and was nicknamed Nero by the Frenchmen at Montreal because of his cruelty.

The French finally captured him near Montreal, but even in captivity his manner was impressive. "This man," commented Father Lalemant, "commonly has nine slaves with him, five boys and four girls. He is a captain of dignified appearance and imposing carriage, and of such equanimity and presence of mind that, upon seeing himself surrounded by armed men, he showed no more surprise than if he had been alone; and when asked whether he would like to accompany us to Quebec, he deigned only to answer coldly that that was not a question to ask him, since he was in our power. Accordingly he was made to come aboard our Vessel, where I took pleasure in studying his disposition as well as that of an Algonquin in our company, who bore the scalp of an Iroquois but recently slain by him in war. These two men, although hostile enough to eat each other, chatted and laughed on board that Vessel with great familiarity, it being very hard to decide which of the two was more skillful in masking his feelings. I had Nero placed near me at table, where he bore himself with a gravity, a self-control, and a propriety, which showed nothing of his Barbarian origin; but during the rest of the time he was constantly eating, so that he fasted only when he was at table."

But this voracious captain was not renowned among the Onondaga as a killer only. He was, on the contrary, also a trusted ambassador, dispatched on occasion to Montreal on missions of peace. He was, in a word, a noted man. He was a killer, but he was not an indiscriminate killer; he killed only those whom it was his right to kill, tortured only those whom he had the privilege of torturing, always as an expression of respect for his dead brother. And although his kinfolk sometimes felt he was a little extreme in his stern devotion to his brother's memory, they did not feel that he was any the less a fine man, or that they had a right to interfere with his impulses; they were willing to entrust the business of peace, as well as war, to his hand.

A century and a half later Mary Jemison, the captive white woman who lived for most of her life among the Seneca on the Genesee River, described her Indian husband in not dissimilar terms. "During the term of nearly fifty years that I lived with him," she recalled, "I received, according to Indian custom, all the kindness and attention that was my due as his wife. — Although war was his trade from his youth till old age and decrepitude stopt his career, he uniformly treated me with tenderness, and never offered an insult. . . . He was a man of tender feelings to his friends, ready and willing to assist them in distress, yet, as a warrior, his cruelties to his enemies perhaps were unparalleled. . . . In early life, Hiokatoo showed signs of thirst for blood, by attending only to the art of war, in the use of the tomahawk and scalping knife; and in practising cruelties upon every thing that chanced to fall into his hands, which was susceptible of pain. In that way he learned to use his implements of war effectually, and at the same time blunted all those fine feelings and tender sympathies that are naturally excited, by hearing or seeing, a fellow being in distress. He could inflict the most excruciating tortures upon his enemies, and prided himself upon his fortitude, in having performed the most barbarous ceremonies and tortures, without the least degree of pity or remorse. . . . In those battles he took a number of Indians prisoners, whom he killed by tying them to trees and then setting small Indian boys to shooting at them with arrows, till death finished the misery of the sufferers; a process that frequently took two days for its completion! . . . At Braddock's defeat he took two white prisoners, and burnt them alive in a fire of his own kindling. . . ."

With this sort of man serving as an ego-ideal, held up by sanction and by praise to youthful eyes, it is not remarkable that young men were ambitious to begin the practice of war. All had seen captives tortured to death; all had known relatives lost in war whose death demanded revenge or replacement. The young men went out on practice missions as soon as they were big enough to handle firearms; "infantile bands, armed with hatchets and guns which they can hardly carry, do not fail to spread fear and horror everywhere." Even as late as the middle of the eighteenth century, Handsome Lake and his brothers and nephews were still busy at the old business of war for the sake of war. Cornplanter became a noted war-captain; Blacksnake, his nephew, was one of the official war-chiefs of the Seneca nation; and Handsome Lake himself took part in the scalping-party pattern as a young man. But Handsome Lake became a sachem and later a prophet, and he never gloried in the numbers of men he killed as his brother Cornplanter (somewhat guiltily) did. "While I was in the use of arms I killed seven persons and took three and saved their lives," said Cornplanter. And Blacksnake, in later life, told with relish of his exploits as a warrior. "We had a good fight there," he would say. "I have killed how many I could not tell, for I pay no attention to or kept [no] account of it, it was great many, for I never have it at all my Battles to think about kepting account what I'd killed at one time. . . ."

The cultivation of the ideal of autonomous responsibility — and the suppression of its antinomy, dependency — began early in life. Iroquois children were carefully trained to think for themselves but to act for others. Parents were protective, permissive, and sparing of punishment; they encouraged children to play at imitating adult behavior but did not criticize or condemn fumbling early efforts; they maintained a cool detachment, both physically and verbally, avoiding the intense confrontations of love and anger between parent and child to which Europeans were accustomed. Children did not so much live in a child's world as grow up freely in the interstices of an adult culture. The gain was an early self-reliance and enjoyment of responsibility; the cost, perhaps, was a lifelong difficulty in handling feelings of dependency.

The Seneca mother gave birth to her child in the privacy of the woods, where she retired for a few hours when her time came, either alone or in the company of an older woman who served as midwife and, if the weather was cold, built and tended a fire. She had prepared for this event by eating sparingly and exercising freely, which were believed (probably with good reason) to make the child stronger and the birth easier. The newborn infant was washed in cold water, or even in snow, immediately after parturition and then wrapped in skins or a blanket. If the birth were a normal one, the mother walked back to the village with her infant a few hours afterwards to take up the duties of housewife. The event was treated as the consummation of a healthful process rather than as an illness. The infant spent much of its first nine months swaddled from chin to toe and lashed to a cradle-board. The child's feet rested against a footboard; a block of wood was placed between the heels of a girl to mold her feet to an inward turn. Over its head stretched a hoop, which could be draped with a thin cloth to keep away flies or to protect the child from the cold. The board and its wrappings were often lavishly decorated with silver trinkets and beadwork embroidery. The mother was able to carry the child in the board, suspended against her back, by a tumpline around her forehead; the board could be hung from the limb of a tree while she hoed corn; and it could be converted into a crib by suspending it on a rack of poles laid horizontally on forks stuck in the ground. The mother was solicitous of the child's comfort, nursed it whenever it cried, and loosened it from the board several times a day to change the moss that served as a diaper and to give it a chance to romp. The children, however, tended to cry when released from the board, and their tranquility could often be restored only by putting them back. Babies were seldom heard crying.

The mother's feeling for her children was intense; indeed, to one early observer it appeared that "Parental Tenderness" was carried to a "dangerous Indulgence." Another early writer remarked, "The mothers love their children with an extreme passion, and although they do not reveal this in caresses, it is nevertheless real." Mothers were quick to express resentment of any restraint or injury or insult offered to the child by an outsider. During the first few years the child stayed almost constantly with the mother, in the house, in the fields, or on the trail, playing and performing small tasks under her direction. The mother's chief concern during this time was to provide for the child and to protect it, to "harden" it by baths in cold water, but not to punish. Weaning was not normally attempted until the age of three or four, and such control as the child obtained over its excretory functions was achieved voluntarily, not as a result of consistent punishment for mistakes. Early sexual curiosity and experimentation were regarded as a natural childish way of behaving, out of which it would, in due time, grow. Grandparents might complain that small children got into everything, but the small child was free to romp, to pry into things, to demand what it wanted, and to assault its parents, without more hazard of punishment than the exasperated mother's occasionally blowing water in its face or dunking it in a convenient river.

The years between about eight or nine and the onset of puberty were a time of easy and gradual learning. At the beginning of this period the beginnings of the differentiation of the roles of boys and girls were laid down. The girls were kept around the house, under the guidance of their mothers, and assigned to the lighter household duties and to helping in the fields. Boys were allowed to roam in gangs, playing at war, hunting with bows and arrows and toy hatchets, and competing at races, wrestling, and lacrosse. The first successes at hunting were greeted with praise and boasts of future greatness. Sometimes these roaming gangs spent days at a time away from the village, sleeping in the bush, eating wild roots and fruits, and hunting such small game as could be brought down by bow and arrow, blowgun, or snare. These gangs developed into war parties after the boys reached puberty. Among themselves, both in gangs and among siblings of the same family, the children's playgroups were not constantly supervised by parents and teachers, and the children governed themselves in good harmony. Said one close observer, "Children of the same family show strong attachments to each other, and are less liable to quarrel in their youthful days than is generally the case with white children."

The parents usually tried to maintain a calm moderation of behavior in dealing with their children, a lofty indifference alike to childish tantrums and seductive appeals for love. Hardihood, self-reliance, and independence of spirit were sedulously inculcated. When occasion presented itself, fathers, uncles, or other elder kinfolk instructed their sons in the techniques of travel, firemaking, the chase, war, and other essential arts of manhood, and the mothers correspondingly taught their daughters the way to hoe and plant the cornfields, how to butcher the meat, cook, braid corn, and other household tasks. But this instruction was presented, rather than enforced, as an opportunity rather than as a duty. On occasion the parent or other responsible adult talked to the child at length, "endeavoring," as a Quaker scribe gently put it, "to impress on its mind what it ought to do, and what to leave undone." If exhortation seemed inadequate in its effect, the mentor might ridicule the child for doing wrong, or gravely point out the folly of a certain course of action, or even warn him that he courted the rage of offended supernatural beings. Obedience as such was no virtue, however, and blows, whippings, or restraints of any kind, such as restriction to quarters, were rarely imposed, the faults of the child being left to his own reason and conscience to correct as he grew mature. With delicate perception the adults noted that childish faults "cannot be very great, before reason arrives at some degree of maturity."

Direct confrontation with the child was avoided, but when things got seriously out of hand, parents sometimes turned older children over to the gods for punishment. A troublesome child might be sent out into the dusk to meet Longnose, the legendary Seneca bogeyman. Longnose might even be impersonated in the flesh by a distraught parent. Longnose was a hungry cannibal who chased bad children when their parents were sleeping. He mimicked the child, crying loudly as he ran, but the parents would not wake up because Longnose had bewitched them. A child might be chased all night until he submitted and promised to behave. Theoretically, if a child remained stubborn, Longnose finally caught him and took him away in a huge pack-basket for a leisurely meal. And — although parents were not supposed to do this — an unusually stubborn infant *could* be threatened with punishment by the great False Faces themselves, who, when invoked for this purpose, might "poison" a child or "spoil his face." "I remember," recalled a Cayuga woman of her childhood, "how scared I was of the False-faces; I didn't know what they were. They are to scare away disease. They used to come into the house and up the stairs and I used to hide away under the covers. They even crawled under the bed and they made that awful sound. When I was bad my mother used to say the False-faces would get me. Once, I must have been only 4 or 5, because I was very little when I left Canada, but I remember it so well that when I think of it I can hear that cry now, and I was going along a road from my grandfather's; it was a straight road and I couldn't lose my way, but it was almost dark, and I had to pass through some timber and I heard that cry and that rattle. I ran like a flash of lightning and I can hear it yet."

At puberty some of the boys retired to the woods under the stewardship of an old man, where they fasted, abstained from any sort of sexual activity (which they had been free to indulge, to the limit of their powers, before), covered themselves with dirt, mortified the flesh in various ways, such as bathing in ice water and bruising and gashing the shinbones with rocks. Dreams experienced during such periods of self-trial were apt to be regarded as visitations from supernatural spirits who might grant *orenda,* or magical power, to the dreamer, and who would maintain a special sort of guardianship over him. The person's connection with this supernatural being was maintained through a charm — such as a knife, a queerly shaped stone, or a bit of bone — which was connected with the dream through some association significant to the dreamer. Unlike many other tribes, however, the Iroquois apparently did not require these guardian-spirit visions for pubescent youths. Many youths were said not to have had their first vision until just before their first war party. Furthermore, any man could have a significant dream or vision at any time. Girls too went through a mild puberty ritual, retiring into the woods at first menstruation and paying particular attention to their dreams. With the termination of the menstrual period the girl returned to the household; but hereafter, whenever she menstruated, she would have to live apart in a hut, avoiding people, and being careful not to step on a path, or to cook and serve anyone's food, or (especially) to touch medicines, which would immediately lose their potency if she handled them.

The Europeans who observed this pattern of child experience were by no means unfavorably impressed although they were sometimes amazed. They commented, however, almost to a man, from early Jesuit to latter-day Quaker, on a consequence that stood out dramatically as they compared this "savage" maturation with "civilized." "There is nothing," wrote the Jesuit chronicler of the Iroquois mission in 1657, "for which these peoples have a greater horror than restraint. The very children cannot endure it, and live as they please in the houses of their parents, without fear of reprimand or chastisement." One hundred and fifty years later, the Quaker Halliday Jackson observed that "being indulged in most of their wishes, as they grow up, liberty, in its fullest extent, becomes their ruling passion." The Iroquois themselves recognized the intensity of their children's resentment at parental interference. "Some Savages," reported Le Mercier of the Huron, "told us that one of the principal reasons why they showed so much indulgence toward their children, was that when the children saw themselves treated by their parents with some severity, they usually resorted to extreme measures and hanged themselves, or ate of a certain root they call *Audachienrra,* which is a very quick poison." The same fear was recorded among the Iroquois, including the Seneca, in 1657. And while suicides by frustrated children were not actually frequent, there are nevertheless a number of recorded cases of suicide where parental interference was the avowed cause. And *mutatis mutandis,* there was another rationalization for a policy of permissiveness: that the child who was harshly disciplined might grow up, some day, to mistreat his parents in revenge.

This theory of child raising was not taken for granted by the Seneca; on the contrary, it was very explicitly recognized, discussed, and pondered. Handsome Lake himself, in later years, insisted that parents love and indulge their children.

STUDY GUIDE

1. Be prepared to discuss European influences on Indian social life, housing, clothing, weapons, and values.

2. What was the role of the Seneca woman in the family, economic life, and government affairs, and how was her position different from that of a European or American woman?

3. Review the introduction to this selection, in which certain myths held by Europeans are discussed. Considering Seneca government, the personality of the Iroquois, and attitudes toward loyalty and war, how does the picture presented by Wallace differ from the myths La Farge noted?

4. Different societies have varied views on child-rearing, marriage, and divorce, and have different ways of controlling such antisocial behavior as crime. How did Seneca practices in each of these areas differ from the patterns in modern America?

5. Like Mary Jemison, who is mentioned in this selection, a great many colonists were adopted as full-fledged members of Indian tribes, remained with them, and rejected opportunities to return to English society. What explanations can you think of for their finding Indian tribal life so attractive?

BIBLIOGRAPHY

One should keep in mind that in this selection Wallace is portraying only one of many Indian societies. Generally, we have tended to see Indian culture as a monolithic system and to ignore important differences among the various tribes. Many people think of all Indians as wearing colorful headdresses, living in tepees, using horses and canoes for transportation, and depending on the bow and arrow for their livelihood. Dress, housing, economy, marital customs, burial rites, and agricultural patterns varied in different regions. Your library may have some of the specialized studies of these aspects of Indian life or books on individual tribes through which you can extend your knowledge of these first Americans.

Wallace's essay on the Iroquois replaces an essay by the distinguished anthropologist Ruth Underhill on the Southeastern tribes that was used in the first edition of this volume. Her book, *Red Man's America* (1953), is one of the best general studies of the various Indian societies. Another very well written, general study of most tribes is Peter Farb, *Man's Rise to Civilization as Shown by the Indians of North America from Primeval Times to the Coming of the Industrial State* (1968). The following are also excellent studies, utilizing both anthropological and historical knowledge: Harold E. Driver, *The Indians of North America*, 2nd ed. (1969); William T. Hagan, *American Indians* (1961); Alvin M. Josephy, Jr., *The Indian Heritage of America* (1968); and Clark Wissler, *Indians of the United States*, rev. ed. (1966).

There are many volumes that deal more directly with topics mentioned in the selection by Wallace. Richard Drinnon, *Facing West: The Metaphysics of Indian-Hating and Empire Building* (1980) describes colonial attitudes toward Indians and examples of cruelty that equaled that of Aharihon. A book by James Axtell, *The European and the Indian: Essays in the Ethnohistory of*

Colonial North America (1981), is a series of fascinating essays on such subjects as scalping, colonists who lived with Indian tribes, and the cultural interaction of Indian and European.

In much historical writing, the American Indian has been treated merely as a "problem" or an obstacle in the path of the more highly advanced civilization of Europe. A very different perspective is given in Francis Jennings, *The Invasion of America: Indians, Colonialism, and the Cant of Conquest* (1975), which treats the European colonists as invaders. Another work which gives a more balanced, and less European-oriented, view of early American history is Gary B. Nash, *Red, White, and Black: The Peoples of Early America* (1974).

The painting "The Old Plantation" shows a slave wedding and the survival of African culture in customs, headties, and the musical instrument.

2

GERALD W. MULLIN

Life Under Slavery

The attitude of British colonials — and later, of American whites — toward blacks, who first landed at Jamestown in 1619, was shaped by myths and stereotypes. Influenced by sexual anxieties, economic self-interest, physical distinctions, and other factors, whites found it impossible to view blacks unemotionally. The first blacks in Virginia were bound to a limited term of service, just as were white indentured servants, but by the 1660s slave codes provided permanent enslavement of African laborers.

The serious study of black history began well before 1900. A number of circumstances limited such study, even by thoughtful scholars who tried to be objective. Black Americans had left some written records and a substantial oral tradition, but most of the sources from which black history was written were left by whites. An equally important limitation was that historians were most interested in those aspects of black history that shed light upon general American history. Thus, their attention was concentrated on slavery. Some understanding of slavery was essential for studying the history of American agriculture, presidential and congressional politics before the Civil War, westward expansion, or the upsurge of social reform after 1830.

Aspects of black life and culture that were only marginally related to white concerns went unstudied. African influences on American culture, black religion, the slave trade, even the impact of slavery on the American black's personality, received scant attention. With the exception of slavery, black history before the Civil War was not considered worthy of intensive study. The mainstream of American social and cultural life clearly came from Europe, as had the ancestors of most Americans, and little note was taken of the early origins of the Afro-American minority.

Yet many black Americans today can assume that their ancestors were in this country before 1800, and most of them can also be certain that those ancestors came in chains. They were rugged pioneers who cherished freedom, but, like no other people, they suffered harrowing hardships involuntarily, helping to establish the foundations of American agriculture under the lash. Disagreement remains concerning some aspects of slavery, but historians have reached a large measure of agreement concerning the life of the slave. By the use of more representative records and new approaches to the study of slavery, they have drawn a graphic portrait of the slaves' family life, housing, food, legal status, rewards and punishments, their work in the fields and in the cities, and their reaction to enslavement.

Gerald W. Mullin's *Flight and Rebellion* is a sensitive study of how African people adapted to, and resisted, enslavement. Mullin deals with slavery in Virginia at the end of the eighteenth century. On one question — whether slaves were contented with their lot or fundamentally rebellious — his work may be more informative than studies of the era just before the Civil War. He writes of a time before the antislavery movement, with its tracts, newspapers, and underground railroad. In the eighteenth century, the slaves reached their own decision. This selection gives a vivid picture of slave life and the determination to gain freedom of a group of our forebears who happened to be black.

The field slave "is called up in the morning at daybreak, scarcely allowed time to swallow three mouthfuls of homminy," wrote the English traveler J. F. D. Smyth. Brief notations like this in travelers' and plantation accounts and record books must suffice for data on the field slave's material condition. Although the records are sketchy, his diet, although probably adequate in bulk, was scarcely nourishing. "Homminy," Indian corn, was the slaves' staple food.

Random accounts of quantities of corn allotted suggest that provisions were sometimes based on the worker's productivity. During the Revolutionary War, "Councillor" Carter asked that "the stronger Shears [shares] men & women" be given one peck of corn per week, "the Remainder of the Black People they to have ¼ Peck per Week each." By 1787 Carter, who was one of the least oppressive slave masters, increased this slightly. He ordered 44 pecks of shelled Indian corn as two weeks' allowance for 26 slaves, less than a full peck per week per laborer. (One peck equals 14 lbs. of Indian corn.)

Meat was seldom given to slaves. Smyth said slaves ate hoecakes and little else; unless their master "be a man of humanity the slave eats a little fat, skimmed milk, and rusty bacon." La Rochefoucauld-Liancourt said that on large plantations the slave subsisted on corn and sometimes on buttermilk. They were given meat 6 times a year. Robert "Councillor" Carter estimated that the common allowance for wheat per hand per year was 15 bushels for those "negroes, who are not fed with animal food" (e.g., meat). These slaves only received meat on special occasions. Joseph Ball wrote his steward that slaves were to "have ffresh meat when they are sick, if the time of the year will allow it." The cuts were to be the least desirable, although not necessarily the least nutritious. When calves were slaughtered, Ball ordered him to give the field hands the "head and Pluck"; the "ffat backs, necks, and other Coarse pieces" of hogs were also to be reserved for the slaves. James Mercer directed his steward to give the slaves the innards of chickens unless he sold them to the local Negro chicken merchants.

Plantation slaves wore clothing usually cut from a heavy, coarse cloth of flax and tow originally manufactured in Osnabrück, Germany. Following the non-importation agreements of the late 1760's, coarse-textured cotton wool weave, "Virginia plains," "country linen," replaced "Osnabrugs." Unlike the colorful variety of many of the artisan's clothing, the notices for runaways after 1770 indicate that field laborers wore uniform pants and trousers. "They are well clothed in the usual manner for Negroes"; "clothed as usual" and "the usual winter clothing for corn field negroes" are representative descriptions from advertisements of that period.

Black women who worked on the quarter wore clothing of the same weight and texture as the men. They usually dressed in a loose-fitting smock or shift, often tied at the waist; a short waistcoat was fitted over this dress. A Dutch blanket used for a sleeping robe and shoes and stockings completed the plantation Negroes' clothing allowance.

Housing for slaves varied widely. But there are frequent references in travelers' accounts to clusters of slave cabins that looked like small villages, and, in plantation records, numerous directions from masters indicating a concern for warm, dry houses with floors, lofted roofs, and on occasion, fireplaces. Slave quarters, however, may have been a late development. Subscribers who used advertisements to sell plantations frequently mentioned "negro quarters," but usually only in those notices published in the last quarter of the century. The plantation's size, location, and wealth were not factors; nearly all had slave quarters. It is likely that the smaller planter's field hands may have slept in the lofts of barns, in tobacco houses, and other outbuildings before the war. Joseph Ball told his nephew that the slaves "must ly in the Tobacco house" while their quarters, 15 by 20 feet with fireplace and chimney, were "lathed & fitted." However, several planters, including George Washington, used a less substantial, pre-fab arrangement. These shacks were small, temporary, and were moved from quarter to quarter following the seasonal crop.

J. F. D. Smyth was forced to take shelter one evening in a "miserable shell" inhabited by six slaves and their overseer. Unlike many slaves' houses "it was not lathed nor plaistered, neither ceiled nor lofted above . . . one window, but no glass in it, not even a brick chimney, and, as it stood on blocks about a foot above the ground, the hogs lay constantly under the floor, which made it swarm with flies."

On the home plantations, "servants," like the crop hands, usually slept in their own quarters. A planter who moved to the valley in 1781 asked his steward to place the "house Servants for they have been more indulged than the rest" with the overseer and his family, "till Such Time as Warehouses can be provided for them." Slaves evidently rarely slept in the great house. . . .

Some idea of a slave's yearly expenses is provided by James Madison's remark to a British visitor earlier in the nineteenth century. "Every negro earns annually, all expenses being deducted, about $257," wrote John Foster. "The expense of a negro including duty, board, clothing, and medicines, he [Madison] estimates from $12–$13."

The lean, spare character of the field slave's material condition was a function of his place in the servile work hierarchy. Most plantation slaves worked in the fields where their tasks were tedious, sometimes strenuous, and usually uninspiring. Although tobacco is a difficult and challenging crop, field laborers — especially the "new Negroes" — were forced into the most routine tasks of transplanting seedlings, weeding, suckering, and worming. Following the harvest their work days extended into the night, when they sorted, bundled, and pressed the tobacco into hogsheads for shipment.

The slave jobber's work assignments were not as routine as the field laborer's chores. Armistead was hired out by his master to "act as a jobber, *viz.* to cut firewood, go to [the] Mill, work in your garden, and occasionally to work in your Corn-field." Jobbers also mended stone and wood fences, patched and whitewashed the plantation's outbuildings, dug irrigation and drainage ditches, and the like. "Councillor" Carter hired John McKenney to "overlook" his jobbers in 1777. Their agreement read:

> the sd Jobbers to make a Crop of Corn Pumpkins, Irish Potatoes, at my plantation called Dickerson's Mill, that is, a full crop fr about 4 Shares — the sd Jobbers to raise Stone to build a tumbling Dam at Dickerson's Mill, they to make ye dirt Dam sufficient, there, and to do several Jobs at Nomony Hall in the course of this year.

McKenney's wages indicate that this type of work was not well paid: he was "to receive f[o]r his services at the rate of 25s/6 per month, [is] to find himself, Board, lodging, Washing &c."

But jobbers were scarcely better off than the field laborers, because they too did not travel outside the plantation. Nor did their menial tasks spur assimilation and a corresponding change in their view of slavery. Regardless of the specific nature of their tasks, the horizons and expectations of most plantation slaves were sharply limited by the plantation environment.

Their tiresome routines in the meager setting of reserve land, in meadow and woods, monotonous rows of tobacco, and temporary, ramshackle buildings, made the quarter a world of its own. But the isolation and work routines of the quarter provided slaves with a convenient means of expressing their unhappiness, so it was also a constant, nagging source of trouble for the planter. Blacks and whites alike knew that the plantation's efficiency and profitability could be seriously impaired simply by a "little leaning" on the slaves' part. "My people seem to be quite dead hearted, and either cannot or will not work"; "my people are all out of their senses for I cannot get one of them to do a thing as I would have it and as they do it even with their own time they have it to do again immediately." These words are Landon Carter's. A tough and competent man, Carter did not bend easily, but this note of resignation is heard early in his diary.

Accounts of the field slave's performance are rare, but one of the best can be found in Jack P. Greene's fine edition of Landon Carter's Diary which tells a dreary story of the crop laborers' quiet and persistently non-cooperative actions. Slaves reported ill every day but Sunday when there were no complaints because they considered this "a holy day"; men treading wheat slept while their "boys," left to do the job, "neglected" it; the "crop people," forced to stem tobacco in the evening hours, retaliated "under the guise of semi-darkness [by] throwing away a great deal of the saleable tob[acco]"; men whom Carter harassed about weeding a corn patch feigned stupidity and leveled thousands of hills of corn seedlings. Carter's slaves, in fact, were so rebellious that he came to question the profitability of slavery. "It is the same at all my plantations," he complained:

> Although I have many to work and fine land to be tended, I hardly make more than what cloaths them, finds them tools, and pays their Levies. Perhaps a few scrawney hogs may be got in the year to be fattened up here. If these things do not require the greatest caution and frugality in living I am certain nothing can do.

William Strickland, an Englishman who visited colonial America in 1800, concurred. As well as any traveler, he succinctly defined the character of the plantation slaves' rebelliousness in a letter to the Board of Trade:

> Any slave that I have seen at work, does not appear to perform half as much, as a labourer in England; nor does the business under which the master sits down contented, appear to be half of what we require to be performed by one. . . . If to this be added the slovenly carelessness with which all business is performed by the slave, the great number of useless hands the slave owner

is obliged to maintain, the total indifference to, and neglect, not to say the frequent wilful destruction, of whatever is not immediately committed to his care. . . . And also the universal inclination to pilfering shown by them, I cannot do otherwise than acquiesce in the received opinion of the country, that slave labor is much dearer than any other.

Lazy, wasteful, and indifferent work was a chronic problem on eighteenth-century plantations. Slaves understood that there was a great deal of time to waste, and little hope of improving their lot. "It will be better to have more eyes than one over such gangs," Landon Carter noted. Following another inspection he complained, "the old trade, take one hour from any job and it makes a day loss in work." Most plantation slaves desired challenging tasks, but once they had them, they dragged out the job as long as possible. Herdsman Johnny, charged with breaking up the quarter patch at Sabine Hall, "does not intend to finish," Carter wrote, "by contriving that all his lambs should get out of the yard that he may be trifling about after them."

Careful planters habitually spot-checked their slaves' productivity. Planters like Landon Carter and George Washington who demanded from their slaves punctiliousness, order, and a high output, were convenient and effective targets for the slaves' piddling laziness and wasteful procedures. A 1760 entry in Washington's diary noted that four of his sawyers hewed about 120 feet of timber in a day. Dissatisfied with this rate of production, and determined to apply gentle pressure, Washington stood and watched his men. They subsequently fell to work with such energy and enthusiasm that he concluded that one man could do in one day what four had previously accomplished in the same length of time.

How many seemingly routine plantation practices were actually concessions to the unreliability of slave labor? For years Landon Carter refused to introduce plows and carts onto his quarters since he felt that these technological innovations would only serve "to make Overseers and people extremely lazy . . . wherever they are in great abundance there is the least plantation work done."

Feigned illness was another remarkably simple but effective ruse. When a slave asked to "lay-in," his master often suspected he was faking, but could never be certain. Too many had stood helplessly by while a strange and lethal "distemper," or "ague," suddenly swept through their slave quarters and carried off numbers of workers. Plantation records are filled with notes on these epidemics: "The mortalities in ties in my families are increased. . . . The number of my dead is now fifteen working slaves. I thank God I can bear these things with a great deal of resignation," or "a grievous mortality of my familys hath swept away an abundance of my people"; and, "we kept the plantations on James River to try to make Crops, but there broke out a malignant fever amongst the Negroes & swept off most of the able Hands;

this threw all into Confusion & there has been little or no thing made since."

Women who feigned illness were usually more effective than men. "As to Sall," James Mercer wrote his steward, "I believe her old complaint is mere deceit, if it is not attended with a fever it must be so unless it is owing to her monthly disorder & then can only last two days, and exercise is a necessary remedy." Washington complained of women who "will lay up a month, at the end of which no visible change in their countenance, nor the loss of an ounce of flesh, is discoverable; and their allowance of provision is going on as if nothing ailed them." Exasperated and uncertain about the health of a black woman, Betty Davis, he explained that "she has a disposition to be one of the most idle creatures on earth, and besides one of the most deceitful." When two of his slave women approached clutching their sides, Landon Carter told them to work or be whipped. He observed that they had no fever (the test of whether or not slaves were ill). "They worked very well with no grunting about pain." But Sarah, one of the women who had pretended to be pregnant for eleven months earlier in the year, soon ran off. When Wilmot used the same stratagem, Carter noted: "it cost me 12 months, before I broke her." This lesson was not satisfactory; for a third woman "fell into the same scheme," and "really carried it to a great length." So Carter whipped her severely; and she was "a good slave ever since only a cursed thief in making her Children milk Cows in the night."

Plantation slaves who "hid out" in the woods and fields as runaways represented a more serious breach of plantation security. They often returned to the quarter in the evening for food and shelter and were an invitation to others to follow their example. But truancy was also inward rebelliousness: it was sporadic, and it was directed toward the plantation or quarter. Unlike the real fugitives, truants had no intention of leaving the immediate neighborhood and attempting to permanently change their status. Truancy was so common that most planters either did not make it a matter of record or simply referred to it in a random manner in their correspondence. "King" Carter actually viewed it as part of his "outlandish" slaves' learning process: "Now that my new negro woman has tasted the hardships of the woods," he observed to an overseer, "she'll stay nearer to home where she can have her belly full." Planters accepted the fact that absenteeism, particularly in the evening hours, was scarcely controllable. In response to Landon Carter's complaint that his pet deer were straying in the Sabine Hall fields, John Tayloe wrote:

Dear Col

. . . Now give me leave to complain to you, That your Patroll do not do their duty, my people are rambleing about every night, . . . my man Billie was out, he says he rode no horse of Master & that he only was at Col. Carter's, by particular invitation, so that the Entertainment was last night at Sabine Hall, & may probably be at Mt Airy this night, if my discoverys do not disconcert the Plan, these things would not be so I think, if the Patrollers did the duty they are paid for.

Plantation slaves probably "rambled" to the "entertainment" in the neighborhood several nights of the week; as long as they reported for work the following day few efforts were made, or could be made, to curtail this practice.

Truants habitually remained very close to the quarter or plantation; but this did not make it much easier for the planter to recapture them. Evidently they were sufficiently clever (and the other plantation slaves were sufficiently secretive) to keep themselves in hiding until they decided to return on their own. Sarah ran off because Carter refused to let her "lie-in" as ill. She spent a week in the woods and ate during the evening hours while visiting the slave quarters. Simon, an ox-carter, also hid beneath the vigilant Carter's very nose. He "lurked" in Johnny's "inner room," and in the "Kitchen Vault."

The outlaw, a far more dangerous type of runaway, used his temporary freedom to inflict punishment on his tormentors. Outlawing a slave was a legal action, placing the runaway beyond the law, making him a public liability, and encouraging his destruction by any citizen. Those who killed outlaws did so without fear of legal prosecution; they also collected a fee from the public treasury and a reward from the slave's owner. The master's advertisements usually did not encourage the slave's preservation: George America was worth forty shillings if taken alive; five pounds if destroyed.

Some slaveowners only threatened to outlaw truants. Recognizing the effective communication between slaves who remained on the quarter and their "outlying" brother, masters used outlawry as a warning for slaves to come in or suffer the consequences. Many did not return, nor were they satisfied with merely "lurking" about and "tasting the hardships of the woods" until hunger brought them back to the quarter. Outlaws destroyed. The omnibus slave codes of the century (four were passed from 1705 to 1797) described these desperate, courageous and "incorrigible" slaves in language which changed only slightly during the ninety years:

WHEREAS many times slaves run away and lie hid and lurking in swamps, woods, and other obscure places, killing hogs, and committing other injuries to the inhabitants . . . upon intelligence, two justices (Quorum unus) can issue a proclamation . . . if the slave does not immediately return, anyone whatsoever may kill or destroy such slaves by such ways and means as he . . . shall think fit. . . . If the slave is apprehended . . . it shall . . . be lawful for the county court, to order such punishment to the said slave, either by dismembering, or in any other way . . . as they in their discretion shall think fit, for the reclaiming any such incorrigible slave, and terrifying others from the like practices.

Newspaper advertisements provide a glimpse of why a few runaways were outlawed: John Smith outlawed Mann because he threatened to burn Smith's house; and John Tayloe's manager at the Occoquan Furnace reported that "Leamon's obstinacy in not delivering himself up when lurking a considerable time about the ironworks, and doing mischief, Induced me to have him outlawed; in which condition he now stands and remains." Other explanations were not as clear as these. Moses and his wife were "harboured" by some "ill disposed" persons in Williamsburg. His master advertised "such notorious offences are not to be borne with any degree of patience." Edward Cary's explanation for outlawing Ben and Alice was even more cryptic. Cary was the chairman of the House of Burgesses committee that reimbursed masters whose slaves were outlawed as public liabilities. "As neither of those slaves have been ill used at my hands, I have had them outlawed in this county and for their bodies without hurt, or a proper certificate of their death, a proper reward will be given."

Some potentially explosive outlaws stayed on the quarters and physically assaulted their overseers. One of Landon Carter's supervisors, Billy Beale, chastised a slave who was weeding a corn patch. Told that his work was "slovenly," the slave replied "a little impudently" and Beale was "obliged to give him a few licks with a switch across his Shoulders"; but the slave fought back, and he and Beale "had a fair box." Subsequently, the laborer was brought before his master; and Carter noted that "it seems nothing scared him." Direct confrontations such as these, between comparatively unassimilated slaves and whites, seem to have been rare; a few, however, are described in detail in the advertisements for runaways. Two fugitives, for example, a husband and wife, were recaptured by an overseer while crossing a field, and were "violently" taken from the overseer and set free by field workers. Another runaway, also a field hand, escaped by "cutting his Overseer in Several Pieces [places?] with a Knife." John Greenhow of Williamsburg lost a slave who "laid violent hands" on him; this man ran off with another field slave who had also beaten his overseer.

Murders, small and unplanned uprisings, and suicides are instances of rebelliousness that was clearly inward-directed in a psychological sense as well as directed against the confines of the plantation. A September 1800 newspaper story graphically illustrates how even the most calculating, courageous, and murderously violent action could be, in a fashion, internalized violence: for after this slave methodically stalked and killed his master he simply "went home."

Captain John Patteson, a tobacco inspector at Horsley's warehouse in Buckingham County, punished his slave for "some misdemeanor"; and from that time, the slave told the court, "he ever after meditated [Patteson's] destruction."

On the evening to which it was effected, my master directed me to set off home . . . and carry a hoe which we used at the place. . . . I concluded to way-lay him. . . . after waiting a considerable time, I heard the trampling of horses' feet. . . . I got up and walked forwards — my master soon overtook me, and asked me (it being then dark) who I was: I answered Abram; he said he thought I had gone from town long enough to have been further advanced on the road; I said, I thought not; I spoke short to him, and did not care to ir-ritate him — I walked on however; sometimes by the side of his horse, and sometimes before him. — In the course of our traveling an altercation ensued; I raised my hoe two different times to strike him, as the circumstance of the places suited my purpose, but was intimidated. . . . [W]hen I came to the fatal place, I turned to the side of the road; my master observed it, and stopped; I then turn'd suddenly round, lifted my hoe, and struck him across the breast; the stroke broke the handle of the hoe — he fell — I repeated my blows; the handle of the hoe broke a second time — I heard dogs bark, at a house which we passed, at a small distance; I was alarmed, and ran a little way, and stood behind a tree, 'till the barking ceased; in running, I stumbled and fell — I returned to finish the scene I began, and on my way picked up a stone, which I hurl'd at his head, face, &c. again and again and again, until I thought he was certainly dead — and then I went home.

The most violent reactions to slavery were small, unorganized uprisings. A newspaper account written in 1770 reported a battle between slaves and free men, which suddenly erupted during the Christmas holidays on a small plantation quarter in New Wales, Hanover County. The re-porter's explanation for the uprising was a familiar one. "Treated with too much lenity," the plantation slaves became "insolent and unruly." When a young and inexperienced overseer tried to "chastise" one of them by beating him to the ground and whipping him the man picked him-self up and "slash[ed] at the overseer with an axe." He missed, but a group of slaves jumped on the white and administered such a severe beating that the "ringleader," the slave whom the overseer had whipped, intervened and saved his life. The overseer ran off in search of reinforcements; and instead of fleeing or arming themselves, the slaves tied up two other whites and "whipped [them] till they were raw from neck to waistband." Twelve armed whites arrived, and the slaves retreated into a barn where they were soon joined by a large body of slaves, "some say forty, some fifty." The whites "tried to prevail by persuasion," but the slaves, "deaf to all, rushed upon them with a desperate fury, armed solely with clubs and staves." Two slaves were shot and killed, five others were wounded, and the remainder fled.

Some slaves took their own lives. The journals of the House of Burgesses contain 55 petitions from slaveowners who sought reimbursement from public funds for slaves who committed suicide. Most of these men were outlawed runaways who, since they feared trial and conviction for capital crimes, hanged or drowned themselves. Since few petitioners reported the circumstances of a slave's death, the journals are not too informative. But one suicide, William Lightfoot's Jasper, was also described in a runaway notice:

> [A] well set Negro Man Slave, much pitted with the Small-pox; he was lately brought from *New-York,* but was either born or lived in the *West-Indies,* by which he has acquired their peculiar Way of speaking, and, seems to frown when he talks; he carried with him different Sorts of Apparel.

If indeed Jasper was a suicide his decision to "dash his brains out against a rock" must have been sudden, for he took a change of clothing with him.

But the field slaves' rebelliousness was not typically violent, self-destructive, or even individualistic. In fact they were much more inclined to attack the plantation in a quietly cooperative and effective way than were the slave artisans. Pilferage was a particularly rewarding and often organized action. "I laughed at the care we experienced in Milk, butter, fat, sugar, plumbs, soap, Candles, etc." wrote Landon Carter. "Not one of these ennumerations lasted my family half the year. All gone, no body knows how . . . thievish servants . . . Butter merely vanishing." Washington estimated that his servants stole two glasses of wine to every one consumed by the planter's visitors. His slaves made a practice of stealing nearly everything they could lay their hands on. Washington had to keep his corn and meat houses locked; apples were picked early, and sheep and pigs carefully watched. . . .

The slaves' traffic in stolen goods was extensive, relatively well organized, and carried on virtually with impunity. The problem was of such proportions that by the 1760's it led to several letters to newspaper editors and to a series of laws. "I suppose every family must have so sensibly felt this evil," noted one letter writer to the *Virginia Gazette.* He observed that in every part of the country, henhouses, dairies, barns, granaries, gardens, and even patches and fields were "robbed in every convenient moonshiny night." Another contributor noted that, in his travels about the country, he had heard "frequent and various complaints" of this "pernicious evil." There was "hardly a family that was not full of enjuries they had received from the numerous thefts of servants and slaves."

Many slaves were fences for stolen goods; they had licenses from "overtender" masters to sell produce. Whites, too, cooperated with the plantation slaves; they were referred to in the newspapers as "common proprietors of orchards," "liquor fellers," and "idle scatter lopping people." One writer made the interesting observation that some slaveowners, with "a modest blush," were so ashamed to sell certain farm products that they gave them to their slaves to dispose of. "Pray why is a fowl more disgraceful," he asked, "in the sale of it at market, than a pig, lamb, a mutton, a veal, a cow or an ox?"

Additional evidence of organized thievery as an outgrowth of the plantation slaves' culture and community is preserved in the Richmond County court records. Between 1710 and 1754 the justices tried and passed sentence in 426 cases. In 1750, although blacks made up 45 per cent of the population and there were nearly twice as many black tithes (1,235) as white (761), only 26 of these 426 actions involved slaves. (It should also be remembered that all slave criminals — with the exception of insurrectionists and murderers who were supposed to be tried by the General Court — were tried by county justices.) Only two trials concerned serious crimes. These were murder trials and both defendants were slave men. One was convicted of stabbing a black woman to death; the other, who later died in jail under very unusual circumstances, was charged with killing his master's young daughter. After his death, the court ordered his body to be quartered and displayed. Most slave crimes in this forty-four year period were petty thefts of the kind described earlier; that is, the charge was nearly always breaking and entering, and the slaves usually took a few shillings' worth of cider, liquor, bacon, cloth, or hogs. One typical case involved a slave who stole five sheets, a fishing line, and a bottle of brandy. Nearly all of these robberies were committed by one person; but the largest theft was conducted by a man and a woman. They took forty gallons of rum and fifty pounds of sugar. Evidently these thefts were well organized; the slaves usually selected such vulnerable targets as the homes of widows, ministers, warehouses, and slave quarters. Only on one occasion did a slave rob his master (who was Landon Carter!). The usual punishment for these crimes was between ten and thirty-nine lashes. For more serious crimes (including a conviction of perjury) slaves lost one or both ears. For capital crimes, slaves were often allowed to plead benefit of clergy.

The plantation slaves' organized burglaries were similar to the rebellious styles of the mobile, comparatively assimilated slaves. These crimes required planning; they took the slaves outside the plantation, and evidently compensated them with money and goods which could be exchanged for articles they needed.

Most field slaves, however, never acquired sufficient literate and occupational skills to move away from the quarter and into the society beyond it. Most were Africans and they remained "new Negroes" all of their lives. There are, then, two possible aspects to the personal dimension of slave life on the quarter. First, from an outsider's point of view, the quarter was a stultifying experience which slowed and restricted the slave's rate of acculturation. Second, from the slave's point of view, life on the quarter was perhaps preferable to daily contact with his captors, because it allowed him to preserve some of his ways.

Household slavery entwined the lives of whites and blacks. In the household more than anywhere else, there were direct and personal encounters that intensified the meaning of slavery for slaves and free alike. For the black servant these situations were often harrowing experiences which threatened to expose a nature sharply divided between enervating fear and aggressive hostility. His inward styles of rebelliousness and such related neurotic symptoms as speech defects were often manifestations of a profound ambiguity about whites and his own "privileged" status. For the white master the intimate presence of so many blacks subtly influenced domestic affairs, particularly his behavior toward his wife and children. The roles developed in household slavery restricted the master's actions toward his servants too. Once a style of discipline and correct order had been established, the master's reactions were often determined by what the slaves had come to expect of him. Highly sensitive to the patriarch's role, servants were quick to exploit any weakness in his performance. If the master was insecure, so were his dependents; but they also kept him that way by their persistent and petty rebelliousness. Household slavery then was the epitome of Professor Tannenbaum's dynamic view of human relationships in slave societies in which slavery was "not merely for blacks, but for the whites [and] . . . Nothing escaped, nothing, and no one."

The greatly enlarged situational (or interpersonal) dimension of slavery in the household is fundamentally important for another reason. Our limited understanding of slave behavior is based almost exclusively on interpretations of these personal encounters. These interpretations, which argue that slaves became the characters they played for whites, that their masters' view of them as infants or Sambos became their self-view, must be used with extreme caution. The interpersonal encounter was only a fragment of slavery's reality for both whites and blacks. When slaves were among their own and using their own resources as fugitives and insurrectionists, it is abundantly clear that much of their true character was concealed or intentionally portrayed in a dissembling manner in the presence of whites.

STUDY GUIDE

1. Differences between black slaves and poor white farmers with respect to freedom are obvious. How would their lives compare with respect to the following: housing; the actual labor they performed; food; health and medical care?

2. What were the various kinds of violent resistance that slaves used to protest enslavement? What were the techniques of "quiet resistance" that they used?

3. How might the following factors have influenced the slave's choice of violent or passive resistance: the master or conditions on the plantation; the slave's personality and character; the slave code and attitudes of a particular region, such as South Carolina as compared to Virginia?

4. How did the household slave's relationship to whites differ from that of the field slave? What were the relative advantages and disadvantages of each position?

5. Though Mullin's selection focuses on the life of the slave, he mentions several times that the institution of slavery influenced every aspect of life in the South for both blacks and whites. How do you think black slavery might have influenced each of the following aspects of southern life: education of whites; relations between whites of different classes; the relative slowness of the South in industrial development; southern politics? Can you think of specific evidence to support your arguments on these points?

BIBLIOGRAPHY

Mullin's book is a study of slavery in eighteenth-century Virginia. The work, the slave code, and the conditions of slave life differed somewhat in other colonies such as New York or South Carolina. Wherever the slave ended up — on a southern plantation or in a port city, as a farmer or a craftsman — the slave's experience began with his or her capture and sale to the captain of a slave ship in Africa. The ghastly conditions aboard such vessels are described in Daniel P. Mannix and Malcolm Cowley, *Black Cargoes: A History of the Atlantic Slave Trade* (1962). Philip D. Curtin, *The Atlantic Slave Trade: A Census* (1969) is a careful study of the number of slaves brought to various parts of North and South America.

Unlike most Europeans who came to the colonies, Africans brought virtually no personal property with them — no jewelry, no utensils, no tools, no musical instruments, no clothes. They did, however, bring their traditions and values — their dances and music, their folklore and religion, and their sense of family and personal relations. Since Melville J. Herskovits published his study of the subject, *The Myth of the Negro Past* (1941), scholars have devoted much energy to identifying African influences upon American Negro culture. The first chapter of John Blassingame, *The Slave Community: Plantation Life in the Ante-Bellum South* (1972) discusses the cultural shock of enslavement, as well as the question of the survival of African culture in the New World.

Another important question is whether racism or slavery developed first in the British colonies. In the very early seventeenth century, Africans were treated as indentured servants and were freed after a number of years of service. Did English colonials force Africans into slavery because of white racism, while allowing Europeans to continue in temporary servitude? Or was it the economic advantage of a wageless, hereditary labor force that led to enslavement, with racism following as a rationalization of white guilt? Anyone interested in this question should read Winthrop Jordan's lengthy study *White over Black: American Attitudes toward the Negro, 1550–1812* (1968) and Edmund S. Morgan, *American Slavery, American Freedom: The Ordeal of Colonial Virginia* (1975).

About half of the people who came to the English colonies in the colonial period were of English descent; Africans were the second largest group, making up nearly 20 percent of the population by 1790. Many other nationalities came in smaller numbers, and your college library is likely to have some of the studies of the Germans, the Scots-Irish, and the other groups that settled the New World. The origins, voyages, and New-World conditions of the European group that most closely paralleled the enslaved Africans are studied in Abbot E. Smith, *Colonists in Bondage: White Servitude and Convict Labor in America, 1607–1776* (1947).

An artist known as the Pollard Limner managed to portray the indomitable spirit of the elderly Puritan woman Ann Pollard.

3

LYLE KOEHLER

Women and Children

As children, most of us take marriage and the family very much for granted — as part of the natural order of things. Eventually, we may come to wonder just how natural matrimony is, whether it exists because of love or social necessity, and what the role of parents and children in the family is and should be. Several factors account for the heightened skepticism about marriage and the family in recent years. One, of course, is the rising divorce rate, and another may be the lessened economic dependence of both women and children upon the father of the family.

In recent years, historians have turned their attention to the makeup of the family and household in earlier times, and have examined how our views have changed with respect to the relations of men and women, child-rearing, and the treatment of older people in society. Some historians believe that women were more highly valued members of the family and had greater equality in earlier centuries, when they were vital to the economy of the household, than in the period since industrialization. Children in the colonial period tended to be treated as "little adults," dressed like their fathers and mothers, from the age of six or seven. There was no recognized period of adolescence, and advice to parents emphasized discipline rather than love and support of children. Fathers, most of whom were farmers or home craftsmen, spent their day in the household, rather than away in factories and offices.

Most of the colonists' views, including those of marital relationships and child-rearing, were heavily influenced by English and continental European traditions. But these customs — like their language, government, and class attitudes — slowly and subtly changed in the New World. The following selection by Lyle Koehler emphasizes the continuity of English traditions in Puritan New England and the pervasive influence of Calvinism upon family life. Koehler argues forcefully that the colonial period was far from being a golden age for women. He views men as striving for male dominance and women as being forced into abject submission.

Other historians might well question these conclusions. Some scholars have suggested that one cannot get a reliable view of the day-to-day life of average people by studying the sermons and laws written by a small elite. Others have suggested that we cannot really speak of a monolithic New England Calvinist society. Some students believe that men and women were closer to having an equal status in the colonial period than in the nineteenth century. In any case, Koehler's article cannot be assumed to give a clear portrait of the family in the middle or southern colonies.

Calvinists in England and in America expected each person to keep his or her proper place in God's social design. They placed virtually everyone on a grid of inferiority and superiority — servant before master, non-church-member before church member, idler before working man, wife before husband, child before adult. Such a system facilitated supervision, because each master was legally accountable for overseeing the behavior of designated subordinates.

Crucial to the maintenance of religious and social order was the Puritans' attention to proper child-rearing. Godly parents were to make sure that their "unstaid and young" charges did not become addicted to the "greasy sensuality" of play — to "rattles, baubles, and such toyish stuff." Pilgrim pastor John Robinson described the difficulty of such a task:

> ... surely there is in all children ... a stubborness, and stoutness of mind arising from natural pride, which must, in the first place, be broken and beaten down; that so the foundation of their education being laid in humility and tractableness, other virtues may, in their time, be built thereon. ...

Reprinted with permission from Lyle Koehler, *A Search for Power: The "Weaker Sex" in Seventeenth Century New England* (Urbana, Chicago and London: The University of Illinois Press). © 1980 by the Board of Trustees of the University of Illinois.

For the beating and keeping down of this stubborness parents must provide carefully.... Children should not know, if it could be kept from them, that they have a will in their own, but in their parents' keeping; neither should these words be heard from them, save by way of consent, "I will" or "I will not."

As Robinson indicated, the parent was to crush the child's drive or desire for self-assertion or independence, for such feelings might advance the child's "natural pride." Instead, adults were to inculcate in youngsters a sense of virtual helplessness before parental whim and God's authoritarian will....

... If children cursed or struck their parents — except "to preserve themselves from Death or Maiming" — Puritan law specified the death penalty. New Hampshire and Connecticut also prescribed hanging for any son who refused to heed his mother's or father's voice after chastisement. The authorities neglected to prosecute youngsters under such capital laws, but they did use the laws to inspire fear. In 1647 the authorities also expended some time and effort attempting to revive "the ancient practice in England of children asking their parents' blessing upon their knees," which would presumably symbolize the child's "Obedience unto the commands" of his or her parents. Ipswich minister Thomas Cobbett went still further, explaining that children "should rise up and stand bare [headed] before their Parents when they come to them, or speak to them.... It stands not with Parents' Honour for children to sit and speak, but rather they should stand up when they speak to Parents." ...

The archetypal Puritan patriarch kept his children in a state of repressive bondage. He was a classic example of what clinical psychologist Diana Baumrind calls the authoritarian parent, who

> values obedience as a virtue and favors punitive, forceful measures to curb self-will at points where the child's actions or beliefs conflict with what he or she thinks is right conduct. He or she believes in keeping the child in his place, in restricting his autonomy, and in assigning household responsibilities in order to inculcate respect for work. This parent regards the preservation of order and traditional structure as a highly valued end in itself. He or she does not encourage verbal give and take, believing that the child should accept the parents' word for what is right.

Such a parent believed that "too much doting affection" distracted children from thoughts of God, or led them to consider themselves their parents' equals. Minister Thomas Cobbett warned that "fondness and Familiarity breeds ... contempt and irreverence in children." Robert Cleaver believed "cockering" children with affection could only ruin them: "For as the Ape doth with too much embracings, well neer kill her young whelpes: so likewise some indiscrete parents, through immoderate love and over-much pampering and cherishing do utterly despoil and mar their children. Therefore, if parents would have their children live, they must take heed that they love them not too much."

Puritans stressed discipline more than affection. In English Puritan households, according to one scholar, "the rod was most favored" as a punitive device. In America, the Massachusetts *Body of Liberties* (1641) prohibited "unnaturall severitie" toward the young, but did not specify when punishment became "severe" or "unnatural." The adult faced prosecution when he broke a child's bones, endangered the child's life, or delivered a cudgeling with "a walnut tree plant, big enough to have killed a horse" — but only three of nearly three dozen such offenders received more than an admonition or a very small fine. Still, New England Puritans did not oppose the use of the "Rod of Correction"; in fact, they considered it "an ordinance of God," suitable to inspire "love and fear." Cotton Mather stated it simply: "Better whipt, than Damn'd." . . .

Growing up in a Puritan home was certainly painful. Strict control through the family and all other social institutions often created a feeling of profound helplessness in children. This phenomenon had wide-ranging impact, for, as psychologist Martin Seligman has shown, repeated and sustained perceptions of an inability to control one's outcomes can lead to a state of chronic despair. Many boys and girls, in true Puritan fashion, lamented their own despicability and great sinfulness. Elizabeth Butcher, aged two and one-half, purportedly asked herself often from the cradle "the question, What is my corrupt Nature? and would make answer to herself, It is empty of Grace, bent into Sin, and only to Sin, and that continually." Jerusha Oliver, "While her infancy was hardly yet expired," professed many sins. Depressed by her backsliding, at age twelve she began sequestering herself for entire days, so that she could repent. Sarah Derby "set up almost all night, crying to the Lord, that he would please apply unto her, by His own Holy Spirit, a Promise, which might Releive the Disconsolations of her Soul." Recurrent melancholia assailed Samuel Sewall's daughter Elizabeth between the ages of seven and fifteen. One minister's son, Nathaniel Shrove, hoped for death, that he might avoid sin — and then decided he was too despicable to deserve even that.

These were anxiety-ridden, insecure, unhappy children — the products of a culture which devalued independent thought, self-satisfaction, exuberance, and real closeness. A consideration of their anguish and preoccupations can help us to understand the Puritan psyche, particularly as it affected attitudes toward the female sex. . . .

Like so many of their European contemporaries, New England's male Puritan leaders assumed that the obvious physical differences between the sexes had important social consequences. Throughout the seventeenth century these authorities argued and acted as if they believed anatomy alone determined destiny. In virtually all avenues of behavior Puritans affirmed the differences and deemphasized the similarities between the sexes — a practice which usually worked to the disadvantage of women. Because Puritan men had a high need to prove that they wielded some sort of power, in the face of the impotence inculcated in childhood and a theology of man's ultimate powerlessness before God, they tended to exaggerate prevailing notions of male superiority. While such men referred to themselves as the "Magnanimous, Masculine, and Heroicke sexe," every woman became a "poore fraile" creature — the "weaker sex." As Elnathan Chauncy scrawled in his commonplace book, "Yᵉ soule consists of two portions inferior and superior[;] the superior is masculine and aeternal. Yᵉ inferior foeminine and mortal." Custom meshed with psychological need for Puritans and non-Puritans alike — with sometimes bizarre results.

Beginning with conception and birth, profound developmental differences were assumed between male and female infants. Some physicians hypothesized that the male child was conceived earlier than the female because the male, as a higher, more sophisticated form of life, needed more time to develop in the womb. On the other hand, some religious leaders asserted that the male embryo, in recognition of its ultimate superiority, received his soul on the fortieth day, while the female embryo had to wait until the eightieth day before she acquired hers. When a woman had conceived twins of each sex, those twins supposedly occupied segregated uterine chambers to breathe into them the "laws of chastity." When the twins or a single child was ready to enter the outside world, the birth of a male was easier, according to the English obstetrical expert Thomas Raynalde. The reason for this was simple: babies were presumed to find their way into the outer world under their own power, and boys, being more vigorous than girls, got out faster. After delivery, the attending midwives cut a girl's navel string shorter than a boy's, "because they believe it makes . . . [females] modest, and their [genital] Parts narrower, which makes them more acceptable to their husbands."

Daughters were "less long'd for" than sons, perhaps in part because English obstetrical guides asserted that mothers who were carrying boys enjoyed fair complexions, red nipples, and white milk, while girls gave them "a pale, heavy, and swarth[y] countenance, a melancolique eye," black nipples, and watery bluish milk. At birth Puritan daughters, in particular, often received names which providentially reminded them of the limitations of their feminine destiny: Silence, Fear, Patience, Prudence, Mindwell, Comfort, Hopestill, and Be Fruitful. No Calvinist girl would ever bear an impressive name such as Freeborne, Fearnot, or Wrestling.

Puritan males, like so many of their English contemporaries, valued those characteristics in women which would insure submissiveness. The ideal woman blushed readily and chose "to be seen rather than Heard whenever she comes." She held her tongue until asked by her father or husband to speak; then only good, comforting words flowed from her mouth. "The greatest Nuisance in Nature," Joseph Beacon unequivocatingly wrote, "is an immodest impudent Woman." The ideal female displayed "an Eminence in Modesty, reserve, purity, temperance, humility, truth, meekness, patience, courtesie, affability, charity, goodness, mercy, [and] compassion," taking special care to avoid the "monstrous" decorative habit of painting the face with "varnish." Tender, consoling, and in need of careful direction, she was viewed as a defenseless creature, "that naked Sex that hath no arms but for imbraces."

In Puritan terms, women needed men, not only for physical protection and financial support but also to prevent themselves from going intellectually astray. Since the woman was presumed less able to ground her spiritual development in the cold logic of reason, Puritan divines told her to consult her father, her husband, or a minister whenever she wished to comprehend a theological issue. In fact, too much intellectual activity, on a theological or any other plane, might overtax her frail mind and thereby debilitate her equally weak body. In 1645 Emmanuel Downing claimed his wife, Lucy, made herself sick "by trying new Conclusions"; he suggested riding as a cure. In the same year Downing's brother-in-law, Massachusetts Governor John Winthrop, asserted that Ann Hopkins, the wife of the Connecticut governor, had lost her understanding and reason by giving herself solely to reading and writing. This statesman commented that if she "had attended her household affairs, and such things as belong to women, and had not gone out of her way and calling to meddle in such things as are proper for men, whose minds are stronger etc., she had kept her wits, and might have improved them usefully and honorably in the place God had set her." ...
Thomas Parker, the Newbury pastor, reacted to his own sister's writing with particular sharpness. "Your printing of a Book," he wrote, "beyond the custom of your sex, doth rankly smell." ...

Many English and American Puritans believed the virtuous woman should walk in the shadow of her male masters from the cradle to the grave. A daughter owed almost complete allegiance to her father's wishes. He was to supervise whom she might choose as friends, direct her to the service of others, and remind her to keep constant watch over the state of her soul. He was expected to reprimand her for tending to become a "Busie-Body" or "Pragmatical." Whatever he commanded (with exception of something sinful), she was to obey. His pleasure was her goal, and "her heart would melt/When she her Fathers looks not pleasant felt." The ideal daughter was like "a nun unprofest," a girl who never read lust-inducing plays and romances, who avoided the comb and the looking glass, and who relished serving her parents with a demeanor of "Virgin Modesty." When she reached a marriageable age, a daughter should "do nothing" without her father's approval; in marriage matters, she should be "very well contented ... to submit to such condition[s]" as her parents "should see providence directing." In every familial relation the father, that "soul of the family," served as "governor of the governed." Apparently to emphasize the potency of such paternal overlordship, John Cotton in 1641 actually suggested hanging any maiden who allowed a lover to have sexual intercourse with her in her father's house.

In marriage the woman traded her father's surname for her husband's, in a symbolic transferral of the male right to "govern, direct, protect, and cherish" her. Her lack of an independent name accented the fact that she could not exist independent of men: as daughter she was to give "Reverence, subjection & Obedience" to her father, and as wife she was to give the same to her marital "master." Since he possessed more "quickness of witte . . . greater insight and forecast," that "Prince and chiefe Ruler" deserved her assistance, "reverand awe," and silent submission — if not outright fear. . . .

Theologians directed the "true wife" to be constantly concerned for her husband's welfare, even at the expense of her own. In Cotton Mather's words:

> When she Reads, That Prince Edward in his Wars against the Turks, being stabbed with a poisoned Knife, his Princess did suck the Poison out of his Wounds, with her own Royal Mouth, she finds in her own Heart a principle disposing her to shew her own Husband as great a Love. When she Reads of a woman called Herpine, who having her Husband Apoplex'd in all his Limbs, bore him on her Back a thousand and three Hundred English Miles to a Bath, for his Recovery, she minds herself not altogether unwilling to have done the Like.

Mather urged the wife to address her husband by the appropriate title of "My Lord." If she felt any "passion" against her mate, she left it unexpressed; but when he was in passion, she quickly strove to mollify it. The virtuous wife was to "carry her self so to her husband as not to disturb his love by her contention, nor to destroy his love by her alienation." She was to be at his beck and call, acting "as if there were but One Mind [His] in Two Bodies." . . .

A wife's major purpose in life, besides working on religious salvation, was to minister to her husband's needs. Her personal identity and social rank were derived through him. She was his appendage, as Cotton Mather explained in a letter to his sister-in-law, Hannah Mather. To be the "best of women in the American World," he urged Mistress Mather, "Go on to love him [her husband], and serve him, and felicitate him, and become accessary to all the Good which *he* may do in the world." . . .

. . . [It] was the Puritan contention that female activities ought to be largely limited to the home's safe environment, even though many non-Puritan women worked in various English agricultural pursuits. William Perkins wrote, "The woman is not to take libertie of wandring, and staying abroad from her owne house, without the man's knowledge and consent." Considering her an ineffective manager of "outward business and affairs," Puritan leaders urged the wife to busy herself with cooking, cleaning, spinning, child care, and other household tasks. Indeed, worldly concerns constituted a potential threat to her health in a way that monotonous household activities did not. A woman achieved respect largely by the extent to which "She looks well to the Wayes of her Household." ...

In the final analysis, the spokesmen for the several Biblical Commonwealths posited an ideology of female weakness, deference, patience, and nurturance. Sex roles were sharply separated, with the male viewed as the stronger, ruling sex, one more protective than nurturant. As much as and perhaps more than their English contemporaries, the Puritan spokesmen of New England viewed male characteristics as expressions of their own "obvious" superiority. Michael Wigglesworth held that women's weakness made them "generally more ignorant, and Worthless." Nathaniel Ward found it hard to view women as anything other than "feather-headed" spendthrifts and "Squirrel-brained" friskers after the latest fashions, ladies "fitter to be kickt ... then either honour'd or humour'd." He called "these nauseous shaped gentlewomen" no more than "gant-bar-geese, ill-shapen-shotten-shellfish, Egyptian Hyeroglyphics, or at the best ... French flurts of the pastery." This acerbic minister maintained that "The world is full of care, much like unto a bubble/Woman and care, and care and Women, and Women and care and trouble." Another minister, William Hubbard, believed women to be little better than property; concerning a case wherein two men claimed the same woman as wife, he wrote that it took much time "to find who was the right *owner* of the *thing* in controversy."

Misogyny in New England had its limits, however. Although they affirmed the need for women to seek male theological advice, Puritans did allow women to work out their individual reckonings with God in the isolation of their closets. Some ministers attacked their male associates for refusing to recognize female worth. Cotton Mather wrote:

> Monopolizing HEE's, pretend no more
> Of Wit and Worth, to hoard up all the store.
> The Females too grow Wise & Good & Great.

This divine informed his readers, "It is a Common, but Causeless report that women's tongues [wag ceaselessly] and are frequently not governed by the fear of God." Similarly, John Cotton asserted that those men who viewed women as "a necessary Evil" were "Blasphemers." Yet another man, John Saffin, in a poem entitled "Cankers touch fairest fruites" directed his male readers away from the belief that women were "Woe to men." ...

The reader may object that I have been painting too bleak a picture of the Puritans' ideas about the "weaker sex." After all, many scholars have pointed out that these religious reformers emphasized the importance of love — an attitude which theoretically facilitated the liberation of women from the shackles of male dominion. On the surface this argument seems plausible, as some Puritans indicated their approval of affection and the emotional closeness which sometimes develops with physical closeness. John Winthrop addressed his wife Margaret as "My Chiefe Ioye in this World" and, when away from her on business, wrote letters containing the following affectionate remarks:

[April 28, 1629] I kisse and loue thee with the kindest affection and rest Thy faithful husbande,

[May 8, 1629] the verye thought of thee affordes me many a kynde refreshinge, what will then the enjoyinge of thy sweet societye, which I prize aboue all worldly comforts,

[February 5, 1629/30] My sweet wife, Thy loue is such to me, and so great is the bonde between vs, that I should neglect all others to hold correspondencye of lettres with thee.

Edward Taylor viewed his relationship with his wife as "the True-Love Knot, more sweet than spice/ And set with all the flowre of Graces dress." To this divine, the wedding knot was the place "Where beautious leaves are laid with Honey Dew./ And Chanting Birds Cherp out sweet Musick true." Thomas Hooker described the ideal husband very romantically, as "The man whose heart is endeared to the woman he loves, he dreams of her in the night, hath her in his eye and apprehension when he awakes, museth on her as he sets at table, walks with her when he travels and parlies with her in each place where he comes." Such a husband cradled his wife's head on his bosom and "his heart trusts in her . . . the stream of his affection, like a mighty current, runs with ful Tide and strength." Thomas Thatcher wrote poetically to Margaret Sheafe, his betrothed, in the 1660s:

Thy Joy I seek, thy comfort's my desire
Whilst to enjoy thy bosom I aspire; . . . .

Puritans like Thatcher, Hooker, Taylor, and Winthrop certainly expressed loving sentiments, quite in accord with those English Puritan divines who described "setled affection," "companionship," and "tender loue" as the "glue" between marital "yoke-fellows." Many a divine directed the husband to support his wife, praise her virtues, honor her, and "bee not bitter, fearce, and cruell vnto her." Yet, when ministers celebrated the mutual delight and concord existing in "louing" union, they considered love "not so much the cause as . . . the product of marriage." A "duty" owed one's spouse and God, it became "nothing but Christian charity, and marriage supplied the chief form for the exercise of that charity." As one minister explained, love was "the Sugar to sweeten every addition to married life *but not an essential part of it. Love was Condition in the married Relation.*" Since a couple need not love to marry, either sex could wed for less romantic considerations. A young man could legitimately search for a "goodly lass with aboundation of money" or a "very convenient" estate, as long as he had a desire to respect his wife-to-be and did not keep his motives from her. And a maiden could accept the hand of a suitor for equally mercenary motives, as long as she was honest about it. Such marriages had little to do with love; it magically appeared at some later date, if at all.

Nor did Puritans view love in egalitarian terms. Although a couple "are combined together as it were in one," Calvinists agreed that, even in the closest human relationship, "one is alwaies higher, and beareth rule, the other is lower, and yeeldeth subjection." . . . William Gouge pointed out that a couple "are yoak-fellows in mutuall familiaritie, not in equall authoritie. . . . If therefore he will one thing, and she another, she may not thinke to haue an equall right and power. She must giue place and yeeld," even if he be "a drunkard, a glutton, a profane swaggerer, an impious swearer, and blasphemer." Gouge and his contemporaries urged the wife, as a specific manifestation of her love, "to guid the house &c. not guid the Husband." The male-centered nature of such love becomes particularly clear in admonitions for her "wholly to depend on him, both in judgment and will." When the husband brought home unexpected dinner guests or failed to take her moods seriously enough, the enduring wife was to grin and bear it, for discontentment over such matters "argueth not a louing affection, nor a wiuelike subjection." Love meant that she empathized with his moods, in a nurturant manner, but that he did not need to reciprocate. In fact, even if she were "wiser, more discreete, and prouident then the Husband," those traits could not "overthrowe the superioritie of the man." The wise wife could advise him, but only with "humilitie and reuerence; shewing her selfe more willing to heare, then to speake."

. . . [T]he disobedient or contentious wife became one of the world's most despicable creatures — not only "an heart-sore to him that hath her," but no better than a wolf, a wart, a cancer, a gangrene, or even excrement. (By comparison, the harsh or churlish husband became only "a wild beast.") Quite revealingly, Puritan Alexander Niccoles explained the prevailing notion of male-centered love: a man "not only unitest unto thy selfe a friend," a "comfort for society" and "a companion for pleasure," but "in some sort a servant for profite too." Thomas Gataker went a step further, referring to the wife as a form of the husband's property. She "must resolue to giue herselfe wholly to him," Gataker wrote, "as her Owner, on whom God hath bestowed her." Still, in their effort to maintain security within the familial unit, as a counterpart to the insecurity occurring in the world outside, many Puritans disliked calling the wifely role "servitude" or "slavery." However, their overt endorsement of female subjection, coupled with affirmations of the husband's "superiority" and "authoritie" in "all things" at home, revealed that Puritans perceived marriage as servitude, although in a slightly different cast.

The Puritan notion of love served, then, not to liberate women; instead, it institutionalized sex-role oppression for both men and women. Whatever the realities of any particular interaction, as an idea it reinforced female submission and made it difficult for males to be anything other than controlling.

Such a concept of love fed male egocentricity. The Puritan male tended to emphasize what his wife could do for him, rather than what he could do for her. He loved her not for her uniqueness but for the extent to which she fulfilled the role expectations of the ideal female, including a self-sacrificing concern for his needs. Joseph Thompson cared for his wife because she studied how "to make my life Comfortable to me, as far as she could." Similarly, Richard Mather's wife was accounted "a Woman of singular Prudence" when she managed his secular affairs so well that he could devote himself totally to his own studying and "Sacred Imployments." Thomas Shepard applauded his mate for her "incomparable meekness of spirit, toward myselfe especially." Edward Taylor's wife, Elizabeth Fitch, was, in his opinion, "a Tender, Loving, Meet,/ Meecke, Patient, Humble, Modest, Faithful, Sweet/ Endearing Help," a woman "Whose Chiefest Treasure/ of Earthly things she held her Husbands pleasure." . . .

. . . Puritans could not agree with the Antinomian and Quaker belief that an intense feeling between husband and wife served as a reflection of, instead of a danger to, love for God. When Antinomian William Hutchinson said he thought more of his wife than of their church, the Puritans could only call him a man of "weak parts," one incapable of constraining his own affection or of regulating his wife's behavior.

Despite the Puritan desire to limit the genuine, earthly love that could develop between two people by subordinating it to the love of God and to demands arising out of sex role dominance and submission, some couples did marry for love and enter into very close relationships. That closeness developed not because of, but in spite of Puritanism. Ideologically, the egalitarian impulse of pure affection was undercut by the Puritan need to regard love first and foremost as duty — not as deep feeling brought to a marriage by the couple, but as a network of obligations imposed upon the couple by God. Such a notion of love, coupled with a belief system which accentuated male superiority, constituted an effort not only to be true to biblical prescriptions and to the sometimes conservative ethos of English culture, but also to countermand the Puritan male's peculiar feelings of impotence. . . .

An important issue arises at this point: Was Puritan sex-role ideology consistent with Puritan practice, or simply an unenforceable vision? Was it a purely intellectual identification with a glorified biblical past, or the genuinely descriptive adjunct of socially institutionalized sex roles? Such questions necessitate an examination of the extent to which the prevailing sex-role ideology was implemented.

Puritan society was organized in a way that explicitly affirmed the belief in sex segregation as a reminder of men's and women's different destinies. In church the men, women, maidens, and youths all sat separately, with the most prominent men sitting in the foremost, highest-status pews. Each sex also entered the meetinghouse by a separate door. . . . When the little girl attended a dame school to learn the rudiments of education, she studied at a curriculum somewhat different from that of the boys; while the latter grappled with Latin, penmanship, spelling, reading, and religion, the former learned cooking, weaving, and spinning, as well as reading, writing, and religion.

... [I]n other realms Puritans used institutional prohibitions to distinguish between the respective roles of men and women. Both spinsters and widows could own property, but neither could vote for public officials. Puritans considered the franchise an important means for protecting of civil liberties, but for men only — as Nathaniel Ward wrote, without such protection, "men are *but* women." Nor could women vote in church affairs, prophesy, or even ask questions in church, for in all such cases "speaking argues power." A woman could speak only when singing hymns or, in a few churches, when she made a public request for the privilege of membership. Male members not only reserved full participation in church affairs for themselves, but also were reluctant to admit to membership women who were "full of sweet affection" but "a little too confident."

Puritan society provided virtually no avenues for women to seek fulfillment outside marriage. The school curriculum emphasized the importance of the woman staying in the home, and the apprenticeship system trained girls for no trade other than housewifery. There is no record of any New England mercantile establishment hiring a maiden to work outside the home until after King Philip's War, although in England a daughter could receive apprenticeship training as a shopkeeper. Maidens, wives, and widows could not hawk or peddle goods throughout the countryside, as was true in their Puritan homeland. An unwed woman could attempt to build some savings by working as a domestic servant, a doctor, or a schoolmistress; however, such occupations were very poorly paid. Without marriage, a woman could hardly expect to have any financial security.

Even if a woman did manage to accumulate a sizeable estate or income (through an inheritance, for example), she faced great social pressure to marry. If a lass remained single until age twenty-three, neighbors called her a "spinster." If she was still unwed at twenty-six, she received the more odious appellation of "thornback." Bookseller John Dunton remarked in 1686 that "an old (or Superannuated) Maid, in Boston, is thought such a curse as nothing can exceed it, and [look'd] on as a Dismal Spectacle." Some of Dunton's Puritan contemporaries believed that deceased old maids could do no better than to lead apes in Hell.

Men were expected to marry also, but community gossip did not focus on the bachelor as it did on the spinster. There was, in fact, no term of opprobrium comparable to "spinster," "thornback," or "old maid." The church members of at least one town, Salem, chose a thirty-six-year-old bachelor, Nicholas Noyes, as their minister (1683). Puritans did, however, establish vehicles for the regulation of bachelors' behavior, since Satan reportedly loved to provide erotic fantasies to tempt the minds of unwed males. Med-field, Massachusetts, set aside segregated housing, a special Bachelors' Row, to facilitate their supervision. The Middlesex County magistrates prosecuted many "singlemen" who failed to place themselves under family government between 1665 and 1679, while Plymouth, New Haven, and Connecticut colonies required bachelors to live with "licensed families." The Connecticut enactment actually specified that bachelors living alone pay a £1 fine each week — which undoubtedly helps to explain why Madame Knight wrote in 1704 that half of Connecticut's males were married by the time they reached twenty years of age.

Despite such pressures to marry, the prospective suitor could not simply court any girl he wished. He first had to secure the permission of the maiden's father, or face prosecution on a charge of "inveigling" the girl. All Puritan-controlled locales except Maine punished by a £5 fine or a whipping any man who "stole away" the affections of a maiden by "speech, writing, message, company-keeping, unnecessary familiarity, disorderly night-meetings, sinful dalliance, gifts, or in any other way." The severity of the punishment for inveigling suggests that Puritans took very seriously the father's right to convey his overlordship to another male, thereby depriving the daughter of any initial decision about whom she wished to woo her. A father could not "wilfullie and unreasonably deny any childe timely or convenient" marriage, but he could largely determine whom she married. The daughter could, of course, reject any suitor allowed to court her, but she then had to deal with the consequences of her decision. For example, when Lucy Downing refused to wed a candidate of whom her parents approved, her mother informed her that such behavior was unwise and disreputable. When a depressed Betty Sewall withdrew from Grove Hirst's suit, her father reminded her that such action would "tend to discourage persons of worth from making their Court" to her. A young woman capable of such independence could hardly be expected to transform herself into a submissive, obedient wife, a fact which further restricted her marital possibilities.

Young men had fewer limitations. Even though a father might attempt to "control" his sons by refusing to give them any of his property, they could hire themselves out to artisans, become fishermen, or enter a number of other occupations. Once a young man decided he wanted to marry, he could secure the appropriate paternal permission to court one or more lasses. His father did not need to approve of his choices, although certainly that was the preferred route.

Once a couple had wed, no law specified that the wife had to obey her husband's every wish. However, the law did give him great supervisory control over her property and behavior. At marriage, a wife had to relinquish control over whatever real estate she possessed or income she received. She could, through a prenuptial contract, attempt to retain some control over her own property, but the English Court of Chancery and the Massachusetts Assistants did not recognize the validity of such an agreement. Not until 1762 did the Bay Colony accept prenuptial contracts as binding, although Connecticut had done so as early as 1673. The authorities of New Haven, New Hampshire, and Plymouth never heard a case concerning the legitimacy of such a contract. Whatever their position on prenuptial agreements, all of the colonies respected the husband's "right" to regulate his wife's realty. Only some of her personal estate — her dresses, quilts, needles, and so on — remained in her hands after marriage.

Puritan legal practice reinforced the notion that a husband was his wife's overseer, and therefore held him accountable if she stepped out of line. When a woman committed a minor crime, the courts usually ordered her husband to pay for it, in a fit punishment for his indiscretion in allowing her to break the law. If a wife did not attend Sabbath services, for instance, her husband was held responsible for failing to bring her to the meetinghouse. If she sold alcoholic beverages without a license, he paid £5 to £10 for tolerating her behavior. With the husband lay the decision of whether to pay a fine assessed against his wife, or to subject her to a whipping instead. In one case the Plymouth General Court actually allowed the husband to punish his wife "att home" after she had beaten and reviled him (1655). The wife had almost no opportunity to discharge a fine by enlisting the aid of her family or a charitable neighbor. Of course, no woman received a trial by a jury of her female peers.

Although, as in English local and customary law, a wife could sue in court for wrongs done her (provided she had her husband's permission), usually her husband brought suit in her behalf. Whenever a wife hurled scurrilous remarks at a neighbor, both she and her husband automatically became parties to the suit. If the husband neglected to take civil action when his spouse was the injured party, her parents might bring suit on her behalf (in a slander suit, for example). Without husbandly or parental allowance, a wife could not seek damages for any injury, irrespective of its severity. Her honor belonged to her father or her husband, who protected it at his discretion. Under no circumstances could a woman sue her own husband for tortious acts (e.g., slander, assault) against her, although she could give evidence against him in a criminal case.

A wife's activity in "outward matters" was always contingent upon her husband's approval. She could contract for rents and wages, sell goods, and collect debts, but only if her husband had authorized her activity. Since Puritans believed the "weaker sex" had little ability in such dangerous matters, they wished to keep women within the home's protective confines. To prevent weak Puritan wives from unwarily responding to some sinner's solicitations, the Massachusetts General Court in 1674 barred any wife, in the absence of her husband, from entertaining any traveler without the allowance of the town selectmen, under the penalty of a £5 fine or ten lashes. She also had to busy herself with household tasks, in order to avoid prosecution on a charge of idleness. . . .

In Puritan ideology and practice, a wife could have few outright belongings. Neither her premarital possessions (with the exception of some personalty) nor her subsequent acquisitions, nor the use of her free time, nor even her criminal sentences were hers alone. Her status semed quite like that of a servant, even though the latter's period of servitude was limited by contract.

. . . Still, despite such disadvantages, women were not completely under male control in Puritan New England. Single, widowed, or divorced women of means could open mercantile shops, own land, and maintain inns. These women could sue on their own behalf in court. Three extant petitions indicate that women attempted to have some political impact by petitioning the Massachusetts General Court or a Connecticut magistrate. In half of all cases where a deceased husband left a widow, she received the right to act as the executor of his estate — a position of some administrative importance.

Even though the husband could restrict his wife's activity in many ways, she retained certain legitimate claims on him (based not on her "rights" but on her supposed weakness, or need for protection). In Plymouth and New Haven, a wife's permission was necessary before a husband could sell their house or any of their land. In contrast, however, Connecticut and much of Massachusetts conceded that property transferral was the husband's prerogative. In his will the Connecticut husband usually referred to the couple's acquisitions as "my" lot or "my" dwelling house. When a husband made his will, he could not leave his wife penniless. In Massachusetts before 1649, Connecticut before 1696, Plymouth, and New Haven, the law reserved to the widow a dower right of one-third of the lands, houses, tenements, rents, and hereditaments her husband possessed. This widow's third was free from all debts, rents, judgments, and executions against her deceased mate's estate. Plymouth and New Hampshire also allowed the widow either all or part of her husband's personal estate, while in Massachusetts after 1649 the magistrates determined what portion she would receive. . . .

A husband could not beat his wife in order to reduce her to abject submission. As early as 1599 the English Puritan Henry Smith asserted, "If hee cannot reform his wife without beating, he is worthy to be beaten for choosing no better." Almost a century later Cotton Mather agreed that for "a man to Beat his Wife was as bad as any Sacriledge. And such a Rascal were better buried alive, than show his Head among his Neighbours any more." The Bay Colony's initial law code, the "Body of Liberties," in 1641 freed the wife from "bodily correction or stripes by her husband, unless it be [given] in his owne defence upon her assalt." Nine years later the Massachusetts General Court specified a fine of up to £10 or a whipping as punishment for any man who struck his wife, or for any woman who hit her husband. None of the other four Puritan colonies enacted such a law, although they did lightly penalize husbands who abused their wives too readily. . . .

We cannot know the extent to which wives possessed real "private power" or derived satisfaction from the marital power arrangement. . . . As a general rule, the specter of male overlordship is so apparent in institutional, intellectual, economic, and family life throughout the seventeenth century that it leaves little room to doubt women's difficulty in achieving, much less exerting, a sense of their own assertive independence. All of woman's protections and the few privileges she enjoyed as a widow did not, in the final analysis, facilitate her development beyond the limitations imposed by her sex-role conditioning.

STUDY GUIDE

1. Summarize the seventeenth-century Calvinist view of the nature of children and proper child-rearing. How do these views differ from the predominant attitudes of American society today, especially with regard to parental concerns about child development?

2. Describe the particular characteristics of the ideal wife in the seventeenth century as set forth in the sermons and laws. Develop an argument as to why such historical sources are or are not reliable guides to the actual relations of men and women in the day-to-day life of the family.

3. What limitations were there on women's equality in economic life, church, government, and social activities?

4. The changing status of women in our time has occurred as a result of a complex variety of factors. Which of the following do you believe to be most important: the decline of traditional religious views, industrialization, creation of new social agencies to handle needs that formerly rested upon the family, modern household technology, or women's suffrage?

BIBLIOGRAPHY

In this edition, Koehler's article replaces a selection from Edmund S. Morgan, *Virginians at Home* (1952), which gives a very different picture of courtship and marriage in a southern colony. A fuller study than Morgan's is Julia C. Spruill, *Women's Life and Work in the Southern Colonies* (1935). Morgan also wrote a work on family life in New England, presenting a somewhat different picture from the one in his study of Virginia: *The Puritan Family: Religion and Domestic Relations in Seventeenth Century New England*, rev. ed. (1966); his chapter on husbands and wives is especially interesting. John Demos, *A Little Commonwealth: Family Life in Plymouth Colony*

(1970) is a fascinating study of nearly all aspects of family life including husband-wife and parent-child relationships, housing, furnishings, and the psychology of life in the seventeenth century.

The women's liberation movement of our time and the revived interest of historians in the history of minority groups have led to a virtual explosion in the study of women's history. Much of the writing has concerned women in nineteenth-century America; these books are cited in the bibliography following the selection by Barbara J. Berg (Reading No. 9). Roger Thompson, *Women in Stuart England and America: A Comparative Study* (1974) is a very full study of male-female relations in the seventeenth century. Nancy F. Cott, *The Bonds of Womanhood: "Women's Sphere" in New England, 1780–1835* (1977) sheds some light on the late colonial period. Mary B. Norton, *Liberty's Daughters: The Revolutionary Experience of American Women, 1750–1800* (1980) and Linda G. DePauw, *Founding Mothers: Women in the Revolutionary Era* (1975) are concerned with the period indicated in the titles.

Both the history of childhood and that of the condition of the aged are of considerable interest to those studying the family in America. The books by Morgan and Demos mentioned earlier have chapters describing how children were viewed and reared in the colonial period. Later views are examined in Joseph F. Kett, *Rites of Passage: Adolescence in America, 1790 to the Present* (1977). Studies of educational history also illuminate attitudes toward children. Among the most interesting of the many volumes on this subject are Lawrence A. Cremin, *American Education: The Colonial Experience, 1607–1786* (1970); Robert Middlekauff, *Ancients and Axioms: Secondary Education in Eighteenth-Century New England* (1963); and James Axtell, *The School upon a Hill: Education and Society in Colonial New England* (1974). Axtell considers the social aspects of childbirth and the effects of postnatal environment on the colonial child. Much less has been written about the aged in American society, but David H. Fischer has attempted a broad survey of social attitudes in his *Growing Old in America* (1977).

T. H. Matteson's painting (1855) portrays the anxiety and excitement accompanying George Jacobs's examination on witchcraft charges at Salem.

4

JOHN C. MILLER

The Witchcraft Scare

One of the striking phenomena of recent years has been widespread interest in witchcraft, the occult, and occurrences beyond normal, sensory perception. Hollywood producers have beaten paths to the bank with the box-office receipts from dozens of films on vampires, ghosts, and satanic possession. Thousands of readers have believed quite as firmly in the reality of supernatural forces haunting the house in Amityville as in the astrological forces in their own lives. One major university has a center for the study of extrasensory perception, and many others offer courses on magic, the devil, and the mystery of evil. If, after all, one believes in God and the forces of good, is it illogical to believe in Satan and the forces of evil?

One might, however, ask why the belief or at least the interest in magic and witchcraft seems to be especially strong in certain periods and to be the subject of skepticism or ridicule at other times. Some scholars have suggested that a society is more likely to turn to supernatural explanations in an especially troubled time and to charge unpopular or deviant members of the society with witchcraft when it needs scapegoats. For many years, this was the fundamental historical explanation of the Salem witchcraft episode that staggered Massachusetts in 1692. In recent years, historians have reexamined Salem witchcraft and have developed a number of other explanations. One writer has suggested that witchcraft was actually practiced in Salem, and that the victims who felt tormented by witches were suffering from hysteria, rather than deliberately misleading the community by false accusations. Another writer has suggested that a peculiar fungus in the rye grain in one part of the town, which some of the citizens used in baking, caused them to experience hallucinations similar to an LSD trip. Others have argued that the witchcraft affair was a religious and socioeconomic conflict between two different parts of the town.

The Salem episode has fascinated novelists and dramatists from Nathaniel Hawthorne to Arthur Miller. Like the historians, they have seen very different things in the outbreak of witchcraft. Miller, writing his play *The Crucible* in the 1950s when Senator Joseph McCarthy was conducting a Communist witchhunt, saw parallels between the events of his own day and those of 1692. In the conclusion of a French film about the affair, a crowd storms the gallows area in a scene reminiscent of events at the Bastille in 1789. Other writers have viewed Salem witchcraft as little more than the logical outcome of a narrow-minded religious outlook, whether in Catholic Europe where thousands perished or in Puritan Massachusetts where twenty men and women died.

The following selection by John C. Miller represents an eclectic, and perhaps a somewhat old-fashioned, point of view in the sea of new interpretations. Miller suggests that socioeconomic conflict, the troubles that the colony had recently experienced, and a lack of enlightenment all contributed to the hysteria. He is a bit harsher on the Mathers than some recent writers, but on the whole, his essay gives a concise and balanced summary of the whole episode. His comments on witchcraft in Europe suggest that some restraint is in order before we label seventeenth-century Salem as an especially dark and bloody chapter of our past.

During the period 1670–1690, among the evidences of backsliding noted by the New England clergy was a growing disposition on the part of the people to take witchcraft lightly. The Reverend Increase Mather observed with alarm that even some church members were beginning to say that people possessed by demons mentioned in the Bible were simply epileptics or lunatics. Taking what he regarded as an extraordinarily tolerant attitude toward these skeptics, Mather said that he would not "suspect all those as guilty of

Reprinted with permission from John C. Miller, *This New Man, The American* (New York: McGraw-Hill Book Co.). © 1974 by John C. Miller.

witchcraft, nor yet of heresie, who call the received opinion about witches into question." But neither did he admit that they had a right to advance such heretical opinions.

To alert these skeptical citizens to their danger, Mather included in his *Essay for the Recording of Illustrious Providences* (1684) a long discourse upon witchcraft. The elder Mather prided himself upon taking a dispassionate, scientific view of witchcraft and of other natural phenomena. He admitted, for example, that many accounts of possession by demons were mere fables, and he denied that it was possible for spirits to generate bodies or beget children or that witches could transform themselves or others into another species of creature such as horse, wolf, cat, and mouse. "It is beyond the power of all the devils in hell to cause such a transformation," he asserted. "They can no more do it than they can be the authors of a true miracle." Moreover, he disapproved of many of the "superstitious and magical ways" of detecting witches — "whereby," he said, "much innocent blood hath been shed." Only by exhaustive cross-examination and scientific appraisal of the evidence, said Mather, could the guilt of witches be proved beyond all doubt.

The "Invisible World" was also very real to Cotton Mather — more real, it sometimes seemed, than the little world of churchgoers over which he presided. He invested commonplace events with supernatural, portentous meaning. For example, when he suffered from toothaches "he considered whether or not he had sinned with his teeth. How? By sinful and excessive eating; and by evil speeches." Thus even a simple case of caries was endowed with theological significance.

In sounding the alarm against witchcraft, Cotton Mather acted under what he supposed was a special mandate from Heaven. In 1686, God appeared to him in a vision and told him that his mission was to fight witchcraft. Accordingly, after protracted fasting and prayer, Mather took up his pen — specially consecrated, he believed, by the Almighty to expose "the whole Plot of the Devil against New England in every branch of it" — to write against witches. The result of his revelation was the publication in 1689 of *Memorable Providences Relating to Witchcraft and Other Possessions*.

Both Increase and Cotton Mather were impressed by the inability of science to explain the phenomena they studied. To them, science left the ultimate mysteries untouched. Lacking a scientific explanation for many baffling events in human affairs, they were driven to the conviction that demons were constantly at work among men and that the Devil, for God's own purposes, had been permitted to act through the medium of witches — always, however, within definite restrictions laid down by the Almighty.

The Mathers tried to buttress the case for witchcraft with pseudoscientific "evidence" derived from their observation of people under seizure. What they recorded were cases of abnormal psychology, but they presented them as irrefutable "proof" of the existence of demons. By their books and sermons they succeeded in inculcating the idea that witchcraft was increasing by leaps and bounds in New England and that God's own plantation might fall before the wiles and stratagems of Satan. "'Tis *our* Worldiness, *our* Formality, *our* Sensuality, and *our* Iniquity," said Cotton Mather, that had provided Satan with an entering wedge into God's own plantation.

In the jeremiads, the clergy portrayed the crusade against sin and worldliness within their favorite frame of reference — the struggle between God and the Devil. All history, as they saw it, consisted of variations on this cosmic theme. Although the last thing the clergy wanted to see was a plague of witches descend upon New England — by their reckoning no greater disaster could befall a country — yet by their books and sermons they inadvertently prepared the way for Salem witchcraft. People who fear witches and who talk about them constantly are likely to be assailed by them sooner or later.

Salem witchcraft was merely an episode — hardly more than a footnote — in the history of an ancient superstition, for evidences of belief in the malefic power of certain individuals has been found in the most primitive societies. But it was not until the late Middle Ages, when witchcraft was identified with heresy and therefore came within the purview of the Holy Inquisition, that a witchcraft mania really began. The Reformation intensified the zeal of the witch-hunters. While Roman Catholics and Protestants disagreed upon many points, they agreed in holding witches in abhorrence and in putting an end to their existence as summarily as possible. In the sixteenth and seventeenth centuries — the age of the Renaissance and the New Science — over 100,000 people charged with having leagued themselves with the Devil were put to death.

Witchcraft was believed to originate in a bargain between a man or a woman and the Devil by which he or she agreed to sell his or her soul to Satan. This transaction, of course, was a great victory for Satan: he had turned against God one of God's own creatures and ensured the damnation of a human being. It was supposed that the Devil insisted that his victims sign a book agreeing to renounce the Christian religion, pay homage to the Prince of Darkness, and join in celebrating the Black Mass. Not until it was all down in writing did Satan feel that the bargain was truly consummated. Everything was neat, orderly and legal, the Devil having served his apprenticeship in Heaven where making contractual obligations — or so the Puritans believed — was the approved procedure. After the signatories signed the "contract," they were permitted to have carnal intercourse with devils, join in the witches' sabbat, revel with the Devil himself, and enjoy the power to subvert God's order on earth. Women who put their signatures to this horrid affidavit became witches; men who joined the Devil's legion were known as wizards.

Witchcraft was therefore treated as a legal crime — an offense against God

— which merited the death penalty. Every country in Christendom enacted laws against witchcraft and hauled suspects into civil or ecclesiastical courts to stand trial. . . . The act need not be malefic or destructive: if it were proved to have been performed through "conference with the Devil," it became a capital offense.

Witches were held responsible for storms, droughts, the death of cattle, sexual impotence, epidemics — and all the evils, in short, that the Devil chose to inflict upon mankind. But, clearly, malice, spite, and unreasoning fear played an important part in determining who were the Devil's agents. Unpopular eccentrics and "far-out" people were always candidates for suspicion. Old women were particularly vulnerable: being accused of practicing witchcraft was one of the hazards of being old, ugly, and unwanted.

The Devil was no respecter of persons. James I, who regarded himself as God's own anointed, also believed that he was the victim of a witches' conspiracy. He was firmly persuaded that they had almost succeeded in drowning him by brewing up a storm while he was at sea. As was his custom when he was particularly exercised by anything from tobacco to theology, James wrote a book against it. *Demonologie,* a dialogue upon witchcraft, appeared in 1597.

As a rule, outbreaks of witch-hunting occurred especially in countries distinguished by clerical power, popular ignorance, the breakdown of government, and the use of torture. Germany, where all these conditions existed, was the site of the most sanguinary efforts to suppress witchcraft. At the height of the mania, no one was safe from the suspicion of being in league with the Devil. The estates of wealthy people made them particularly vulnerable, and a lenient judge was liable to incur the charge of being an accomplice of the accused. Even the expression of disbelief in witchcraft was apt to be construed as circumstantial evidence of guilt. As James I said in *Demonologie,* the author of a book casting doubt on the existence of witches betrayed himself to be "one of that profession."

In whipping the people into a frenzy of fear of witches, intellectuals played a vital role. The belief in witches and the determination to stamp them out was in part a by-product of the scholarship of the age: the more learned and religious the individual, the more zealous and remorseless was his attitude toward witches likely to be. In the great witch-hunts of the sixteenth and seventeenth centuries, the prime instigators were men of learning who instilled their fear of the prevalence of witchcraft into the minds of the common people.

Vast ingenuity was expended by scholars upon the problem of determining how a witch could be detected. While such signs as moles or warts, an insensitive spot which did not bleed when pricked, a capacity to float in water, and an inability to recite the Lord's Prayer constituted only circumstantial evidence, they gave witch-hunters a clear lead in tracking down the Devil's agents.

On the European continent, torture was used to extract confessions from those accused of witchcraft. The rack, red-hot pincers, thumbscrews, scourges, leg-crushing machines — the familiar appurtenances of torture — together with a novel instrument, the witches' chair (a seat under which a fire was kindled), were the ultimate resorts of judges and inquisitors confronted with people who obstinately protested their innocence. By express orders of the Pope, issued in 1468, there were no limits upon the amount or degree of torture that could be applied. But the inquisitors were not content with a confession procured under torture: the accused had to be tortured until he or she confessed voluntarily.

In England, although those accused of witchcraft were not tortured, they were subjected to intensive interrogation, sometimes lasting for weeks or even months without benefit of habeas corpus. Those convicted in England were hung rather than burned at the stake — a distinction which, however finely drawn, was important to those who suffered the penalty. Moreover, James I and other authorities on witchcraft enjoined judges and juries strictly to observe the rules of evidence. Even so, about 30,000 people were convicted of witchcraft in the British Isles.

During the centuries when witchcraft was in flower, the professional witch-hunter and informer flourished in Europe. Judges welcomed the services of these itinerants who ferreted witches out of their deepest lairs. One of the most successful witch-hunters on record was Matthew Hopkins, who, during the 1640s, was personally responsible for the death of over 200 English witches. But Hopkins enjoyed an unfair advantage over his rival witch-hunters: he was said to have secured the Devil's own list of witches commissioned to operate in England.

As a result of the bloodletting of the period 1600–1660, when the mania reached its height, a reaction against witch-hunting set in. On the Continent, torture had been carried to such lengths that the confessions which had brought thousands of men and women to their deaths seemed worthless. During this period, thousands of people saw one or more of their relatives suffer death under one of the most terrible charges that could be made against a human being — selling his or her soul to the Devil and contracting to aid the Devil against God.

Being the most militant of English Protestants in the struggle against the Roman Catholic Counter-Reformation, the Puritans were peculiarly prone to believe in witchcraft and the ubiquitous power of Satan. Literal believers in the Bible, they took the injunction "Thou shalt not suffer a witch to live" to mean that they were under a religious duty to exterminate witches. As Calvin said, "The Bible teaches that there are witches and that they must be slain. . . . God expressly commands that all witches and enchantresses shall be put to death; and this law of God is an universal law." In Geneva, Calvin suited the action to the word. Before he came to that city, little had been heard of witchcraft, but in the 60 years that followed, over

150 witches were burned. It is not therefore merely coincidental that the most destructive witch craze in English history occurred during the period of Puritan ascendancy.

By the last quarter of the seventeenth century, the maniacal phase of witchcraft was clearly on the wane. Fewer and fewer of the "Accursed tribe" were sent to the stake or the gallows. As Montaigne said, "After all, it is rating one's conjectures at a very high price to roast a man alive on the strength of them." In the late seventeenth century, Holland abolished witchcraft trials altogether. In Geneva, the final witch burning occurred in 1652, and the last mass holocaust took place in Germany in 1679 when the Archbishop of Salzburg consigned 97 witches to the flames. In 1672, Louis XIV of France ordered that all prisoners recently condemned to death for witchcraft by the Parlement of Rouen should have their sentences commuted to banishment.

But the belief in witchcraft could not yet be dismissed as a mere peasant superstition. What had really changed was not the belief in witchcraft but confidence in the effectiveness of the methods used to detect it. While few doubted that many of those who perished at the stake were genuine witches who richly deserved their fate, it began to dawn upon the sober-minded, particularly after the mania had spent itself, that many had fallen victim to biased evidence, rumor, hearsay, envy, and malice.

What is truly remarkable about Salem witchcraft is that it occurred so late in the history of an ancient superstition. Far from playing a leading part in the mania, the Puritans did not enter upon the stage until the final act. That, in part, is why they became so conspicuous: most of the other actors, having already played out their terrible parts, had left the scene.

In Puritan New England, the outbreak of witchcraft occurred in a social context characterized by instability, clerical power, tension, and fear. The decade 1680–1690 had seen the loss of the Massachusetts charter, the establishment of the despotic Dominion of New England, the revolution of 1688–1689, and an abortive expedition against Quebec. The "great fear" abroad in the land was the fear of crypto–Roman Catholics in high places who were believed to be plotting the overthrow of the Protestant religion. It is significant that the witch-hunt was preceded by a hunt for Roman Catholics. To a marked degree, Salem witchcraft was a continuation of the anti–Roman Catholic agitation. Puritans would have been hard pressed to tell which of the two — Roman Catholics or witches — was more malefic. In any event, at the very time that the threat of Roman Catholicism was approaching its climax, the country was infested with swarms of witches.

In Salem Village — now Danvers, Massachusetts — the anxiety and apprehension felt by all the people of the colony were aggravated by dissension between the pastor and his congregation (just before the outbreak of witchcraft, two ministers had successively taken their parishioners to court to collect their salaries, and both had won judgments); by educational backwardness; by petty squabbles among the villagers over land, animals, and crops; and by the presence of Tituba, a slave woman of mixed black and Indian ancestry whose mind was filled with the primitive lore of her people. Tituba was a slave in the household of the Reverend Samuel Parris, who had come to Salem Village in 1689 and who, like his predecessors, had quarreled with his parishioners over his salary. The Reverend Mr. Parris's family consisted of his wife, his daughter, and his niece. Tituba regaled these highly impressionable adolescents with tales of the occult: Salem witchcraft was the product of the conjunction of the pagan superstition of Africa with the Christian superstition of Western Europe.

The Reverend Mr. Parris was a firm believer in witchcraft, and his young daughter and niece had probably learned at his knee all about black magic and the Invisible World. It certainly seemed very real to them; at the age of twelve they were experts on demonology. Growing up in the narrow world of a country parsonage in an intellectual atmosphere that came straight from the Middle Ages, with overtones of voodooism, and living in a backward, tension-ridden, credulous, quarrelsome community, these girls were in a strategic position to start a witch-hunt. Not surprisingly, they were seized with fits and convulsions, pinched and choked by unseen hands, pricked with invisible pins and needles, and visited by specters who tried to entice them into selling their souls to the Devil.

In 1691, few people doubted that the long-heralded assault on New England by the Invisible World had begun. . . . The most dismal predictions of the jeremiads seemed mild in comparison with the horrible reality. Cotton Mather declared that "prodigious Witch-Meetings" were being held all over the country at which "a fearful knot of proud, ignorant, envious and malicious creatures" volunteered for the Devil's service. But Mather was not surprised by this untoward event: "Where," he asked rhetorically, "will the Devil show most Malice, but where he is hated, and hateth most?" Mather rejoiced at the prospect of a decisive encounter with his old enemy who, he was persuaded, had sent the witches "as a particular Defiance unto *my* poor *Endeavours* to bring the Souls of men unto Heaven." . . . But at least the enemy was identifiable. From reports he had heard, Mather pieced together a picture of the Devil: "a short and a Black Man . . . no taller than an ordinary Walking-Staff," wearing "a High-Crowned Hat, with strait Hair, and had one Cloven-Foot."

In May 1692, at the advice of the clergy, Governor Phips appointed a special court of oyer and terminer in which those accused of witchcraft could be tried. This court was composed of merchants, public officials, and doctors. Most of the members were college graduates. There was not a lawyer among them, but this circumstance was not accounted important: college graduates were deemed sufficiently learned in the law to qualify as judges, and in any event, the problem of ridding the country of witches was thought to transcend the skill and erudition of any mere lawyer. Only the most pious, God-fearing men could cope with this assault.

In Salem witch trials, despite the strong sense of urgency and crisis, no precipitate action was taken. There was a three-month delay between the first accusations and the first trial. During this interval, the bodies of the accused were carefully examined for such telltale evidence of guilt as insensitive spots, supernumerary teats, warts, or moles. The physical checkup over, the accused were asked to recite the Lord's Prayer. If they stammered, stuttered, or missed a word, it was all up with them, for it was a well-known fact that the Devil could not get through the Lord's Prayer without stumbling. Inability to shed tears was likewise accounted an incriminating sign, since the Devil was incapable of feeling remorse for any of his misdeeds. Those who failed to clear themselves of suspicion were indicted and bound over for trial. Without legal counsel, they conducted their own defense — no easy task in view of the fact that the judges and jurors, who were all church members, were strongly inclined to regard them as guilty until proved innocent.

Among the accused was a backwoods preacher, the Reverend George Burroughs. Burroughs was alleged to be the "black man" who sounded the trumpet that summoned the witches to their rendezvous, and he was also accused of having successively murdered his two wives by incantation. The first witness against Burroughs was his own granddaughter! During his examination and trial, spectators cried out that he was biting them — and, wonderful to relate, marks made by his teeth were found on their arms even though he had not stirred from the dock. Evidence was presented that Burroughs had performed feats of running and weightlifting clearly beyond the powers of mortal man unless aided by the Devil.

For Cotton Mather, the clinching evidence against Burroughs was supplied by five witches from Andover who testified that he was their ringleader and that in that capacity he had presided over their infernal get-togethers. Thenceforth, Mather took a personal interest in seeing Burroughs brought to the gallows, unusual as it was for one clergyman to display such zeal for putting a halter around the neck of another wearer of the cloth.

Burroughs was duly convicted and sentenced to death. But as he was being prepared for the noose, he made a moving plea of innocence and recited the Lord's Prayer without making a single mistake, and the spectators were almost persuaded that Burroughs was not a wizard after all. At this point, Cotton Mather, mounted on a horse, proved that he was as effective an orator in the saddle as in the pulpit. He turned the crowd against Burroughs by pointing out that the condemned man was not really an ordained minister and that all the persons hitherto executed had died by a righteous sentence. Burroughs was strung up, and Cotton Mather rode home satisfied with having done a good day's work for the Lord.

A convicted witch could save herself by confessing; indeed, the object of the prosecution was not to kill witches but to extract confessions from them. Some of the accused took this easy way out, implicating others in their accounts of their dealings with the Devil. These confessions brought an ever-widening circle of people under suspicion. As in England, torture was not used to procure confessions, but wizard or witch could go to the gallows protesting his or her innocence or stubbornly refusing to speak.

Confession, while it usually saved a person's life, led to forfeiture of property. Giles Cory, who would have been found guilty in an ordinary court of law of nothing more serious than eccentricity, refused to answer his accusers when charged with entering into a compact with the Devil — in the hope thereby of preserving his estate for his heirs. By English law (not repealed until 1772), *peine forte et dure* — pressing by weights until a confession, or death, was forthcoming — was prescribed for those who stood mute. The weights were placed upon Cory, and after several days of torture, he died without opening his lips. At that incredible cost, he made it possible for his heirs to inherit his property.

Salem witchcraft was not merely the result of a welling up of ignorance, superstition, and fear from the depths of society. The clergy, the magistrates (including Governor Phips himself), and educated people in general shared the conviction of the most ignorant and deluded people that they were witnessing an outbreak of "horrible Enchantments and Possessions" instigated by Satan.

As long as the accusations were made against friendless old women and people of low degree, the clergy hallooed on the witch-hunters and sanctified the good work by quoting the injunction of the Book of Exodus: "Thou shalt not suffer a witch to live." In the trials, every kind of "evidence" — hearsay, gossip, old wives' tales — was admitted provided that it indicated the guilt of the accused. Some of this so-called evidence went back many years and obviously originated in personal spite. None of the defendants had counsel to raise objections to the admission of this kind of evidence or, indeed, to question the legality of the procedure or the jurisdiction of the court. As a result, there was no one to contest the legality of "spectral evidence."

In their confessions, or in giving evidence on the witness stand, many people alleged that they had been approached by people who passed as respectable members of society yet who now appeared in the guise of the Devil's agents urging their victims to sign the Devil's book and to commit other enormities. This was "spectral evidence," and if it were indiscriminately admitted to be valid, there was obviously no limit to the number of people who might be accused of witchcraft. The weighty question raised by spectral evidence was whether or not the Devil could assume the shape of an innocent person or whether or not every person who appeared to the afflicted actually served the Devil's purposes.

When their opinion was asked, the Mathers recommended that the judges observe "a very critical and exquisite caution" lest they be taken in by the Devil's legerdemain. Caution was especially important, they warned, in cases of "persons formerly of an unblemished reputation." "It was better for a guilty witch to live," said Increase Mather, "than for an innocent person to die." Cotton Mather admitted that the Devil might, by God's permission, appear in the shape of an innocent person, but he thought that this permission was rarely given.

In essence, Cotton Mather took the position that spectral evidence merely offered grounds for suspicion and, at most, a presumption of guilt but that corroborative evidence was required before a verdict could be rendered. The immediate danger, as he saw it, was that evil spirits would confuse the judges by appearing in the guise of innocent people, thereby permitting bona fide witches to escape scot-free. Chief Justice Stoughton, much as he revered the Mathers, did not accept their views on the admissibility of spectral evidence. In his opinion, the fact that the Devil assumed the form of a respectable individual, even though he was a pillar of the community, must mean that that individual had sold his soul, for, he declared, the Devil could not impersonate an innocent man or woman. He therefore instructed the jury that "as the Devil had appeared in the form of many of the accused, according to the eye-witnesses there, the defendants must be guilty." This instruction resulted in the conviction of several of the accused.

Nor did the people follow the Mathers in drawing these fine distinctions regarding the admissibility of spectral evidence. To them, any person who took the form of a specter must be an agent of Satan. In consequence, Massachusetts was gripped by a reign of terror. Ties of friendship and of blood ceased to matter. It was a case of every man for himself and the Devil take the hindmost. Wives testified against their husbands; children charged their parents with practicing witchcraft; a wife and daughter gave evidence against their husband and father in order to save themselves; and a seven-year-old girl helped send her mother to the gallows. When two young men would not confess, they were tied together by the neck until they accused their own mother. The roll of specters began to read like a *Who's Who* of New England. Captain John Alden, the eldest son of John and Priscilla Alden, was accused of being a wizard on the strength of spectral evidence, but the resourceful captain escaped from jail. Dudley Bradstreet, the son of a former governor, fled the colony before he could be brought to trial. The wife of the Reverend John Hale, secretary of the colony of Connecticut, was denounced as a witch, and one woman who was hung at Salem was a church member. Cotton Mather himself was not safe: in October 1693, a young woman swore that Mather's image threatened and molested her. "I cried unto the Lord," Mather wrote in his Diary, "for the Deliverance of my *Name,* from the Malice of Hell." Thus the work of casting out devils seemed likely to lead to the depopulation of Massachusetts. Who would be alive to hang the last witch?

Clearly, events were escaping from the control of the clergy and magistrates. Witch-hunting had reached the height of mass hysteria: the people clamored for more victims, and no one was safe from their zeal and fear.

To add to the danger, although Salem Village continued to be "the Chief Seat of these Diabolical Vexations," witches began to expand their operations until all Massachusetts reeled under "the horrible Assaults made by the Invisible World." The citizens of Gloucester, expecting to be attacked by an army of witches, took refuge in a stockade. In Andover, where an epidemic was blamed on witches, more than 50 people were accused of having had dealings with the Devil. One of the magistrates who dared to defy public opinion by refusing to institute proceedings against the suspects was himself accused of sorcery. But the mania was short-lived: one of the accused instituted action for defamation of character against his accusers. "This wonderfully quenched zeal," it was observed, "the accusers saw *his* spectre no more."

By September 22, 1692, the Salem judges had tried 27 suspects, one-third of them church members; all had denied being witches. All 27 had been sentenced to death, and of this number 19 had been hanged and 1 pressed to death. A man accused of bewitching a dog barely escaped with his life, but the dog, presumably possessed by devils, was killed. None of the 50 who confessed that they were witches had been executed; 100 persons accused of being witches were in jail awaiting trial; and an additional 200 had been accused but had not yet been imprisoned. Two judges had resigned from the court of oyer and terminer to protest the course the proceedings had taken. Among the suspects were Lady Phips, the wife of the Governor of the province, and the Reverend Samuel Willard of Boston, the president of Harvard College. Willard was under suspicion because he had questioned some of the evidence presented at the trials.

On September 22, 1692, at the advice of the clergy, now thoroughly alarmed by the use to which spectral evidence was being put, Governor Phips suspended the proceedings of the court of oyer and terminer. In December the accused were brought before the Superior Court for trial. Spectral evidence was sparingly admitted, with the result that of the 52 persons brought to trial, 49 were acquitted. Only three were found guilty and condemned, but Phips first reprieved them and then granted a general pardon to all under suspicion. In 1957, the Massachusetts Legislature adopted a resolution absolving all the Salem witches of wrongdoing.

Chief Justice Stoughton bitterly lamented the decision to call a halt to the trials: "We were in a way to have cleared the land of them," he said. "Who it is that obstructs the cause of justice I know not; the Lord be merciful to this country!"

It is ironical that Cotton Mather, who wished to be known above all as a man of God and a do-gooder, should be remembered chiefly for his part in the Salem witch trials and therefore held to be typical of all that was most narrow, bigoted, and repellent in Puritanism — the very epitome of the black-frocked, bluenosed zealot. He was by no means the most remorseless and bloodthirsty of the witch-hunters; indeed, his position on spectral evidence marks him as a moderate and a stickler for the observance of legal formalities. The people, and some of the clergy, demanded more witch trials and more executions, but Mather tried to calm the storm he had helped create. In his poem dealing with Salem witchcraft, Longfellow makes Mather say:

> Be careful. Carry the knife with such exactness, That on one side no innocent blood be shed By too excessive zeal, and, on the other, No shelter given to any work of darkness.

Yet Cotton Mather did not question the justice of the verdicts handed down at Salem, nor did he doubt that all who had been executed were guilty. Those who asked God to attest to their innocence were guilty, in his opinion, of "monstrous impudence." Lest it be supposed that innocent people had been condemned on the basis of inadequate evidence, Mather wrote a book entitled *Wonders of the Invisible World* (1692). Yet Mather was not as sure as he professed to be that justice had been done: in 1696, he recorded in his diary his fear that God was angry with him for "not appearing with Vigor enough to stop the proceedings of the Judges, when the Inextricable Storm from the Invisible World assaulted the Country."

The period of the Salem witchcraft marked the last occasion on which witches and wizards were executed in the colonies, but the belief in witchcraft did not end, nor did the indictment and trial of suspects stop. In Virginia in 1705, a woman was accused of practicing witchcraft. The court ordered that her body be examined for witch marks and that she be subjected to the trial by water. The incriminating marks were found, and she floated while bound — strong evidence of guilt. Nevertheless, she was not tried as a witch, nor, for that matter, was she given an opportunity to clear her reputation.

Nevertheless, even during the trials at Salem, doubts had been expressed by one of the judges and by some clergymen regarding the guilt of some of the condemned. Not, however, that they doubted the existence of the Devil and of witchcraft: their reservations extended only to the kinds of evidence held admissible by the court. Yet the feeling gained ground that New England lay under the heavy indictment of having shed innocent blood. For this reason, some of the jurors and witnesses publicly repented their part in the proceedings at Salem. In 1697, Judge Samuel Sewall stood before his congregation and acknowledged his "blame and shame . . . asking pardon of men, and especially desiring prayers that God, who has unlimited authority, would pardon that sin and all others his sins." On the other hand, Chief Justice Stoughton went to his death insisting that he had been in the right.

It was the educated laity rather than the clergy who took the lead in discrediting witchcraft. In 1700, Robert Calef, a Boston merchant, published *More Wonders of the Invisible World,* an attack upon Cotton Mather and witchcraft. Calef believed that a great deal of innocent blood had been shed at Salem, and he held Cotton Mather primarily responsible for it. The girls who had started the frenzy he called "a parcel of possessed, distracted, or lying Wenches, accusing their Innocent Neighbours." Cotton Mather denounced Calef's book as "a firebrand thrown by a madman," and Increase Mather, as president of Harvard College, ordered the book publicly burned in the College Yard.

The eighteenth-century Enlightenment completed the rout of witchcraft. Science shifted the attention of educated men from the supernatural to the natural world, thereby resuming a process which, having begun with the Renaissance, had been interrupted by the Reformation. Satan suffered the second of the two great disasters that befell him in his long and checkered career: having been cast out of Heaven, his power to control human events now began to be questioned. In short, Satan lost the thing upon which his power over men had always depended — his credibility. Witchcraft, after a long and bloody history, was relegated to the ignominious status of a mere superstition, and the thousands of men and women who had perished in the flames or on the scaffold were seen to have been the victims of a great delusion.

STUDY GUIDE

1. In the opening section of this essay, Miller suggests certain broad social conditions that are likely to exist in a country in which witch-hunting arises. What are these conditions, and to what extent did they exist in Massachusetts in the 1690s?

2. Miller says witch-hunting died out, not because people no longer believed in witchcraft, but because they doubted the tests used to discover witches. What were these tests? Which were used in the Salem trials and which were not?

3. The special court appointed in Salem had no lawyers on it, though witchcraft was a crime. On the other hand, clergymen played a prominent role in advising the court and in other respects. Can you think of ways in which the participation of trained attorneys might have affected the evidence, the examination of witnesses, or the outcome? Or would the lawyers, in that society, have acted much the way laymen did?

4. Some modern cults embody elements of satanic worship and witchcraft; others do not, but some of the psychological motivation of the cultists may be similar to that exhibited at Salem. Considering such recent phenomena as the Moonies and the mass suicide at Jonestown, how do you explain the psychology of the modern cult member?

BIBLIOGRAPHY

The editors selected the preceding excerpt from John C. Miller's book because, in a relatively brief space, it presents a balanced view of the many different facets of the witchcraft affair. There are, however, a number of more specialized books that you might like to investigate. One of the best short accounts of the affair ever written is by Marion L. Starkey, *The Devil in Massachusetts: A Modern Inquiry into the Salem Witch Trials* (1949). More recently, there have been a number of books and articles, each with a distinctive point of view. Chadwick Hansen, in *Witchcraft at Salem* (1969), argues that the symptoms described by the bewitched suggest that they were suffering from hysteria. Making use of psychological theory, John Demos suggested that the accusers — many of whom were adolescent girls — exhibited an Electra complex against the older women accused of witchcraft in "Underlying Themes in Witchcraft of Seventeenth-Century New England," *American Historical Review* LXXV (1969–70). Still another suggestion by Linnda R. Caporeal — which appeared both in *Science* CXCII (April 2, 1976) and in *Horticulture Magazine* (Fall 1976) — was that some of the rye grain in the community was contaminated by the fungus ergot. The hallucinations and other symptoms of the bewitched, Caporeal argued, were owing to a disease called convulsive ergotism.

While each of these explanations can be argued quite logically, it is difficult to find evidence to prove hysteria, psychological anxiety, or ergotism. Historians have been more receptive to a recent study that suggests that the affair arose because of religious and social-economic conflicts within the small village. In *Salem Possessed: The Social Origins of Witchcraft* (1974), Paul Boyer and Stephen Nissenbaum examined disputes over land and other matters to argue this position. The same two authors edited the anthology *Salem-Village Witchcraft: A Documentary Record of Local Conflict in Colonial New England* (1972). This anthology and another by David Levin — *What Happened in Salem?* 2nd ed. (1960) — will give you some flavor of the times. John P. Demos, *Entertaining Satan: Witchcraft and the Culture of Early New England* (1982) tells us more about witchcraft in places *other than* Salem than does any previous study.

Naturally, witchcraft should be understood within the broader context of American religious and social life. Both the great Puritan movement of the early seventeenth century and the revival movement known as the Great Awakening, which followed some decades after the witchcraft scare had abated, have a very extensive literature, which cannot be listed here. Any college library, however, is likely to have some of the key studies by Perry Miller, Edmund Morgan, Larzer Ziff, David E. Stannard, and others on Puritanism. Books by Edwin S. Gaustad, Wesley M. Gewehr, Clarence C. Goen, and Charles H. Maxson cover the Great Awakening in the New England, Middle, and Southern colonies. The bibliography of an American history textbook will list many of the titles of these works.

II THE NEW NATION

The quarter-century that followed the start of the War for Independence in 1775 is a remarkable period in American history. Seldom has there been a time in this country when the future seemed so promising and the problems so profound. Having broken from the mother country, Americans thought of themselves as in something of a state of nature, with a clean slate on which they could design new, republican institutions of government. By the end of the eighteenth century, every state except Connecticut and Rhode Island had written a new constitution. Together, the American people had adopted a federal constitution, established a government that was truly national in its operation, and enunciated political ideas that became so deeply embedded in the national consciousness that they are referred to as the American Credo.

Besides the enduring monuments of American political and constitutional practice that were raised, these twenty-five years also witnessed remarkable achievements in other areas. The break from England did much to accelerate the development of American democratic thought and equalitarian social attitudes. It also encouraged a spirit of nationalism in literature, architecture, and other aspects of American cultural life. Basic directions in foreign policy were enunciated, and there were significant developments in American economic life.

Of course, our American ancestors could not foresee the extraordinary economic and political success of the United States. Indeed, between 1775 and 1800, there was a question as to whether the republic would survive. The first essay in this section gives us a sense of the initial optimism and nationalism of the revolutionary forces as well as of the frightening prospect that Washington's army would not succeed. Many Americans questioned the wisdom of declaring independence, and the fifty thousand colonists who fought on the side of the British were but a small reflection of the deep division in American society. The treatment of the Loyalists is described in the second selection. The third and fourth essays discuss the beginnings of the Industrial Revolution and the movement toward egalitarianism during the late eighteenth and early nineteenth centuries. The third reading describes two key inventions of Eli Whitney, and gives insight into the broader technological achievements of nineteenth-century America which were to make this country preeminent in industrialization. The fourth reading describes the emergence of broad-based national denominations of American Protestantism that appealed to common men and women. Growing out of the great religious revival that swept the country after 1800, these religious groups held forth to all people a promise of salvation that the closed sects of the seventeenth century had not.

"Valley Forge, 1777" by A. Gibert depicts the suffering of Washington's soldiers that made it difficult to enlist large numbers of volunteers.

5

CHARLES ROYSTER

Building an Army

During much of their history, Americans have considered themselves to be a special people, destined by God to serve as an example for the rest of humanity. The religious sects who settled here, including the Puritans, saw their colony as "a Citty upon a Hill, the eyes of all people uppon us." In the eighteenth century, many revolutionary leaders believed that there was a conspiracy in England aimed at suppressing colonial liberties and that they had a sacred duty to defend America as the last bastion of freedom. Americans, they felt, were a virtuous people who were destined by God to lead the world in establishing a free and noble republic that would abolish the kings, armies, and corrupt ministries that enslaved Europe. The defense of liberty would be made by untrained citizen-soldiers, moved to courageous deeds by their love of freedom and their faith in God. Their fear of regular, standing armies gave rise to a long tradition of anti-militarism, a commitment to civilian control of the military, and a belief that American wars could be fought by voluntary enlistment of average citizens. It also perpetuated a myth that the Revolutionary War was won by patriotic farmers who turned out in large numbers to promote the glorious cause.

During the first year of the war, a considerable amount of such enthusiasm was displayed in the patriotic songs and poetry, in the parades and celebrations, and even in the number of men who joined the ranks. By 1776, however, the enthusiasm had waned, and men deserted, went home on leave and never returned, or refused to enlist unless a bounty was paid for their doing so. Washington's army seldom exceeded 25,000 troops and was frequently much smaller. Increasingly Washington saw the need for a regular army of long-term enlistees, and increasingly the war was fought not by middle-class patriots, but by others who were hired to fight — the slave and servant who thus bought their freedom, or the young and the poor who saw so few opportunities in civilian life that even the meager pay in the Continental army looked good. If the enthusiasm of the volunteer soldier soon flagged, so too did that of the civilian population, which complained about taxes and sometimes sold food and supplies to the British army rather than donating them to Washington's forces.

Charles Royster has written a book on the ideals of the American people during the Revolutionary War and how these ideals were eroded as the war progressed. The opening of the following selection from his volume describes the initial enthusiasm of the colonists as war broke out in 1775. Much of the remainder of the article discusses problems in maintaining this spirit, and the growing realization among Americans that, if the war was to be won, it would have to be by a regular army. The picture he paints is not very flattering, but as in every war, there were selfless men and women who persisted through thick and thin. The selection concludes with a vignette of a dashing, romantic hero whose life demonstrates that nearly every myth — including that of our patriotic ancestors — is based upon some kernel of truth.

From the Battle of Lexington to the Declaration of Independence, all kinds of military exercises, uniforms, and threats aimed at the British enjoyed a wide vogue among Americans. A letter from Philadelphia assured the British that "the Rage Militaire, as the French call a passion for arms, has taken possession of the whole Continent." Although commitment to American independence grew during the war, this popular *rage militaire* vanished by the end of 1776 and never returned. Even in 1776 it was a weak echo of its loudest moments in 1775. Months before the Lexington and Concord skirmishes, Americans had begun militia drills to prepare for armed resistance. As mobilization progressed, they enthusiastically celebrated the citizens'

From *A Revolutionary People at War: The Continental Army and American Character, 1775–1783* by Charles Royster. Copyright 1979 The University of North Carolina Press. Published for the Institute of Early American History and Publisher. Reprinted by permission of the publisher.

rapidly acquired skill in the manual of arms and in field maneuvers. An observer who believed what he heard would have concluded that the survival of liberty depended on widespread voluntary submission to military discipline.

After war began, the Continental Army, most of which besieged Boston until March 1776, became the focus of Americans' announced determination to surpass the British in military prowess as in virtue. Two strengths, they claimed, ensured this superiority: Americans used only the essentials of drill without an intricate, unnecessary dumb show; and Americans possessed "natural" or "native" or "innate" courage.

The printed manuals of arms and evolutions that Americans used — especially Lewis Nicola's *Treatise of Military Exercise* and Timothy Pickering's "easy" plan, adapted from an English model — emphasized simplicity, not show, by using the fewest possible movements to load, fire, and maneuver. General Charles Lee assured Americans that they could dispense with "the tinsel and show of war" and learn the essentials — to load and fire, to form, to retreat, to advance, to change front, to rally by the colors, to reduce from a line of fire (two deep) to a line of impression (four, six, or eight deep) — all in three months. The Massachusetts Council adopted Pickering's plan because it was not "clogged with many superfluous motions, which only serve to burthen the memory and perplex the Learner." . . .

The revolutionaries could not equal the complexity of British parade and decided they did not want to, but they greatly enjoyed what they had left. Judging from a few loyalist witnesses and from the long time it took the Continental Army to learn to drill, the countless town-square parades and maneuvers of 1775 must have looked pretty poor. In the *Virginia Gazette*, Robert Washington, who wanted a job training soldiers, acknowledged that Americans' early use of firearms, knowledge of the country, and "native Courage" made them superior in the woods. But he warned, "Let us not plume ourselves with this Conceit, that we shall always have the Bush to fight behind." He went to a muster to see "the *Prussian Exercise,* as they call it" but only saw men forming six deep, turning about-face, marching eighteen paces to the rear, opening ranks, and going through slow parade motions of prime and load — "you may call it *Prussian Exercise* if you please; but . . . to lead a Body of brave men, with such counterfeit Discipline, to face a disciplined Enemy, would, in my Opinion, be downright Murder." . . .

Reviews and drill attracted many spectators; Congress watched parade-ground evolutions on June 8, 1775. Companies drilled by moonlight. Boys between the ages of thirteen and sixteen volunteered. They were commended but turned away. Younger boys played soldier and organized their own companies for drill. One militiaman remembered 1775, the year of his thirteenth birthday: "I obtained a pamphlet in which this exercise was fully explained, according to the best system of the day, which was the Prussian. . . . I made myself so much a master, that I had the honour of standing before the company as *fugleman*." Everywhere revolutionaries reported rapid progress in discipline. . . . Some people who saw reviews wrote that Americans were or soon would be equal to any troops in the world.

People could believe this, despite the shortcomings in drill that they must have seen, because they thought that American soldiers were courageous by nature. The Americans' claim to have native courage later became grounds for questioning the importance of the Continental Army, but in 1775 it made the army, with its growing discipline, the main representative of American resistance. The revolutionaries' courage was bolstered by their conviction that God had given them the ability to choose and the zeal to defend liberty for themselves and for mankind. . . . Revolutionaries felt sure that against such strength the British could muster only the artificial courage of force, pay, and rote, while the loyalists had no courage at all. . . .

Early in the war, Americans, especially revolutionary leaders, talked freely about large numbers of casualties. The revolutionaries argued not only that death in a glorious cause was rewarding and that risking death was imperative, but also that they did not fear death. They would, according to the spirit of 1775, rush to the field of combat, eager to conquer or to die: "A spirit of enthusiasm for war is gone forth, that has driven away the fear of death." . . . Neither living nor dying in the cause of liberty proved so uncomplicated and easy as the ideals of 1775 announced. A revolutionary would need sources of strength besides native courage or would suffer for the lack of them.

Captain Joseph Jewett found it so as he took thirty-six hours to die of bayonet wounds in his chest and stomach after the Battle of Long Island. On the last morning, he "was sensible of being near his End, often Repeating that it was hard work to Die." In one of the battles of Saratoga, Captain John Henry, Patrick Henry's son, distinguished himself in combat. Afterward he walked among the American dead, pausing to recognize men he had known. Then he drew his sword, broke it, threw it on the ground, and raved, mad. Nine months later, his "ill state of Health," according to Washington, caused him to resign his commission. . . .

The army's experiences in 1775 and 1776 quickly revealed the contrasts between the ideals of 1775 and the conduct of the war. The first year of fighting the British and creating a regular army began the test of Americans' response to the problem of reconciling lapses in revolutionaries' conduct with the rigor of absolute ideals. Two kinds of failure threatened to undermine the cause: battlefield reverses, which called Americans' native courage into doubt, and the army's lack of discipline and decorum, which fell far short of the revolutionaries' hope for an army of Israel.

When Washington arrived at Cambridge in July 1775, the Massachusetts legislature apologized for the state of discipline in the army. The representatives told him that the men were "naturally brave, and of good understanding," but "the completion of so difficult and at the same time so necessary a task is reserved to your Excellency." Even before reaching camp, Washington could notice one of his difficulties: the sound of sporadic musket fire. The shots did not mean combat or even sniping at sentries. The firing was just what it sounded like — men shooting off muskets at random in camp. One of the revolutionaries' most often-repeated claims to superiority over the British army said that Americans learned the use of firearms from childhood. These claims exaggerated both American marksmanship and its usefulness in combat against a disciplined bayonet charge. Whatever the extent or the advantage of early familiarity with weapons, muskets in the hands of idle men proved very dangerous. Men used them to start fires; men discharged them to empty them; men fired at wild geese flying overhead. Some soldiers wounded or killed themselves by accident. Many men enjoyed snapping flintlocks for the fun of it; sometimes the musket was loaded and a nearby soldier was killed or wounded. In 1776 Washington was still saying in general orders, "Seldom a day passes but some persons are shot by their friends."

The Massachusetts legislature had warned Washington that the soldiers were "youth . . . used to a laborious life," who had not learned "the absolute necessity of cleanliness in their dress, and lodging, continual exercise, and strict temperance, to preserve them from diseases." Some soldiers felt that washing clothes was women's work; so they wore what they had until it crusted over and fell apart. Others sent their laundry home. Washington wanted the soldiers to bathe; those who would bathe wanted to swim all day and show off naked in front of "ladies of the first fashion" who happened to be crossing the bridge in Cambridge. Prolonged swimming threatened the men's health, as did refusing to bathe or to wash their clothes. . . . Throughout the war soldiers and officers suffered from "the Itch," a product of poor hygiene and sleeping on the ground. It could become so severe as to cover a man with scabs or strip off his skin. It left large numbers of men hardly fit for duty. Soldiers "Ointed for the Itch" with hog's lard or pine tar and brimstone — a process that made "the Devil of a Stink" and, in one case, "over came them so that we Thought they would a Died in the Night."

Every soldier's health was endangered by persistent problems with camp sanitation, which did most harm in the early years of the war. Open latrines for thousands of men were bad enough, but many soldiers would "Set Down and Ease themselves" wherever they felt like it. The remains of slaughtered cattle often rotted unburied. When the army stayed in one place for long, it sat amid a smoky miasma rising from green wood fires, gunpowder smoke, urine, feces, and animal offal. At first Washington thought that Massachusetts men were "an exceeding dirty and nasty people"; he later found that soldiers from all states would freely foul their own camp. The Continental Army became much cleaner in the years after 1777, but in 1781 Americans could still marvel at how clean their French allies managed to keep a camp.

Neglect of cleanliness, like carelessness with firearms, was a self-destructive response to the unforeseen hardships of life in camp. General Philip Schuyler put the soldiers' attitude in one word: "nonchalance." We might call it anxiety. Americans' inexperience in war caused many of their early problems, and the revolutionaries' respect for personal independence worked against quick, strict obedience to orders. Men who had shared the *rage militaire* of 1775 remained reluctant to master the soldierly skills that would help to keep them alive in the army. Even those soldiers who put self-preservation first by deserting a few weeks or months short of their discharge date risked, by their departure, the self-destruction of the army. Late in June 1775, eighteen men from Captain Winthrop Rowe's New Hampshire company deserted outside Boston, saying "that they didn't intend when they enlisted to join the Army, but to be station'd at Hampton" on the New Hampshire coast. . . .

Generals and doctors found that homesickness meant just that — sickness. The symptoms were loss of appetite, restlessness, and melancholy. Few of the New England soldiers had been far from their hometowns before; they would seldom have gone away for long; they would never have lived with thousands of others in new and uncomfortable constraint. The soldiers' strong local attachments came not only from their affection for family and friends but from lives wholly shaped by experience within a small area. Private Barber said of his company, "Most of us had not . . . been twenty miles from home." The ardor that had moved them to defend their beloved homes against the threat of invasion could not alone sustain all of them. They fell ill, yet recovered when discharged. No doubt some were malingering, but most who suffered from homesickness must have found it as real as smallpox or dysentery. Their longing was not just the disappointment or temporary low spirits we usually mean by the word "homesick." It was a lasting obsession. Repeatedly during 1776 and 1777 newspaper advertisements for deserters described soldiers as having a "dejected" look, a "down look," a "prodigious down look." One colonel reported from camp, "The Officers and Soldiers are possessed to get Home." . . .

The most notorious departers were the Connecticut soldiers who refused a request to stay beyond the end of their terms. The generals tried patriotic appeals, flattery, shame, drinks, and blows, but Colonel Jedidiah Huntington found that "we shall not with all our Rhetorick be able to retain many." When the soldiers marched, the generals encouraged the citizens and tavern keepers along the road to deny service to the soldiers and to express contempt for their conduct. In Connecticut people were glad to see the soldiers for a visit, but expected them to go back to camp. Many condemned the soldiers' departure from camp and shamed some men into reenlisting. . . .

Apart from the handling of army supplies, recruiting introduced more corruption into American society than any other activity associated with a standing army. But in this kind of corruption, we do not see a ruler taxing the people in order to employ favorites to support his rule. We see the people buying freedom from the demands of their own government. Everyone knew that this was happening, and even men who applauded the widespread suspicion of open-ended enlistments deplored the traffic in short-term recruits. They wanted men to enlist and reenlist for a fixed bounty. Some men did, but not enough. . . .

In 1776 the army again enlisted for one year. Against the wishes of the generals and the New England delegates, Congress resolved that "no bounty be allowed to the army on reinlistment." During the early months of 1776 the states tried to fill their regiments without a bounty. In January the Massachusetts legislature forswore both a bounty and a draft, while the *Connecticut Courant* addressed potential recruits, "Will it not be criminal, at a crisis like the present, to bury your martial talents because more of your money is not taxed from you and returned as a bounty. . . . The pay of the soldiery, though not equal to intentions of bribery, is equal to all the purposes of comfortable and manly subsistence." At first Virginia and North Carolina wanted to recruit even more battalions than Congress had asked them for. But the states failed to fill their regiments, and Congress acknowledged the failure on June 26, 1776, when it voted to grant ten dollars to men who enlisted for three years. . . .

An annual pattern of recruiting began in 1777. Congress assigned a quota to each state, which then assigned quotas to the towns. The commander in chief, the delegates in Congress, and Continental Army officers from the state wrote letters urging prompt compliance. The local militia commander held a muster and called for volunteers. A few men enlisted. Then weeks of dickering started. The state or the town or private individuals or all three sweetened the bounty. Meanwhile, citizens who did not want to turn out with the militia were looking for militia substitutes to hire. Continental Army officers were in the countryside trying to build their own company or regiment. As men held out for an offer they liked, Washington and the officers in camp wrote more letters urging the state to fill its quota promptly so that men could be trained before the fall campaign. By late spring or summer, all of the men who were going to enlist that year on any terms had done so, whereupon the state found that it had not filled its quota. Washington called for militia reinforcements. Drafting began in 1777 and sent men for terms ending in December, which ensured that the whole process would begin again next January. . . .

. . . Desertion . . . had many forms. Bounties inspired some soldiers to enlist several times with several units within a few days. Men bought or forged illegal discharges. Soldiers went to the enemy. More often, they went home. The army sent small detachments to catch them. Although the British and the loyalists encouraged men to desert and promised to reward or shelter them, deserters were most commonly helped by revolutionaries themselves, especially relatives. People not only refused to help army detachments apprehend deserters, but also helped the deserters escape arrest. In "many instances," according to Washington, "Deserters which have been apprehended by Officers, have been rescued by the People." Citizens also bought deserters' arms and clothing. States offered rewards for the arrest of deserters and threatened to draft, fine, and flog people who sheltered them. Trying another expedient, from time to time Washington offered amnesties. None of these measures, nor the whipping of captured men, nor the execution of some deserters, had any lasting effect. The most thorough study of the official returns estimates an average desertion rate of between 20 and 25 percent. The army's returns showed desertion to be declining in the later years of the war, as the army developed a core of long-term soldiers. . . .

The camps around Boston introduced both soldiers and civilians to a problem of discipline that followed the army throughout the war — the theft and destruction of property. The private homes and Harvard College buildings that were used for quarters inevitably got damaged. For a mile around Cambridge, soldiers pulled down every fence and cut down every tree for firewood. They threatened to start on houses until the legislature empowered the army to seize loyalists' woodlots. Soldiers also stole things on their own. Private Daniel Barber later said that "home and plenty are very different from the close quarters and deprivations to which a soldier is liable. The devil would now and then tell us, that it was no harm sometimes to pull a few potatoes and cabbages, and pluck, once in a while, an ear of corn, when we stood in need." . . .

Continental generals tried European discipline because they wanted to achieve their idea of a regular army and because they thought that the vulgar could best be restrained by force. Continental soldiers often were rough men, toward the enemy or toward civilians and each other. Throughout the war, people in the neighborhood of the army felt this harshness often. They withstood three kinds of plunder: official plunder, casual plunder, and private plunder. Official plunderers, following orders, took livestock and grain and left a paper certifying that they had done so; casual plunderers burned fence rails for firewood, turned horses loose in grain fields, and fouled buildings; private plunderers beat people up and robbed them.

Supply shortages and lack of pay encouraged men to take what they could find, as commanders and civil officials knew. However, some soldiers, abetted by junior officers, stole in order to turn a quick profit. They enjoyed threatening or using force against people who seldom could resist. Soldiers argued that, since property would soon fall under British control, they might as well take it. To conceal theft from private homes, they set fire to the houses. "How disgraceful to the army is it," Washington said in one of his many futile orders against theft and destruction, "that the peaceable inhabitants, our countrymen and fellow citizens, dread our halting among them, even for a night and are happy when they get rid of us?" A few of the Continental Army's casualties occurred when citizens defended their property against looting soldiers, and soldiers who met resistance sometimes fired on citizens. . . .

[There were frequent quarrels and bloodshed within the army, as well as between soldiers and civilians.]

Much of the violence in camp took place when men were drunk. When Private James McCormick was tried for shooting and killing Private Reuben Bishop while drunk, his defense was that he had not intentionally murdered Bishop because he had meant to kill his company commander. Rum — West India for officers, New England for enlisted men — was the most common drink, but all ranks took stinking whiskey hot from the still, wring-jaw cider, or whatever they could get. A week before the Battle of Brandywine, General Peter Muhlenberg said that "many Soldiers [are] making a practice of getting drunk regularly once a Day and thereby render themselves unfit for duty." Men sometimes pleaded drunkenness, itself a crime in the army, as an excuse or extenuation for other crimes.

Alcohol in moderation, people then thought, promoted health. To treat "putrid fevers" army doctors prescribed, among other things, "wine (two or three bottles a day in many cases)." One gill, or four ounces, of rum was part of the daily ration when available. At Valley Forge, Henry Knox urged the commissary to provide this ration: "We have found by experience that this would support the men through every difficulty." Sutlers who followed the camp sold more to those who had money; a man without cash could drink up his pay in advance. Washington tried twice to ban liquor dealers and then tried to license some, control their prices, and keep others away from the soldiers. None of these efforts succeeded for long. Men stole liquor, stole things to buy liquor, even sold their clothes to buy liquor. During the war, some of the biggest fortunes were made getting European manufactured goods for civilians, but some of the surest were made selling liquor to soldiers.

From the beginning the Continental Army disturbed many Christians because so many men swore. Today, the revolutionaries' admonitions against profanity may seem naive or futile. British soldiers had long been famous for their oaths. To Godfearing Americans, this was all the more reason for the Continental Army to reflect the righteousness of its cause by superior piety and self-restraint. Instead, all observers agreed, the Americans imitated the British more effectively on this score than on any other.

To judge by surviving examples, revolutionary profanity would sound mild to many people now. The same words were stronger then because they had not lost their religious meaning: profanity still permitted important theological distinctions. After Eli Showell was jailed for refusing to enlist, an officer came to him with a drawn sword and said, "Eli, now God damn your soul but . . . your life is your own, if you do not enlist I will run you through." Two sergeants worked the "son of a bitch" over, and Eli enlisted. Anthony Wayne may have been the greatest swearer among senior officers. Lieutenant Ebenezer Elmer got it this way: "Col. Wayne . . . finding no sentry, (as we have not kept one in the day time) he damned all our souls to hell, and immediately ordered two by night and one by day, which I immediately put in execution — but shall not forget his damns, which he is very apt to bestow upon people; but my great consolation is, that the power thereof is not in his hands, blessed be God for it." . . .

Against all these forms of disorder, officers relied mainly on one device: flogging. By British standards, which went up to 1,000 lashes, the Continental Army was lenient. Congress stuck to the Mosaic law of 39 lashes until 1776. For the rest of the war, the articles allowed 100. . . . For punishment of crimes such as plundering and firing guns in camp, Washington tried to make whipping more effective by authorizing lashes on the spot. He also kept asking Congress to raise the maximum to 500 because men could take 100 and remain defiant, leaving him no effective punishment short of death. The request, which had the support of James Madison, was never granted. Washington considered punishing men by confinement at hard labor, but this was not implemented, perhaps because it would have been hard to tell from routine service in the Continental Army.

Men were either whipped with a cat-o'-nine-tails or made to run the gauntlet. Since Washington believed that witnessing punishment deterred crime — a common assumption of the time — the soldiers were assembled and, after the adjutant read the sentence, either watched a drummer whip a guilty man tied to a post or whipped him themselves with sticks as he was marched between two lines of men. A bayonet in front of him kept him from going down the gauntlet too fast. One soldier, after undergoing the gauntlet, was "in a miserable situation . . . not able to move." The 100 lashes at the post might be spread over four days, with salt rubs between the four floggings. Before 50 lashes the back was "like a jelly," and the cat got clogged with blood. A dry one was substituted to cut more sharply. The soldiers had a name for the post to which they were tied: they called it "the Adjutant's Daughter." . . .

. . . One of Washington's arguments for raising the maximum number of lashes to 500 was that such authorized rigor would decrease the excesses of officers' arbitrary punishments. Most generals approved of calculated blows to correct stubborn men. However, some officers seemed to have succumbed simply to rage. At West Point one writer saw an officer and a subordinate beat a soldier bloody; "many officers gathering round, said *lay on,* and damning him that dare say otherways," until one officer stopped them. To this witness, beating a man who dared not resist was the sure sign of a coward. A few officers who inflicted especially cruel beatings were court-martialed. One who was found guilty of "a malevolence of temper scarcely to be equalled" got a severe reprimand. . . .

Courts-martial imposed many death sentences, but most condemned men were pardoned. Estimates of the number of executions in the Continental Army during the war range from forty to seventy-five. Mutiny, fighting for the enemy, and plundering were most likely to get a man hanged or shot.

Washington and his generals used capital punishment as an example to discourage others from committing like crimes. Since Washington did not intend to execute all the men guilty of capital crimes, he tried to preserve the effect of the example. Soldiers were assembled for an execution; drummers marched the condemned man to the gallows or the firing squad; the adjutant read the sentence; the chaplain addressed the condemned man and the army; and when the blindfolded man was ready for execution, the general's pardon was read. In asking for a five-hundred-lash penalty, Washington complained that through overuse this charade had become ineffective. Hardly any evidence suggests that it ever had been effective, except to excite curiosity among most onlookers, sympathy among a few, and fainting or tears among the recipients of the commander's clemency. Several of the pardoned men were later hanged for new capital crimes. Executions followed some mutinies and, the generals believed, forestalled others by catching leaders, who were eliminated while the men returned to duty, glad to escape death. Hangings had little noticeable effect on desertion or plundering. Throughout the war, the Americans' use of capital punishment fluctuated between prolonged forbearance and abrupt severity. . . .

Neither corporal punishment nor capital punishment achieved the smooth system of interlocking wheels that Washington wanted for Continental Army discipline. Yet these punishments and the soldiers' consent to serve were the main supports of the new Articles of War. The generals had complained to Congress that the first "Rules and Regulations" of 1775 were too weak, and Congress strengthened them in a new set of articles in August 1776. The new articles showed increased attention to the idiosyncrasies of American soldiers. The penalty clauses mentioned punishment by death more frequently than the old articles did, and increased the limit on flogging to one hundred lashes rather than thirty-nine. New sections tried to regulate sutlers, 'to stop fights, and to prevent or punish the new forms of graft that had appeared in the first year of war. Congress responded to the commanders' requests and tried to transform Americans into regular soldiers by bringing the government of the Continental Army closer to that of other armies. Congress was ready to experiment with firmer military law, but the "more severe and rigorous" articles that, according to President John Hancock, conveyed Congress's determination "to introduce obedience and regularity among the troops" could not change the independent minds of the soldiers. . . .

By the end of the first year of hostilities, the Continental Army had begun to develop the character that it retained throughout the war. We see fewer signs of a whole populace marching against the invader and more calculated measures to raise a distinct body of soldiers; we hear less about ardent volunteers for regular army service and more about negotiations for pay, bounties, and conscription; we read less about young gentlemen who wanted to be privates and more about youths who wanted to become gentlemen; we find less hope for the soldiers' constant self-restraint and more fear of their casual violence. In the remaining years of the war, the army's survival, discipline, and patriotism helped to sustain the revolutionaries' perseverance. But in several troubling ways that army grew more like other armies than like the popular *rage militaire* of 1775. Some recurring elements of the soldiers' conduct violated the ideals that the Continental Army was supposed to promote. Before 1776 had ended, the war had permanently linked the achievement of American independence to this flawed military institution. Americans' reactions to both the victories and defeats of that year claimed to distinguish the revolutionary cause from the army on which it depended. At the same time, the public's response to battles and marches made that dependence ever clearer. Thus, the second year of war left the ideals of the revolution inextricably tied to the vicious as well as the virtuous elements of the Continental Army.

On July 15, 1779, Major John Stewart led an advance party following the forlorn hope in the assault on Stony Point. He often said that he did not want to live to be an old man, but Crazy Jack Stewart and Mad Anthony Wayne and the Light Infantry carried the fort and lived to hear their countrymen's praise. Congress voted Stewart a silver medal. It showed America, personified as an Indian queen, giving him a palm branch. In 1789 Thomas Jefferson brought the medal from France — too late for Stewart to receive it. In 1790 President Washington sent it to Stephen Stewart, saying that "it must afford some pleasing consolation when reflecting upon the loss of a worthy Son."

Two years before the action at Stony Point, Stewart had been taken prisoner by the enemy on August 22, 1777, while commanding a detachment covering the withdrawal from Staten Island following General John Sullivan's unsuccessful raid. Lieutenant William Wilmot said that Stewart "had never gave them an inch before he found that he had nothing left to keep them of[f] with." Placing a white handkerchief on the point of his sword, he walked forward to surrender, "as cool as if he had been going to shake hands with a friend." But Stewart did not long remain a prisoner. While confined aboard a prison ship, he "made his escape by descending silently to the water, and swimming to the New Jersey shore."

Already in 1776, when he was a lieutenant, Stewart had become known for "the most fashionably cut coat, the most *macaroni* cocked hat, and hottest blood in the union. . . ." He was six feet tall, well made, "handsome," and had "a fine presence for an Officer." Fifteen months after Stony Point, he almost got married. According to a friend, he "was damn'd nigh it. How he escaped I know not . . . her wedding Cloth[e]s are made, but . . . poor Kitty Crane, you must hug your sheets."

Stewart went south with the Maryland troops and made lieutenant colonel. He was well known and "much beloved" among officers of the southern army, who told "many extraordinary stories" of his bravado. Citizens who crossed him got arrested or beaten up or horse-whipped. He commanded the First Maryland Regiment at the liberation of Charleston in December 1782.

On Friday, March 21, 1783, a few weeks before the southern army was to disband, Stewart rode down a steep hill at a hard gallop in a stunt that looked certain to kill him and his horse. But he made it. Saturday evening, Colonel William Washington invited the officers to an entertainment near Sandy Hill, South Carolina. Stewart was riding there, on a level road, when his horse fell and threw him head first into a ditch, injuring his neck. Sunday morning Stewart died, at the age of twenty-five.

STUDY GUIDE

1. The conduct of war — like governmental institutions and class attitudes — may reflect the national characteristics of different societies. Some people, for example, believe there is a distinctive Prussian, English, or American way of making war. Do you see any peculiarly "American" traits in the attitudes of revolutionary soldiers?

2. The kinds of extraordinary disciplinary, recruiting, and desertion problems described by Royster are not usually associated with our army in World Wars I and II. Tell how the following factors might help to explain the apparent contrast: differences in governmental authority and organization, the backgrounds of the soldiers in the two periods, and developments in propaganda.

3. The Revolutionary War might also be compared to the Vietnam War. Some people today see the former as the embodiment of selfless sacrifice and patriotism, while viewing the widespread draft-dodging and dissent during the Vietnam conflict as a national disgrace. How does Royster's article modify your view of these and other American wars?

4. What evidence do you see in modern America that our society has seriously modified its distrust of a standing army and militarism?

BIBLIOGRAPHY

Royster's book is a broad study of how the need to establish a regular army to fight the war conflicted with the revolutionary ideals of a citizen-soldiery and a virtuous republic. James K. Martin and Mark E. Lender, *A Respectable Army: The Military Origins of the Republic, 1763–1789* (1982) is one of several recent studies to argue that in this war, as in many later American wars, the fighting was done by the poor and unfortunate, rather than by the middle and upper classes. There are several books that give one an idea of the life of the average soldier, including C. K. Bolton, *The Common Soldier under Washington* (1902); Lynn Montross, *Rag, Tag, and Bobtail* (1952); Larry G. Bowman, *Captive Americans: Prisoners during the American Revolution* (1976); and Alfred H. Bill, *Valley Forge: The Making of an Army* (1952).

Military history used to be written as the story of battles and heroes. In recent years, historians have studied military history as it is related to the political, social, and economic life of a nation, and the way in which it may reflect the national character of a people. Walter Millis, *Arms and Men* (1956) covers most of American military history in this way, while Marcus Cunliffe, *Soldiers and Civilians* (1968) deals with American thought from 1775 to 1865. Don Higginbotham, *The War of American Independence* (1971) is an excellent study of the Revolution that utilizes the perspective of the "new military history." If you enjoy studying history through biography, you might look at two books edited by George Billias which give sketches of the principal general officers in the Revolution: *George Washington's Generals* (1964) and *George Washington's Opponents* (1969). For some of the topics covered in your textbook and *The Social Fabric,* you should take a look at some primary sources, written by people who lived through the events of an earlier time. In *Private Yankee Doodle* (1962), George F. Scheer has edited the journal of Joseph Plumb Martin, a revolutionary soldier.

*"The Bostonians Paying the Excise-Man" by Philip Dawe, 1774,
shows the punishment of John Malcolm.*

6

WALLACE BROWN

Social War

One of the most elusive goals of the historian, and of the human mind in general, is objectivity. In our time, most historians recognize that, try as they may to avoid it, some prejudice and personal values are bound to creep into their thought and into the history they write. One illustration of this is in the difference in treatment that history accords to the winners and losers in any revolution. Rebels who fail don't get a very good press from historians, since their society is likely to denounce the revolutionary leaders as traitors or madmen. If the revolution succeeds, the same men may be celebrated as patriots and statesmen, while the ruling group that is overthrown is castigated as oppressive or corrupt.

Between 1765 and 1775, British colonial society developed some serious internal divisions and antagonisms. Upon the outbreak of war, provinces, towns, and families were split, and brother fought brother with all the hatred that civil war can engender. By 1783, as many as 80,000 people had been driven out of the colonies; farms and businesses of Loyalists were confiscated, and thousands of these British adherents were intimidated and mistreated. Many of them had been distinguished contributors to colonial society — governors, judges, ministers, farmers, craftsmen, and laborers. Had the British won the war, Thomas Hutchinson, Joseph Galloway, William Franklin, and Jonathan Boucher would today be as celebrated as are John Adams, Thomas Jefferson, Patrick Henry, and John Hancock.

One question worth pondering is what American society may have lost by the exile of the Loyalists and the victory of the Patriot cause. A substantial reservoir of political talent and experience certainly evaporated, but among the many who cast their lot for independence were an extraordinary number of men of talent to take the Loyalists' places. More difficult to judge is the loss to American thought and culture. A number of Loyalists were able or distinguished scientists, artists, writers, and religious leaders who made their contributions in Canada or Europe rather than here. More important than such individuals was the effect of the break upon American political and constitutional thought, which — it has been argued — suffered the loss of a valid conservative tradition with the exile of the Loyalists.

Another question that has interested historians since the Revolution began is just what a Tory or Loyalist was. The simplest definition is that he was one who remained loyal to England. This raises the question of why they were loyal, whereas immediate neighbors of similar background and position became revolutionary leaders. Many answers to this question have been offered — that it was one's religion that made the difference, or one's wealth, age, occupation, national origins, or temperament. Yet for all the Loyalists who were influenced by such factors, there were at least as many men of the same class who chose the Patriot side.

Wallace Brown, a contemporary student of these questions, has made use of statistical techniques to try to determine the percentage of Loyalists of different occupations, religions, and so forth. Since the statistical parts of his studies are based on fragmentary records, they have been criticized by some historians. However, his book *The Good Americans,* from which the following selection is taken, is a general study of Loyalism that is less dependent than his earlier work upon statistics. Chapter 5 of *The Good Americans* presents a vivid account of the suffering that Loyalists endured during the American War for Independence. If few groups have since been subjected to such direct violence, the persecution of the Loyalists nonetheless reminds one of the fate of many another unpopular minority in later American history. And it should make us cautious about accepting only a "winner's" view of historical losers.

In November, 1777, the Continental Congress recommended the confiscation of Loyalist estates, a suggestion already made by Thomas Paine, and in some

Abridgment of pages 127–146 from *The Good Americans: The Loyalists in the American Revolution* by Wallace Brown. Copyright © 1969 by Wallace Brown. By permission of William Morrow & Company, Inc.

places already acted upon. All states finally amerced, taxed, or confiscated much Loyalist property, and in addition New York and South Carolina taxed Loyalist property in order to compensate robbery victims. Some towns simply raffled off Tory property. Patriot officers requisitioned horses and supplies from Loyalists rather than Whigs, and, of course, there was much old-fashioned looting, particularly of the property of exiles. . . .

Although the majority of active Loyalists suffered much loss of property, some attempted by various subterfuges to preserve their estates quite apart from having a wife or third party act as purchaser. One scheme was to make over one's property, or make a sham sale, to a sympathetic, moderate friend who had escaped suspicion.

Much commoner was the device used by exiles of leaving their wives or relatives behind in order to keep a foot in both camps. For example, Benjamin Pickman fled from Salem, Massachusetts, in 1775, but left his wife behind to look after their property, to which he returned ten years later. Some brothers may even have chosen opposite sides for such a reason. As the British claims commissioners commented on one split family, "it is possible that this may be a shabby family Compact . . . to preserve the property whether Great Britain or America prevailed."

The overall severity of the various laws against the Loyalists has been estimated as follows:

"Harshest" — New York, South Carolina.
"Harsh" — Massachusetts, New Jersey, Pennsylvania.
"Light" — Rhode Island, Connecticut, Virginia, North Carolina.
"Lightest" — New Hampshire, Delaware, Maryland, Georgia.

With some exceptions, notably Georgia, laws were harshest in states where Loyalists were most powerful, and as the war progressed, the purpose of the laws changed from conversion to "revenge and hate." Similarly, enforcement varied and was usually severest where danger was greatest and civil war bitterest.

A prominent Southern Tory reported that in Virginia, where the Loyalists were weak and little problem, the property of those who joined the British army went to their wives and children "on the Spot . . . as if the Father was dead," and he noted that his own wife "had never been molested but on the contrary treated with the utmost Kindness and Respect." Other Loyalists described being turned off their property with only the clothes on their backs.

But perhaps more typical was the fate of the Chandler family of Worcester, Massachusetts. Colonel John Chandler, a very prominent citizen of distinguished Massachusetts pedigree, dubbed "Tory John" and later in England the "Honest Refugee," fled from Boston with the British army to become a permanent, proscribed exile. For over two years his wife and family continued to enjoy their property undisturbed, until the Worcester Committee of Correspondence began a process that resulted in the confiscation of all but a third of their real and personal property, which third was reserved for Mrs. Chandler's use as long as she remained in the United States. Her husband did not return (he was forbidden to by an act of October, 1778), and on her death special legislation was needed to secure her property for her children.

A myriad of particularities could play a part in determining the extent of persecution. A well-liked or respected Tory (and there were a few such) might well escape, as might someone whose skills were especially valued, for example, a doctor. Influential but quiet Loyalists were more apt to avoid penalties than those of lower social standing or those more vociferous in their beliefs.

The zeal of the patriots could be extremely capricious and, as always with witch-hunts, frequently ridiculous and heavy-handed. One citizen was accosted for naming his dog "Tory," the implication being that a Tory was forced to lead a dog's life. In 1776 at Stratford, Connecticut, an Episcopal minister was brought before the local committee because he had officiated at a baptism where the child was named Thomas Gage. The committee viewed the action as a "designed insult" and censured the cleric. In the same state Zephaniah Beardslee reported that he was "very much abused" for naming his daughter Charlotte, after the queen. It may be noted that Beardslee, apparently a very serious Loyalist, had also been found drinking the king's health. The frequent persecution of Tories for this activity, however, is not as picayune as it seems, because toasts presuppose groups in taverns and the chance of Loyalist plots and associations. Thus, Abraham Cuyler held a gathering in Albany, New York, in June, 1776, that featured drinking and the singing of "God Save the King." At last the enraged Whig citizens crashed the party and carried the royal merrymakers off to jail. . . .

The results of Loyalism might simply be social ostracism — being sent to Coventry — as, for instance, happened to James Allen, who noted in his diary for February 17, 1777: "I never knew how painful it is to be secluded from the free conversation of one's friends"; and to George Watson, a mandamus councillor, when he entered a church at Plymouth, Massachusetts, and "a great number of the principal inhabitants left." Or it might mean serious loss of services, as when the blacksmiths of Worcester County, Massachusetts, refused to work for any Loyalists, their employees, or their dependents; or an economic boycott, as in Connecticut, where the local committee forbade "all Persons whatever viz. Merchants Mechanicks Millers and Butchers and Co. from supplying . . . John Sayre or Family with any manner of Thing whatever." Lawyers, teachers, doctors, apothecaries, and others often lost their customers and hence their livelihoods. Mathew Robinson, a Newport trader, from the first branded as "a Rank Torey," suffered several indignities, including the pulling down of his fences by a "multitude . . . under colour of laying out a Highway" and climaxing in 1781 when, after "*a New England Saint*" charged that Robinson "drank the King's Health, and damn'd the Congress and call'd them damn'd Rebels and Presbyterians," he was imprisoned by the rebels without examination, this being even "against their own Bill of Rights."

In many areas — for example, New York — the Loyalists were allowed to sell their property before departing, but such hurried, desperate sales were unlikely to net a fair price, and the result amounted to confiscation.

All wars and revolutions cause great mental strain and suffering, most of which goes unmeasured. The history of the Revolutionary era is liberally punctuated with stories of Loyalists who succumbed to melancholia, became mad, died, or committed suicide.

Alexander Harvey, a Charleston lawyer, wound up in a private English madhouse, having been "driven to Distraction" by his experiences as a Loyalist; George Miller, a North Carolina merchant whose fright had conquered his Loyalist principles, was thrown "into Convulsions" by the strain of serving in the American militia; Peter Harrison's death came after the shock of Lexington, and with it America lost its greatest colonial architect; several Loyalists, including the wife of William Franklin, simply died of "a Broken Heart"; the widow of Dr. Robert Gibbs of South Carolina recounted that the prospect of the loss of his property "so preyed upon his Spirits" that he died. Andrew Miller, of Halifax, North Carolina, was estranged from all his friends by his Loyalism, which literally killed him; others chose suicide — Millington Lockwood of Connecticut was wounded in the head, lost his reason, and drowned himself, while some years later, in London, after years of fruitless waiting for compensation, an unnamed, ruined Loyalist shot himself in despair, blaming an ungrateful country.

Although Americans at the time of the Revolution would clearly have found it odd, today one of the sharpest historical debates is over the question of how far the American Revolution was a *real* revolution. Even those historians who, noting the social dislocation, argue that the American Revolution was rather like the French Revolution stress the absence of the Terror. Mass executions there were not, a guillotine there was not, yet atrocities and terror there most certainly were. It is fitting that in the beginning the rebels "hoisted the Red Flag or Flag of Defence."

Leaving aside civil-war aspects such as the execution and maltreatment of prisoners and the burning of towns (by both sides: for example, the Americans fired Norfolk and Portsmouth; the British, Falmouth and Fairfield), we can cite a great range of fates that awaited the Loyalists; they were catalogued by "Papinian" as tarring and feathering, rail riding,

> . . . chaining men together by the dozens, and driving them, like herds of cattle, into distant provinces, flinging them into loathsome jails, confiscating their estates, shooting them in swamps and woods as suspected Tories, hanging them after a mock trial; and all this because they would not abjure their rightful Sovereign, and bear arms against him.

Tarring and feathering (pine tar and goose feathers) became the classic Whig treatment of the Tories, and the British Government believed there was "no better proof of Loyalty" than suffering this punishment. A famous instance of it occurred in Boston on January 25, 1774, and is worth recounting in some detail.

At about eight o'clock in the evening a club-wielding mob milled along Cross Street. Their objective was John Malcolm, a distinguished but hot-tempered veteran of the French and Indian War, a native Bostonian, an ex-overseas merchant turned royal customs official, and a highly unpopular man for many reasons connected with both his personality (he was inordinately quarrelsome) and his job.

His recent arrival in Boston had been preceded by the unpopular news that in 1771 he had helped the governor of North Carolina against those reputedly Whiggish rebels known as the Regulators and that in October, 1773, he had officiously seized a brigantine at Falmouth (now Portland), Maine. Malcolm waited, ready and armed, behind barred doors. Undeterred, the mob raised ladders, broke an upstairs window, captured their prey, dragged him onto a sled, and pulled him along King Street to the Customs House, or Butcher's House, as it was popularly known, where the spectators gave three mighty cheers.

Although it was "one of the severest cold nights" of the winter, so cold that both Boston Harbor and even the very ink as it touched paper had frozen hard, the wretched man was put in a cart, stripped "to buff and breeches," and dealt the punishment of tarring and feathering, which American patriots were soon to convert into a major spectator sport. Malcolm, self-styled "Single Knight of the Tarr," as opposed to English Knights of the Garter, had already suffered the same indignity the year before for his conduct at Falmouth. He later claimed to be the first in America tarred for loyalty.

A contemporary description gives a good idea of how Malcolm and many others were treated:

> The following is the Recipe for an effectual Operation. "First strip a Person naked, then heat the Tar until it is thin, and pour it upon the naked Flesh, or rub it over with a Tar Brush, *quantum sufficit*. After which, sprinkle decently upon the Tar, whilst it is yet warm, as many Feathers as will stick to it. Then hold a lighted Candle to the Feathers, and try to set it all on Fire; if it will burn so much the better. But as the Experiment is often made in cold

Weather; it will not then succeed — take also an Halter and put it round the Person's Neck, and then cart him the Rounds."

Malcolm, flogged and otherwise molested at intervals, was paraded around various crowded streets with his neck in a halter and was finally taken to the Liberty Tree, where he refused to resign his royal office or to curse Thomas Hutchinson, the hated governor of Massachusetts.

The crowd then set off for the gallows on Boston Neck. On the way Malcolm gasped an affirmative when one of his tormentors asked if he was thirsty and was given a bowl of strong tea and ordered to drink the king's health. Malcolm was next told to drink the queen's health; then two more quarts of tea were produced with the command to drink to the health of the Prince of Wales.

"Make haste, you have nine more healths to drink," shouted one of the mob.

"For God's sake, Gentlemen, be merciful, I'm ready to burst; if I drink a drop more, I shall die," Malcolm implored.

"Suppose you do, you die in a good cause, and it is as well to be drowned as hanged," was the reply.

The nine healths, beginning with the "Bishop of Osnabrug," were forced down the victim's throat. Malcolm "turned pale, shook his Head, and instantly filled the Bowl which he had just emptied."

"What, are you sick of the royal family?"

"No, my stomach nauseates the tea; it rises at it like poison."

"And yet you rascal, your whole fraternity at the Custom House would drench us with this poison, and we are to have our throats cut if it will not stay upon our stomachs."

At the gallows the noose was placed in position around Malcolm's neck and he was threatened with hanging, but he still refused to submit, whereupon he was "basted" with a rope for a while, and finally, on pain of losing his ears, he gave in and cursed the governor. The stubborn, brave man was further carted around the town, made to repeat various humiliating oaths, and finally deposited back at his home just before midnight, half frozen, an arm dislocated, and, as he said, "in a most mizerable setuation Deprived of his senses." Five days later, bedridden and "terribly bruised," he dictated a complaint to Governor Hutchinson, which his injuries obliged him to sign with an X.

The frost and tar caused an infection that made his skin peel extensively. However, he was careful to preserve a piece of skin with the tar and feathers still adhering (the stuff was the very devil to get off), which he carried to England as proof of his sufferings when, somewhat recovered, he set sail on May 2, 1774, to try to gain compensation for his loyalty.

Another Tory punishment that became traditional was the gruesome riding on a rail that sometimes followed tarring and feathering, but was severe enough in itself. It consisted of jogging the victim roughly along on "a sharp rail" between his legs. The painful effect of these "grand Toory Rides," as a contemporary called them, can readily be imagined. Seth Seely, a Connecticut farmer, was brought before the local committee in 1776 and for signing a declaration to support the king's laws was "put on a Rail carried on mens Shoulders thro the Streets, then put into the Stocks and besmeared with Eggs and was robbed of money for the Entertainment of the Company."

Persecution of the Loyalists came in many forms. In 1778 prisoners in Vermont were made to tread a road through the snow in the Green Mountains. The wife of Edward Brinley was pregnant and waiting out her confinement at Roxbury, Massachusetts, accompanied by "a guard of Rebels always in her room, who treated her with great rudeness and indecency, exposing her to the view of their banditti, as a sight 'See a tory woman' and striped her and her Children of all their Linens and Cloths." Peter Guire, of Connecticut, was branded on the forehead with the letters *G. R.* (George Rex). Samuel Jarvis, also of Connecticut, related that the following treatment made his whole family very ill:

> That your Memorialist for his Attachment to constitutional Government was taken with his Wife and Famely, consisting of three Daughters and one little Son by a Mob of daring and unfeeling Rebels from his Dwelling House in the dead of Night Striped of everything, put on board Whale Boats and Landed on Long Island in the Month of August last about 2 oClock in the Morning Oblieging them to wade almost to their Middles in the Water.

Probably the best-known mobbing in Philadelphia was that of Dr. John Kearsley, whose widow finally submitted a claim to the commissioners. Kearsley, a leading physician, pill manufacturer, and horse dealer, was a pugnacious American with strong Loyalist views. He was seized by a mob in September, 1775, and had his hand bayoneted; then he was carried through the streets to the tune of "Rogue's March." Sabine reports that he took off his wig with his injured hand and, "swinging it around his head, huzzaed louder and longer than his persecutors." This display of spirit notwithstanding, he nearly died following this treatment, according to his widow. His house was later ransacked, he was arrested, and he finally died in jail.

Atrocious punishments of Loyalists were sometimes carried out by local authorities in semilegal fashion — it was noted that the tarring and feathering of a New York victim in 1775 "was conducted with that regularity and decorum that ought to be observed in all publick punishments." But just as often mobs, drumhead courts, and all the horrors of vigilante policing were found. Indeed it is possible that the term "lynch law" derives from Charles Lynch, a Bedford County, Virginia, justice of the peace who became renowned for his drastic, cruel action against neighboring Tories.

The number of Loyalists subjected to cruel, often extra-legal, punishments can only be estimated, and likewise the number of those murdered or executed "legally" will never be known, but no one familiar with the sources — Whig newspapers are full of accounts of executions — can doubt that it is substantial, although the statement by a New York Loyalist that the rebels "made a practice of hanging people up on a slight pretence" is no doubt an exaggeration. Probably only fear of reprisals kept numbers from being much larger than they were. The carrying out of the supreme penalty was usually reserved for some overt aid to the British such as spying, piloting ships, guiding troops to the attack, recruiting, counterfeiting.

One of the most notorious executions of a Loyalist was that of John Roberts, a native-born Pennsylvania Quaker, who had aided the British occupying forces in Philadelphia and rather foolhardily had not departed with them. His trial was in 1778, and even many Whigs petitioned the authorities for a pardon, but in vain. A contemporary described the situation thus:

> Roberts' wife, with ten children, went to Congress, threw themselves on their knees and supplicated mercy, but in vain. His behaviour at the gallows did honor to human nature. He told his audience that his conscience acquitted him of guilt; that he suffered for doing his duty to his Sovereign; that his blood would one day be demanded at their hands; and then turning to his children, charged and exhorted them to remember his principles, for which he died, and to adhere to them while they had breath. This is the substance of his speech; after which he suffered with the resolution of a Roman.

In 1792 the state of Pennsylvania restored Roberts' confiscated estate to his widow, Jane, a belated act of justice, for it seems Roberts had been a scapegoat, only one among so very many who had cooperated with the British. Roberts' behavior would doubtless have made him a remembered hero had he suffered for the other side. Similarly, in Connecticut, Moses Dunbar was tried and hanged for accepting a British commission and recruiting troops at about the same time that Nathan Hale suffered the same penalty. Connecticut honors Hale but forgets Dunbar. One of the more bizarre executions was reported by the *Boston Gazette* for November 3, 1777, under the date line Fishkill: "Last Thursday, one Taylor, a spy was hanged at Hurley, who was detected with a letter to Burgoyne, which he had swallowed in a silver ball, but by the assistance of a tartar emetic he discharged the same."

But perhaps more moving across the years than accounts of atrocities are the more pedestrian misfortunes of war. Women in particular are always the great sufferers, being separated from their husbands and sons, living in constant dread of bereavement. In 1780 Mary Donnelly petitioned the British authorities in New York for relief. Her husband had been serving on board a privateer when "about seven months ago as my youngest Child lay expireing in my Arms an account came of the Vessil being lost in a Storm." Mrs. Donnelly was now destitute, "frequently being affraid to open my Eyes on the Daylight least I should hear my infant cry for Bread and not have it in my power to relieve him. The first meal I had eat for three days at one time was a morsel of dry bread and a lump of ice."

On June 6, 1783, Phebe Ward, of East Chester, wrote to her husband Edmund, a native of the province of New York:

> Kind Husband
>
> I am sorry to acquant you that our farme is sold. . . .
> thay said if I did not quitt posesion that thay had aright to take any thing on the farme or in the house to pay the Cost of a law sute and imprisen me I have sufered most Every thing but death it self in your long absens pray Grant me spedy Releaf or God only knows what will be com of me and my frendsles Children
> thay say my posesion was nothing youre husband has forfeted his estate by Joining the British Enemy with a free and vollentary will and thereby was forfeted to the Stat and sold
> All at present from your cind and Loveing Wife
>
> > phebe Ward
> > pray send me spedeay anser.

One of the most pathetic stories of all concerns Filer Dibblee, a native-born lawyer, and his family. In August, 1776, they fled from Stamford to Long Island, but a few months later the rebels turned Dibblee's wife and five children "naked into the Streets," having stolen the very clothes from their backs as well has having plundered the house. The family fled to New York City, where Dibblee obtained sufficient credit to settle at Oyster Bay, Long Island, but in 1778 the rebels plundered the family a second time and carried Dibblee as prisoner to Connecticut, where he remained imprisoned six months until exchanged. With further credit the family established themselves at Westhills, Long Island, where they were "plundered and stripped" a third time; then came a move to Hempstead, Long Island, and in 1780 a fourth ravaging. Dibblee now, for the first time, applied for relief from the commander in chief and received about one hundred dollars. In 1783 the whole family moved to St. John, New Brunswick, where they managed to survive a rough winter in a log cabin, but Dibblee's "fortitude gave way" at the prospect of imprisonment for his considerable indebtedness and the fate his family would suffer as a consequence. The result was that he "grew Melancholy, which soon deprived him of his Reason, and for months could not be left by himself," and finally in March, 1784, "whilst the Famely were at Tea, Mr. Dibblee walked back and forth in the Room, seemingly much composed: but unobserved he took a Razor from the Closet, threw himself on the bed, drew the Curtains, and cut his own throat."

Shortly afterward the Dibblee house was accidentally burned to the ground, was then rebuilt by the heroic widow, only to be accidentally razed again the same year by an Indian servant girl.

It is not surprising that imprisonment and escape loom large in Loyalist annals. The most celebrated prison was in Connecticut at the Simsbury (now East Granby) copper mines, where the ruins still afford a dramatic prospect. The isolated and strongly Whig back country of Connecticut was considered a good spot to incarcerate important Loyalists from all over the Northern colonies, and the mines, converted into a prison in 1773, were ideal. The "Catacomb of Loyalty," to quote Thomas Anburey, or the "woeful mansion," to quote an inmate, contained cells forty yards below the surface, into which "the prisoners are let down by a windlass into the dismal cavern, through a hole, which answers the purpose of conveying their food and air, as to light, it scarcely reaches them." The mere threat of the "Mines" could make a Loyalist conform. One prisoner regarded being sent there as a "Shocking Sentence (Worse than Death)." The mines received such celebrated Loyalists as Mayor Mathews of New York and William Franklin, who wrote of his "long and horrible confinement" and was described on his release as "considerably reduced in Flesh."

In May, 1781, there was a mass breakout. The leaders of the escape, Ebenezer Hathaway and Thomas Smith, arrived in New York some weeks later, and their alleged experiences were reported by Rivington's newspaper. Hathaway and Smith recalled that they had originally been captured on a privateer, sentenced, and marched the seventy-four miles from Hartford to Simsbury. The entrance to the dungeon was a heavily barred trap door that had to be raised

> by means of a tackle, whilst the hinges grated as they turned upon their hooks, and opened the jaws and mouths of what they call Hell, into which they descended by means of a ladder about six feet more, which led to a large iron grate or hatchway, locked down over a shaft about three feet diameter, sunk through the solid rock. . . . They bid adieu to this world,

and went down thirty-eight feet more by ladder "when they came to what is called the landing; then marching shelf by shelf, till descending about thirty or forty feet more they came to a platform of boards laid under foot, with a few more put over head to carry off the water, which keeps continually dropping." There they lived for twenty nights with the other prisoners, using "pots of charcoal to dispel the foul air" through a ventilation hole bored from the surface until the opportunity to escape came when they were allowed up into the kitchen to prepare food and rushed and captured the guards.

Some colorful Connecticut escapes in other places are also recorded. Nathan Barnum avoided appearing for trial in 1780 by inoculating himself with smallpox, whereupon he was "sent to the Hospital, where he was chained to the Floor to prevent his Escape, he found Means to bribe one of the Nurses, who not only brought him a File to cut off his Irons, but amused the Centinal, placed over him while he effected it. . . ."

Samuel Jarvis and his brother got out of prison "by the assistance of Friends who had privately procured some Women's apparel which they Dressed themselves in, and by that means made their escape through the Rebel Army." James Robertson asserted that while he was in jail at Albany, the British attacked and set the building on fire, whereupon, unable to walk, he managed to crawl into a bed of cabbages "and chewing them to prevent being suffocated" was found three days later badly burnt.

There was even a series of Tory hiding places between New York and Canada, rather in the fashion of the "Underground Railroad" of the pre-Civil War days.

The treatment of imprisoned Loyalists ranged over the widest possible spectrum. Simsbury was notoriously the worst prison, almost the Andersonville of the time. Many Loyalists suffered close confinement in much pleasanter conditions; others merely underwent house arrest; others were only prevented from traveling; some were on parole and, if banished to some remote part of America, were boarded with reluctant Whigs. Some worked in the normal way by day and simply spent the night in jail. In 1776 Thomas Vernon, a fanatically early riser, was removed, with three other prominent Rhode Island Loyalists, from Newport to Glocester, in the northern part of the state, because he had refused the test oath. The foursome's journey and their few months' stay in Glocester were pleasant and gentlemanly, almost Pickwickian. The friends walked and admired the countryside, ate, drank, and conversed well in the local inn where they lived; they planted beans, killed snakes, trapped squirrels, fished, played Quadrille (a card game); they were very well treated by the ladies of the house and by neighboring females. Their chief complaints were the lack of books, some local abhorrence of Tories, particularly by the men (their landlord said "the town was very uneasy" at their being there), a few fleas, tedium from the lack of friends and family, and some stealing of their food by their far from genial host. . . .

The Whigs suffered as the Tories did — legal persecution, mob action, imprisonment (the British prison ships were particularly horrible and gave rise to effective propagandist literature), and all the excesses of civil war. Adrian C. Leiby, the historian of the Hackensack Valley, for example, reports that there was barely a Whig family there that had not lost someone to a Tory raiding party. There is at least one recorded tarring and feathering of a Whig by British troops — of one Thomas Ditson, Jr., in Boston in March, 1775. In June, 1779, the *Virginia Gazette* reported the murder of a Whig captain by a party of Tories whom he had discovered robbing his house. A sentinel wounded him with a gunshot; then, after taking all the horses from the stables, the Tories pursued the captain into the house, where he was lying on a bed, and

immediately thrust their bayonets into his body several times, continuing the barbarity while they heard a groan; and lest life might still be remaining in him, they cut both his arms with a knife in the most inhuman manner. The villain who shot him, had been his neighbour and companion from his youth.

The victim lived another two days.

STUDY GUIDE

1. Be prepared to discuss the following quotation from Sir John Harrington, who lived two centuries before the American Revolution:

   Treason doth never prosper; what's the reason?
   Why, if it prosper, none dare call it treason.

   Evaluate Harrington's epigram with respect to Loyalists and Patriots in the War for Independence; and second, explain why the favorable historical reputation of the losing Civil War general Robert E. Lee is an exception to Harrington's view.

2. Summarize the various devices used to punish the Loyalists — both in their persons and in their property. What was the relation between official policy by state governments and actual treatment of Loyalists by neighbors and townsfolk?

3. Does the picture presented in this chapter modify your view of the American Patriots? If so, how?

4. Is there any evidence here that would support the view that the Revolution was a civil war between different groups of colonials, as well as a war for independence from England?

BIBLIOGRAPHY

As suggested in the introduction to this selection, the Loyalists have not received very sympathetic treatment from American historians. Even more important than this is that they have generally been ignored. It was not until 1974, for example, that an extended biography of the distinguished Massachusetts Loyalist Thomas Hutchinson was finally published. Aside from the works of a few early scholars such as Claude Van Tyne, the serious study of Loyalism is a very recent phenomenon. A growing number of historians in the last two decades have devoted their attention to these forgotten Americans, most notably William H. Nelson, in *The American Tory* (1961); Wallace Brown, in *The King's Friends: The Composition and Motives of the American Loyalist Claimants* (1966); Paul H. Smith, who describes the military involvement of the Loyalists in *Loyalists and Redcoats: A Study in British Revolutionary Policy* (1964); and Mary B. Norton, in *The British-Americans: The Loyalist Exiles in England, 1774–1789* (1972). An earlier work that attempts to identify the character of the Tory mind and psychology is Leonard W. Labaree, *Conservatism in Early American History* (1948).

Anyone who is interested in the antagonisms in British colonial society can find a comprehensive survey in Elisha P. Douglass, *Rebels and Democrats: The Struggle for Equal Political Rights and Majority Rule during the American Revolution* (1955). Since 1950, however, many historians have argued that this was simply a war for independence, rather than an internal social revolution, and have suggested that eighteenth-century colonial society was characterized by broad consensus rather than conflict. This view has been argued in studies of individual colonies, in studies of revolutionary ideology, and in studies of the consequences of the Revolution. For some years the views of Edmund S. Morgan, Daniel Boorstin, Robert E. Brown, and other scholars were so widely accepted that a general consensus as to the conservative nature of the American Revolution seemed in the offing. More recently, this view has been challenged by a group of younger historians, frequently identified as the "New Left." In a series of articles, Jesse Lemisch and Staughton Lynd, among others, have argued that conflict did in fact exist in the revolutionary period, and that the laboring men of urban areas were as important as farmers in the uprising.

The views concerning the causes and character of the American Revolution are so varied and the important books so numerous that they cannot be mentioned here. The bibliographies of most textbooks will refer you to the more important studies, or you can find a good bibliography, with selections from various historical writings, in Robert F. Berkhofer, Jr., *The American Revolution: The Critical Issues* (1971).

The genius of Eli Whitney and other early inventors culminated in an extraordinary display of American technology at the Philadelphia Exposition of 1876.

7

JOSEPH AND FRANCES GIES

Beginnings of Industrialism

When it was first used, the term "Industrial Revolution" had a very limited meaning. An English writer, Arnold Toynbee, used it to describe the development of steam power and its application to coal mining and transportation, new inventions in the textile industry, the factory system of production, and the formation of new capital. He found the origins of this revolution in England between the mid-eighteenth century and 1830. Eventually historians realized that those developments were only limited facets of much broader changes that are still taking place and that have spread to much of the world. The rudimentary development of the factory system and mass production that took place before 1830 has now progressed to completely automated production lines that produce, among other things, McDonald's hamburgers with scarcely any human intervention. Today, the Industrial Revolution is seen as including new ways of organizing business and capital; new inventions and technology in office machinery as well as on the production line; new sources of power and raw materials, including man-made synthetics; a vastly expanded labor force; and new patterns of transportation and distribution. Many historians, in fact, consider the entire Industrial Revolution as only a part of a broad social, political, and economic development that they refer to as "modernization."

By any standard, the Industrial Revolution must rank with the invention of the wheel and the opening of the Western Hemisphere as one of the most influential changes in world history. Throughout most of history, only a very small elite had more than a bare subsistence level of living, while most of humanity was doomed to hereditary poverty. It is the wealth of modern industrialism that has enabled society, for the first time, to consider educating most people, providing a nourishing diet, good medical care, and adequate housing. Virtually every aspect of modern existence, from skyscrapers to jet planes, reflects the influence of industrialization. Before the invention of steel, reinforced concrete, and the elevator, few residential or commercial buildings in the world were higher than six or seven stories. Transportation was such that most people never saw any part of the world other than the isolated valley or village in which they were born, lived their lives, and died. Industrial changes of the past century have had so radical a social impact that the changes in this period might be greater than the accumulated changes of the previous nineteen centuries.

Toynbee was correct in identifying eighteenth-century England as the seedbed of industrialism, but since that time the American people have embraced the movement with unparalleled enthusiasm. From the dawn of the republic, Americans seem to have had a special knack for fiddling with machinery and for developing ingenious inventions to solve practical problems. In the early nineteenth century, a whole host of American tinkerers invented or contributed to the development of steamboats, vulcanized rubber, the telegraph, and new textile machinery. Eli Whitney was one such, and his invention of the cotton gin and his contribution to the principle of interchangeable parts for machines were to have a far-reaching impact upon American agriculture, manufacturing, and social life. In the following essay, Joseph and Frances Gies indicate the tremendous implications that machine precision and interchangeable parts were to have upon labor and mass production. The selection opens with a description of the great Philadelphia Centennial Exposition of 1876, where American and foreign visitors were awed by the technological marvels that Eli Whitney and his successors had developed.

After speeches and more music, at noon the flags were raised on all the buildings, and a hundred-gun salute thundered. Then President Grant and the emperor [Pedro II of Brazil] led the way down the length of the cavernous Main Building, out the far end, and past one of the Exhibition's many fountains, to another immense new building, Machinery Hall.

Here George H. Corliss, wealthy Providence industrialist and Centennial Commissioner for Rhode Island, waited on another platform. Behind him towered his personal gift to the Exhibition, the Corliss Double Walking-Beam Steam Engine, whose 30-foot, 56-ton flywheel was designed to supply the power for all the machinery exhibited in Machinery Hall. With deferential pride, Corliss showed the president and the emperor how to turn a pair of wheels and, when as much of the crowd as could squeeze in was in place, gave a hand signal. The two heads of state obediently turned their wheels, and overhead the twin walking beams began to rock, stirring the mighty flywheel into silent motion. Throughout the vast hall belts began to move and wheels to spin, and in a few moments hundreds of machines were humming and clacking. Spontaneously, the crowd burst into a long, delighted round of applause.

The tableau was perfect. Those who had come to Philadelphia bemused with images of Betsy Ross and the Liberty Bell were awakened at a stroke to the reality of America's first century — the transformation of the country from a scattering of seaboard towns and farms on the edge of a continental wilderness to an industrial colossus, bestriding North America and rivaling, or rather surpassing, the old European powers.

Machinery Hall was the true heart of the Exhibition. Understandably, Great Britain and the continental European nations were limited in their contributions by the expense of shipping, but it was not short of amazing that three-fourths of the whole mighty display was American.

Lathes, presses, power looms, steam hammers, milling machines, pumps — the variety and profusion were impressive without the numerous superlatives attached to them. The steam-hydraulic cotton press of the Taylor Iron Works of South Carolina was "the most powerful in the world." The section of wire cable for John A. Roebling's famous Niagara suspension bridge was the largest in the world, and about to be surpassed by that for the new Brooklyn Bridge, whose 1,595-foot main span dwarfed all the bridges of Europe. As a sort of analogue to the Corliss engine, a 7,000-pound pendulum clock by Seth Thomas acted as electrical master to twenty-six slave clocks around the building.

The central aisle was crowded with the latest models of one of America's most valued inventions, the sewing machine, a portrait of whose chief inventor, Massachusetts's Elias Howe, gazed benevolently down on visitors to the exhibit. Several other makes of sewing machine were also represented, but the largest manufacturer, Isaac Singer, had so many new models that he had built his own pavilion elsewhere on the grounds.

An array of locomotives and equipment included George Westinghouse's revolutionary air brake, just introduced on the Pennsylvania Railroad. Christopher Sholes's new "type-writer," manufactured by the Remington Arms Company, astonished visitors by printing neat and legible characters at the touch of the operator's fingers. Massive rotary presses of the Bullock and Hoe companies demonstrated their prowess by turning out thousands of copies of the *New York Herald* and the *Philadelphia Times.* A group of machines exploiting the invention of the late Charles Goodyear fashioned "India rubber" boots and shoes for visitors.

To the connoisseur of technology, perhaps the most telling display in Machinery Hall was in the area containing the products of William Sellers & Company of Philadelphia and Pratt & Whitney of Hartford, Connecticut, America's foremost manufacturers of machine tools — the machines that make machines. Sober black iron monsters whose varying steel edges could cut, chip, stamp, mold, grind, and otherwise shape metal, they had made possible the world-famous "American System of Manufacture," meaning high-speed mass production with interchangeable parts. In the separate U.S. Government Building nearby, workers and machines from the Springfield Arsenal demonstrated the system itself by assembling rifles from identical parts machined to a thousandth of an inch tolerance.

Between the Sellers and Pratt & Whitney displays the Midvale Steel Works of Philadelphia showed off its largest axles, shafts, and chilled-steel bars, demonstrating a sophisticated American capability with this once-exotic metal whose quantity production had first been achieved by an American. Steel's birth as a structural material was the subject of another display, a model showing how the steel arches of Captain James Eads's mighty St. Louis Bridge had been formed and joined.

Baffling to the layman, but nonetheless impressive, was an 8-foot-long mechanism mounted on a pair of trestle legs and looking like the insides of a thousand-keyed piano. This was George B. Grant's "Calculating Machine," an American version of Charles Babbage's much-talked-about British calculator. Grant's creation was considered an improvement on Babbage's, though certainly less original, but it suffered from the same inherent defect, the unsuitability of mechanical components to perform the lightning-swift operations that only electronics would permit. No one guessed the future relationship of the perforated paper rolls that programmed the twelve-piece "Electro-Magnetic Orchestra" in Horticultural Hall with the Babbage-Grant machines. . . .

The country had come so far so fast it found itself a little taken aback. No nation had ever before undergone an experience like America's first hundred years, and the more one looked back at 1776, the more the question seemed in order: how did it all happen? [To answer that, one must examine the origins of American technology in the early inventions and primitive mills of men like Samuel Slater, Eli Whitney, and David Wilkinson, nearly a century before the Philadelphia Exposition.]

At the moment when Samuel Slater's mill machinery was suddenly enlarging the demand for raw cotton, the tobacco, rice, and indigo planters of the South were encountering marketing difficulties that made them eager to turn to cotton as a staple. Unfortunately, there was a problem. Of the two great cotton-plant varieties, long-staple and short-staple, the first resisted cultivation and the second resisted cleaning. Only at Sea Island, Georgia (which gave its name to the variety in the United States), and along the Georgia-Carolina coast as far as Charleston did the long-staple plant flourish. The short-staple grew in more or less any warm, moist climate, but its seeds stuck like glue to the lint, from which they had to be torn or cut by hand. It took one person a day to clean a pound of the stuff.

The smooth seeds of Sea Island cotton were removed mechanically. The lint was run through a pair of wooden rollers, grooved lengthwise, and turned by a hand crank in opposite directions, like a clothes wringer. The cleaning device was neither an American nor a European invention, but a product of India, where for hundreds of years it had been known as a churka. In 1790 Dr. Joseph Eve of the Bahamas and Augusta, Georgia, fitted up the churka with accessories that permitted it to be powered by a horse or waterwheel, but though Dr. Eve and others who tinkered with it claimed that their improvements made it effective with short-staple cotton, they vastly exaggerated. The obstinate short-staple seeds either passed through or clung and broke between the cylinders, scattering fragments throughout the cotton.

Yet the churka supplied a basic starting point, and Carolina planters felt with a sort of gambler's prescience that an improvement was due any moment. In 1793 many actually raised short-staple cotton in the hope that someone would invent an effective gin ("gin" in the sense of trap) in time for the crop.

Throughout the planting country, people were talking about such a machine. Consequently, it was not surprising that three planters gathered at Mulberry Grove, Georgia, in the winter of 1792–93 fell to discussing it. Retired army officers, Majors Bremen, Forsyth, and Pendleton, they were paying a call on Catherine Greene, widow of their old commanding officer, General Nathanael Greene. Nathanael and Catherine were originally Rhode Islanders, and had settled in the South as a direct result of Greene's famous Southern campaign against Cornwallis in 1780–81 that had led to Yorktown. Mulberry Grove, the property of a Tory lieutenant governor, was a gift of the state of Georgia to the general for his services.

Captivating Catherine Greene was one of the most prominent and popular ladies in the South, famed for her charm as a hostess and remembered for her courageous spirit at Valley Forge. Listening to her guests, she had a sudden inspiration. "Gentlemen," she said, "apply to my young friend Mr. Whitney — he can make anything." She displayed an embroidery frame that the mysterious Mr. Whitney had made for her needlework, and several toys he had made or repaired. The gentlemen expressed a desire to meet the young mechanic, and Whitney himself was produced. He proved to be a handsome young fellow with a Yankee beak, luminous dark eyes, a firm chin, and a well-proportioned figure.

Although fresh out of Yale College, Eli Whitney was twenty-seven years old. Like Samuel Slater and Oliver Evans, he was the son of a prosperous farmer. On his farm in Westborough, Massachusetts, the elder Whitney had a workshop equipped with a lathe and other tools to make and repair household furnishings and farm implements. As a boy, Eli showed the mechanical curiosity and aptitude of Slater, Evans, and John Fitch, once feigning illness and staying home from church to take apart and reassemble his father's watch. At twelve he fashioned a violin that made, he recalled, "tolerable good musick." The oldest of four children, he was a reliable performer of chores, watering sixty head of cattle every morning. According to his sister, he was "remarkable for thinking and acting for himself." At fourteen he installed a forge in his father's workshop to make nails, in demand because the war had shut off the British supply, while the American industry had been handicapped by the old Parliamentary restraints. So successful was his nailmaking that he hired an assistant, and when the war's end brought a flood of British nails on the market, he switched his production to hatpins and walking sticks.

In 1783, at the age of seventeen, when an American boy's schooling was normally over, he suddenly decided he wanted some higher education. Answering an advertisement for a schoolmaster in nearby Grafton, he got the appointment and, by studying nights to stay ahead of his pupils, earned enough salary — $7 a month, poor pay even for 1783 — to finance a summer term at Leicester Academy. For three years he taught winters and learned summers, until he had enough arithmetic, Latin, and Greek to qualify "to keep a Grammar School." It was also enough to win admittance to college, and Whitney had decided he wanted to go to Yale. . . .

Yale consisted of a dormitory (Connecticut Hall), houses for President Stiles and the one other professor, a refectory, and the chapel, which doubled as repository for the library and the "philosophical apparatus," i.e., scientific equipment. To the college collection, consisting of a set of the basic machine components (lever, wheel and axle, cord and pulley, toothed gear wheels, plane, wedge, screw), a quadrant, a theodolite, an air pump, and a variety of natural curiosities such as mammoth tusks and snakeskins, Dr. Stiles had personally added a three-foot telescope, a micrometer, and an orrery — a model for demonstrating the motions of the planets. Stiles and Professor

Josiah Meigs conducted all lectures, while three tutors drilled students in grammar and composition, history and geography, disputation and theology. Because the jail was next door in crowded College Square, recitations and prayers were often accompanied by the audible groans, curses, and screams of the jail's mixed population of debtors, felons, and lunatics.

The library boasted 3,000 books, most of them comprising a gift dating from 1733, but including a copy of Newton's *Principia* donated by Newton himself, a volume that may have enlightened Whitney about the failure of a perpetual-motion machine he had once invented. Despite the cost of college — nearly $400 a year including bed and bedding, board, candles, fuel, laundry, and books, of which his father apparently paid half or more — Yale was not only a great experience but promised to provide him with a substantial reward in the shape of a legal career. At the graduation exercises in September 1792, marked by a fireworks display to celebrate the state's forgiveness of the college's back taxes ($40,000), Eli appeared in new store-bought clothes — pants, coat, waistcoat, cotton shirt, slippers, and silk hose. Following commencement, he received a disappointment that proved one of destiny's silver-lined clouds — a teaching post Dr. Stiles had lined up for him in New York to provide for him while he studied law had evaporated. Something vaguer and much farther off, a tutoring job in South Carolina, had turned up to replace it. The intermediary for the tutoring job was a recent Yale alumnus named Phineas Miller, who though only a year older than Whitney was manager of the estate of the late General Nathanael Greene. At the moment Miller was in New Haven, and suggested that Whitney accompany him, Mrs. Greene, and the children, who were summering at Newport, back to Mulberry Grove, across the Savannah River from the household that was seeking the tutor. . . .

Exactly when General Greene's ex-officers introduced Whitney to the cottonseed problem is not clear from his account, written almost a year later, except that it was shortly after his arrival at Mulberry Grove in November 1792. His response was a modest disclaimer to the effect that he had never seen either cotton or cottonseed in his life. But he promised to study the problem, and soon after went to Savannah, brought back a parcel of cotton, and talked the problem over with Phineas Miller, who strongly urged him to try. His tutorial post had meantime disappointed him by promising only fifty guineas instead of the hundred he had anticipated. He soon "struck out a plan of a machine," and communicated it to Miller, who enthusiastically offered funds and a room in the basement for a workshop. "In about ten days I made a little model, for which I was offered, if I would give up all right and title to it, a Hundred Guineas. . . ." Putting Miller off, he returned to work, surrounded by the inquisitive Greene children, and produced a full-scale machine that one man could operate to clean "ten times as much cotton as he can in any other way before known and also clean it much better than in the usual mode. This machine may be turned by water or with a horse . . . and one man and a horse will do more than fifty men with the old machines."

Essentially Whitney approached the problem of separating seeds from cotton from the reverse side, designing a machine that pulled the cotton from the seeds rather than the seeds from the cotton. The principal element in his gin was a horizontal cylinder set in a frame and (like the churka) turned by a crank, armed with iron spikes or teeth that matched the slots in an iron guard on the face of the lint box, positioned directly in front of the cylinder. The spikes speared the cotton and yanked it through the slots with such force that the lint was torn from the seeds, leaving the seeds in the box. No plate iron was available, so he made his teeth from a coil of iron wire that "one of the Miss Greenes had bought . . . to make a bird cage."

The full-size machine (its cylinder was 26 inches long and 6 inches in diameter) gave scope for a full-size trial, and a problem immediately developed. The fibers caught by the teeth rolled up around the cylinder, clogging it and preventing it from turning. A popular story, origins unknown but not confirmed by Whitney, had it that Catherine Greene suggested the solution by picking up a stiff-bristled hearth brush and asking him why he did not try that. What Whitney actually did was to add a small supplementary cylinder, set with bristles, attaching it to the crankshaft by means of a belt that caused it to turn in the opposite direction to the main cylinder. It worked — the bristles pulled the lint free of the teeth.

Catherine Greene invited the neighbors in to admire the new invention. Their exclamations began to make clear the dimensions of its value and even the dangers. Though they urged Whitney to take advantage of the new United States patent law, their excitement was a warning of potential piracy. Shortly after, on May 27, 1793, Whitney and Phineas Miller signed an agreement to share profits on the cotton gin while Miller continued to pay for the work of development. Whitney then sailed for the North.

Their idea was to establish a factory in New Haven to manufacture cotton gins. The first gins would be set up in Mulberry Grove to gin the district's 1794 cotton crop, whose planting Miller would stimulate by appropriate advertising. After that, they would gradually extend their operation into the Carolinas. It seemed a reasonable plan, but they entirely underestimated the demand for the gin.

Landing in New York, Whitney proceeded first to Philadelphia by stage, filing a patent application with Secretary of State Jefferson. En route to New Haven he stopped off in New York to witness an examination of cotton ginned by his machine at Mulberry Grove; the cotton was declared of good quality and sold at auction at "the highest price." At New Haven he set to work with energy and ingenuity, building a wire-drawing block, a lathe, and special turning tools. After waiting vainly for the yellow fever epidemic that had driven the government from Philadelphia to subside, he sent his full patent description to Jefferson on October 15, 1793. . . .

At New Haven that winter Whitney had to battle serious difficulties. Determined to make his new gins as large as possible, he repeatedly cracked the wooden cylinders with the hundreds of iron wire teeth driven into them. To solve the problem, he built another machine, one for cutting wire teeth uniformly. By February of 1794 he had completed six large gins to take to Georgia and a miniature for the Patent Office. On March 14 Edmund Randolph, the new Secretary of State, granted the patent.

Two weeks earlier Miller published his announcement in the Georgia *Gazette,* stating that he would gin any amount of green-seed cotton on the basis of one pound of cleaned cotton for every five pounds delivered. Since it normally took three pounds of raw cotton to produce one pound of clean, Miller proposed to keep two-thirds of a pound for each five pounds cleaned, or two-fifths of the cleaned cotton. Such payment in kind was the time-honored arrangement for millers, fullers, sawyers, and other processers. Miller's proposition may have been a little too greedy, but the terms were not really the problem. Planters did bring their cotton, in large quantities. Whitney crated his disassembled gins in New Haven, two gins to three large boxes, and Miller set them up in pairs, each pair turnable by a horse or waterwheel. Miller was successfully expanding the business in Georgia and had established one operation in South Carolina when in the spring of 1795 a fire destroyed Whitney's New Haven shop, with tools, materials, and twenty unfinished gins. At the same time Miller, trying for a quick fortune in another direction, lost heavily in the Yazoo land speculation that exploded in a scandal over bribes to the Georgia legislature. Catherine Greene came to his rescue by putting her resources, consisting of several plantations, at Miller's disposal, an arrangement formalized by their marriage in 1796.

Fire and scandal were remediable disasters. A worse catastrophe building for the firm of Whitney, Miller, and Greene was not. Using Miller's high charges as an excuse, and the mechanical simplicity of the gin as a means, the planters of Georgia and Carolina industriously set to work copying it. One pirate, Edward Lyon, not only stole the design through espionage but fabricated and sold gins that he brazenly declared to be "improved models." Another, Hodgen Holmes, actually did improve the gin by using teeth cut from sheet iron, Whitney's original preference, and won a patent from the federal government, even though he had actually copied Whitney's device from drawings. Dr. Eve and others who had made the earlier churka-type gins "improved" their models by adding all Whitney's features. Injury was compounded by insult as the swarm of imitators launched an incredibly malicious propaganda campaign in England to persuade British manufacturers that Whitney's original gin damaged cotton fibers, and for a time Whitney and Miller were unable to sell cotton in England. Miller sued Georgia trespassers only to have the local jury impertinently sustain the planters, using a loophole provided by faulty wording of the Patent Act, which read, "If any person shall make, devise, *and* use . . ." where it should have read "*or* use." Even the South's slave code helped protect pirates. Slaves, barred from testifying in court, could operate a cotton gin in a loft, where no white witness ever saw it. Whitney later wrote Robert Fulton about an occasion on which the rattle of three nearby pirate gins could be heard on the steps of the Georgia courthouse in which Whitney was vainly trying to prove that the machine had been used in Georgia. By 1800 Whitney succeeded in getting the Patent Law reworded, and eventually Miller and Whitney won substantial awards from the legislatures of South and North Carolina. A licensing arrangement, suggested by a Yale classmate of Miller's, also brought in revenues. By that time Miller and Catherine Greene had had to sell Mulberry Grove, and Miller died shortly after, a victim of fever. The awards and licensing fees mostly disappeared in litigation costs, and Whitney bitterly concluded that "An invention can be so valuable as to be worthless to the inventor." As he described the situation to Fulton, "The use of this Machine being immensely profitable to almost every individual in the Country all were interested in trespassing & each justified & kept the other in countenance."

Whitney of course was right, but what he could scarcely be expected to see was the degree of justice on the planters' side. An invention that the whole community badly needed had to be made available to it, if possible on terms favorable to the inventor, otherwise on terms unfavorable to him. Watt's steam engine was pirated; Samuel Slater and others plagiarized Arkwright's textile machinery; Oliver Evans's automatic flour mill was freely copied; and many other nineteenth-century inventors suffered similarly. The fatal characteristic of Eli Whitney's cotton gin was that it was so wonderfully simple. Given a good look at it, or a good drawing, any carpenter or smith could make one, in any size, to suit the pirate's needs and purse.

If Whitney got little profit, he at least got much honor. Yale awarded him a Master of Arts degree in 1795, when the gin's national importance was already apparent. Ultimately the economic benefit conferred on the South, and on the United States, was beyond anyone's most optimistic calculation. The 2 to 3 million pounds of green-seed cotton that a few upland planters in South Carolina and Georgia had grown hopefully in 1793 spread by 1820 to a cotton belt far expanded west and north that produced 80 million pounds, nearly a third of an immensely increased world supply. By this time a large part of the crop was going to the factories lining the New England river valleys, where copies of Samuel Slater's machinery, driven by the splashing waterwheels and tended by ex-farm women and children, were turning out cotton thread. That same year the Missouri Compromise signaled one of the major effects of the gin — the formal, fatal division of the United States over slavery, a result produced, strangely enough, by the economic partnership created between North and South by Samuel Slater and Eli Whitney. . . .

Chance had led Whitney to his first invention; need drove him to his second, of an entirely different order, but of a significance fully comparable to that of the cotton gin. The John Adams administration's quarrel with revolutionary France in 1798 disclosed the national weakness in arms manufacture. The new Springfield (Massachusetts) Armory had turned out scarcely a thousand muskets in three years, and the newer Harpers Ferry (Virginia) none at all in two. The government turned frantically to private gunsmiths, appropriating the huge sum of $800,000. But the few skilled gunsmiths in the country, fabricating weapons one at a time, lock, stock, and barrel, would take years to equip an army.

In a letter to Oliver Wolcott, Secretary of the Treasury, written May 1, 1798, Whitney put forward a remarkable proposal: "I am persuaded that Machinery moved by water adapted to this business would greatly diminish the labor and facilitate the manufacture of this article — machines for forging, rolling, floating, boreing, grinding, polishing, etc. may all be made of use to advantage.

"Cartridge or Cartouch Boxes is an article which I can manufacture. I have a machine for boreing wood of my Invention which is admirably adapted to this purpose. The making of swords, hangers, Pistols etc. I could perform."

Whitney proposed to make 10,000 "stand of arms" — musket, bayonet, ramrod, wiper, and screwdriver, the complete arms needed to equip a soldier — for $134,000 or $13.40 apiece, not a particularly low price since in 1795 the government had imported muskets for $9 apiece. But with the French Revolutionary War peaking in intensity, imports could no longer be had, and Congress jumped at Whitney's offer. A contract was signed in Philadelphia after just three weeks' negotiations, including correspondence with Whitney's lawyer in New Haven. The government would supply a model, the French Charleville 1763, of Saratoga-Yorktown fame, and would furnish black walnut gunstocks at 25 cents apiece. Four thousand muskets with bayonets and ramrods were to be delivered by September 30, 1799, the remaining 6,000 by the following September. A $5,000 advance permitted Whitney to pay off pressing debts.

Implicit in Whitney's proposal to use "Machines for forging, rolling" and other operations was the momentous idea of interchangeable parts. With his waterpowered machines — which remained to be created — Whitney meant to manufacture rapidly large numbers of each part of a musket, then assemble the muskets. For Whitney, the beauty of the plan lay less in the speed with which powered machinery could turn out the parts than in the elimination of scarce, expensive skilled labor.

As in the case of John Fitch and Oliver Evans, Whitney had European forerunners of whom he apparently knew nothing. As early as the 1720s, Christopher Polhem, a Swedish scientist and engineer, built a mechanized factory that employed the principle of interchangeable parts to produce clocks, padlocks, knives, forks, scissors, files, and nails. In 1722 a French gunsmith, name unknown, undertook to apply interchangeability to musket manufacture; the idea was taken up again by Honoré Blanc, superintendent of the Royal Manufactory of Arms at St. Etienne, who established a special factory to produce musket locks in 1778. In 1785 Blanc demonstrated his method to Thomas Jefferson, then American ambassador to France, who wrote, "I put several [musket locks] together myself, taking pieces at hazard, as they came to hand, and they fitted in the most perfect manner. . . . He effects [interchangeability] by tools of his own contrivance, which at the same time abridge the work, so that he thinks he shall be able to furnish the musket two livres cheaper than the common price." Jefferson vainly "attempted to remove this Artist to the United States."

Jefferson's acquaintance with Blanc's work was of benefit to Eli Whitney when unforeseen difficulties plagued his enterprise. He had trouble acquiring a good mill site, and when he found one, at Mill Rock, on Mill River near New Haven, early winter stopped construction, Philadelphia's yellow fever epidemic delayed delivery of his gunstocks, and Connecticut floods prevented his Canaan machine-part contractors from fulfilling their contract. Despite his $5,000 advance, he could not work out credit arrangements that would permit buying in quantity. Finally, he had problems with his labor, and had to ask for an extension of his own contract deadline. He wrote Oliver Wolcott on July 30, 1799, "I must . . . candidly acknowledge that much more time must necessarily be taken up in the first establishment of the business than I had at first any conception of . . . I must not only tell the workmen but must show them how every part is to be done."

Wolcott sent Captain Decius Wadsworth, the army's inspector of muskets, to Mill Rock to determine if Whitney's excuses were valid. Captain Wadsworth was a Yale classmate of Phineas Miller who knew Whitney's cotton gin well and brought a sympathetic understanding to Mill Rock. On his recommendation, Wolcott granted Whitney's request for a reprieve from the contract, writing sensibly, "I should consider a *real improvement* in machinery for manufacturing arms as a great acquisition to the United States." Wolcott enclosed a letter of credit on the Collector of the port of New Haven for $1,500 to ease Whitney's financial problems.

The first batch of muskets was not in fact delivered until September 1801, two years after the original contract date, and numbering only 500 instead of 4,000. Twenty-six other contractors had delivered only about a thousand muskets (so it was just as well that the French war threat had passed) but Whitney felt he should make an explanation in person, and as a result a memorable incident took place. Setting out for the new capital on the banks of the Potomac, where Jefferson had now assumed office as president, Whitney took along one complete musket and the parts for several locks. At either the White House, the War Department, or possibly at the incomplete Capitol building, he deposited the lock components on a large table, then choosing parts at random, assembled a lock. He invited the officials present (who included Jefferson and new Secretary of War Henry Dearborn) to do the same. They were all delighted with the result — the parts were so uniform that a musket lock could be assembled from any appropriate group.

The demonstration was decisive as far as the government was concerned, Whitney was given further extensions and more money, and Jefferson wrote James Monroe, the governor of Virginia:

"Mr. Whitney . . . has invented moulds and machines for making all the pieces of his locks so exactly equal, that take 100 locks to pieces and mingle their parts and the hundred locks may be put together as well by taking the first pieces which come to hand . . . Leblanc, in France, had invented a similar process in 1788 & had extended it to the barrel, mounting & stock. . . ."

The machinery by which Whitney achieved his delayed but impressive performance in production remains obscure because, perhaps out of exasperation with his cotton-gin experience, he took out no patents. All we know is a description written by ten-year-old nephew Philos Blake to Blake's sister: "There is a drilling machine and a bouring machine to bour berels [barrels] and a screw machine and too great large buildings, one nother shop to stocking guns in, a blacksmith shop and a trip hammer shop. . . ."

Whitney set down the theory of his machine organization in a letter to Wolcott:

"One of my primary objects is to form the tools so the tools themselves shall fashion the work and give to every part its just proportion — which when once accomplished will give expedition, uniformity and exactness to the whole. . . . In short, the tools which I contemplate are similar to an engraving on copper plate from which may be taken a great number of impressions exactly alike."

For all his enlightened enthusiasm, Jefferson did not really grasp the significance of interchangeable parts in manufacture. In his letter to Monroe, he laid stress on the value of interchangeability in musket repair — "out of ten locks, e.g. disabled for the want of different pieces, 9 good locks may be put together without employing a smith." That advantage seems modest. After a battle, the army left in possession of the field might perhaps do such repair work, but would be more likely to salvage whole muskets from the casualties. Whitney himself was inclined to stress the economy of dispensing with skilled labor, a point of great importance to any manufacturing operation and especially valuable in early America. Blanc in France actually grasped the advantages of interchangeability better than did Whitney. The true economic sense of mass production, the dramatic lowering of unit costs, was as yet difficult to perceive.

Even in his limited aim, Whitney gained only a qualified success. The handicraft technique survived and for a while was credited with better results in the sense of more reliable weapons. Wood and iron machines could not yet attain — or maintain — the precision necessary for a really satisfactory mass-production operation, and standard gauges did not yet exist.

Whitney's impressive demonstration for Jefferson was probably partly rigged by a careful selection of parts. His normal procedure was apparently to do some hand-finishing on parts at the moment of assembly. Whether he ever achieved genuine interchangeability remains in doubt.

Yet Whitney had started something and he had started it in fertile soil. In France Honoré Blanc and his successors made many thousands of muskets by interchangeable-parts manufacture, but French industry, dedicated to old-fashioned handicraft production of fine goods, made no attempt to adapt the technique. In Britain a Frenche émigré engineer, Marc Brunel, manufactured pulley blocks for the British navy by a well-thought-out system of interchangeable parts production in which he made use of the gifted British machine-tool expert Henry Maudslay. But though the experiment was technically a brilliant success, the Brunel-Maudslay system was no more copied by British industry than was the Blanc system by French.

Only in America did the idea take hold. Whitney had an imitator almost at once (possibly even a coinventor) in Simeon North, a gunsmith of nearby Berlin, Connecticut, who made pistols under government contract. Of far more significance was the adoption of the technique by the New England clock industry, whose craftsmen had always followed the European tradition of hand-fabricating their wheels and gears with compasses, saws, and files. In 1806 Eli Terry of Plymouth, Connecticut, built a waterpowered factory, installed lathes and other machinery, and by 1807 was astounding his competitors by turning out 200 wooden-movement clocks a year, a figure that ultimately rose to thousands, with movements of brass as well as wood. Any debt owed by Terry to Whitney remains conjectural, despite an assertion by Terry's onetime partner and later rival Seth Thomas that the Plymouth factory's machinery "was hinted to him by Eli Whitney."

Whitney's system had an important implication for the development of another basic component of American industry: machine tools. To make machinery, metal-working machines were needed. Britain was at this moment in the midst of creating these basic tools, adapting some from the lathes, planes, bits, augers, awls, chisels, and gouges of woodworking, and inventing others. Henry Maudslay was the leader in the development. Maudslay has generally received credit for originating the important "slide-rest lathe," in which the cutting tool was carried on a sliding carriage, advanced by a long screw that ran parallel to the axis of the workpiece.

But Samuel Slater's young friend, brother-in-law, and mechanic, David Wilkinson, invented a lathe very similar to Maudslay's in 1796, at least a year earlier than Maudslay, and it was Wilkinson's lathe that diffused in America (and in many other places in the world). In 1786–87 Wilkinson's father had started making large iron drive screws for paper-manufacturing presses, sending young David to Hope Furnace, in Scituate, Massachusetts, to cast the screws in clay molds, David then finishing them by hand in Pawtucket. The Wilkinsons expanded to making drive screws for clothiers' presses and oil mills. "But they were imperfect," David wrote, "and I told my father I wanted to make a machine to cut screws on centers [in other words, on a lathe], which would make them more perfect."

The project took several years and was interrupted by David's other activities — helping Samuel Slater, building lock machinery for the Middlesex Canal, even an early steamboat. In 1794 Oziel Wilkinson built a rolling and slitting mill in Pawtucket, and here David put into operation his new machine "on the principle of the gauge or sliding lathe now in every workshop almost throughout the world. . . . I cut screws of all dimensions by this machine, and did them perfectly."

Wilkinson was especially proud of the rocklike stability of his device. In 1797, he journeyed to Philadelphia to apply for a patent, returning home to find that the well-known ironmaster Jacob Perkins had come to see his machine, and had been so delighted with it that he had "laughed out, and remarked that he could do his engraving on cast steel for Bank Note plates with that machine, — that he could make a hair stroke with [it], for it would never tremble. . . ." Another visitor, a master machinist from England, had quite a different reaction: He "advised me as a friend to abandon my new machine, for said he, 'you can *ner* do it, for we have tried it out and out at *ome,* and given it up; and don't you think we should have been doing it at *ome* if it could have been done?' "

Wilkinson made patterns for his lathe and had it cast, "and it worked to a charm." He sold the patterns for ten dollars to Richard and William Anthony, sons of the Daniel Anthony for whom he had helped build a model of the Arkwright spinning frame in 1789 — "And this is all I ever received for so valuable an invention." It was all he received up to the time of writing his memoir in 1846, but two years later, when he was almost seventy-eight years old, he was the recipient of a significant as well as gratifying award of $10,000 by resolution of Congress "for the benefits accruing to the public service [i.e., the arsenals] from the use of the principle of the gauge and sliding lathe of which he is the inventor."

As for Eli Whitney, through the early years of the new century his life continued to be full of hard work, anxiety, and frustration. He wrote a friend:

"You will find me a solitary Being, without a companion & almost without a friend . . . living on plain fare in a humble cottage. . . . If I had a house, a wife & a home —." He referred to himself as "Old Bachelor." The fact seems to be that he had fallen in love with the magnetic Catherine Greene, but never to have dared tell her so. Twice-widowed Catherine would have been receptive to an offer from Whitney. Her letters were transparent. "I wish to god my dear friend you were married," she wrote. ". . . I am prepared to love any woman who would make you happy." And again, "Never — Never shall I Cease Considering you My Son — and never never Cease lamenting that you were not born so," a gross exaggeration of their twelve-year age difference. And, "I wish also to whisper other secrets in your Ear — which I certainly should do if you were seting by me. . . . I comfort myself sometimes in looking at your picture and mentally conversing with it — and sometimes in the Lover stile give it a kiss." And, "You see how little I can do without you — and I can see how much I could do — if I had your advice and assistance for a month . . . Save my life in saving your own — for I find I can not comfortably be in this world if you are not of it." And, "Your picture ornaments my toilet table — It is every day looked at and some times kissed — that is to say when you are sick." But Whitney, diffident, obtuse, or distracted by a large government contract resulting from the outbreak of the War of 1812, let Catherine die in 1814 without ever seeing her again.

Two years later he married, at the age of fifty-two. His bride, Henrietta Edwards, whom he had known since she was a little girl, was twenty years younger, not renowned for her beauty, and on the verge of becoming a spinster. Yet they were evidently happy in their eight years of married life. Whitney's death in 1825 left three children (another had died), of whom Eli Whitney, Jr., grew up to take over his father's arms business.

Despite the cataclysmic effect of his cotton gin on the South, Whitney never took any interest in politics, and the word *slavery* is not even mentioned in his correspondence. The indifference was mutual. The gin-created cotton kingdom, driven to expand to escape exhausted soil, took slavery with it westward, and created fatal conflict with the wheat and corn farmers of the old Northwest over the trans-Mississippi territories. Press and pulpit of the whole country debated slavery and bandied secession, but the man whose invention had loosed the whirlwind was largely forgotten.

In 1832 a South Carolinian published an article about Whitney with the avowed aim of rescuing the South's benefactor from oblivion, but it was not till the end of the century that American schoolchildren learned that "Eli Whitney invented the cotton gin in 1793."

Even longer delayed was recognition of his role in the history of mass production, partly perhaps because of his casual failure to patent machinery, but mostly because the significance of mass production was so tardily appreciated.

STUDY GUIDE

1. Some inventions may be a single stroke of the imagination of one creative mind, but many seem to develop through the cumulative contributions of several people. To what extent were Whitney's cotton gin and interchangeable parts original with him?

2. Some American inventors were uneducated farm boys, others were college graduates, though none had the equivalent of a modern engineering education. Yet there may have been some similarities in their backgrounds or turn of mind that account for their imaginative solutions to practical problems. What do you see in Whitney's youth that foreshadows his later career?

3. Some of the inventions of the early Industrial Revolution had been developed in England and France, but not much used there as compared to their rapid and wide acceptance in the United States. What factors can you think of in those countries — such as labor, tradition, markets, and the like — that might explain a somewhat more conservative attitude toward new inventions?

4. Suppose the cotton gin had never been invented, and it had proved impossible to grow the long-staple, or Sea Island, cotton any place except along the coast of South Carolina and Georgia. How would this have affected slavery, westward expansion, and American social and political life?

5. How do the life, the rewards, and the conditions of one's work differ for an inventor in today's corporate, industrialized world? What examples can you think of, in inventions or improvements of products, that are not used because they would affect a company's sales or profits? What problems does a single, independent inventor face today in developing such improvements?

BIBLIOGRAPHY

The Gieses' book, from which the preceding selection is taken, is a delightful series of sketches of American inventors from John Fitch and Robert Fulton to Charles Goodyear and Thomas Edison. But the Industrial Revolution cannot be understood only through the lives of inventors and great business leaders. A volume that does provide a survey of the many factors involved, including transportation and labor as well as technology and business leadership, is Thomas C. Cochran and William Miller, *The Age of Enterprise: A Social History of Industrial America* (1942). Technology in early America is discussed in Brook Hindle, ed., *America's Wooden Age: Aspects of Its Early Technology* (1975). Roger Burlingame has written several books on the history of technology; his *March of the Iron Men: A Social History of Union through Invention* (1938) emphasizes the social environment of inventions. If you like a biographical approach to history, you might enjoy reading a full biography of Samuel Slater, Samuel F. B. Morse, or some other American inventor. Two of the best studies concern Eli Whitney: Jeannette Mirsky and Allan Nevins, *The World of Eli Whitney* (1952) and Constance Green, *Eli Whitney and the Birth of American Technology* (1956).

The literature on American economic development is too vast to be listed here. There are scores of fine studies of manufacturing, agriculture, railroads and canals, labor, the factory system, and finance. Gilbert C. Fite and Jim E. Reese, *An Economic History of the United States*, 3rd ed. (1973) has individual chapters on these subjects and an excellent bibliography. One classic work on the pre–Civil War period is George R. Taylor, *The Transportation Revolution, 1815–1860* (1951).

As you might imagine, the people who actually confronted the Industrial Revolution experienced considerable conflict and anxiety. Carefully acquired skills were outdated by the new machines, women and children competed with men for jobs, new and distant markets developed, the place of employment was now outside of the home, and the industrial system seemed to be in conflict with some deeply held social and ethical beliefs. These sorts of concerns are studied in three volumes: Marvin Fisher, *Workshops in the Wilderness: The European Response to American Industrialization, 1830–1860* (1967); John F. Kasson, *Civilizing the Machine: Technology and Republican Values in America, 1776–1900* (1976); and Leo Marx, *The Machine in the Garden: Technology and the Pastoral Ideal in America* (1964). Your library might also have some of the works of Lewis Mumford, whose sweeping studies range over industrialization and urbanization, the social and psychological changes brought about by invention, and the European scene as well as nineteenth-century America. Two other works that relate aesthetics to industrialization are Siegfried Giedion, *Mechanization Takes Command: A Contribution to Anonymous History* (1948) and John A. Kouwenhoven, *Made in America: The Arts in Modern Civilization* (1962).

Finally, some scholars have attempted to understand the impact of industrialism by cameo studies of individual towns or factories. Three exemplary works of this type are Alan Dawley, *Class and Community: The Industrial Revolution in Lynn* (1976); Stephan Thernstrom, *Poverty and Progress: Social Mobility in a Nineteenth Century City* (1964); and Anthony F. C. Wallace, *Rockdale: The Growth of an American Village in the Early Industrial Revolution* (1978).

"Sing-Sing Camp Meeting" by Joseph B. Smith, 1838. (Detail) One of the faithful is "treeing the devil."

8

EVERETT DICK

Religious Democracy

Religious organizations, like most institutions, reflect the social forces of their particular society and time. Even such a world-wide organization as the Roman Catholic Church has differed in doctrine and rites of worship in different countries, and most churches that survive a century or more undergo subtle changes. American Protestantism has been substantially transformed since it was first brought to these shores, and few of the changes have been so profound as those that came about in the first half of the nineteenth century.

Both New England Calvinism and the pietistic religions of Pennsylvania were brought to the colonies by small, tightly knit groups of devout believers. But the churches soon faced the question of whether or not to modify their doctrines and soften their requirements in order to retain the membership of later generations who held the beliefs less intensely and found the worship less satisfying. By the early 1700s, many people felt that the churches had compromised too much, and they responded enthusiastically to the first "Great Awakening," a religious re-vival movement that attracted many followers in the 1730s. The second major revival movement, which began about 1800, had its roots in a society that seemed to be increasingly secular and among a people who found a highly rational religion emotionally barren. Yet the remarkable religious awakening that swept across the country at the beginning of the nineteenth century was quite different from the earlier revival and had a much longer-range impact upon American Protestantism.

Theologically, one of the characteristics of the Second Great

Awakening was the new emphasis upon Jesus, rather than upon God the Father or the remote Creator of the Deists, an emphasis that has dominated Protestant thought and worship ever since. Preaching the salvation of all men, Protestant churches in the early nineteenth century outgrew the boundaries of a single colony or state and developed broad, national denominations. Between 1800 and 1850, Protestantism also assumed a new sense of mission and destiny, as did the American secular philosophy of the period. Bible, tract, and missionary societies were formed to carry the Word to the unsettled West, and each denomination established a multitude of colleges to provide a Christian education for the young.

Many of these developments took place after the most emotional revivalism had subsided. Yet the whole first half of the century witnessed a strong element of religious emotionalism and democratization, as evidenced in the founding of several new faiths. Spiritualism, Mormonism, and Adventism all had distinctive appeals, but like the revival itself, they succeeded because they found a people who were receptive to an emotional religious experience. Evidence of the revival was seen in the eastern states even before 1800, but the frenzy took its most distinctive form in the frontier communities farther west. In the following selection, Everett Dick discusses religion on the American frontier.

Various causes operated to promote an unreligious atmosphere on the frontier. Often the less pious moved west. The lack of women had a tendency to remove the steadying influence normally present. Very rude surroundings, with an intense struggle for existence, tended to promote ungodliness.

Contemporary writers in early Kentucky noted with amazement the lack of piety in the country. A most liberal estimate of the number of church members in 1792 still left two thirds of the population outside the fold of the church.

In some instances in Alabama preachers were driven off. There is a tradition that at St. Stephens a Baptist minister was rowed across the river and told that if he ever returned he would be tarred and feathered. A minister

From *The Dixie Frontier: A Social History of the Southern Frontier*, by Everett Dick. Copyright 1948 by Everett Dick. Reprinted by permission of Alfred A. Knopf, Inc.

by the name of Sturdevant labored a year without organizing a "society" or enrolling a member.

Timothy Flint complained that in Arkansas in 1819 part of the audience listened for a time to his sermon and then returned to the billiard room. . . .

The Baptists were the pioneers in religion in Kentucky and the most numerous body of Christians in the early settlement of the state. The first Methodist conference west of the Alleghenies was established by Bishop Asbury in the state of Franklin (now eastern Tennessee). He wrote of the work in Kentucky that "the Methodists do but little here, others lead the way." Despite slow growth in early years the Methodists became the leading denomination throughout the southern and southwestern frontiers. The Baptist church was next in size and influence.

. . . Under the leadership of Samuel Doak, the Presbyterians early possessed the field in eastern Tennessee. Educated at Princeton, he walked through Maryland and Virgina, driving before him a "flea-bitten gray horse loaded with a sack full of books." The Presbyterian belief was rigid, formal, and austere. The doctrine of predestination was not so popular on the frontier as the free-will doctrine of the Baptists and Methodists. As a result of the revival of 1800, however, a free-will branch of the Presbyterians, known as the New Lights, grew up.

When there were enough people in a neighborhood to support a church, all hands turned out and raised the walls for a meeting house. These churches were log cabins without floors and in the lower South were without any heating apparatus. Of these churches John Poage Campbell said:

> Numbers of them were open to everything and more like hog pens and stables, than places where men can worship God. . . . A pane of glass to let in the light and keep out the wind and rain is scarcely seen, a pew or decent seat about as rare. . . .

Preaching appointments were happy occasions. The people lived far apart, and there was preaching only as often as the itinerant came to the neighborhood, which usually was only once a month. It was a day of social communion as well as spiritual uplift. When the minister arrived he saw the fence and the yard around the building crowded with men, women, and children. Numerous guns leaned against the log cabin, with strings of squirrels, a few opossums, and numbers of partridges. In Indian days every man took his place on a bench wearing his shot-pouch, tomahawk, and scalping knife, and with his gun in his hand. Most of the congregation had on neither shoes nor stockings and were clad in apparel that was unlike that worn in more civilized areas. Every man brought his dogs. In that period an average congregation would consist of perhaps fifteen families. Each couple had an average of five children, two of whom were infants and a third was too small to keep quiet during services. It would be conservative to estimate five dogs to a family. As one minister facetiously remarked, there were in a congregation "forty-five babies and seventy-five dogs, with only sixty adults to police the mob." The preacher had his hands full to compete with quarreling dogs without and squalling children within.

There was much handshaking in the yard before meeting and much visiting there afterward. To smoke in church was not considered impious or out of order. On a hot summer day a new minister noticed a boy on his way to church swinging a firebrand to keep it burning. He was at a loss to know why fire was needed in summer. When he arrived in the yard after caring for his horses, he found the fire had been placed in a large stump and was burning freely. Old and young took out their pipes and, drawing from their roomy pockets home-cured tobacco, lighted their pipes at the stump and sat down to enjoy a smoke and visit before going in to the service. During the sermon he noticed a woman but a few feet in front of him nudge the one next to her, who nudged the one next to her, and the nudge was carried on down the bench. During this time every eye was fixed on the speaker. Soon the signal was repeated. Then all rose from the bench with almost military precision, quietly moved to the burning stump, lighted their pipes, and sat on the ground near by, smoking. During all this time they paid perfect attention, apparently never missing a word.

The people were fixed in their ideas of worship, anxious that the program be carried out in the old way, and informal and democratic enough to speak out if the minister forgot anything. When a new minister attempted to dismiss a service, a brother rose and in a loud voice drawled: "Ain't you goin' to give out no app'intment for the nixt round?" "Yes, brother," replied the preacher, "my colleague will be here in four weeks." Another brother called: "Give out the class meetin' for nixt Sunday." "At what hour?" "Three o'clock," was the reply. The minister then announced: "Let us be dismissed!" "Not yet! Not yet," implored a man with a red bandanna over his head. All was silence. "Ain't you goin' to give out prayer meetin' for next Thursday night?" "Yes; there will be prayer meeting in this house next Thursday evening." Someone offered: "Not in this house, brother; it will be at Brother M.'s, in the lower end of town." Finally the congregation was dismissed.

When the itinerant did not arrive at the announced time, the crowd would patiently await his coming for hours. John Mason Peck got lost while on his way to an appointment in 1818. He arrived at the clearing just at sunset and found more than twenty people who had waited since noon to hear the strange preacher. Often at church service business announcements, notices of lost stock, and other secular matters were "given out."

Although there were the beginnings of class distinction in social life, religion was one common plane upon which all classes met. The plantation-owners, their slaves, and "poor white trash" all worshipped together. The names of the slaves appear on the same church records as those of their masters and they were baptized together. As time passed, however, there was a tendency to hold a morning meeting for the whites and an afternoon session for the servants, although this was not a clear-cut rule. Negroes were often allowed to attend the morning sermon. In some instances a colored minister even preached to mixed congregations. Many Negro preachers could not read, of course, and it was necessary for them to get someone in the big house to read the Bible to them until a text was struck that suited them. Then they memorized it and other Scripture, and by means of homely but often apt illustrations they built up their sermon. . . .

At the conclusion of the service the Negroes could not separate without the breaking exercises, so called from breaking up the meeting. One who attended such an exercise said they sang the grandest, wildest, most beautiful African music he had ever heard. They began to sing and move in a procession by the pulpit, shaking hands with the minister as they passed. As the long column filed by, faces shone with delight as the music rose wilder and more exciting. Finally the handshaking ended, the meeting "broke," and the service was over.

The duties of church membership were taken seriously. If a man did not live up to his profession he was summoned to answer for his conduct. The Baptists held a monthly business meeting and the Methodists held one quarterly on Saturday. On these occasions the private lives of the members came up for review. Those whose conduct was deserving received a ticket admitting them to the communion the next day, and the black sheep were disciplined. These tickets were taken up by a sentinel at the door. . . .

The rules adopted by the Buffalo Lick Baptist Church of Kentucky provided for a moderator and efficient sensible rules of order covering all conceivable cases. Church trials were held regularly at these meetings. Witnesses were summoned and sworn in, they gave their testimony, and judgment was rendered by a vote of the church. Sometimes the offenses were church cases and warranted discipline by the church. Some, however, were of the nature of lawsuits or trials between individuals and were settled without cost or fees. Some of the cases that came before the Cooper Run Baptist Church in Bourbon County, Kentucky, for discipline were: neglecting to attend worship, chastising a slave too severely, playing the fiddle for dancing, horseracing, telling a lie, committing adultery, forging the father-in-law's name on a marriage permit in order to get the girl, permitting gambling in one's house. The women were disciplined for slander, tale-bearing, whispering, and quarreling; one married woman was hailed before the brethren for "unjustifiable familiarity with a young man in permitting him to kiss her three times." At the Bent Creek Church, Lucy Clark was excluded for adulterating beeswax with tallow. James Carter was suspended for not settling a personal debt where he came from.

The churches apparently regarded dancing as a sin and sufficient cause for excommunication, while placing their endorsement on distilling whisky. In 1795 a Kentucky church minute book recorded the fact that a certain woman was summoned to answer before the church for her disrespectful remarks about the distilling business. At the second meeting thereafter the same woman was excluded from membership for permitting dancing in her home.

Sectarianism arose after the Great Revival, and members were disciplined for hospitality to ministers of other churches. On a Mercer County, Kentucky, church minute book appear charges against a brother "for having Barton Stone preach his wife's funeral within the bounds of the church." His plea was that it was done at his wife's dying request, but would a like occasion arise again, he would be more circumspect.

Ministers, the Methodists in particular, were against the wearing of jewelry, ornaments, and fine apparel, which were considered an indication of pride. The Reverend Silas Drake pronounced earrings the devil's stirrups. One day at a meeting he saw a woman with large brown bows of ribbon on her hat and reproved her publicly, charging that her bows were of absolutely no use. She countered by charging that the buttons on his sleeves and the back of his coat were just as useless. He immediately pulled off his coat, cut off the buttons, and never wore them again.

The question whether a master could whip a black brother instead of taking the gospel steps was raised in one church and settled in favor of whipping. The marital status of slaves who had been married and separated from their spouses by sale and then married again came up at the Tick Creek Church in Kentucky. It was voted that the slave brethren were not guilty of adultery, but the masters were out of order in separating husbands and wives.

The Buffalo Lick Church, in Kentucky, voted to treat slaves the same as any other brother in the church in settling differences; that is, masters should settle a grievance with them as they would with a free brother.

Since drinking was almost as common as eating, it is not surprising that nearly all good church people drank. One never thought of entertaining without liquor in some form. A minister reported a conversation between two prominent church members who had been to market to lay in supplies for the annual revival. One asked the other: "How much 'sperits' did you git?" "Ten gallons," his brother replied. The other retorted: "Jest sech stinginess as that will spile the meetin' and kill the church. I got twenty gallons myself an' you are jest as able to support the gospil as I am, if you wuzn't so dog stingy." Ministers regularly took their morning eye-opener and their nightcap in the evening. Some even made whisky or trafficked in it.

By 1825 a consciousness of the evils of liquor began to arise. The Methodist church was the outstanding denomination in its advocacy of temperance and teetotal abstinence. In other churches the discussion over the use of liquor grew so heated that it was a red-hot issue for years, causing wrangling and ill feeling. St. Paul's admonition to Timothy to take a little wine for his stomach's sake was a tower of strength to those who liked their toddy. Disputes over one thing and another grew so spirited that churches were split. . . .

Worship was extremely informal. Loud shouts of "Hallelujah!" "Amen!" "Glory!" and other exclamations of praise and joy in Christ arose spontaneously. At a "love feast" of the Cumberland Presbyterians, a minister present said the procedure was for a man to rise, give his testimony, and then start out shaking hands with everyone in the church, continuing his remarks and ejaculations. A sister would rise, speak of the love of God, and then start out to embrace the other sisters. Before long almost the entire church was shaking hands and embracing, keeping time in their movements with a wild Western melody they were singing. Handshaking or kissing was very cordial when someone was converted, or "came through," as they called it.

... [A] "call to preach" was thought to exceed, by far, any preparation that might be made in the matter of education. There was a prejudice even against preparation for a particular sermon. A parishioner in visiting with a circuit rider remarked that since the minister had only one appointment a day and two on Sunday, he would have plenty of time to visit the homes of the people, and that if he did not "the sisters would be down on him." "But," replied the young minister, "I must have some time for rest and study." "As to study," replied the good brother, "I don't believe in it any way. It's no use; just get up, and look to God, and fire away."

A representative of the American Bible Society said that the deeper he got into the brush and the denser the ignorance of the people, the greater was the number of preachers. Some of them could not read at all and many mispronounced a large number of the longer words. An Indian man said that one of these inspired clergy, standing before the congregation, would recite this homiletic creed:

> Yes, bless the Lord, I am a poor, humble man — and I doesn't know a single letter in the A B C's, and couldn't read a chapter in the Bible no how you could fix it, bless the Lord! — I jist preach like old Peter and Poll, by the Sperit. Yes, we don't ax pay in cash nor trade nither for the Gospel, and arn't no hirelins like them high-flow'd college-larned sheepskins — but as the Lord freely give us, we freely give our fellow critturs. . . .

The mispronunciation of words and ignorance of their meaning often led the backwoods preacher into the most fantastic interpretations. One word, wrongly interpreted, often served as material for a whole sermon. One pious minister took for his text: "Wherefore, gird up the loins of your mind. . . ." He confused the word "loins" for "lines" and dwelt at length on the different kinds of lines: lines by which carpenters carried on their work, lines to divide land, stage lines for travelers, and lines with which to drive horses. In all these uses of the word he unfolded a deep mystery, to the delight of his hearers.

A preacher was explaining the reference in Ecclesiastes xii, 6: "Or ever the silver cord be loosed. . . ."

"The doctors say that there is a cord that runs from the nape of the neck, down the backbone, through the small of the back, into the heart, right thar; and that when a man dies that cord always snaps: That is the silver cord loosed."

"Ah," said a sister, her face radiant with delight, "Brother P— has studied *that*."

The delivery of a written sermon was little short of a disgrace. Old Peter Cartwright said that "it made him think of a gosling that had got the straddles by wading in the dew." Some of the ministers of the Disciples of Christ were alarmed because they felt their brethren studied the Bible too much. One of these Bible students on his way to meeting was joined by one of the fearful, who told him he hated to see him take the Bible to church. When asked why, he said he was afraid someone would think he was going to preach from it.

Strong lungs, vigorous gestures, copious tears, a ready flow of language, and an ability to describe in picturesque language the horrors of a literal, eternal, burning hell and the joys and bliss of a home in the Heavenly Canaan were the chief stores of ordnance in the backwoods minister's arsenal. And yet his message was powerful. He spoke in the common language of the people and seasoned it with illustrations familiar to all. . . .

When Bishop Asbury traveled to Kentucky, the old general got a taste of the lot of the rank and file of his army. He wrote in his journal that among other trials he had "taken the itch; and considering the filthy houses and filthy beds . . . it is perhaps strange I have not caught it twenty times." Later he wrote: "Oh, the rocks, hills, ruts and stumps! My bones, my bones!"

The route of the itinerant was often through uninhabited country and he spread his blanket on the moss at the foot of a tree, arranged his saddle for a pillow, and slept beneath the stars. At four he was stirring. First he knelt in prayer, then rubbed down his horse. As soon as it was light enough, he took the Bible from his saddlebags and studied it before starting. By noon perhaps he reached his appointment.

Sometimes an Indian arrow or tomahawk laid low the man of God. In 1794 on the road from Kentucky to Tennessee two Baptist ministers were ambushed by the Indians and killed while traveling with a group.

Singular as were these "brush preachers," they did not quail at the duty of thundering out against sin in its various forms. They blasted dueling, drunkenness, dishonesty, immorality, and worldliness in general. Their lives of sacrifice bore fruit in the experiences of their congregations, who appreciated their labors.

The Great Revival of 1800 and its attendant institution, the camp-meeting, were pure products of the frontier of the Old Southwest. Although accounts vary, camp-meetings seem to have been started two or three years previously in various places in a small way. In the summer of 1800 in the Cumberland country of southwestern Kentucky they appeared in full bloom.

At the sacramental solemnities of a Presbyterian church on the circuit of the Reverend James M'Gready, two brothers named John and William McGee, one a Methodist and the other a Presbyterian minister, were in attendance. The two brothers preached, and such a stirring experience followed that when the time came for the next meeting the ministers appointed to preach were unable to do so. There were cries and sobs all over the house and excitement indescribable. The inhabitants round about, on hearing of the stirring times, flocked in in such numbers that the church house was unable to accommodate the crowd. The people were so anxious about their salvation that these woodsmen soon cleared out the underbrush, felled the pine trees for pews, improvised a platform of poles, and erected an altar in the forest. After enjoying the spiritual refreshing, the people did not want to go home, and while some went foraging for provisions, others began the erection of temporary abodes made of poles and boughs. Such bedding as had been brought was used to improvise tents. Near-by farms were visited to secure straw for beds. This gave the meeting a new impulse; others flocked in bringing camp equipage. People came fifty to one hundred miles in carriages and wagons and on horseback. The meeting lasted several days in spite of the fact that it was harvest time. The movement soon swept beyond the borders of Kentucky into the neighboring states. These camp-meetings during the Great Revival were interdenominational, with the Presbyterians, Methodists, and Baptists taking the lead. Sectarianism was wiped away. Later the Presbyterians dropped the camp-meeting plan, leaving it to the Methodists and Baptists.

For some years previous to this, certain strange religious phenomena had cropped out at times. Now, with the gathering of great crowds and a general revival sweeping the whole region, these spiritual "exercises" burst into full flower. The "falling exercise" appeared at the McGee meeting mentioned above. In this experience the individual felt the constriction of the large blood vessels, a shortness of breath, an acceleration of breathing, and dropped prostrate. The hands and feet were cold. He lay from one to twenty-four hours. Upon returning to normal he was sometimes in a state of despair and felt he was such a sinner he could never be saved. More often he rejoiced that his sins were forgiven and immediately began to exhort others to give their lives to Christ. Timid people without apparent talent often showed great ability in praying and exhorting at that time. Scoffers and unbelievers as well as those seeking salvation were "struck down." Whole families at home, individuals in bed asleep, on the road, or plowing in the field, were stricken. Children at school where there were no religious exercises were seized. John McGee in speaking of it said: "The people fall before the word like corn before a storm of wind; and many rose from the dust with Divine glory shining in their countenances. . . ."

The next most common phenomenon was known as "the jerks." It was similar to the falling exercise in affecting all kinds of people everywhere. Like the falling exercise, it frequently fell upon people at meetings, but those far from the meetings were stricken. Elder Jacob Young said he had often seen ladies take it at the breakfast table as they were pouring tea or coffee. They would throw the whole up toward the ceiling, sometimes breaking both cup and saucer. As they left the table their heads would be so violently jerked that their braided hair, hanging down their backs, would crack like a whip. Witnesses say that some were taken up in the air, whirled over on their heads, coiled up so as to spin about like a cartwheel. They endeavored to grasp trees or saplings, but were carried headlong and helplessly on. J. B. Finley said that as many as five hundred of these subjects might be seen in one congregation in west Tennessee, bending the whole body first backward and then forward, the head nearly touching the ground forward and back alternately.

The Reverend Samuel Doak, an educated conservative Presbyterian of east Tennessee, went north on a visit about 1804, and when he returned was welcomed by a large assemblage to hear him preach. In the midst of a moving sermon, he was seized with a strange convulsion that made his limbs jerk and twist. He soon began to jump and finally went jerking and rolling off the platform down the hill while his congregation stood awe-stricken. After a while he finished his sermon, but he continued to jerk more or less for some time.

Lorenzo Dow had heard of the strange doings in Tennessee and said that he, like the Queen of Sheba, went to see for himself and found it was the real thing. . . . As Elder Dow passed a camp-meeting site he noticed from fifty to one hundred saplings cut off about breast-high. This seemed a slovenly way to clear an area and he asked the cause. When informed that they were left for people to jerk on, he went to see and found the people had laid hold and jerked so powerfully that they had kicked up the earth like a horse stamping flies.

In the "barking exercise" the victim would bark like a dog as he chased the devil. One who saw this said the person affected jerked, foamed at the mouth, rolled into a hog wallow, and then rose and with arms uplifted began to bark as he took the trail through the woods. Half a mile off he found a creek and, still barking, stopped at a tree, placed his hands on it, and looking up exclaimed: "I have treed the devil."

Sometimes a whole congregation would be thrown into side-splitting convulsions of laughter. When it got started in an audience, everybody would be seized with hearty natural laughter. It would last for hours sometimes. This was known as the "holy laugh." The "holy dance" was probably a variation of "the jerks" and was ungovernable until it ran its course.

In some instances children ten years of age mounted a log and preached with eloquence and the wisdom of the learned.

Some, while lying on the ground as a result of the exercises, had visions and, on regaining their normal composure, told of having been taken to heaven, of the delightful scenes there and whom they saw. Others brought back reports of a trip to hell with its horrors. While in this supernatural state they were able to do astonishing feats. Many of these phenomena kept popping up on the frontier for the next third of a century and were carried into the new territories and states. The "holy dance" and other ecstasies appeared among both white and black worshippers in Alabama and Mississippi as late as 1835.

As a frontier institution the camp-meeting developed a standard pattern during the first few years of the nineteenth century. A forest area was selected near a sparkling stream with plenty of shade and grass for the hundreds of horses. A large square clearing was made and over this was constructed an immense brush arbor or, as a camp-ground became permanent, a long shed covered with clapboards. The logs were laid end to end in rows lengthwise, and rough slabs, split from other logs with wedges, were laid across these in tiers the full length of the arbor. At one end was a high platform, known as "the pulpit-stand," made of poles or poles and slabs. At the foot of the stand was a straw-floored enclosure about thirty feet square, known as "the altar" or "penitent's pen." A rail fence was built down the center of the arbor to separate the men from the women.

Forming a quadrangle or large ellipse of about two acres including the arbor, and some distance from it, were the dwelling-places of the worshippers. These were called "the tents," although in a permanent camp they were often pole pens covered with clapboards. Many, however, were tents made of tow, or improvised tents made by stretching quilts, sheets, and counterpanes around and over crude pole frames. On the fourth side of the quadrangle, behind the pulpit-stand, were the dwelling-places of the ministers. The women cooked with Dutch ovens, pots, and skillets around fires in the open air and served the meals on long clapboard scaffolds. At night the grounds were lighted by pine-knot fires built on wooden altars covered with dirt or flat rocks. As roads were improved enough to permit vehicles, many people came in covered wagons, which were their home for the following few days. The underbrush was cleared for a great area around, permitting retirement for secret prayer. . . .

The day's program was regulated by the blowing of a cow's horn or tin trumpet. There were prayers at the general assembly before breakfast. After breakfast there ensued an hour of secret prayer in the woods. At ten and two were general meetings. At four came another hour of secret prayer in the woods. The big meeting of the day was at candle-lighting time in the arbor. It did not often adjourn until after midnight and during stirring times lasted until broad daylight.

The night meeting was picturesque, with the deep shadows of the primeval forest lighted up by lurid flames which cast a glare on the earnest ministers and their vast congregation. This scene, with its background of the majestic forest, presented an imposing effect. In this setting the great throng worshipped in a primitive way.

The meeting in the early evening proceeded with a good degree of decorum, but as the night progressed, wilder and wilder became the disorder. As the minister began to warm up to his subject, which itself was often a hot one — an eternal burning hell in which the wicked were suffering — people began to respond. So realistically was the destiny of sinners portrayed that the listeners could fairly feel its scorching breath and smell its brimstone. . . . When the call for penitents was made, sinners pushed forward until the pen was filled with those seeking forgiveness. Then ensued in that enclosure the greatest confusion — shouting, screaming, leaping, jerking, clapping of hands, falling, and swooning away. Ministers and other workers stood by and urged those under conviction to "come through." . . . Thus the wild confusion continued, many times until daybreak. Between meetings in the large assembly the same sort of work for sinners and the same sort of exercises took place in the living-quarters.

So popular was the movement that everybody came. Although the primary objective was religious, the curious were there too. The ambitious and influential attended, for public opinion was all-powerful on the frontier and their presence was demanded in order for them to hold and extend their influence. Aspirants for office were there to gain popularity and electioneer in a quiet way. Young ladies were there to show themselves and their costumes. The young men went to see the girls and frolic in a quiet way. Couples promenaded about the camp-ground between meetings. It was an enjoyable social season as the long isolated frontiersmen met together for a time in the warmth of Christian fellowship.

Unfortunately some unconverted ones almost always caused trouble for the campers. These "rowdies," as they were termed, would fortify themselves with whisky illicitly obtained somewhere near by. They engaged in all sorts of devilment, from pranks down to riotous conduct and stealing horses and rigs. It was necessary to post a line of sentries around the quadrangle and sometimes the ministers slept on their arms, so to speak, by keeping clubs at hand in order to be able to rush out in the night as a sort of auxiliary police force to assist in clearing the grounds of evil-doers. Peter Cartwright had many an adventure with rowdies. Once he captured the whisky that they were drinking and thus dried up the mischief at its source. Another time he gained the victory by strategy. He appointed the leader of the rowdies captain of the camp guard. On still another occasion, when a timid officer feared to arrest a whisky-seller, Cartwright got the sheriff to appoint him and four other preachers as bold as himself a posse to arrest the trouble-makers. They took the culprit and never left him until he had paid a fine and costs. When the rowdies in retaliation attempted to rout the preachers from their quarters at night, he drove off one of their leaders by hitting him a violent blow with a "chunk of fire" and another a blow on the head that drove out his "dispensation of mischief." One rowdy leader was "struck down" by an unseen hand just as he came up quietly to hang a necklace of frogs around a preacher's neck, and he got up a converted man.

The Great Revival reached its crest with the tremendous camp-meeting at Cane Ridge in Bourbon County, Kentucky. A vast crowd variously estimated at from twelve to twenty-five thousand gathered. That vast sea of human beings seemed agitated as by a storm. The noise was like that of a giant waterfall. Hundreds were swept down in a moment as though batteries had swept the crowd with grapeshot, and then followed shrieks and shouts that fairly rent the very heavens. It was estimated that three thousand fell at that meeting. The congregation was so large that it had to be split up, and twenty-six ministers occupied various improvised pulpits such as stumps, fallen trees, and wagons as they each preached to good-sized groups.

The Cane Ridge meeting lasted seventeen days. Later camp-meetings usually lasted from four to ten days. At the close of the meeting it was customary to gather for a final blessing where so many had been enjoyed. Then with tears, benedictions, hearty handshakes, and fond embraces the worshippers took their way homeward.

There was a wide difference of opinion as to the Great Revival and camp-meetings that sprang from it. Many felt that the meetings and the exercises that accompanied them were of the devil. As an overview from the vantage point of several years' observation, perhaps the evaluation of Timothy Flint sums up the situation as well as any. Flint, a Harvard graduate, had little sympathy for camp-meetings on principle at first, but said of them:

> Notwithstanding all that has been said in derision of these spectacles so common in this region, it cannot be denied, that their influence, on the whole, is salutary, and the general bearing upon the great interests of the community, good.... Whatever be the cause, the effect is certain, that... these excitements have produced a palpable change in the manners and habits of the people.

STUDY GUIDE

1. We often think of churches as performing basically a religious function. What functions, social and otherwise, did religion perform on the American frontier?

2. What evidence does Dick provide that religion on the frontier was equalitarian and democratic? How does frontier religion compare with that of such colonial groups as the Puritans and Quakers?

3. What types of misbehavior and moral transgressions did the frontier churches tend to condemn? Explain why they might disapprove of dancing, but tolerate liquor.

4. Different observers have given different explanations of religious exercises such as falling and barking. What arguments can you develop to support each of the following explanations: (a) the exercises represented a strong religious response by people who could not attend worship regularly; (b) the exercises provided people who lived in social isolation for an extended period with a means of "letting off steam"; (c) the exercises were a result of poor diet, poor health, and exhaustion produced by the camp-meeting environment?

5. Consider the reform movements of the 1830s, such as abolitionism and women's rights, and then think about the words of the Civil War song "Battle Hymn of the Republic." Is it legitimate to suggest that the sense of mission and the emotional urgency of Protestantism in this period shaped these other aspects of American life? Or was American religious life simply a reflection of the broader sense of missionary zeal and destiny among all of the American people in that period?

BIBLIOGRAPHY

There are a number of works on religion in the West and the great religious revival of the nineteenth century. One of the most prolific writers on American religious history was William W. Sweet, who wrote *Revivalism in America: Its Origin, Growth and Decline* (1944) and also edited four volumes of writings entitled *Religion on the American Frontier* (1931–1946). Among the most interesting books on the revival are Bernard A. Weisberger, *They Gathered at the River: The Story of the Great Revivalists and Their Impact upon Religion in America* (1958) and Charles A. Johnson, *The Frontier Camp Meeting* (1955). William G. McLoughlin, Jr., *Modern Revivalism: Charles Grandison Finney to Billy Graham* (1959) is a delightful series of sketches of revivalists from the early nineteenth to the mid-twentieth century. Among special studies on certain regions or aspects of revivalism, two of the best are Timothy L. Smith, *Revivalism and Social Reform in Mid-Nineteenth Century America* (1957) and Whitney R. Cross, *The Burned-Over District* (1950), which concerns the revival spirit in New York State.

Besides the studies of individual denominations, there are several general books on American Protestantism. Winthrop S. Hudson, *American Protestantism* (1961) is a general survey which provides an excellent introduction to the subject. Another book by Hudson, *Religion in America* (1965), is also worth reading, as are the works of two distinguished scholars — H. Richard Niebuhr, *The Kingdom of God in America* (1937) and Sidney E. Mead, *The Lively Experiment: The Shaping of Christianity in America* (1963).

There are two basic introductions to Catholicism and Judaism in the United States, the bibliographies of which contain references to many other works: John T. Ellis, *American Catholicism*, 2nd ed. (1969) and Nathan Glazer, *American Judaism* (1957). In *Freedom's Ferment: Phases of American Social History to 1860* (1944), Alice Felt Tyler describes some of the many smaller sects and new religions that arose in the early nineteenth century. Many of the special works on those subjects lack objectivity, but two good works on the Mormons are Thomas F. O'Dea, *The Mormons* (1957) and Fawn M. Brodie, *No Man Knows My History: The Life of Joseph Smith, the Mormon Prophet* (1945).

The most comprehensive book on the religious history of American blacks was published more than fifty years ago: Carter G. Woodson, *The History of the Negro Church* (1921). Shorter studies include E. Franklin Frazier, *The Negro Church in America* (1963) and Chapter 42 of the newest general survey of American religious history, Sydney E. Ahlstrom, *A Religious History of the American People* (1972).

III THE AGE OF REFORM

One of the questions frequently asked of historians is how closely their reconstruction of the past approximates the past as it truly was. We seldom think of ourselves as being part of an "age," and we are scarcely aware of the patterns of development that later historians may detect. Fifty years from now, historians may look back on our times as a revolutionary period, an age of reform, a period of cultural decay, or a turning point in the disintegration of American society. Any such characterization of a period is somewhat artificial. It ignores many contradictory developments of the time and applies simple labels that are not always helpful to those trying to understand the period.

The last decade of the eighteenth century and the first quarter of the nineteenth century are generally regarded as a period of centralization and nationalism. Following the adoption of the Constitution in 1788, the Federalist period of Washington, Hamilton, and Adams was characterized by the strengthening of the national government in both domestic and foreign affairs and by the development of national interests quite distinct from those of European powers. This nationalistic thrust was continued under the Virginian presidents from Jefferson to Monroe, though support for a domestic program along these lines was stronger in Congress than in the executive mansion.

The second quarter of the nineteenth century has proved to be more difficult to characterize. Though some historians emphasize the democratic features of the "Age of Jackson," others have suggested that it was basically an age of business entrepreneurs and social inequality. There is little doubt that the years from 1830 to 1850 were a time of great social ferment, and such a startling variety of reforms were undertaken that some historians call it "The Age of Reform."

As the first reading indicates, there were ambivalent attitudes toward the position of women in American society during these decades, but the first women's rights movement originated then. The second reading, discussing an area in which reform was needed but not attempted, traces the callous and sometimes brutal treatment accorded the American Indian in the nineteenth century. A host of other concerns, including pacifism, help for the handicapped, abolitionism, and the temperance crusade grew into national movements during this period. The temperance movement, which had one of the longest influences upon American thought, is discussed in the third reading. Many Americans believed that reform could best be achieved by creating local and state institutions to care for orphans, delinquents, the insane, and other unfortunates, while others attempted to form ideal, small communities to serve as a model for a perfect world. The last two readings discuss these two very different approaches to reform.

143

Like many American women trying to live up to romantic ideals of womanhood, Harriet Beecher Stowe suffered serious psychological and physical illness.

9

BARBARA J. BERG

The Status of Women

The reform crusade of the 1830s, to aid the handicapped and unfortunate, was undertaken largely by committed individuals and private humanitarian societies, rather than by the national government. In this and succeeding decades, women were especially active in the various reform organizations. Dorothea Dix traveled thousands of miles investigating the care of the insane and petitioning legislatures for improved facilities. Angelina Grimké filled a Boston theater as she preached against slavery, while Harriet Beecher Stowe wrote her emotionally appealing *Uncle Tom's Cabin* and actively assisted runaway slaves.

Some of the women of the period extended their concerns to areas such as the antislavery crusade after they had become aroused by the discrimination they experienced as women. Many others first began working in abolition and humanitarian reform movements and turned their attention to the women's rights crusade only after discovering that their "meddling" in these areas evoked taunts, threats, and disparagement of women in public affairs. Their reforms ranged from dress styles that afforded more freedom to equality in marriage, law, and employment. Women entered industry, journalism, medicine, teaching, and other areas. Both women's colleges and coeducational institutions were founded before the Civil War to afford educational opportunities to women, and some changes were made in state laws on property holding, marital rights, and the like.

Yet, throughout the nineteenth century, the majority of American women continued to see their roles as those of wives and mothers. The "cult of true womanhood" created separate spheres for men and women, with females being expected to devote all of their time and strength to providing a cultured retreat in the home for husbands and children. Womanly virtues included sexual innocence, healing the sick, teaching morality, and elevating the rougher nature of man. To write or lecture or engage in political causes was unfeminine. Though some women built up strong systems of support with other women, most languished at home, and the lack of meaning in their lives had devastating psychological and medical effects. Despite the reforms of the Jacksonian period, there is little evidence of substantial changes in either male or female attitudes toward women. They did not achieve the right to vote until after World War I, and women's liberationists of our time have contended that such legal changes are largely meaningless because of the continuation of discriminatory social attitudes toward the roles of men and women.

In the following selection, Barbara J. Berg describes the position of women in the early nineteenth century. Much of the selection describes the artificial ideal that women were expected to personify, but it also discusses the reality of daily life and the demands for change that were beginning to be voiced.

The greatest trial . . . is that I have nothing to do. Here I am with abundant leisure, and capable, I believe, of accomplishing some good, and yet with no object on which to expend my energies. . . . I cannot be happy without being employed. Alone as I am, my mind seems to prey upon itself until I am weary of life.

With these words, one female expressed the sense of stagnation and misery that scarred the lives of many nineteenth-century American women. The decrees of genuine womanhood, tyrannically governing feminine existence, thwarted efforts at self-realization. Women could neither control their own destinies nor help to free one another from society's bonds as long as the myths of the woman-belle ideal remained embedded in the nation's consciousness.

The contradictory mandates generated severe tension. Intense inner turmoil sought an outlet and impelled women to ameliorate their intolerable

Excerpted from *The Remembered Gate: Origins of American Feminism, The Woman and The City, 1800–1860* by Barbara J. Berg. Copyright © 1978 by Oxford University Press, Inc. Reprinted by permission. (Footnotes omitted)

condition. This search for personal fulfillment assumed different forms, sometimes even affording temporary abatement. But remaining individual and insular, it did nothing to improve the general plight of women until the interactions of the city brought a new understanding of woman's position.

Before the dynamics of urban growth would enable women to gain new insights and support from their shared experiences, nineteenth-century females suffered alone. Their numerous ailments became the observable symptoms of inner malaise. Visitors and residents alike expressed astonishment at the extent of ill health among American women. A British actress, Fanny Kemble, remarked that women in the United States "look old and faded" by the time they reach twenty-five years of age, while the "pallid and unhealthy complexions of the American ladies" struck her compatriot Richard Cobden with amazement. A journal reported that "foreigners who visit this country [comment] that American ladies have, almost without exception, a delicacy of complexion and appearance, amounting almost to sickness." Citizens concurred with these European observations.

Both James Fenimore Cooper and Nathaniel Hawthorne expressed dismay at the precarious health of American females. Other, less eminent writers voiced similar views. Joel Hawes described the "puny forms . . . feeble frames and sickly faces," as well as the "dismal train of ills," which characterized women of the "higher classes." Rev. Anson Smyth thought the "health of [the] American woman poor compared to what it used to be," and his colleague, Rev. Dr. Hawes of Hartford, bemoaned the fact "that the muscular vigor and strength of our . . . women have, for a long time past been undergoing a melancholy change. . . . But a small proportion of our adult females enjoy complete health." . . .

Doctors directed their attention to the womb, holding the reproductive system responsible for most female ills. Her uterus exercises a "paramount power" over her physical and moral system, and its grasp is "no less whimsical than potent," believed William P. Dewes, professor of midwifery at the University of Pennsylvania. Because doctors agreed that woman "is constantly liable to irregularities in her menstrua, and menaced severely by their consequences," they focused medical treatment on uterine and menstrual disorders. Female sexual organs bore the onus for headaches, nervous disorders, indigestion, insomnia, depression, and backaches.

The pages of the *Water-Cure Journal*, a contemporary periodical heralding the benefits of hydropathy, document the nineteenth-century obsession with "uterine-related diseases." Articles on such topics as "chlorsis or green sickness . . . the non-appearance of the menstrual discharge . . . [which] inevitably results in the serious derangement of the general health," "menstrual cramps" to which the "luxurious and idle are more subject," and "leucorrhoea and uterine catarrh" dominated the publication. The water-cure offered such novel therapy as "hip baths," "cold injections into the urethra," and "rubbing of the back, loins, and abdomen." Its remedies contrasted sharply with the practices of orthodox medicine, which often used "leeching" and "cauterization" to alleviate feminine discomfort.

Much female physical anguish did indeed relate to the reproductive system, particularly as the prevailing codes of delicacy prevented physically sick women from seeking help. Dr. Charles Meigs "rejoiced" at the difficulty of making a "local examination" as it gave "evidence of a high and worthy grade of moral feeling." Women, conforming to the dictates of modest behavior, suffered in silence rather than endure the "mortification" of a gynecological examination, as propriety combined with ignorance to make the womb a source of much distress.

The conventional wisdom of the era preached that "conception . . . is much more likely to happen from intercourse a few days before or after the menstrual period." Accordingly, women who wished to practice some form of birth control intentionally had sexual relations in the middle of the menstrual cycle. They no doubt found their repeated pregnancies not only surprising but physically difficult as well. The diverse ailments attending birth ranged from minor irritation, to severe infection, to prolapsus uteri, but doctors responded to all uterine disorders with the same antiquated and often harmful treatments. Even a normal, uncomplicated birth could prove debilitating. The traditional medical practices insisted upon complete inactivity for long periods of time following delivery. A Mrs. O. C. W. reported to the *Water-Cure Journal* that she was "kept confined to . . . bed nearly two months" with the birth of her first child, and "it was not until about the middle of the following summer that [she] attained [her] former health and strength."

Clearly, childbearing did have painful and dangerous aspects. Scholars seeking to understand the roots of feminine maladies have sympathetically suggested that women used the "pretext of being 'delicate' as a way of . . . closing the bedroom door," "an elaborate strateg[y] for limiting the occasions of sexual intercourse . . . and thus limiting their families." Undoubtedly some women fabricated illness to shield themselves from unwanted pregnancies. Others, obviously, were physically ill. Still others were merely dupes of subtle economic and social pressure to keep women nonproductive and dependent. But the prevalence of poor health among women of leisure, the comments of a few sensitive observers, and the strong psychological component of the various described afflictions, all combine to invite further investigation into the causes of feminine illness.

George Combe, the Scottish phrenologist, believed that "nervous disease of which females of the middle and upper classes were the most frequent victims" could be attributed to "inactivity of intellect and feeling." Dr. W. A. Alcott, the noted nutritional reformer, urged that ladies be given "some employment . . . to save them from ennui, and disgust, and misery — sometimes from speedy or more protracted suicide." Harriet Martineau blamed the "vacuity of mind . . . among women of station and education in the most enlightened parts of the country" for a host of problems.

Catharine Beecher, whose "extensive tours in all portions of the Free States" had "brought [her] into most intimate communion" with countless women, exclaimed "And oh! what heartaches were the result of these years of quiet observation of the experience of my sex in domestic life. How many hearts have revealed the fact that what they had been trained to imagine the highest earthly felicity, was but the beginning of care, disappointment, and sorrow, and often led to the extremity of mental and physical suffering." And, above all, Beecher wondered why she found so many women in comfortable circumstances "expressing the hope that their daughters would never marry."

Some thoughtful individuals, therefore, stated or implied that many women's ailments had a psychological rather than physical origin, and the personal experiences of nineteenth-century females seem to support this hypothesis. The private journals, letters, and case studies of diverse women . . . detail the symptoms of hysteria, severe anxiety, and constant depression. "I was quite ill, and my spirits depressed," wrote Sarah Connell Ayer often in her diary, revealing the perpetual mental anguish of this middle-class wife and mother. The phrase "my spirits were unusually depressed" covered the sheets of her journal. Ayer frequently confessed having to curtail activities because of her emotional state, "for which [she] could not account."

Having little understanding of the causes or nature of their afflictions, women described anger and anxiety. In 1841, Elizabeth Payson Prentiss, who later became an author of children's books, wrote of her constant nervousness, which often made life "insupportable." "I . . . think mother would not trust me to carry the dishes to the closet, if she knew how strong an effort I have to make to avoid dashing them all to pieces," she confided. "When I am at the head of the stairs I can hardly help throwing myself down. . . . Tonight, for instance, my head began to feel all at once as if it were enlarging till at last it seemed to fill the room. . . . Three days out of seven I am as sick as I . . . can be — the rest of the time, languid, feeble, and exhausted by frequent faint turns, so that I can't do the smallest thing in my family."

"My spirits are . . . depressed this forenoon," wrote Ann Warder countless times in her journal. Sarah Stearns suffered from "anxiety [and] vexation" and felt "quite unable to attend the concerns of [her] family." A brilliant student, Nancy Maria Hyde constantly complained that "[her] spirits have been unusually depressed, and [her] feelings have been those of languor and despondency." Susan Huntington's memoirs describe her perpetual battle with "distressing nervous depression," while Laura Clark's journal entries divulge a suffering so great that she states: "I sometimes . . . wonder that I am alive."

. . . Few women consciously expressed the wish to "flee" or escape from a life they found unbearable, but thousands of nineteenth-century females fell victim to a particular form of psychoneurosis. Manifesting itself in disabling symptoms, this illness gave women no choice but to retreat from their daily routines. The *Water-Cure Journal* disclosed the case histories of numerous females who had suddenly and inexplicably become totally incapacitated. Miss Elizabeth Pott was "an excellent scholar [who] had not been able to read or write for years," and Miss Isabella Thompson suddenly "could not do anything." These furnished but two examples of the thousands of women invalids who experimented with hydropathy. Among those who flocked to the flourishing water-cure centers was Harriet Beecher Stowe. Her case study provides an interesting illustration of the nature of much feminine malady.

The daughter of Lyman Beecher, a fiery minister who infused his children with a passionate desire to reform humanity, Harriet suffered from a tormenting apprehension that she could not fulfill her father's expectations. To her sister Catharine she confessed the fear that she might not be "fit for anything." Fortunately Catharine, ten years her senior, had plans to open a school for girls and very much needed Harriet's help. The two young women worked together until 1836, when Harriet married Calvin Stowe, a classics professor. Demanding, domineering, and irascible, Professor Stowe expected complete obedience from his wife. Within their first ten years of married life, Harriet bore three children and agreed to have Calvin's aged and complaining mother live with them. Then, suddenly, at the end of this decade, which Harriet described as filled with "pain, confusion, disappointment and suffering," when all she "proposed was met and crossed and in every way hedged up," her right side became totally paralyzed.

Harriet went to the famous water-cure sanitarium in Brattleboro, Vermont, for therapy. There, the "shattered broken invalid, just able to creep along by great care," began to reexamine her life. In the serene atmosphere, removed from the perpetual exactions of a domestic martinet, Harriet Beecher Stowe started her slow recovery. "Not for years have I enjoyed life as I have here," she wrote, ignoring her husband's repeated entreaties to return home. After a year away from her life of "constant discouragement," of "hasty and irritated censure," Harriet came to realize that she could not make her family "my chief good and portion."

During her stay in Brattleboro, Harriet gained the emotional strength to insist that her husband make certain concessions as a prerequisite for resuming cohabitation. He agreed to accept a teaching position at Bowdoin College in Maine and apparently pledged not to inhibit Harriet's fledgling career as an author. She began work on *Uncle Tom's Cabin* shortly after rejoining her family in Maine; her ailments, not surprisingly, disappeared. Until her death in 1896 at the age of eighty-five, she enjoyed vigorous health, free from all signs of her affliction.

Harriet Beecher Stowe's paralysis emanated from deep emotional distress.

Clinically called conversion hysteria, or conversion reaction, this crippling psychoneurosis is characterized by the tendency to represent inner psychological conflicts by means of symbolic somatic disturbances. Hysteria, then, as well as depression and anxiety, singularly or collectively, incapacitated Jacksonian women. Stowe benefited from a stable childhood, an indulgent, if somewhat awe-inspiring father, and an ambitious and supportive sister. Additionally, she had a comfortable economic situation that enabled her to remain in Brattleboro for over a year, a conciliatory husband, occupying interests, and a strong will. Harriet Beecher Stowe thus managed to overcome the more obvious, debilitating symptoms of illness brought on by the conflicts of her life. But most women did not share this good fortune and languished in their chambers alone and afraid.

Contemporaries could not understand why females, with every comfort and no responsibility, became so desperately ill. Yet an abundance of psychoneurotic symptoms plagued American women. These ailments afforded visible evidence of stifled anger, unassuaged guilt, and unfilled emotional and physical drives. Fear of punishment and loss of love from the realization of repressed drives and wishes, the overwhelming feeling of stagnation, and the lack of self-esteem became manifested in profound psychological and related physical distress. . . .

Female journals of this period reveal both woman's struggle to accept and comply with the era's concept of feminine nature and behavior and the harvest of unhappiness that her efforts inevitably reaped. The persistent vigil to conform to the precepts of the woman-belle ideal produced severe tension: "How soon one is wearied of the constant exertion to be agreeable, even when conscious of admiration!" complained one woman. Another believed that "it is the struggle to be patient and gentle and cheerful, when pressed down and worn upon and distracted that costs so much."

Taught from childhood that the true woman always sacrificed her self-interest for the happiness of others, women worried incessantly that they might not have these angelic virtues and blamed themselves for their apparent failings. "I think that to give happiness in married life a woman should possess oceans of self-sacrificing love and I, for one, haven't half of that self-forgetting spirit which I think essential," confided Elizabeth Prentiss to a friend in 1843. The introspection of one diarist exposed her "fear that this power of enjoying myself makes my pleasure too independent of others, and consequently renders me too little solicitous about them," while her contemporaries berated themselves for similar "shortcomings."

Another axiom of feminine nature — woman's innate desire to tend the sick — demanded compliance. Antebellum females constantly ministered to ill friends and family. Their diaries disclose irritation with these tasks and also the strain women experienced from the need to perform these duties with the cheerfulness required of them. Elizabeth Prentiss frequently confessed vexation at having "to drag one's self out of bed to take care of a sick baby," and Harriet Beecher Stowe complained that her choleric son acted like a "great fellow who thinks women [were] made for his especial convenience." The conflict between society's vision of the female happily and indefatigably caring for the sick and woman's resentment at these chores finds full eloquence in the diary of Hannah Backhouse. Feeling an overwhelming sense of repugnance at ministering to sick relatives, Hannah struggled to cultivate the "appropriate" feelings. When her brother became ill she had an opportunity to test her endurance. Her diary records a mixed success. "I often felt my aversion to trifles, and the want of employment and ideas made me feel it a great cross; this sometimes overcame me," she admitted.

Yet this young woman ardently hoped she would develop the requisite qualities: "Beginning to act from duty in such cases, one may end by acting from affection, and then it becomes necessary to one's satisfaction to do so. A woman who cannot suffer the confinement of a sick room, leaves unfulfilled one of her most marked duties and can never be fit for a wife. It is a difficult task when one is not spurred onward by the continual impulse of the heart, or in short, when self is a dearer object than the invalid. . . . I could often wish my heart were more susceptible of kindness and compassion than it is."

Secretly protesting the demands made upon them, women also writhed under the decrees of the era that fettered their activities. "How painfully sensitive am I to not being free to act as I like," asserted Hannah Backhouse. She admitted that as a child she most enjoyed "using the hammer and saw with dexterity, and [found] the greatest pleasure [in] being victorious in a game of trapball." When admonished against the unladylike nature of her amusements, she wrote: "I fell into a sulky mood in my own mind, growling over the misery of . . . restraint. I sometimes feel my want of freedom rather galling." . . .

Feminine thralldom assumed many forms, but economic deprivation emerged as one of the most visible signs of oppression. With opportunities for employment severely limited, impoverished women, as well as those whose families had recently suffered financial reversals, found themselves victimized by the prevailing legal and social codes. Nancy Maria Hyde, considered by her contemporaries to have been an exceptionally able student, endured great hardship after her father's death. Creditors pressed upon Nancy and her mother for the payment of debts, and "neither in the family of her father, her mother, or herself, was there a son or a brother, to stand up as their helper."

. . . Desperate for an income and unable to find work as a teacher, Nancy took a job painting artificial fruit. But as she explained to her journal: "Choice would never have instigated me to this employment." Other women, similarly situated, tried to support themselves by writing. Yet, like Hannah Adams, the gifted author whose scholarly works included *History of Reli-*

gions, they found that the "penalties and discouragements attending authors in general fall upon woman with double weight. To the curiosity of the idle, and the envy of the malicious, their sex affords a peculiar excitement."

The ethos of the woman-belle ideal prohibited women from most forms of financially remunerative endeavor. It also denied the value of independent feminine achievement and criticized females for developing pride in their accomplishments. The prevailing codes deemed few tasks ladylike. Embroidering, painting, playing musical instruments, and perhaps writing some trivial verses probably did not appeal to most women. Yet those who demonstrated talent and an eagerness to follow these limited, acceptable pursuits had still other restrictions. The perfect female never exhibited self-assurance nor even allowed herself to feel confident. "The love of painting has been uppermost in my mind for some weeks past," wrote Hannah Backhouse. After completing a canvas that gave her special satisfaction she admitted: "I did so well that I felt most uncomfortably elated with it. . . . How I disliked myself. . . . I strove much against my feelings." . . .

Women could expose neither mental ability nor knowledge, but the craving for intellectual stimulation forms a constant litany running through their private journals and letters. "Write me a long letter," Sarah Ayer begged her friend Maria. "Tell me everything . . . what books you have been reading, your opinion of them, and indeed everything that interests you." Before sealing the letter, Ayer enclosed a proposed reading list and asked Maria to comment on her selections. Hannah Backhouse records the "delightful hour" she spent "reading Locke," and Catharine Sedgwick's correspondence with her women friends contain frequent references to current authors.

Not surprisingly, most women could not satisfy intellectual needs within the narrow limits allowed them. And many anguished over insipid conversation resulting from women's lack of education and involvement. "I cannot bear talking about trifles," exclaimed Hannah Backhouse. Other women echoed these feelings. In a letter to her confidante, Sarah Ayer wrote: "I hate large parties, such as we have both frequently attended, where . . . improving conversation, and all intellectual enjoyments were banished, and trifling amusements fit only to please a child supplied their places." "How much more real pleasure and advantage is to be derived from solid and refined conversation," she continued, "than from that empty, unmeaning *chit-chat* which I am sorry to say so frequently forms the greater part of female conversation." . . .

Women who tried to "cultivate" their "mental powers" in a social milieu that mocked their attempts and undermined their efforts often experienced profound frustration and, ultimately, resignation. "My mind grows inactive and lethargic," complained Sarah Stearns, and Elizabeth Prentiss had the same grievance. "Don't ask me if I have read anything else," she wrote shortly after her marriage and subsequent relocation in New Bedford, Massachusetts. "My mind has become a complete mummy, and therefore, incapable of either receiving or originating a new idea." Wedlock had brought the end of her previous attempts to indulge intellectual curiosity. "Just what I expected would befall me has happened. I have got immersed in the whirlpool of petty cares and concerns which swallow up so many other and higher interests, and talk as anxiously about good 'help' and bad, as the rest of 'em do. . . . I sometimes feel really ashamed of myself to see . . . how my time seems to be wasted if I venture to take up a book. . . . [W]ives who have no love and enthusiasm for their husbands are more to be pitied than blamed if they settle down into mere . . . [household] managers."

Substantially barred from satisfying the requirements of her mind, the middle- and upper-class woman had to endure the agony of relentless boredom. "There is such a sameness in my life . . . that the particulars of it are hardly worth the pains of writing," recorded one young woman. And Ellen Parker of New Hampshire grieved that "another long day has passed into eternity. How slowly time passes to me." Mary Peacock's diary reflects her disgust at having to "sit idle," considering it as "the most tiresome thing a person can do." Hannah Backhouse, describing her friends who came to tea, exclaimed: "What dull worldly people they seem to be!" "Having done nothing all day, and being all assembled in the evening, vacancy pervaded the whole room to such a degree, that I wished I had been obliged to work for my bread, that my duty might not be in the listless inactivity of a parlour."

Forced leisure generated an oppressive sense of uselessness and caused the nineteenth-century woman to "[wonder] why [she] was made, and if anybody on earth [would] ever be a bit happier for it." Plagued by feelings of worthlessness, but immersed in the ethos of the woman-belle ideal, she could not appreciate the intricate origins of her anguish. She therefore accepted the wisdom of contemporary theorists and attributed all unhappiness to her individual failings. This self-blame ultimately intensified her conflicts and sense of isolation. Elizabeth Prentiss confessed to feeling "mentally and spiritually alone in the world," and Sarah Ayer, writing in Concord, Massachusetts, complained: "[I have] lived so much in solitude . . . that my mind has become somewhat enervated."

As women attempted to meet society's expectations, they resolved to become more self-sacrificing and patient and endeavored to enjoy their sickbed duties. They restrained themselves from exhibiting wit and intellect and tried to find meaning in a life of futility. And throughout this lonely search for fulfillment women entrusted their troubled emotions and thoughts to personal diaries. The myriad of confidential writings provided an outlet for stifled feelings but did little to enable women to challenge the womanhood myths. The persistent urge to find understanding could not be absorbed by scattered pages of private journals. And the need to communicate came streaming forth, eventually eroding the carefully constructed dam of male authorship. Feminine anguish flowed into countless novels and short stories; woman's creative literature emerged as a confluence of anger and sadness, hope and despair.

The astonishing outpouring of writing by females at once annoyed and amazed those accustomed to dominating the literary field. Predictably, resentment against women authors rose up to meet their hesitant efforts. Nathaniel Hawthorne damned the entire "mob of scribbling women." Articles warned women that they could not "be too cautious in assuming the privilege of presenting their thoughts to the world." And essays, cautioning those who "[devoted] themselves to studies and research" that they would soon "despise their duties and neglect them altogether," appeared frequently. . . .

The existence of voluminous printed material signed by women afforded evidence that middle- and upper-class females did not find domestic life engrossing or enriching. The theme of feminine tedium dotted the pages of woman's writings. "Oh, the weary years of unused life to which so large a portion of the human race is remorselessly consigned!" bemoaned the author of the novel *Three Sisters*. Written in the first person, this tale traces the maturation of three women. The author indicted the system that created and encouraged the useless lady: "I returned home . . . to find my elder sisters leading that living death to which it is the fashion to consign females of the wealthy middle-class . . . an aimless life."

Vesta, the courageous heroine of Charlotte Chesebro's *Children of Light,* sighed: "I'm tired of reading, and tired to death of embroidery; and one can not be forever praising the work of another." She asked her companions if they would "acknowledge that idle persons are, of all, most miserable?" Chesebro infused her character with a yearning for excitement and fulfillment. "If I were a man, I would very soon discover what there was for me to do. . . . I would be clear of dragging out my life in the kitchen, or of putting myself down to the mending of old clothes, or of finding my recreation in walking over the lawn and garden, for all the world like a stupid animal, . . . a well-trained dog! When I feel like rushing out — strong enough to fight all the battles of the world, and with some little disposition that way too." Yet, Vesta had to face the reality of her existence:

> But here I am, only a woman — a housekeeper, the mistress of an hospital as I might say, to be kept in my 'proper sphere' and 'place,' and never to stir an inch out of it in any direction, for fear that all creation would turn against me, and hunt me down, as they would a wild beast! Oh, these laws of propriety — these ridiculous customs.

. . . Women writers recognized the era's insistence upon matrimony as the only acceptable path to feminine fulfillment, but many attempted to invalidate this decree through their literature. Mary Howitt, author of "Single Sisters," printed in the 1845 edition of the *Keepsake,* objected to "fairy tales which portray 'old maids' as cruel and ugly." Indeed, Ada Lester, in a story bearing her name, did not marry and achieved much recognition. Leopoldine of Julia Delafaye-Brehier's "Two Sisters" claims that she does not regret being single, for "that condition, which appears to you so frightful, has its happiness. . . . I have called into my aid the arts and letters which it is so difficult for married females to cultivate with constancy." In another tale, the married Emily confesses to her spinster sister: "You have had years of happiness while I have never felt a single moment of unalloyed felicity." On her deathbed, Emily pleads: "My sister, teach my children the moral of our story."

Emily's small children might have required an explanation of their mother's dying words, but the countless stories of females forced into marriage by a deleterious dictate made the message clear to antebellum readers. The *Amulet* of 1846 relates the sad history of a sixteen-year-old girl "who abides her parents' wishes and marries a man she can't love." An autobiographical sketch appearing in the *Ladies' Wreath*, "A Life Without Love," tells of a woman who never loved her husband-to-be and whose wedding day, rather than bringing her joy, filled her with dread and a feeling of "strange repulsion." And Catharine Sedgwick expressed her opinion by writing that Grace "will soon be married, and then, like Eleanor, mere wife and mother to the end of her life." . . .

The narrator of *Three Sisters* longed to become a doctor and as a child performed operations on dolls. "Had I been a boy instead of a girl, these early indications would have been hailed with satisfaction as pointing unerringly to my future vocation. As it was, they procured me only reprimands and punishment for mischief; and as I could not play properly with my dolls, they were taken from me altogether." Eliza Woodson of Eliza Farnham's fictionalized autobiography had no books for her own. Desperate for reading material, she "devoured" congressional debates, political newspapers, and cabinet reports brought in by the men in her family. But her relatives, finding these pursuits "curious," ostracized Eliza and labeled her a "fool."

Fear of derision and exclusion forced women to hide their knowledge and skills. "Amelia's frosty reception in the best Philadelphia drawing rooms" led this character of the novel *Ferdinand and Elmira* "to warn her friends to display no learning or sentiment, for the moment it is discovered, your reputation is lost forever." Ruth Hall, the literary creation of the indefatigable Fanny Fern, aroused the curiosity of her friends. They "wonder[ed] . . . why she took so much pains to bother her head with those stupid books, when she was every day growing prettier" and would not be able to use or exhibit her imagination or learning.

"The Mysterious Picture," appearing in the 1832 edition of *Affection's Gift*, is a sensitive study of one young woman caught between her own needs and society's dictates. Josephine Vericour had "an ardent ambition to excel" in the painting of miniatures, but she "was the victim of a painful and unconquerable timidity, and entire want of confidence in herself." Josephine could not believe she was capable of producing anything of value. And, indeed, the work done under the scrutiny of her instructor was quite mediocre. Then one night a miraculous event happened. When Josephine awakened, she found the unfinished painting she had left on her easel transformed into a magnificent work of art. At first the startled young woman said and did nothing about this extraordinary occurrence. But she arose on several subsequent mornings to discover that more of her own undistinguished miniatures had been changed into truly beautiful paintings. Baffled, Josephine decided to stay awake and catch the artistic intruder who furtively worked in her bedroom each night.

When darkness gave way to dawn and no one appeared, the confused and tired Josephine confided these mysterious incidents to a friend and begged that her schoolmate keep vigil the next night. The friend agreed, and the scene she witnessed astonished her. In the dead of night Josephine, sleepwalking, approached an incomplete canvas and worked with a proficiency and talent never displayed in public. With the first rays of morning, the young artist finished her work. She crept back into bed and slept, having no awareness of her marvelous accomplishment. At first Josephine refused to believe her friend's story. Finally, however, when convinced of its authenticity, she "made vigorous efforts to conquer her timidity in the presence of her master. . . . [In] time she was able to paint as well under his inspection as she had done when alone and asleep in the gloom of midnight."

The story of Josephine Vericour seems to be no more than a charming tale of a gifted schoolgirl. But its author, Eliza Leslie, skillfully wove together many separate strands of the rope that bound her countrywomen. Josephine's master symbolized the antebellum male who watched, instructed, and inhibited the talents and needs of women. Josephine, the legitimate child of the woman-belle ideal, felt acute inferiority. Although wishing to excel in a loved activity, she could not perform well in her teacher's presence. She knew that a woman who displayed talent evoked scorn and contempt. Her artistic impulses, unable to be denied, manifested themselves in such a manner that they neither brought credit to Josephine nor enhanced her self-image. Yet Leslie implied that if woman could somehow be numbed or made impervious to the prohibitions against her abilities, the long-stifled talents would surely burst forth. Ironically then, somnambulism aroused Josephine's dormant skills. Confronted with the reality of her achievement, she was able to develop the self-assurance to shield her from society's disapproval. But most of Josephine Vericour's living counterparts did not share this good fortune and passed their lives unfulfilled and unhappy.

STUDY GUIDE

1. Today American women tend to be viewed as active and healthy, engaging in all sorts of sports, working at "men's" jobs, and perhaps less neurotic than in times past. Berg suggests that a lot of the physical ill health of women in the nineteenth century reflected an inner psychological anguish. What were the causes of the anger and depression that seemed so common?

2. How did nineteenth-century medical men view the causes of female sickness, and what cures were used?

3. Describe the behavior, education, and proper pursuits of a "true lady." What do these reveal about the nineteenth-century idea of a woman's mind and sensibilities? What changes in behavior and the like did these educated women advocate?

4. What changes do you see in the status of women and in male-female relations in the nineteenth century as compared to the earlier period described by Lyle Koehler in his essay on colonial Massachusetts (Reading No. 3)?

5. What differences do you see in the goals of the women Berg writes of and those of women's liberationists today, as represented by such organizations as NOW? Are the goals of either group relevant to the welfare of poorer, less well-educated women?

BIBLIOGRAPHY

Very few historical fields have developed so rapidly and resulted in the publication of as fine a body of scholarship as has women's history in the last ten years. Berg's book is on the woman and the city, but the selection you have read is a good summary of two of the central themes in women's history — the views that men and women had of women's proper role, and the relationship of women to American medical practices. Barbara Welter wrote influential essays on these and other topics which are collected in her book *Dimity Convictions: The American Woman in the Nineteenth Century* (1976). One of the limitations of women's history is that it has tended to focus primarily on middle- and upper-class women, as exemplified in Barbara J. Harris, *Beyond Her Sphere: Women and the Professions in American History* (1978) and Susan Conrad, *Perish the Thought: Intellectual Women in Romantic America, 1830–1860* (1976). There are exceptions, such as a popular work by Barbara M. Wertheimer, *We Were There: The Story of Working Women in America* (1977), and one by Walter O'Meara, *Daughters of the Country: The Women of Fur Traders and Mountain Men* (1968).

In the nineteenth century, male physicians took childbirth out of the hands of midwives, women were refused admission to medical schools, and a great deal of writing warned against the dangers of masturbation, prostitution, birth control, and the intemperate use of sex in marriage. A number of physicians recommended and performed an operation that removed the clitoris of women. Various aspects of these themes are covered in the following books: G. J. Barker-Benfield, *Horrors of the Half-Known Life: Male Attitudes Toward Women and Sexuality in Nineteenth-Century America* (1976); Jane B. Donegan, *Women and Men Midwives: Medicine, Morality, and Misogyny in Early America* (1978); John S. and Robin M. Haller, *The Physician and Sexuality in Victorian America* (1974); James Reed, *From Private Vice to Public Virtue: The Birth Control Movement and American Society since 1830* (1978); Mary R. Walsh, *"Doctors Wanted: No Women Need Apply": Sexual Barriers in the Medical Profession, 1835–1975* (1977); and Ronald G. Walters, *Primers for Prudery: Sexual Advice to Victorian America* (1974).

There are several general works dealing with women's rights and the suffragist movement, including Eleanor Flexner, *Century of Struggle: The Woman's Rights Movement in the United States* (1959); Keith E. Melder, *Beginnings of Sisterhood: The American Woman's Rights Movement, 1800–1850* (1977); Robert E. Riegel, *American Feminists* (1963); William L. O'Neill, *Everyone Was Brave: The Rise and Fall of Feminism in America* (1969); and Andrew Sinclair, *The Better Half: The Emancipation of the American Woman* (1965). There are also specialized studies on other aspects of women's history. Anne F. Scott, *The Southern Lady: From Pedestal to Politics, 1830–1930* (1970) is on the romanticized idea of Southern womanhood. Although the history of black women has been given less attention than that of white women, Gerda Lerner does discuss it in her short work *The Woman in American History* (1971). She has also published a separate book of readings, *Black Women in White America: A Documentary History* (1972).

On women's history, as with many subjects in this volume, some of the best writing has been in the form of articles in historical journals. There are several collections of such articles: Jean E. Friedman and William G. Shade, eds., *Our American Sisters: Women in American Life and Thought*, 2nd ed. (1976); Mary Hartman and Lois Banner, eds., *Clio's Consciousness Raised* (1974); and Nancy F. Cott and Elizabeth H. Pleck, eds., *A Heritage of Her Own* (1979). If you wish to read anything further on women's history, there is no better place to start than with some of the articles by Barbara Welter and Carroll Smith-Rosenberg that are reprinted in such anthologies.

Woolaroc Museum, Bartlesville, Oklahoma

Robert Lindneux's "The Trail of Tears" vividly depicts the suffering of the Cherokees during their removal from their ancient homeland.

10

DALE VAN EVERY

Trail of Tears

In the Declaration of Independence, Jefferson had written that "all men are created equal" and are divinely endowed with the rights of life, liberty, and the pursuit of happiness. The members of the Continental Congress who signed their names to that proclamation were concerned with the rights of the colonists in relationship to the governing power of England. Few of them considered these ringing phrases as guaranteeing social or political rights to minorities within American society. Some few voices were raised to suggest that women, blacks, and Indians might have a greater cause to revolt than did the planters, lawyers, and merchants who led the revolution against the authority of King George III. Throughout much of American history, various national, racial, and religious groups were treated as less than equal and beyond the protection of the Bill of Rights.

The Age of Reform exhibited some striking contrasts in American sentiment. In many respects, it is a most revealing period for judging both the achievements and the failures of the American people in living up to the philosophy expressed in the Declaration. The 1830s witnessed the first great period of American social reform, with scores of organizations founded to assist the handicapped and the unfortunate. But it is also a decade that, one might say, lives in historical infamy, because American Indian tribes were removed from their ancient homelands, as whites coveted and took over their lands.

In the selection that follows, Dale Van Every suggests that this is the ultimate catastrophe that can befall a people. Being torn from the land of one's birth, losing most or all of one's belongings, being forced to find a livelihood as best one can in an

161

unfamiliar country, and losing one's very sense of identity are experiences we can hardly comprehend. The story of the removal of the Civilized Tribes of the southeastern United States — the Creeks, Chickasaws, Choctaws, Seminoles, and Cherokees — to new territories beyond the Mississippi River, and the numerous casualties they suffered along the "Trail of Tears," is one of the most famous and tragic in American history. In the North, the same story was repeated with different characters on a somewhat smaller scale. Whatever the Declaration of Independence meant to white, male Americans in the early nineteenth century, it must have appeared to be a bitter mockery to the native Americans who were forced out of their homes by this cruel invasion.

History records the sufferings of innumerable peoples whose country was overrun and possessed by alien invaders. There have been relatively fewer recorded occasions, as in the instance of the Babylonian Captivity of the Jews, of an entire people being compelled to abandon their country. This has been universally regarded as the ultimate catastrophe that can befall a people inasmuch as it deprives them of the roots which sustain their identity. Upon the exiles has been pronounced a sentence that by its nature denies all hope of reprieve or relief. To Indians, with their inherited conception of the land of their birth as the repository of those spiritual links to their ancestors which were holy and therefore indissoluble, the prospect of expulsion was clothed with added dreads beyond human evaluation.

The threat was in all its aspects so monstrous that in the spring of 1838 the bewildered masses of the Cherokee people, homeless, hungry, destitute, still remained incredulous that so fearful a fate could actually impend. Outrageously as they had been harassed for the past ten years by Georgia and Alabama white men, they still clung to their trust that most white men wished them well. This was a confidence instilled in them by the reports of John Ross [a respected Cherokee chief] who had been made more conversant with the apparent truth by his wide travels across the immense white nation stretching beyond the Cherokee horizon. They had been further prepared to accept his judgment on the inherent goodness of the white race by their own experience with the many white men who had lived among them as teachers, missionaries and counselors, sharing their struggles and tribulations. Their more recent experience with [General

Adaptation of Chapter 18 from *Disinherited: The Lost Birthright of the American Indian* by Dale Van Every. Copyright © 1966 by Dale Van Every. By permission of William Morrow & Company, Inc.

John] Wool and his officers and with [General R. G.] Dunlap and his Tennesseans had strengthened their impression that the white race could not be wholly committed to their destruction.

Ross was still in Washington engaged in a final frantic effort, with some dawning hope of success, to wring from the administration a temporary postponement of removal. His followers were continuing to obey his injunction that they persist in their nonviolent resistance. Most continued to refuse even to give their names or a list of their belongings to the agents commissioned to organize the details of the migration. May 23, two years from the date of the President's proclamation of the Senate's ratification of the treaty, was the day, as all had for months been warned, when their residence in the east would become illegal but they still could not believe that a development so frightful could be given reality by that day's sunrise. Even after five regiments of regulars and 4,000 militia and volunteers from adjacent states began pouring into their country they still could not believe.

Major General [Winfield] Scott arrived May 8 to take command of the military operation. His May 10, 1838 address to the Cherokee people proclaimed the terrible reality in terms no Cherokee could longer mistake:

> Cherokees — The President of the United States has sent me with a powerful army, to cause you, in obedience to the treaty of 1835, to join that part of your people who are already established in prosperity on the other side of the Mississippi. Unhappily, the two years which were allowed for the purpose, you have suffered to pass away without following, and without making preparations to follow, and now, or by the time this solemn *address* shall reach your distant settlements, the emigration must be commenced in haste, but, I hope, without disorder. I have no power, by granting a farther delay, to correct the error that you have committed. The full moon of May is already on the wane, and before another shall have passed away, every Cherokee man, woman, and child . . . must be in motion to join their brethren in the far West. . . . My troops already occupy many positions in the country that you are to abandon, and thousands and thousands are approaching from every quarter, to tender resistance and escape alike hopeless. . . . Chiefs, head men, and warriors — Will you then, by resistance, compel us to resort to arms? God forbid. Or will you, by flight, seek to hide yourself in mountains and forests, and thus oblige us to hunt you down? Remember that, in pursuit, it may be impossible to avoid conflicts. The blood of the white man, or the blood of the red man, may be spilt, and if spilt, however accidentally, it may be impossible for the discreet and humane among you, or among us, to prevent a general war and carnage. Think of this, my Cherokee brethern. I am an old warrior, and have been present at many a scene of slaughter; but spare me, I beseech you, the horror of witnessing the destruction of the Cherokees.

Scott sincerely hoped that the enforced removal could be accomplished not only without bloodshed but without undue hardship inflicted upon the unfortunate thousands being ejected at bayonet's point from their homes. He had been impressed by Ross during conferences with him in Washington and like most professional soldiers of his time had developed a genuine regard for Indians. In his May 17 general orders to his troops he sternly admonished them to practice restraint:

> Considering the number and temper of the mass to be removed together with the extent and fastnesses of the country occupied, it will readily occur that simple indiscretions, acts of harshness, and cruelty on the part of our troops, may lead, step by step, to delays, to impatience, and exasperation, and, in the end, to a general war and carnage; a result, in the case of these particular Indians, utterly abhorrent to the generous sympathies of the whole American people. Every possible kindness, compatible with the necessity of removal, must, therefore, be shown by the troops; and if, in the ranks, a despicable individual should be found capable of inflicting a wanton injury or insult on any Cherokee man, woman, or child, it is hereby made the special duty of the nearest good officer or man instantly to interpose, and to seize and consign the guilty wretch to the severest penalty of the laws. The major-general is fully persuaded that this injunction will not be neglected by the brave men under his command, who cannot be otherwise than jealous of their honor and that of their country.

Scott's intentions were humane but the larger portion of his army were state levies unaccustomed to discipline and without his professional susceptibilities. The nature of the operation required the army's dispersion in scattered detachments over a wide area. Most of the Cherokee to be removed were inhabitants of Georgia and their apprehension was conducted by Georgia militia who had long as a matter of policy been habituated to dealing harshly with Indians. Prison stockades had been erected at assembly and embarkation points in which the Cherokee were to be herded and confined while awaiting transportation west. There was little or no likelihood of attempted resistance. Most had been disarmed during Wool's regime and the irresistible military power that had been brought to bear was self-evident. The classic account of what next transpired is that recorded by James Mooney. His contribution to the Bureau of American Ethnology, eventually published in the 19th Annual Report in 1900 under the title *Myths of the Cherokee,* included a history of the Cherokee based upon years of field work. His narrative of the 1838 expulsion was drawn from personal interviews with survivors, white officers as well as Cherokee victims, and had therefore much of the vitality of an eyewitness report:

> The history of this Cherokee removal of 1838, as gleaned by the author from the lips of actors in the tragedy, may well exceed in weight of grief and pathos any other passage in American history. Even the much-sung exile of the Acadians falls far behind it in its sum of death and misery. Under Scott's order the troops were disposed at various points throughout the Cherokee country,

where stockade forts were erected for gathering in and holding the Indians preparatory to removal. From these, squads of troops were sent to search out with rifle and bayonet every small cabin hidden away in the coves or by the sides of mountain streams, to seize and bring in as prisoners all the occupants, however or wherever they might be found. Families at dinner were startled by the sudden gleam of bayonets in the doorway and rose up to be driven with blows and oaths along the weary miles of trail that led to the stockade. Men were seized in their fields or going along the road, women were taken from their wheels and children from their play. In many cases, on turning for one last look as they crossed the ridge, they saw their homes in flames, fired by the lawless rabble that followed on the heels of the soldiers to loot and pillage. So keen were these outlaws on the scent that in some instances they were driving off the cattle and other stock of the Indians almost before the soldiers had fairly started their owners in the other direction. Systematic hunts were made by the same men for Indian graves, to rob them of the silver pendants and other valuables deposited with the dead. A Georgia volunteer, afterward a colonel in the Confederate service, said: "I fought through the civil war and have seen men shot to pieces and slaughtered by thousands, but the Cherokee removal was the cruelest work I ever knew." To prevent escape the soldiers had been ordered to approach and surround each house, so far as possible, so as to come upon the occupants without warning. One old patriarch, when thus surprised, calmly called his children and grandchildren around him, and, kneeling down, bid them pray with him in their own language, while the astonished onlookers looked on in silence. Then rising he led the way into exile. A woman, on finding the house surrounded, went to the door and called up the chickens to be fed for the last time, after which, taking her infant on her back and her two other children by the hand, she followed her husband with the soldiers.

Within days nearly 17,000 Cherokee had been crowded into the stockades. Sanitation measures were inadequate in those makeshift concentration camps. Indian families, accustomed to a more spacious and isolated existence, were unable to adapt to the necessities of this mass imprisonment. Hundreds of the inmates sickened. The Indian was by his nature peculiarly susceptible to the depressions produced by confinement. Many lost any will to live and perceiving no glimmer of hope, resigned themselves to death. Those who had become converts found some comfort in the ministrations of their white and native pastors. In every stockade hymn singings and prayer meetings were almost continuous.

All physical preparations had been carefully planned in advance by the federal authorities in charge of the migration so that little time might be lost in getting the movement under way. In the first and second weeks of June two detachments of some 800 exiles were driven aboard the waiting fleets of steamboats, keelboats and flatboats for the descent of the Tennessee. They passed down the storied waterway by the same route taken by the first white settlers of middle Tennessee under John Donelson in 1780. In the shadow of Lookout Mountain they could survey the wilderness vastnesses from which for 20 years bands of their immediate forebears had sallied to devastate the white frontier, some of them commanded by war chiefs who had lived to be condemned to this exile. Then, at Muscle Shoals there came an ironic contrast between the past and the future as Indians being driven from their ancient homeland were committed to transportation by the white man's newest invention. They disembarked from their boats to clamber, momentarily diverted, aboard the cars drawn by the two puffing little locomotives of the railroad recently constructed to move freight and passengers around the rapids. Returning to other boats, they resumed their seemingly interminable journey in the debilitating heat of an increasingly oppressive summer. The attendant army officers, however sympathetic, were helpless against the waves of illnesses. Scott, moving new contingents toward embarkation, was appalled by the reports he received of the mounting death rate among those who had already been dispatched.

The troops assembled for Cherokee expulsion had been by considered governmental design so numerous as to present a show of military power so overwhelming as to provide no faintest invitation to Indian resistance. By the army's first pounce more than nine tenths of the population had been rounded up and driven into the stockades. There remained only a handful of the wilder and more primitive residents of the higher mountains still at large. This handful, however, represented a problem causing Scott serious concern. Were they provoked to resist they might among their remote and cloud-wreathed peaks prove as difficult to apprehend as were the Seminole in their swamps. From this tactical threat sprang the one heroic action to gleam across the otherwise unrelieved despondency of the removal scene.

Tsali was an hitherto undistinguished mountain Cherokee who suddenly soared to an eminence in Cherokee annals comparable to the homage accorded an Attakullaculla, an Old Tassel, a Sequoyah or a John Ross. The stories of his inspired exploit, drawn from eyewitnesses, survivors and references in contemporary official records, vary in detail and have become encrusted by legend but coincide in most essentials. According to the more generally accepted version, a young Cherokee woman upon being assaulted by two soldiers killed both with a hatchet. Tsali hid the weapon under his shirt and assumed responsibility for his kinswoman's act. Scott could not permit the death of his soldiers to remain unpunished and served notice on the band of mountain Cherokee of which Tsali was a member that a scapegoat must be produced. The band felt that it had a reasonable chance to elude pursuit indefinitely but its councils were impressed by the advice of a white trader, William Thomas, a friend of his native customers in the notable tradition of Ludovic Grant, Alexander Cameron and John McDonald. Thomas pointed out the advantage that could be taken of Scott's demand. Tsali was prepared to offer his life for his people. His fellow tribesmen thereupon notified Scott that he would be turned over to American justice in return for American permission to remain unmolested in their mountains. Scott, eager to escape the uncertainties of a guerrilla campaign in so difficult a terrain, agreed to recommend this course to Washington. Tsali was brought in, the voluntary prisoner of his compatriots. His Cherokee custodians were required to serve as the firing squad by which he, his brother and his eldest son were executed. The story became one of the few Indian stories with a happy ending. Thomas continued for years to interest himself in the prolonged negotiations with the governments of the United States and North Carolina which eventually resulted in federal and state recognition of Cherokee title to their mountain holdings. Tsali's sacrifice had permitted this fraction of the nation to become the remnant of the East Cherokee [and] to cling to their homeland where they still are colorful inhabitants of the North Carolina mountains.

Aside from the Tsali episode the roundup of the Cherokee proceeded without interruption. By June 18 General Charles Floyd, commanding the Georgia militia engaged in it, was able to report to his governor that no Cherokee remained on the soil of Georgia except as a prisoner in a stockade. Scott was able to discharge his volunteers June 17 and two days later to dispatch three of his five regular regiments to sectors where military needs were more pressing, two to the Canadian border and one to Florida.

Meanwhile so many migrants were dying in the drought and heat to which the initial removal was subjected that Scott was constrained to lighten the inexorable pressures. The Cherokee Council, which though technically illegal still spoke for the Cherokee people, begged for a postponement to the more healthful weather of autumn. Scott agreed. In July Ross returned and in conferences with Scott worked out a further agreement under which the Cherokee would cease passive resistance and under his supervision undertake a voluntary migration as soon as weather permitted. Scott was glad to be relieved of further need to use military force. The administration was glad to be offered some defense against the storm of northern criticism. Even Georgia made no serious protest, inasmuch as the Cherokee had already been removed from their land to stockades and there remained no questioning of the state's sovereignty. The one remonstrance, aside from the complaints of contractors, was voiced by the aging [Andrew] Jackson from his retirement at The Hermitage in a letter of August 23, 1838 to Felix Grundy, Attorney General of the United States:

> . . . The contract with Ross must be arrested, or you may rely upon it, the expense and other evils will shake the popularity of the adminstration to its center. What madness and folly to have anything to do with Ross, when the agent was proceeding well with the removal. . . . The time and circumstances under which Gen'l Scott made this contract shows that he is no economist, or is, *sub rosa,* in league with [Henry] Clay & Co. to bring disgrace on the administration. The evil is done. It behooves Mr. [President Martin] Van Buren to act with energy to throw it off his shoulders. I enclose a letter to you under

cover, unsealed, which you may read, seal, and deliver to him, that you may aid him with your views in getting out of this real difficulty.

Your friend in haste,

Andrew Jackson

P.S. I am so feeble I can scarcely wield my pen, but friendship dictates it & the subject excites me. Why is it that the scamp Ross is not banished from the notice of the administration?

Ross, having at last recognized the inevitable, gave to his preparations for the voluntary removal the same driving energy and attention to detail he had until then devoted to resisting removal. All phases of the organization of the national effort were gathered into his hands. All financial arrangements were under his supervision, including the disbursement of the basic federal subsistence allowance of 16 cents a day for each person and 40 cents a day for each horse. For convenience in management en route the 13,000 Cherokee remaining in the stockades were divided into detachments of roughly a thousand to head each of which he appointed a Cherokee commander. At a final meeting of the Cherokee Council it was provided that the constitution and laws of the Nation should be considered equally valid in the west.

The first detachment set out October 1, 1838 on the dreaded journey over the route which in Cherokee memory became known as The Trail of Tears. The last started November 4. The improvement in weather awaited during the tedious summer months in the stockades did not materialize. The spring migration had been cursed by oppressive heat and drought. The fall migration encountered deluges of rain followed by excessive cold. To the hundreds of deaths from heat-induced diseases were now added new hundreds of deaths from prolonged exposure.

The most vivid general account of the 1838 migration is again that of James Mooney, assembled from the recollections of participants:

. . . in October, 1838, the long procession of exiles was set in motion. A very few went by the river route; the rest, nearly all of the 13,000, went overland. Crossing to the north side of the Hiwassee at a ferry above Gunstocker creek, they proceeded down along the river, the sick, the old people, and the smaller children, with the blankets, cooking pots, and other belongings in wagons, the rest on foot or on horses. The number of wagons was 645. It was like the march of an army, regiment after regiment, the wagons in the center, the officers along the line and the horsemen on the flanks and at the rear. Tennessee river was crossed at Tuckers (?) ferry, a short distance above Jollys island, at the mouth of the Hiwassee. Thence the route lay south of Pikeville, through McMinnville and on to Nashville, where the Cumberland was crossed. Then they went on to Hopkinsville, Kentucky, where the noted chief White-path, in charge of a detachment, sickened and died. His people buried him by the roadside, with a box over the grave and poles with streamers around it, that the others coming on behind might note the spot and remember him. Somewhere also along that march of death — for the exiles died by tens and twenties every day of the journey — the devoted wife of John Ross sank down, leaving him to go on with the bitter pain of bereavement added to heartbreak at the ruin of his nation. The Ohio was crossed at a ferry near the mouth of the Cumberland, and the army passed on through southern Illinois until the great Mississippi was reached opposite Cape Girardeau, Missouri. It was now the middle of winter, with the river running full of ice, so that several detachments were obliged to wait some time on the eastern bank for the channel to become clear. In talking with old men and women at Tahlequah the author found that the lapse of over half a century had not sufficed to wipe out the memory of the miseries of that halt beside the frozen river, with hundreds of sick and dying penned up in wagons or stretched upon the ground, with only a blanket overhead to keep out the January blast. The crossing was made at last in two divisions, at Cape Girardeau and at Green's Ferry, a short distance below, whence the march was made on through Missouri to Indian Territory, the later detachments making a northerly circuit by Springfield, because those who had gone before had killed off all the game along the direct route. At last their destination was reached. They had started in October, 1838, and it was now March, 1839, the journey having occupied barely six months of the hardest part of the year.

President Van Buren in his December 1838 message to Congress announced the administration's view of the event:

> . . . It affords me sincere pleasure to apprise the Congress of the entire removal of the Cherokee Nation of Indians to their new homes west of the Mississippi. The measures authorized by Congress at its last session have had the happiest effects. By an agreement concluded with them by the commanding general in that country, their removal has been principally under the conduct of their own chiefs, and they have emigrated without any apparent reluctance.

A traveler who had encountered the Indians en route was moved by the President's words to write his own eyewitness report which was published in the January 26, 1839 *New York Observer* under the heading. "A Native of Maine, traveling in the Western Country":

> . . . On Tuesday evening we fell in with a detachment of the poor Cherokee Indians . . . about eleven hundred Indians — sixty wagons — six hundred horses, and perhaps forty pairs of oxen. We found them in the forest camped for the night by the road side . . . under a severe fall of rain accompanied by heavy wind. With their canvas for a shield from the inclemency of the weather, and the cold wet ground for a resting place, after the fatigue of the day, they spent the night . . . many of the aged Indians were suffering extremely from the fatigue of the journey, and the ill health consequent upon it . . . several were then quite ill, and one aged man we were

informed was then in the last struggles of death. . . . The last detachment which we passed on the 7th embraced rising two thousand Indians with horses and mules in proportion. The forward part of the train we found just pitching their tents for the night, and notwithstanding some thirty or forty wagons were already stationed, we found the road literally filled with the procession for about three miles in length. The sick and feeble were carried in wagons — about as comfortable for traveling as a New England ox cart with a covering over it — a great many ride on horseback and multitudes go on foot — even aged females, apparently nearly ready to drop into the grave, were traveling with heavy burdens attached to the back — on the sometimes frozen ground, and sometimes muddy streets, with no covering for the feet except what nature had given them. . . . We learned from the inhabitants on the road where the Indians passed, that they buried fourteen or fifteen at every stopping place, and they make a journey of ten miles per day only on an average. One fact which to my own mind seemed a lesson indeed to the American nation is, that they will not travel on the Sabbath. . . . The Indians as a whole carry on their countenances every thing but the appearance of happiness. Some carry a downcast dejected look bordering upon the appearance of despair others a wild frantic appearance as if about to burst the chains of nature and pounce like a tiger upon their enemies. . . . When I past the last detachment of those suffering exiles and thought that my native countrymen had thus expelled them from their native soil and their much-loved homes, and that too in this inclement season of the year in all their suffering, I turned from the sight with feelings which language cannot express. . . . I felt that I would not encounter the secret silent prayer of one of these sufferers armed with the energy that faith and hope would give it (if there be a God who avenges the wrongs of the injured) for all the lands of Georgia. . . . When I read in the President's Message that he was happy to inform the Senate that the Cherokees were peaceably and without reluctance removed — and remember that it was on the third day of December when not one of the detachments had reached their destination; and that a large majority had not made even half their journey when he made that declaration, I thought I wished the President could have been there that very day in Kentucky with myself, and have seen the comfort and the willingness with which the Cherokees were making their journey.

The first migrants reached their destination on the plains beyond the western border of Arkansas January 4, 1839. Other contingents continued to straggle in until late in March. Examination of all available records by Grant Foreman, outstanding authority on Indian removal, led him to conclude 4,000 Cherokee had died either during confinement in the stockades or on their 800-mile journey west.

While the Cherokee were traversing their Trail of Tears their fellow southern Indians were committed to afflictions as dismal. The processes of removal were grinding out the cumulative calamities that had been visited upon a race by governmental fiat.

The Chickasaw had at length embarked upon their self-governed migration. They were the aristocrats of the Indian world, long noted for the prowess of their warriors, the beauty of their women and the speed of their horses. They had bargained shrewdly until they had wrung every possible advantage from federal authorities, including uninterrupted control over their affairs and a good price for their lands in western Tennessee and northwestern Mississippi. When finally they started west it was a movement under their own leadership undertaken at a time of their own choosing after repeated inspections of their new territory and the route to it by their own representatives. They traveled in comfort, well supplied with equipment, food and money. It might have been expected that were removal ever to be conducted under acceptable conditions it might prove so in their case. But it did not. Their relative prosperity became one of the major causes of their undoing. Sensing unusual profits, contractors gathered stockpiles of supplies along the way in such quantities that the food spoiled before it could be eaten. The travelers were charged exorbitantly for transportation and their every other requirement. They picked up smallpox en route and the disease reached epidemic proportions after their arrival. Most had arrived too late to get in an 1838 crop and they were soon as hungry as their poorer fellow colonists. The move west had made plaintive beggars of the once proud and warlike Chickasaw.

Nearly 2,000 Seminole, rounded up by various devices, pseudo-agreements and military pressures, were also on the way west in 1838. Having suffered so much more than other migrants before their start, they continued to suffer more en route. Many had scarcely emerged from their swampland refuges before they were crowded, naked and undernourished, aboard ship. Others had already endured long periods of imprisonment by which they had been weakened. Most were detained for weeks and months en route in noisome concentration camps in Tampa, Mobile and New Orleans. In addition to all their other privations and afflictions they were continually harassed at every stop and in every new state jurisdiction by the claims of slave dealers to the ownership of Seminole prisoners who showed evidence of Negro blood. A considerable proportion of Seminole were Negroes who had for generations been considered members of the tribe and even though they were closely guarded prisoners each group of exiles fiercely resisted every attempt to single out any of their number for delivery into slavery. The problem of identification had been complicated by the flight to the Seminole of many actual slaves during the war. Some of the slave traders' claims were thus clothed with a species of legitimacy which made adjudication of every dispute more difficult. As one controversial example, among the Seminole prisoners of war taken by the Creek auxiliaries in 1837 had been 90 black Seminole whom they had sold to traders. In all these disputes federal and state authorities, except for the attendant army officers, in their anxiety to expedite the removal tended to support the traders' claims to an extent that provoked a congressional investigation. Meanwhile, in Florida the war went on, with American troops now under the command of Brigadier General Zachary Taylor, later President of the United States, continuing their attempts to run to earth the some 2,000 Seminole still in hiding.

The year 1838 also witnessed the initiation of a companion Indian removal in an adjoining country. Bowl's band of Cherokee, the first recorded migrants who had fled their homelands in 1794, had eventually settled on the Texas side of the Red River in what was then Mexican territory. Joined by other Cherokee and other Indians, the colony had increased to some 8,000. At the outbreak of the Texas revolution Sam Houston had negotiated a treaty of friendship with Bowl's Cherokee which saved the Americans in Texas from possible attack by Indians at the precarious moment they were being assaulted by Santa Anna in return for a Texan recognition of Cherokee title to the land on which they had settled. But in 1838 Mirabeau Lamar, upon succeeding Houston as President of Texas, immediately proclaimed his intention of expelling all Indians from the republic. In the ensuing 1839 campaign the aged Bowl was killed, still clutching the tin box containing the documents and deeds relating to the 1836 treaty of friendship with Texas. The Texas Cherokee were driven across the Red River to share the fortunes of the West and newly arrived East Cherokee on the upper Arkansas.

Indian removal had now been accomplished. Aside from a few scattered remnants, such as the Seminole fugitives in the Florida swamps, the few mountain Cherokee in North Carolina, the Choctaw residue in Mississippi and an occasional tiny enclave in the north, every Indian nation which had originally occupied the immense expanse of woodland extending across the eastern half of the United States had been compelled to seek new homes on the plains beyond that woodland's western margin. It had required a persisting effort over a period of 15 years, distinguished not only by the sufferings inflicted upon Indians but by the virulent disagreements excited among Americans, to give effect to the outwardly plausible policy announced by [James] Monroe and [John] Calhoun in 1825. Removal had been a contemporary success in the sense that the national government had proved able to impose its will and the states concerned had been rid of unwanted Indian inhabitants. But for the Indians and for the larger interests of the United States it had been a deplorable failure. The opportunity for Indians to become useful and valued members of American society, an achievement many had seemed on the verge of attaining in 1825, had been heedlessly postponed for more than a century.

Most informed Indians had long realized that such an assimilation represented the one lingering hope that Indians might ever regain comfort and security. The mass of Indians, less aware of the economic and political realities, had as long clung despairingly to the more appealing hope that they might yet contrive some escape from the white incubus. Removal dealt crushing blows to both hopes. In the west progressive Indians were compelled to begin again, under far greater handicaps, the painful climb toward citizenship and all Indians were subjected to white exactions more distracting than any they had known in the east. It was only after decades of miraculously patient struggle that Indians were finally to gain recognition of the principle that the rights of the conquered are even more precious than the prerogatives of their conquerors.

During the three centuries Indians had been retreating before the inexorable advance of alien invaders they had been bitterly conscious that they were suffering greater deprivations than the loss of their lands and lives. Their entire way of life, their whole world as they had known it, was in the course of obliteration. They understood, as could nobody else, by how wide a margin their post-invasion opportunities to pursue happiness failed to match the opportunities they had known before invasion. There was little enough comfort in the reflection that these opportunities were being denied them by a force physically too strong for them to resist.

In their despair Indians had sought consolation in resort to the supernatural. Native prophets, such as those who had inspired the followers of Pontiac and Tecumseh, had emerged again and again to preach the doctrine of original blessedness. They had exhorted Indians to eschew every compromise with white influence, especially by forswearing the use of white tools, weapons and alcohol, so that by a return to their ancient purity they might regain the strength to regain their former freedoms. These movements had been frustrated by their adherents' realization that obedience left Indians even more defenseless than before. By the time of the removal Indians were increasingly addicted to more extravagant religious phantasies. A favorite conceit, intermittently erupting for generation after generation until its final resurgence as the Ghost Dance excitement among the Plains Indians in the late 1880's, envisioned the evocation, by appropriate prayers, dances and rites, of the innumerable spirits of all Indian dead who would return to earth as a mighty host capable of expelling the white invaders and thus restoring the land of peace and plenty Indians had once enjoyed.

Even so superior an intellect as Sequoyah's was subject to wishful fancies. He had from his youth believed that the one Indian hope to retain their identity as a people was to withdraw from white contamination. He had himself moved west nearly 20 years before removal and all his life had sought by advice and example to persuade Indians to shun intercourse with whites. In his declining years he became obsessed with the possibility that the Lost Cherokee, reputed by tribal legend to have disappeared into the farthest west in the forgotten past, still lived in innocence, freedom and security in some distant land. In his frail old age, still in pursuit of this relic of the Indian golden age, he set out on a two-year journey in search of a remote Cherokee colony reported to have found sanctuary in the mountains of Mexico. His 1843 death in a Mexican desert was giving ultimate poignancy to the discovery all Indians were being required to make. For them there was no way back. There was only the way ahead.

STUDY GUIDE

1. Describe where each of the Indian tribes discussed in this essay — the Cherokee, Seminole, and Chickasaw — lived before removal and how each of these nations reacted to the forced removal.
2. What problems did the Indians face with respect to weather, supplies, health, and transportation on the trail west?
3. How did the sentiment of General Scott, who was directly responsible for supervising the Indian removal, differ from that of Andrew Jackson? How does a knowledge of the politics of the period help in understanding the views expressed in Jackson's letter?
4. Discuss the deeper, psychological impact of removal upon the Indian tribes. Explain what factors in the nineteenth century made it difficult for the Indian to resist removal.
5. What differences can you think of between the removal of the Indians in this period and the forced removal of Japanese-Americans from their homes on the Pacific coast to concentration centers during World War II?

BIBLIOGRAPHY

A great deal has been written about the removal of the eastern Indian tribes to lands beyond the Mississippi. As Van Every's selection indicates, it is a gripping story. Unfortunately, some of the books that are most reliable are not very interesting, and some of the most interesting are not very reliable. Grant Foreman has probably written more on this subject than anyone. The first of his titles cited here is on the removal of the tribes north of the Ohio River, and the second is on the situation of the Indians in their new homelands following removal: *The Last Trek of the Indians* (1946); *The Five Civilized Tribes* (1934); and *Indian Removal: The Emigration of the Five Civilized Tribes of Indians* (1932). R. S. Cotterill, *The Southern Indians* (1954) is one of the best general works on the Civilized Tribes of the Southeast. Three other works dealing directly with those tribes are Arthur H. De Rosier, Jr., *The Removal of the Choctaw Indians* (1970); Angie Debo, *The Rise and Fall of the Choctaw Republic*, 2nd ed. (1967); and Gloria Jahoda, *The Trail of Tears* (1975). Alvin M. Josephy, Jr., *The Patriot Chiefs* (1961) is a series of nicely written sketches of Indian leaders from Hiawatha to Chief Joseph.

Much of the recent writing in the field of Indian history has tried to "get inside" Indian life and culture. Valuable as such works are, it is also necessary to study white attitudes and government policy. Several works examine these subjects, both in earlier American history and in the 1830s, when the eastern Indians were removed. Two of the best works on the earlier period are

Reginald Horsman, *Expansion and American Indian Policy, 1783–1812* (1967) and Bernard Sheehan, *Seeds of Extinction: Jeffersonian Philanthropy and the American Indian* (1973). Two volumes on Indian policy during Jackson's administration are Ronald N. Satz, *American Indian Policy in the Jacksonian Era* (1975) and Michael P. Rogin, *Fathers and Children: Andrew Jackson and the Subjugation of the American Indian* (1975). Politics and government policy, even in the nineteenth century, frequently reflect the values and attitudes of the American people, or a substantial majority of them. The popular beliefs that made Andrew Jackson such a hero with the American people are set forth in John W. Ward, *Andrew Jackson: Symbol for an Age* (1962), a very readable volume that includes some suggestive passages on Jackson's personal attitude toward Indians. In recent years, legal suits by various Indian tribes in federal courts have raised the question of who actually owns parts of the United States. Wilcomb Washburn, *Red Man's Land, White Man's Law* (1971) is a study of land titles and Indian policy. Another work, not directly related to removal but containing information of considerable interest on Indian-white relations, is Wilbur R. Jacobs, *Dispossessing the American Indian* (1972).

The bibliography following the essay by Anthony F. C. Wallace, "Indian Life and Culture" (Reading No. 1), lists several general works on Indian history. Two other readable works of this sort are William Brandon, *The American Heritage Book of Indians* (1961), which includes many illustrations, and Angie Debo, *A History of the Indians of the United States* (1970).

This cartoon, "Drunkard's Progress," expresses the belief of prohibitionists that intemperance was the leading cause of personal tragedy and social ills.

11

MARK E. LENDER
JAMES K. MARTIN

America: Wet and Dry

In the last decade, the American people have become extraordinarily health conscious. Millions have kicked the smoking habit, and many more have modified their eating habits in order to lose weight and decrease their intake of sugar, salt, and fats. Fish and chicken have grown in popularity on restaurant menus, and even modest-sized towns may have one or more vegetarian restaurants. Vitamin and health food stores, once hard to find, are now a common fixture of shopping malls. The national craze for jogging and other ways of keeping fit has provided a new stimulus to sporting goods manufacturers who once catered largely to team sports. Americans, it seems, are being converted from sports spectators to active participants. Whether these occurrences represent passing fads or long-range changes in American lifestyles is still an open question. A skeptic might note that among the most avid handball players are a significant number who stop off for two martinis after work.

One person's reform may be considered radical nonsense or reactionary folderol by another. Thus, the Age of Reform was also an age of serious divisions in American society. Some people founded a peace society, and others went off to war against Mexico; some women struggled to expand their opportunities and assert their rights, and were taunted for their efforts; abolitionists preached in small towns and large cities, and found their lives in danger. One movement, the attempt to control alcoholic consumption, crossed many of these lines of division. Protestants and Catholics, abolitionists and their opponents, and Northerners and Southerners could be found in the ranks of the temperance crusade.

The following selection from the book *Drinking in America: A History,* by Mark E. Lender and James K. Martin, covers the history of the temperance movement from the late eighteenth century to the Civil War. The authors describe the easygoing attitude of most Americans toward the Devil's brew, which many people felt was actually beneficial, as well as the growing abuse of alcohol in the nineteenth century and the movement to dry up the country. Eventually, the prohibitionists achieved passage of an amendment to the United States Constitution to make America dry, but widespread violation of the Volstead Act during the 1920s suggested that many Americans were still wringing wet.

The bitterest denunciation of distilled spirits came in the immediate aftermath, and as part of the zeitgeist, of the Revolution. The Revolutionary period witnessed heightened concern that society's traditional values were being lost — that luxury and vice were threatening public virtue and liberty itself. A great many people traced these unwanted developments to American links with the British nation, which supposedly had grown increasingly decadent over the years, thus representing a corrupting influence on America. The result was what Revolutionary leaders often described as a rise in social dissipation and a decline in public spirit. . . . They hoped that the Revolution would represent a cleansing process for Americans and that it would fire a rebirth of individual and public virtue.

"Virtue" was the catchword of republicanism. It dictated that citizens act, vote, and think not out of hopes for personal gain but out of a sense of public duty and concern for the general good. A nation founded on this premise had to maintain traditional concerns about order and stability, and republicans believed that true liberty could exist only in a society composed of such a virtuous people. Providence, they held, would certainly shepherd the fortunes of such a republic as long as it adhered to these principles.

Yet victory in the War for Independence failed to allay many republican fears. . . . Society as the colonials had known it was hardly falling apart, but the old deferential patterns — and voluntary compliance with them — were clearly giving way to a more individualistic, pluralist set of values. The doctrine of liberty espoused during the Revolution went a long way toward weakening communal responsibility for individual behavior in many areas. But while republicans cherished the ideals of the Revolution, no one (who was willing to admit it) wanted these ideals to proceed to anarchy or to a decline in general morality or civil order. And in this concern for social stability and virtue, few things seemed to have more disruptive potential than the intemperance that apparently was accompanying the startling rise in the use of distilled spirits.

This unsteadying fear lay behind America's classic early stricture of drunkenness: *An Inquiry into the Effects of Ardent Spirits on the Human Mind and Body* (1784), by Dr. Benjamin Rush of Philadelphia. Rush commanded attention. An ardent republican, he had been active in Revolutionary politics, signed the Declaration of Independence as a Pennsylvania delegate, and served for a time as Continental army surgeon general. Rush enjoyed a reputation after the war as perhaps the new nation's foremost physician. His interests ranged widely — his writings on mental illness earned him the title "Father of Psychiatry" — but most Americans of his time came to know him for his work on behalf of temperance. Rush had spoken out publicly against the use of hard liquor since at least 1772, but his masterpiece was the *Inquiry*.

The tract represented a radical challenge to previous thinking; it assaulted the old dictum that alcohol was a positive good. Rush had no quarrel with beers and wines, which he believed healthful when consumed in moderate amounts, but he correctly pointed out that Americans were now drinking primarily "ardent spirits," and, he argued, these did more than cause drunkenness. Consumed in quantity over the years, they could destroy a person's health and even cause death. More important was how alcohol went about its lethal business: For Rush was the first American to call chronic drunkenness a distinct disease, which gradually, but through progressively more serious stages, led drinkers to physical doom. In fact, he described an addiction process and specifically identified alcohol as the addictive agent. As Rush claimed, once an "appetite," or "craving," for spirits had become fixed in an individual, the victim was helpless to resist. In these cases, drunkenness was no longer a vice or personal failing, for the imbiber had no more control over his drinking — the alcohol now controlled him. In Rush's view, the old colonial idea that drunkenness was the fault of the drinker was valid only in the early stages of the disease, when a tippler might still pull back; once addicted, even a saint would have a hard time controlling himself. . . .

As a good republican, he abhorred intemperance (and the strong drink that caused it). It was a personal and social vice, and it struck at the very heart of the Revolutionaries' vision of the good republican society. Allow drunkenness to flourish, Rush cautioned, with its attendant crime, degraded individuals, broken families, economic loss, and other disruptions, and the Revolution would have been fought in vain. "Our country," he warned, would soon "be governed by men chosen by intemperate and corrupted voters," rather than by citizens of virtue. "From such legislators the republic would soon be in danger," openly susceptible to demagoguery. Nor, of course, would the Almighty look favorably on a people who preferred to drink whiskey when they had the opportunity to build a golden edifice dedicated to liberty and a moral republican order. To avert such a calamity, Rush advocated not only personal abstinence from hard liquor but also a return to strict communal sanctions against drunkards. Drunkards, Rush pointed out, were the antithesis of virtuous citizens; they were incapable of managing their own affairs, could become mentally enfeebled, and certainly could not be responsible enough to vote. Better, Rush said, to lock them up in special asylums until they regained whatever faculties remained (he suggested the name "Sober House" for the asylum he envisioned for Philadelphia). He also urged that "good men of every class unite and besiege" their leaders with demands for fewer taverns and heavy taxes on "ardent spirits" as further means to stem the tide of intemperance. So while Rush was no prohibitionist, he saw considerably more at stake in American drinking practices than did the vast majority of his countrymen. . . .

As the nineteenth century dawned, the drinking habits that had so worried Dr. Rush continued unabated. Relatively heavy and frequent drinking, with the very American preference for hard liquor, had become common throughout the nation. In fact, the period from the 1790s to the early 1830s was probably the heaviest drinking era in the nation's history. Consumption estimates tell the story dramatically: From an annual average of 5.8 gallons of absolute alcohol per capita (for people aged fifteen or older) in 1790, mean absolute alcohol intake rose to 7.1 gallons a year by 1810 and, with minor fluctuations, remained at about that level until at least 1830. Of these amounts, as Samuel Dexter noted in 1814, "the quantity of ardent spirits . . . surpasses belief." And Dexter, who in 1814 was president of the Massachusetts Society for the Suppression of Intemperance — he had earlier served as treasury secretary and secretary of war — apparently knew what he was talking about, even if he was an interested source.

Dexter's data closely approximate modern consumption estimates . . . which suggest that by 1800 (and possibly earlier) about half the absolute alcohol consumed was in the form of distilled liquor; this proportion was well over half after 1810. In 1830, for example, when average annual consumption was about 7.1 gallons (absolute), some 4.3 gallons were in hard liquor, while only 2.8 came from beer, cider, or wine. Again, however, as in dealing with the colonial drinking figures, it must be kept in mind that these were national averages, based on the entire population over fifteen years old. So, if, as Dexter insisted was necessary, we adjust our figures by excluding slaves and "others who, through disrelish, delicacy, or principle, drink little or none," average consumption levels for actual drinkers would have been much higher.

These figures seem almost too high. To drink enough whiskey, beer, or whatever to reach seven gallons of absolute alcohol in a year would be, for most people, a genuine feat, and we cannot be sure how accurate the estimates of nineteenth-century consumption really are. But at the same time, an extensive body of evidence (in the form of local histories, diaries, and travel reports) suggests that our best estimates are not far off the mark and that drinking had reached unparalleled levels. It seems clear that most Americans of the early nineteenth century drank pretty much as their Revolutionary period brethren had. They simply drank at an accelerated rate.

The question becomes why? For one reason, the old notion that alcohol was necessary for health remained firmly fixed. It was common to down a glass of whiskey or other spirits before breakfast, "and so conducive to health was this nostrum esteemed," noted a journalist in 1830, "that no sex, and scarcely any age, were deemed exempt from its application." Instead of taking coffee or tea breaks, Americans customarily stopped every morning and afternoon for eleven o'clock ("eleveners") and four o'clock drams. At the appointed hours, laborers in fields, offices, and shops halted and picked up the jug. Even school children took their sip of whiskey, the morning and afternoon glasses being considered "absolutely indispensable to man and boy."

Ardent spirits were a basic part of the diet — most people thought that whiskey was as essential as bread. In the evenings plenty of liquor was drunk during and after dinner to aid digestion and sleep; before retiring one took a "strengthening" nightcap, with one recipe calling for "whiskey, maple syrup, nutmeg, and boiling water, the whole dashed with rum." Taking a "healthful" dram, then, could have people drinking all day — a fact not unnoticed by many contemporary commentators. In "every corner," one Englishman recorded while traveling the Mississippi in the 1820s, "north or south, east or west, was the universal practice of sipping a little at a time, but frequently."

Social drinking, if anything, was even more prevalent in the nineteenth century than it had been in the colonial era. Even nondrinkers generally kept a supply of whiskey on hand for guests, and it was a rare occasion on which people got together without a bottle of spirits. "The friend who did not testify his welcome, and the employer who did not provide bountifully" in liquor "for his help, was held niggardly," one commentator noted. "The consequence was that, what the great majority indulged in without scruple, large numbers indulged in without restraint." According to a British observer, the Americans believed the British could settle nothing save over a good dinner; the Americans, he found, did nothing except over a drink. "If you meet you drink," he said, "if you part you drink; if you make an acquaintance you drink. They quarrel in their drink, and they make it up with a drink." . . .

. . . [C]ontemporary sources also indicate that early in the nineteenth century not very many persons saw disgrace in a binge; few, unlike Dr. Rush, considered such behavior a real threat to the moral fabric of the republic. Behavioral norms had in fact evolved to the point that imbibing citizens could take in stride quite a bit of what we would today consider problem drinking. This phenomenon was partly a reflection of the newer noncommunal, individualistic orientation that was emerging with the Revolutionary era — an outlook that put greater emphasis on personal liberty, self-reliance, and equality of opportunity among free citizens unfettered by unreasonable social and governmental restraints. This more latitudinarian world view stood in stark contrast to the community centered ethos of the colonial period and to the republicanism of Benjamin Rush, which emphasized a society of moral-political harmony and common purpose. Politically, this credo became more apparent with the election of Thomas Jefferson in 1800 and perhaps reached its zenith with the presence of Andrew Jackson in the presidency after 1828. The new mood exalted the rights of the common person, fostered a diversity of ideas, and preached the hatred of any form of privilege; it encouraged people to employ their wits and seek their fortunes individually, restrained only by their natural abilities. . . .

In this age of nascent democracy, drinking and beverage choice served to enrich the egalitarian ethos. For some citizens, downing American whiskey took on connotations of national feeling. "Good rye whiskey," one patriotic toper advised in 1814, "or high-proof apple-brandy," rather than wines or imported spirits, were the drinks for loyal men and women of the republic. Corn whiskey, particularly bourbon, earned yet more honors as a national drink. Harrison Hall, one of the most prominent distillers of the early 1800s, never tired of singing the praises of corn spirits. The French sipped their brandy, he noted, "the Hollanders swallowed gin; the Irish glory in their whiskey"; the English had their beloved porter. So, Hall reasoned, "why should not our countrymen have a national beverage?" Hard cider had its partisans for the honor, especially in New England. Whether enjoying cider or bourbon, however, many drinkers consciously identified their preferred beverage with a keen sense of nationhood, and they thus saw their imbibing as a patriotic act. . . .

In the presidential race of 1840, the Jacksonian opponents of William Henry Harrison printed an article alleging that the old man would be better off in a log cabin with a jug. The insult was a monumental blunder. In the "log cabin campaign" that followed, Harrison's managers played up the imagery — it had a certain common touch that voters liked. Harrison's supporters even passed out thousands of small bottles of hard cider just to make sure the voters remembered who their best friend really was. Harrison won easily.

Even earlier, at rough-hewn Andrew Jackson's inauguration gala in 1829, the imbibing crowds in the White House had become so rowdy that officials feared the revelers would tear the place apart. The solution was masterful:

The staff carried the liquor out to the lawn; the gathering followed (naturally); and the mansion's doors swung shut. Few doubted, then, that America was in good hands as long as its leaders were willing to have drinks with the populace. . . .

As acceptable as drinking was to most Americans, it nevertheless had its critics. . . . In Litchfield County, Connecticut, for instance, some two hundred of the "most respectable farmers," challenging the wisdom of the day, concluded that drinking on the job did more harm than good and, in 1789, discontinued the customary liquor rations for farm labor. In 1808, a small group in Moreau, New York, founded the nation's first temperance society, also citing the deleterious impact of liquor on farm productivity.

Indeed, as these first temperance groups were being born, the United States was getting ready to enter an era of intense social reform activity — activity that merged temperance with goals as diverse as school reform, abolition, and women's rights. This ferment, growing out of the times, left the young republic in turmoil over a host of new social forces — forces that moved the nation steadily toward its modern character as a pluralist democracy. Thousands streamed toward the frontiers and beyond the influence of Eastern institutions; the increasingly powerful Jeffersonians (followed by the Jacksonians of the 1820s and thirties) offered citizens a democratic ideology stressing unfettered individualism as the basis of freedom, as opposed to the communal ideals of traditional republicanism; the arrival of major immigrant populations, unfamiliar with American values and having their own creeds and customs, also seemed likely to affect the character of the young nation; and around the corner loomed the industrialization process, with unknown consequences for the largely agrarian order of the postrevolutionary generation. While no one could predict where these trends would eventually lead, many Americans rejoiced at the apparent evolution of old social relationships and values and saw in the dawning age new and greater political and economic opportunities for all citizens. On the other hand, the specter of change also left a great many people, especially older native American families, perplexed and apprehensive.

Those who questioned the wisdom of these potentially radical changes were the nineteenth-century heirs of the old republicans. . . . Like Benjamin Rush, former President John Adams, and others of the Revolutionary generation (many of whom were still alive in the early 1800s), they worshipped basic political liberty and the institutions of the republic, but only in the context of a stable social-moral order governed by men of sufficient character and virtue to appreciate what was needed for the welfare of all citizens. . . .

For many neorepublicans, safeguarding society depended, as they frankly admitted, upon social and governmental leadership by men such as themselves — men of proven distinction, who would set high examples of personal conduct and had the courage to act vigorously in defense of accepted standards. Historians have termed this strain of thought the "stewardship tradition"; that is, a moral elite would act as stewards for the rest of the nation, guiding and correcting their behavior. . . .

These moral stewards honestly thought that they knew best how to order the affairs of other men and women. And they were equally convinced that reform would be a vital step in fulfilling the old republican dream of establishing the United States as a beacon of promise for the rest of humanity. If they could see to it that Americans acted in a manner worthy of their destiny, Providence itself — working largely through the major Protestant denominations — would guide the fortunes of the nation. . . .

The reform impulse flowed into a number of channels and became a hallmark of the American experience before the Civil War. Any condition or situation labeled evil generated an effort — and frequently a formally organized national society — to set it right. Temperance was only one facet of this general phenomenon: Peace, abolition, the elimination of profanity and Sabbath-breaking, women's rights, mental health, the rekindling of orthodox Protestantism, concern over immigration (including, in its extreme forms, some of the anti-Catholicism noted earlier), education, and other causes all attracted champions. Temperance reform, however, as the period advanced, became one of the most popular causes. As drunkenness lay demonstrably at the root of other social ills, or at least symbolized such aspects of rampant pluralism as immigration and the roughhouse lifestyle of the American West, the attack on intemperance appeared particularly important. How, for example, could the nation logically promote better care for the mentally ill or the imprisoned if it allowed people to drink themselves to insanity or to a life of crime? Why reform public education when children returned each day from school to besotted parents, or end poverty when the poor squandered their pay on liquor? It seemed impossible to cure national ills without acknowledging the centrality of the liquor question, and legions of reformers quickly came to accept what Rush had pointed out long before: The elimination of drunkenness would prove crucial to avoiding internal civil disruption — thus literally preserving the republican experiment itself. . . .

A formal national temperance movement emerged in 1826: the American Society for the Promotion of Temperance (later known as the American Temperance Society). Leadership rested firmly in the hands of socially prominent clergy and laymen, whose proclaimed purpose was the reformation of the nation under the guidance of "holy men" who would "induce all temperate people to continue temperate" through abstinence from ardent spirits. The early temperance movement, then, was *not* a prohibitionist crusade; in adopting this moderate approach, the new society had taken a page right out of Benjamin Rush. Rush, whose memory the society revered and whose writings became movement gospel (he would eventually be known as the "Father of Temperance" and the "True Instaurator"), had counseled precisely such a course. Permitting the measured use of nondistilled beverages would prevent the drinking excesses associated with hard liquor.

Armed with this moderate doctrine, the Society for the Promotion of Temperance performed admirably. It virtually assumed the national leadership of temperance activities. The society helped organize local units, sent lecturers into the field, distributed literature (including the *Inquiry*), and served as a clearinghouse for movement information. Within three years, in large measure inspired by society proselytizing, 222 state and local antiliquor groups were at work across the land. The crusade was by no means at peak strength numerically, nor did it have any appreciable political influence at this stage; yet temperance reform now constituted a burgeoning national movement. . . .

Fear of alcohol addiction, the enslavement to drink that Rush had described, was instrumental in bringing about a crucial change in the meaning of temperance — the shift from temperance as abstinence from distilled beverages to temperance as total abstinence. . . .

The most forceful statement of this position came in Lyman Beecher's *Six Sermons on Intemperance*. Beecher delivered them from the pulpit in Litchfield, Connecticut, in 1825. In 1826 he published them, and the *Six Sermons* took their place with Rush's *Inquiry* as temperance movement classics. Any drinking, he argued, was a step toward "irreclaimable" slavery to liquor; people simply could not tell when they crossed the line from moderate use to inebriety — could not tell, that is, until too late. Look out, he said, if you drank in secret, periodically felt compelled to drink, and found yourself with tremors, inflamed eyes, or a "disordered stomach." "You might as well cast loose in a frail boat before a hurricane, and expect safety," Beecher explained, and "you are gone, gone irretrievably, if you do not stop." But most could not stop; the power of alcohol was too strong. This fact, he noted, coupled with the abolition of the liquor traffic, would at least end the country's alcohol problem, as the "generation of drunkards" would "hasten out of time." Total abstinence, Beecher concluded, was the only sure means of personal salvation and societal stability.

The temperance movement controversy over total abstinence gave rise to one account of the origin of the term "teetotaler." In Hector, New York, the local temperance society debated the matter in 1826. To compromise, it allowed members a choice of pledges, one foreswearing all liquor, the other just distilled spirits. However, those going completely dry received a T — for total abstinence — next to their names on the society rolls, thus becoming known locally as "T-totalers." The term spread generally as other societies introduced total abstinence pledges. . . .

. . . At a . . . national temperance convention in Saratoga, New York, in 1836, the delegates formally endorsed total abstinence as the movement's interpretation of temperance. There was still some resistance among the rank and file, but by the end of the decade the issue was virtually closed. Temperance reform, for the first time, had gone fully "dry."

More remarkable, however, was the extent to which the rest of the nation followed suit. In 1835 the national temperance society estimated that two million people had renounced the use of distilled liquor (causing some four thousand distilleries to close), while nearly a quarter of a million persons had become total abstainers. Membership in temperance organizations had climbed to about 1.5 million. Thousands of others, without any temperance affiliation or signing any pledge, also cut back on their drinking, even if they did not stop entirely. The cumulative effect sent national liquor consumption plummeting. From a high of just over seven gallons of absolute alcohol per capita annually in 1830, consumption estimates fell to slightly more than three gallons by 1840 — the largest ten-year drop in American history. . . .

While the temperance movement mulled over the question of prohibition, events transpired that temporarily took the antiliquor initiative away from the established reform societies. A dry revival, led by men with no prior temperance connections, swept the nation in the 1840s, catching reformers almost completely by surprise. This remarkable dry explosion was the "Washington movement," founded by six Baltimore topers in 1840. Sitting in Chase's Tavern one evening, or so tradition has it, these gentlemen turned to a discussion of their tippling ways, which they admitted were undermining their lives. As a consequence — and perhaps as a lark — one of the group, charged with reporting back to his companions, attended a nearby temperance lecture. The delegate emerged from the lecture a new man, not only taking the pledge himself but also persuading his friends to do the same. They decided to work for the reform of other drinkers, and calling themselves the Washington Temperance Society (in honor of the first president), they drew up a total abstinence pledge.

The group succeeded beyond its wildest expectations. Over a thousand men took the society's pledge by the end of the year, and "missionaries" then carried the Washingtonian theme to New York City, where they attracted thousands. After this, the Washingtonians came to represent a full-fledged revival. Societies patterned on the Washingtonian model sprang up everywhere; churches opened their sanctuaries for meetings; and Washingtonian lecturers, such as the spellbinding John B. Gough and John Hawkins, joined the ranks of the most sought-after speakers in the country. . . .

The Washingtonians were unlike other regiments in the antidrink army. Their emphasis was on saving individual alcoholics, not general social reform. To them, alcoholism was a problem of the isolated drinker, not part of a broader social malaise or a matter of ideological neorepublicanism. Helping the drunkard was the end in itself. At a time when the formal temperance movement was advocating prohibition, the Washingtonians remained cool toward legislatively oriented solutions to the problem. Indeed, to keep the focus on alcoholics and their problems, Washingtonians often closed their meetings to clergy and to members of other temperance organizations. . . .

Yet the meteoric rise of the Washingtonians held the seeds of their eventual decline. Like all other revival phenomena, the movement lost momentum, and by 1844 its activities were on the decline. By 1847 almost all the local societies had stopped meeting (although the Boston chapter continued to gather until 1860). More important than declining momentum was the loss of church and non-Washingtonian temperance support. The established churches, which had been allies, had come to resent Washingtonian opposition to their presumed leadership of the dry struggle, and they began to close their doors to movement activities. This prompted Washingtonian attacks on the church, which in turn exacerbated bad feelings. Some clergy envied the success of the lay movement, hurt that ex-alcoholics proved better reformers than learned ministers. "As [the clergy] were neither the originators nor the leaders in the movement," wrote one temperance man, "they felt themselves ignored, [and] therefore refused to have any affiliation for, or lend any assistance to it." At the same time, and for the same reasons, the older temperance societies also began to withdraw support. The societies worried further that the Washingtonians had drained off energies that might otherwise have flowed to them and that the revivalist-oriented group lacked the institutional structure and the wider reform vision necessary to preserve the republic. The neglect of legal authority in the fight against liquor was a mistake, they insisted. Even a generally sympathetic temperance observer felt compelled to note that the "triumph of moral suasion was short and doubtful." In that the emotional appeal of the Washingtonians had diverted attention from the societies working toward legal suasion, their activities were actually an "evil." It was true that the Washingtonians had neither long-range programs nor a central organization to sustain what they had won. To save drunkards and then to see thousands of them relapse because liquor was still freely available made less and less sense to the stewardship-oriented societies. In their eyes, the Washingtonian experience was proof that real progress could be attained only through legislation. . . .

. . . Thousands of people, who before had merely dreamed of a dry republic, now saw this goal as within the realm of possibility. They began to bombard state legislatures with demands for the abolition of demon rum. Among some politicians, support for prohibition was already there. As early as 1846, temperance forces in Maine, under the leadership of Neal Dow, had persuaded the legislature to outlaw the manufacture and sale of distilled liquors. Although the law lacked penalties harsh enough to compel full compliance, the response of the legislators was enough to make temperance advocates in other states optimistic. . . .

Enthusiasm and political pressure finally came to a head in 1851. Neal

Dow's Maine Law of that year gave prohibition advocates their first great legislative breakthrough, and they moved quickly to follow up on their victory. In August 1851, another temperance convention met in Saratoga Springs and issued a battle cry for the passage of Maine Laws throughout the nation. Lobbying at the state level redoubled, and prohibition became the goal of what was now clearly one of the most comprehensive political efforts the nation had ever seen. After an enthusiastic campaign directed in part by old stalwart Lyman Beecher, Massachusetts went dry less than a year later. Maine Laws next carried the day in Vermont, Minnesota Territory, and Rhode Island (1852); Michigan (1853); Connecticut and Ohio (1854); and Indiana, New Hampshire, Delaware, Illinois, Iowa, and New York (1855). Similar measures almost won in Wisconsin (where prohibition twice cleared the legislature in 1855, only to meet a governor's veto), Pennsylvania, and New Jersey; across the border, the Canadian provinces of Nova Scotia and New Brunswick added their names to the dry column as well.

Politicized morality thus seemed well on its way to rolling back the tide of over two hundred years of American drinking habits. By the mid-1850s, many dry reformers were congratulating themselves on having destroyed the old consensus on drinking as a positive good, and they eagerly looked forward to national prohibition. Their confidence appeared fully justified. During the 1850s, enough Americans had stopped or moderated their drinking to drop national annual consumption levels well below three gallons of absolute alcohol per capita. These were the lowest rates in the nation's history. . . .

But those who prophesied a dry millennium were wrong. The Maine Laws in fact marked the high tide of temperance influence in the antebellum years — a tide that ebbed quickly with the approach of the Civil War. By the late 1850s, masses of people feared a violent confrontation over slavery and the preservation of the Union. Most Americans, including some important temperance leaders, increasingly gave the impending sectional struggle a higher priority than they did the battle against the traffic. Popular interest in the cause, so keen in the early fifties, was fading fast by the latter part of the decade as "Bleeding Kansas," the Dred Scott case, John Brown's Harper's Ferry raid, and Southern rumblings about secession began to dominate newspaper headlines. Also aiding the disenchantment with prohibition were a number of European medical reports that concluded that alcohol, while dangerous in excess, was not deleterious in moderation. All this caught the temperance movement off guard. Opponents of prohibition took heart. . . .

Events in Maine were typical of those in other locales. The original Maine Law lasted only a few years. It was replaced in 1858 by a measure that kept prohibition on the books in name alone. There was neither popular nor political support for a stiffer law, and even Dow admitted that any effort to achieve real prohibition would have to wait until the nation had sorted out its sectional differences. Indeed, by the time Confederate guns opened on Fort Sumter in April 1861, prohibition had all but collapsed as a major public issue.

Yet the legacy of the prohibition struggle remained. The movement had indelibly etched total abstinence on much of the popular mind. It had convinced many that the dry doctrine held the key to the stability and prosperity of the republic. And if its political manifestation, prohibition, had fallen on hard times, thousands remained loyal to the idea nonetheless. In fact, the antebellum movement set an important precedent: Few temperance advocates in subsequent years would seriously advance any other method than legal prohibition as a solution to the liquor question.

STUDY GUIDE

1. In this selection, the authors use a number of what may be unfamiliar terms, each of which has a broad and important concept behind it. Look back over the essay, and be prepared to explain the meaning of the following terms and what period or group each is associated with: republican ideology; noncommunal, individualistic orientation; egalitarian ethos; stewardship tradition.

2. In what ways did the arguments of Benjamin Rush and Lyman Beecher differ?

3. Contrast the early groups, such as the American Temperance Society, with the Washingtonians with respect to techniques, social backgrounds, and attitude toward religion.

4. The above selection (as well as Reading No. 12 on the creation of asylums and Reading No. 19 on abolitionism) suggests that there was a very strong element of Protestantism in the reform movements of this period. How can you explain this in terms of traditional Christian thought or in terms of the changes taking place in American society in the nineteenth century that threatened the position of Protestantism?

BIBLIOGRAPHY

The bibliographies following other readings in this section list some of the general works on reform, many of which have one or more chapters on the temperance crusade. Besides the book from which the above selection was taken, two other book-length studies of the pre–Civil War crusade have been published recently: Ian R. Tyrell, *Sobering Up: From Temperance to Prohibition in Antebellum America, 1800–1860* (1979) and W. J. Rorabaugh, *The Alcoholic Republic: An American Tradition* (1979). An older work that is fuller in some ways than the recent studies is John A. Krout, *The Origins of*

Prohibition (1925). The concern of nineteenth-century Americans with other aspects of health is delightfully summarized in Chapter 9, "The Body and Beyond," of Ronald G. Walters, *American Reformers, 1815–1860* (1978), and is more fully detailed in Stephen Nissenbaum, *Sex, Diet, and Debility in Jacksonian America: Sylvester Graham and Health Reform* (1980).

It is not surprising that much more has been written about drinking and prohibition in the 1920s than in the nineteenth century. History is largely the study of changing developments over time, and studies that are limited to one chronological period can sometimes be misleading. Thus, on a topic such as prohibition, one should compare the pre–Civil War period with the twentieth century to understand the evolution of laws and attitudes. Many of the comical aspects of the 1920s are told in Henry Walsh Lee, *How Dry We Were: Prohibition Revisited* (1963). Andrew Sinclair's study, *Prohibition: The Era of Excess* (1962), published in paperback as *Era of Excess: A Social History of the Prohibition Movement,* emphasizes the nativistic and backward-looking tendencies of the movement. A similar point of view is taken by Joseph R. Gusfield in *Symbolic Crusade: Status Politics and the American Temperance Movement* (1963) and by Norman Clark in *The Dry Years: Prohibition and Social Change in Washington* (1965). James H. Timberlake, in *Prohibition and the Progressive Movement, 1900–1920* (1963), makes a case for prohibition as a facet of progressive reform. In "New Perspectives on the Prohibition 'Experiment' of the 1920's," *Journal of Social History* (Fall 1968), pp. 51–68, John C. Burnham disagrees with those who have labeled the prohibition movement a failure. Burnham offers a number of statistical studies to prove his contention that as a consequence of prohibition, the social and medical health of the nation — and particularly that of lower-income groups — improved markedly.

*Scores of new prisons, asylums, and reformatories, like the New York
House of Refuge, were established in the pre–Civil War period.*

12

JOSEPH M. HAWES

The Reform Impulse

Every society has to deal with social problems, which might range from controlling those who disobey its laws and mores to assisting the poor, aged, or orphaned who cannot care for themselves. In the Seneca culture described by Anthony Wallace (Reading No. 1), ridicule, as when Red Jacket was nicknamed Cow-killer, was often sufficient to enforce tribal mores. The British colonists used religion and law as tools of social control, but the family was the single most important social agency. In the absence of the many institutions that now exist, the colonial family served as a hospital for the care of the sick, an orphanage and retirement home, a house of correction and reform, and a school and apprenticeship program. By the nineteenth century, various social changes, including the rise of cities, made it impossible for the family to handle all these services.

By 1830 the needs had become quite apparent, and a remarkable group of men and women undertook — in some cases, singlehandedly — to do something about the growing social problems. In every major city, societies sprang up to reform conditions in jails and almshouses, to help the handicapped, to combat alcoholic intemperance, to fight for women's rights, and to abolish slavery. Thomas Gallaudet established a school to help the deaf and mute, while Samuel Gridley Howe developed methods to assist the sightless. Dorothea Dix was scandalized by the treatment of the mentally ill, who were frequently jailed, sometimes in shackles, rather than treated in hospitals. It is estimated that she traveled 40,000 miles and investigated more than eight hundred jails and almshouses. Her petitions to legislatures led twenty states to adopt her recommendations, and thirty-two new hospitals were established. Thousands of lesser-known women and men worked in the antislavery crusade, the peace movement, and other reform organizations of the Jacksonian era.

Whether a society tries simply to punish its deviant members or to reform and care for them can help us in understanding the values and the view of human nature in that society. Through much of Western history, the individual has been viewed as having free will to do good or evil. The possible influences of social and psychological factors upon behavior were not recognized, so criminals were considered entirely responsible for their crimes and punishments were often severe. The hand of a thief might be cut off, the tongue of a gossip pierced, or, in a later period, an adultress required to wear a scarlet A. The holding of people in slavery, the shackling of the insane, and the use of execution and mutilation were not regarded by most people as either unusual or abhorrent.

Change began in the eighteenth century, on both sides of the Atlantic, with the development of a new feeling — a concern for other human beings that we call humanitarianism. A number of sensitive men such as John Howard, John Woolman, Anthony Benezet, and Philippe Pinel questioned traditional ideas and provided a social philosophy directed toward a more humane world. The number of capital crimes was reduced, imprisonment rather than mutilation became more common, and institutions were developed that might reform offenders. Prisons at Philadelphia and at Auburn, New York, became models that attracted Alexis de Tocqueville and scores of other foreign travelers interested in reform. In the selection that follows, Joseph M. Hawes describes the institutions established in the 1820s and 1830s to care for homeless children and to separate juvenile offenders from hardened criminals. He discusses the nineteenth-century view of children and of why they became delinquent, as well as the daily routine and the system of discipline in these early reformatories. Newspaper headlines about juvenile delinquency, the criminal "repeater," and prison riots indicate that despite these noble efforts of the 1830s, the problems remain today.

In the fall of 1822 two men met in one of New York City's parks. They were James W. Gerard, a young lawyer, and Isaac Collins, a Quaker, and both were members of the Society for the Prevention of Pauperism. Every year this Society presented a public report to suggest ways of carrying out its purposes. Usually, one man, with the assistance of two others "for form's sake," wrote this report. Gerard was talking to Collins about the street children of New York because he was going to write the report for 1822 on "the reformation of juvenile delinquents." Collins, whose father was a Philadelphia printer, became interested in the treatment of juvenile delinquents after reading the annual report of an English institution for young offenders. Gerard had become interested in juvenile crime as a result of the very first case he tried, that of a fourteen-year-old boy accused of stealing a bird. The young lawyer won acquittal for his client by arguing that prison would corrupt the boy. The case so interested Gerard that he began to investigate the facilities for detaining prisoners in New York. He also decided to join the Society for the Prevention of Pauperism.

Gerard presented his report at a public meeting held in the ballroom of the City Hotel in February, 1823. "Those who are in the habit of attending our criminal courts, as jurors or otherwise," Gerard said,

> must be convinced of the very great increase of juvenile delinquency within these few years past, and of the necessity of immediate measures to arrest so great an evil. . . . It is with pain we state that, in five or six years past, and until the last few months, the number of youth under fourteen years of age, charged with offenses against the law, has doubled; and that the same boys are again and again brought up for examination, some of whom are committed, and some tried; and that imprisonment by its frequency renders them hardened and fearless.

This was hardly surprising, Gerard said, if one knew the conditions of the prisons and the Bridewell. (A Bridewell then had about the same functions as a county jail in twentieth-century America.) At the Bridewell persons awaiting trial because they could not afford to pay bail were all packed into one large room, "the young and the old . . . promiscuously crowded together. . . . Boys who have been charged with picking pockets, stealing watches, and the like crimes," Gerard continued, "have declared before the police when [asked] how they came to such things, that they learned the art from the experienced offenders they met in [the] Bridewell."

Every year one to two hundred children between the ages of seven and fourteen appeared in the criminal courts of New York City. Some were homeless and most of them were "the children of poor and abandoned parents" whose "debased character and vicious habits" caused them to be "brought up in perfect ignorance and idleness, and what is worse in street begging and pilfering." Gerard concluded with a recommendation that a "house of refuge" for young convicts be established where juvenile delinquents might be reformed. "Unless the heart is corrupt indeed, and sunk deep in guilt," Gerard said, "the youth would undergo a change of feeling and character, and he would look on crime with greater abhorrence, because he himself had been a criminal." Gerard's report led to the creation of the first separate institution for juvenile delinquents in the United States, the New York House of Refuge. . . .

The act incorporating the Society for the Reformation of Juvenile Delinquents in the City of New York outlined the procedures for membership in the Society and made the Board of Managers responsible for the operation of the House of Refuge. Thus, America's first institution for juvenile delinquents was a "mixed" institution. That is, a private philanthropic group established and operated it, but the state had chartered it and provided for the conditions of its operation. The act of incorporation also contained the first statutory definition of juvenile delinquency in the United States. It authorized the Managers "to receive and take into the house of refuge to be established by them, all such children who shall be taken up or committed as vagrants, or convicted of criminal offenses" if a judge thought they were "proper objects." The Managers could also "place the said children committed to their care, during the minority of such children at such employments, and cause them to be instructed in such branches of useful knowledge, as shall be suitable to their years and capacities." The Managers had the power to bind out children (with their consent) as apprentices until they reached legal maturity. The children remained under the control of the Managers until the boys were twenty-one and the girls were eighteen, or until the officials at the House of Refuge decided that they were "reformed" and agreed to their discharge. Thus, the New York House of Refuge began the use of the indeterminate sentence long before penal reformers advocated it in the late nineteenth century as a necessary innovation in American penology.

The House of Refuge began its operations in the old arsenal building on January 1, 1825, with six boys and three girls. By the end of the first year, a total of seventy-three children had come to the Refuge, fifty-four boys and nineteen girls, and fifty-six remained in the institution. Of the seventeen children who left during the first year, nine had been indentured as apprentices or servants, four had been discharged, and four boys had "absconded."

Most of the children who came to the House of Refuge that first year and most of the ones who came later were "very ignorant." Even those few who had learned to read "had acquired no relish for intellectual improvement. Their habits, as it [sic] respects skill and useful industry, were still more deplorable." Particularly surprising was the fact that the girls could not perform any of the standard feminine tasks; they could not cook, sew, or iron. For the first year the boys spent most of their time cleaning up the grounds and helping to erect a new building and make the wall higher. When they were not busy with their newly learned domestic tasks, the girls planted grass. Once the maintenance tasks were finished, the boys began to learn shoemaking and tailoring, and the girls found themselves doing all of the mending and laundry for the institution.

The schedule, which the superintendent had worked out, allowed two hours a day, one in the morning and one in the evening, for formal instruction. The curriculum included spelling, reading, writing, and cyphering (arithmetic). To some extent the inmates taught themselves, since the Lancastrian or monitorial system was used. Apparently, the combination of labor and instruction and the system of discipline at the House of Refuge were effective. The *Annual Report* for the first year noted that "of the whole number in the house, the superintendent reports that [only] eleven are still restless and refractory." Four of the boys had run away, but the Managers and the superintendent were apparently satisfied with the other children, who had been in the House of Refuge at one time or another in 1825.

Methods of discipline varied; the superintendent sometimes put the "subjects" on a ball and chain. He also used handcuffs, leg-irons, and the "barrel." On January 28, 1825, Superintendent [Joseph] Curtis noted in his daily journal that six subjects, two of whom were girls, had been talking during a meal. He "took each of them to the barrel which supports them while the feet are tied on one side and the hands on the other. . . . With the pantaloons down [this device] gives a convenient surface for the operation of the 6 line cat." On that same day a boy wearing handcuffs made himself a key. The superintendent "put him in prison," locked his leg iron to the wall, and instructed the staff to feed him on bread and water. In spite of these restraints, however, the boy broke out of "prison," but the police soon recaptured him. Curtis refused to have this boy back at the House of Refuge, and so he went to the penitentiary. Corporal punishment was not confined to boys. On March 13, 1825, the superintendent put leg-irons on a girl who "does not obey the orders of coming when called, and neglects her work for playing in the yard." Curtis also gave one "sullen, ill-natured and disobedient" girl "a dose of salts" — apparently aloes, a purgative. She came to the House of Refuge in March, 1825, and was "very trying." She did not "transgress in things of importance" but she was "artful and sly" and told "many equivocating stories." Her conduct exasperated Superintendent Curtis and he "gave her a ball and chain and confined her to the house." She escaped twice; once the police recaptured her, and once she returned on her own. She went out as a servant, but voluntarily returned to the House of Refuge. Another indenture took the girl to her majority, but on December 26, 1829, the superintendent wrote that "she is said to be on the town."

The situation at the Refuge made some of these punishments necessary. The walls presented no real barrier, and the superintendent had to appoint some of the boys as guards. There were, consequently, a number of escapes. On October 4, 1825, Superintendent Curtis noted in the daily journal that "this evening has been spent in making confessions on the repeated attempts of escaping." As a result,

> great freedom of speach [*sic*] and frankness appeared to our entire satisfaction, all the movements and plans as well as the persons who have manifested

a desire to go has [*sic*] been fully exposed. . . . It tells us that the insecurity which we have daily felt on this subject has been well grounded; and that there is no security with our present encumbrances.

The fact that the magazine of the old arsenal still contained powder also added to the superintendent's worries. In addition many of the inmates in the House of Refuge were boys over sixteen, for legally any boy under twenty-one could be sent there. In September, 1826, the superintendent complained about the "large notorious & hardened villains" who came to the Refuge. "I fear," he said, "that our extended wish to do good will in consequence of introducing these ill bred hardened boys among the first and young offenders, will prove a curse rather than a blessing." Since the old arsenal building was clearly inadequate, the Acting Committee (which functioned as a board of trustees for the House of Refuge) decided to erect a new building which would provide "greater security." In April, 1825, the Committee resolved to add workshops and small utility buildings to their construction plans and decided that the new main building should contain "cells and accommodations for a number of delinq'nts not exceeding one hundred." In that same month the United States Army sent a man to remove the powder from the magazine, which somewhat reduced the "insecurity."

To pay for the new building the managers of the Society appealed to the public for more money. In May, 1825, they issued an *Address to Annual Subscribers* in which they claimed that "already the number of vagrant children who beg and steal in our streets is perceptibly diminished." There were thirty-five boys and eleven girls in the House of Refuge at that time "in a situation where there is no temptation to vice . . . and, where, instead of being left to prey on the public, they will be fitted to become valuable members of society." To continue this important work the managers felt compelled "to erect . . . an additional stone building with separate dormitories for each child, on a plan somewhat resembling the State Prison at Auburn. . . ." To be sure that their contributions were worthwhile "subscribers and the public" were invited "to call at the House of Refuge, and see that idleness has become changed to industry, filth and rags to cleanliness and comfortable appearance, [and] boisterous impudence to quiet submission."

The Acting Committee directed the superintendent to employ a foreman and four to six masons to erect the building with the assistance of the boys. The masons and the boys finished the new cell house in April, 1826. It was a two-story stone building with barred windows and heavy doors. Inside were small "dormitories" — three feet, three inches wide — for each boy. The new building did make it more difficult to escape and brought about the complete separation of the male and female departments. "We find ourselves in possession and enjoyment of all the long wished advantages of the new building," Superintendent Curtis wrote, "and we also find (as we may allways [*sic*] expect) that our anticipations are not realised." The boys now had to do their own cooking, and for a time they proved less adept than the girls.

From the first the House of Refuge attracted a stream of visitors, distinguished and otherwise. Soon after the Refuge opened, a father appeared and demanded the return of his son. Only after he had secured a writ of habeas corpus did the superintendent permit the man to take his boy. In May, 1826, Governor De Witt Clinton of New York, the Governor of Ohio, the Mayor of New York, "and various other dignitaries and their wives" came to the House of Refuge and left apparently well pleased. In July three men from Pennsylvania came to study the House of Refuge because they were planning to establish a similar institution in Philadelphia. "They left us highly gratified," the superintendent noted in the daily journal, "with a determined resolution to advance the same good cause they had witnessed." A week later, the sister of a former inmate came by to see some of her old friends. She was wanted by the police, however, and the superintendent arranged to have her detained. Such guests must have appeared frequently for on July 26, 1826, Superintendent N. C. Hart (Joseph Curtis had resigned on July 11, 1826) noted in the daily journal that "it is found that now and then improper persons get into our yard on visiting days. I have given direction to the gate-keeper not to permit any to enter (even on visiting days) Unless they are very respectable looking persons." . . .

At the end of the second year, in the *Annual Report* the Managers explained the theories which guided the efforts to reform juvenile delinquents at the House of Refuge. "The young offender," they said, "should, if possible, be subdued by kindness. His heart should first be addressed, and the language of confidence, though undeserved, be used towards him." They added that the young inmate should be taught that "his keepers were his best friends and that the object of his confinement was his reform and ultimate good. If he is made to believe that he is still of some use and value, he will soon endeavor to act up to the character which is set upon him." This kind of discipline, the managers argued, "will be willing, cheerful and lasting." The remarkably gentle — and from the lights of modern psychology, appropriate — methods espoused by the Managers of the New York House of Refuge came from a nineteenth-century theory about children and the development of their personalities. As the Managers explained, men of the early nineteenth century believed that "the minds of children, naturally pliant, can, by early instruction, be formed and moulded to our wishes. An inclination can there be given to them, as readily to virtuous as to vicious pursuits." Not only can the plastic minds of children be turned to vice or virtue, but earlier inclinations can be altered if the child is not too old: "The seeds of vice, which bad advisers may have planted, if skill is exercised, can yet be extracted . . . and on the mind which appeared barren and unfruitful may yet be engrafted those principles of virtue which shall do much to retrieve the errors of the past, and afford a promise of goodness and use-fulness for the future."

The Managers also reminded their readers that "these little vagrants, whose depredations provoke and call down upon them our indignation, are yet but children, who have gone astray for want of that very care and vigi-lance we exercise towards our own." They were, nonetheless, misbehaving children, whose actions had to be condemned. Furthermore, "a regard for our property and the good of society, requires that they should be stopped, reproved and punished. . . . But," the Managers continued, "they are not to be destroyed. The public must in some measure take the place of those who ought to have been their natural guardians and protectors." Here the Managers of the New York House of Refuge anticipated one of the key con-cepts of the Illinois Juvenile Court Act of 1899 — the idea that the public (in the Illinois law it was the state) has a collective responsibility to and for society's misbehaving children. Ironically, this provision of the Illinois law was hailed as a great innovation in the legal treatment of delinquent chil-dren.

In order to carry out their theories, the officials at the New York House of Refuge adopted rules which prescribed continuous activity for the inmates during their waking hours. They were to be employed "every day in the year, except Sundays, at such labor, business, or employment as from time to time [would] be designated by the Acting Committee." Other rules indi-cated that all the children wore "coarse but comfortable apparel of the cheapest and most durable kind," which was made on the premises. Inmates who refused to work or who used profane or indecent language, or who fought with their fellow delinquents, would be punished. Punishments in-cluded deprivation of play periods, being sent to bed without supper, and bread and water. In more serious cases, the officials might force the recal-citrant boy or girl to drink a bitter herb tea which caused them to sweat profusely, or they might put the offender in solitary confinement. In ex-treme cases, corporal punishment or iron fetters might be used. The rules provided that corporal punishment could only be inflicted in the presence of the superintendent (or the matron in the case of misbehaving girls). The rules also indicated that "the females shall eat their meals and lodge in a separate building from the males, with whom they shall have no intercourse or communication, except at family or public worship."

Scarcely a week passed without some sort of incident. On September 5, 1826, one of the worst troublemakers in the girls' department returned of her own accord after having escaped. She and the schoolteacher got into an argument, and he began whipping her. According to Superintendent Hart,

She commenced swearing most bitterly, tore his shirt considerable & made battle with her fists — having a pen knife secreted about her, she succeeded in opening it with her mouth, & made several attempts to stab him in his breast — to no purpose, but finally got it in the flesh of his arm and ripped a gash at least 1½ inches long and very deep.

The superintendent put the girl in irons. In December, 1826, two boys escaped through the attic of the male cell house, and an officer went to town to look for them. He found one of the boys "in a small rum hole in Anthony St. with girls and other company of ill fame." The boy drew out a knife, while one of the patrons of the establishment shouted "Stick him [!] Stick him [!]." The boy cut the officer severely on the arm and on the neck "near the jugular vein." When the police had returned this boy to the House of Refuge, the superintendent punished him "with a cowskin upon his bare back" and then put him in solitary confinement "without a book to divert his mind" on a bread-and-water diet. The boy remained in solitary for three days, after which the superintendent put him in a cell in the upper tier. The boy then attempted another escape:

> [He] tied three sheets & a cord together — broke through the plastered wall into the garret — again fastened the cord to the same place where he had been successful in making his escape but a few evenings since — but alas! no sooner than he had . . . [placed] his weight upon the cord thus fastened, it broke & he fell about 30 feet upon frozen ground & stones — broke his foot badly — pitched upon his face cut a hole over his eye to the skull bone & fractured it, broke his nose & drove the bones so deep as to endanger his life — cut his lip through nearly up to his nose. Thus he rolls in agony.

To prevent similar escape attempts the officers moved the older boys to the first tier and put the younger boys in their place.

The House of Refuge, following the penal theories of men like Thomas Eddy, also instituted a rudimentary classification system. When they entered, the officials placed the inmates in one of four grades, ranging from "those who are vicious, bad and wicked" in class four to "the best behaved and most orderly boys and girls; those that do not swear, lie, or use profane, obscene or indecent language or conversation," in class one. Every Sunday, the superintendent, his assistant, and the teacher reclassified the children according to their behavior. The upper classes enjoyed extra recreation, and the lower classes found themselves on a reduced diet and suffered from the loss of other privileges. The system of treatment at the New York House of Refuge, rudimentary as it was, is another example of an improvement in penal practice made in a juvenile institution which would later be hailed as an "innovation" in adult reformatories.

A typical day in the Refuge illustrates this system. A bell would ring at sunrise to arouse the sleeping children. They had fifteen minutes to dress, make their beds, and straighten up their cells; then they assembled in the corridors and marched off to the washrooms. After washing, the inmates lined up for a personal inspection. They were at best a motley group. Their clothing had been cut from "a coarse, cheap material" to six standard sizes. In 1848 Elijah Devoe, formerly an assistant superintendent, recalled that they had "collectively a slovenly and untidy appearance." From inspection the children went to morning prayers, after which they went to school for an hour and a half. Then they sat down to a breakfast which usually consisted of bread, molasses, and rye coffee. After breakfast, the inmates trooped off to their various workshops, where they worked until noon. Washing up again and the noon meal occupied the next hour, after which the children returned to work. During this afternoon work period the children could gain extra recreation time if they finished their assigned tasks early. The work period ended at five o'clock; then there was a half-hour for supper and another hour and a half of school. Following the evening school session, there were evening prayers; the inmates then marched back to their cells, turned in, and followed a rule of silence for the night.

The labor of the children in the House of Refuge was let out to contractors, who then paid the institution for the value of the work done by the children. While the contractors taught the children the skills necessary to perform their tasks, the officials of the House of Refuge maintained discipline. The girls worked mostly at sewing; and the boys made cane bottoms for chairs, various kinds of brushes, shoes, and boxes for soap and candles. The contractors represented an outside presence in the House of Refuge and an unending source of difficulty. On July 22, 1826, for example, two girls claimed that the shoemaker took them "into his dwelling & there perpetrated that heinous crime of seduction." An investigation quickly followed and on August 6, Superintendent Hart wrote that the shoemaker had "closed his business with us." On October 16, 1827, Hart noted in the daily journal that the parents of some of the boys in the House of Refuge had complained that their sons were not learning a trade since the shoemaker had set up an assembly line, assigning a separate task to each boy. "The remarks are in considerable degree true," Hart wrote, "& how the difficulty is to be obviated I cannot tell." It would take nearly half a century to eliminate the contract system.

When the officials at the New York House of Refuge concluded that a boy or girl had sufficiently reformed to be trusted outside the institution itself, they often bound them out as apprentices. Some of the boys signed on as sailors in whaling ships, a practice which the managers endorsed heartily in the *Fifth Annual Report* because such a boy would find himself under "wholesome restraint and discipline" and would have the examples of "moral, industrious, and religious companions." Most of the boys, however, were apprenticed to farmers, including some in the West — a practice which anticipated the placing out system of Charles Loring Brace and the Children's Aid Society. Generally, the girls became servants in families not too distant from the House of Refuge. Boys were indentured until they were twenty-one, girls until they reached eighteen. To explain the purposes and methods of the New York House of Refuge, the superintendent sent a form letter to the masters of the apprentices, which warned against the overuse of corporal punishment and reminded the masters that "it has not been concealed from you, that this child has been a delinquent." The superintendent also addressed a form letter to the apprentice. "We should not have consented to part with you at this time," it began, "had not your conduct given us reason to hope, that the religious and moral instruction you have received since you have been under our care, have disposed you to lead an honest, industrious, and sober life." The letter to the apprentice also cautioned him against bad company, especially his former associates. . . .

What distinguished the House of Reformation in Boston from the New York House of Refuge and the House of Refuge established in Philadelphia in 1828 was its system of discipline. As Tocqueville and Beaumont noted, "the Boston discipline belongs to a species of ideas much more elevated than that established in New York and Philadelphia"; but it was difficult to practice because it was "entirely of a moral character." The Boston House of Reformation used a classification system based on the conduct of the inmates, but unlike the New York House of Refuge it required each child to evaluate his own conduct, and a jury composed of children in the institution tried cases of serious misconduct. In the House of Reformation there were six grades of conduct — three good ones and three bad ones. Each of the good grades carried with it certain privileges; boys in the highest grade could go outside the bounds of the House of Reformation by themselves. Conversely, each of the bad grades carried a degree of privation; boys in the two lowest grades were not allowed to speak unless it was absolutely necessary. Before the boys could participate in this system of discipline, they went through a period of probation. A new arrival met with the superintendent, who interviewed him to determine his moral condition. Then, if the new inmate had been found guilty of a serious offense, he was placed in solitary confinement for two weeks so that he could reflect on his vices. Superintendent Wells then told him why he was in the Boston House of Reformation and explained the system of discipline. If the boy rebelled against the officials during his probationary period, they whipped him. Only at this first stage did the superintendent permit corporal punishment. At the end of the probationary period, the superintendent assigned the child one of the bad grades and encouraged him to move up. . . .

The public image of an institution, derived in part from the reports of well-publicized visitors and investigations and also from the institution's own annual reports, is rarely a complete picture of its daily life. In a book that amounted to a polemic against the New York House of Refuge, Elijah Devoe, a discharged assistant superintendent, contended that the New York institution had deliberately falsified its public face. He charged that officials had altered the records to give a higher rate of reformation and that the day-by-day practices in the institution were far more cruel than any outsider realized. The routine was "a stern, brutal, coercive government and discipline, entirely the opposite of that paternal establishment so amiable and ingeniously pictured in the 'annual reports.' " Devoe also indicated that the rule prohibiting corporal punishment unless in the presence of the superintendent was a dead letter: "Corporal punishments are usually inflicted with the cat or a ratan. The latter instrument is applied in a great variety of places, such as the palm and back of the hands, top and bottom of the feet, and lastly, but not rarely or sparingly, to the posteriors over the clothes, and also on the naked skin." Rattans were readily available and "liable to be used everywhere and at all times of the day." In addition, Devoe deplored the mixing of "hardened culprits over fifteen years" of age with "small, younger, and less corrupt children." The older boys were just as likely to corrupt the younger ones as hardened adult criminals were to corrupt juveniles in prison; it was therefore an injustice that "boys under a certain age, who become subject to the notice of our police, either as vagrants or houseless, should be thrust into the society of confirmed thieves, burglars, and robbers, and subjected to the same discipline and punishments."

Devoe's account, which was the work of an unhappy former employee, nonetheless provides an "inside view" of an early nineteenth-century juvenile institution. It seems probable that the annual reports of these institutions, which were made in response to state law and which represented to some extent arguments for state appropriations, presented only the most favorable aspects of houses of refuge and ignored the day-to-day activities which deviated from the high ideals set by the managers. In some respects, however, the view of juvenile institutions presented in their annual reports is more valuable than the "inside story," because the annual reports gave the public its only look at juvenile institutions. Thus, they are a rudimentary index to what nineteenth-century Americans knew about institutions for juvenile delinquents.

The creation of special institutions for juvenile offenders in the second decade of the nineteenth century indicated a growing awareness on the part of American city-dwellers of the problem of juvenile delinquency, and the new institutions also represented a modification in the application of criminal laws to young people. Under the common law as Blackstone explained it, children under seven were presumed to be unable to distinguish between right and wrong. Between the ages of seven and fourteen, "though an infant shall be *prima facie* adjudged to be *doli incapax* [not mentally competent]; yet if it appear to the court and jury that he was *doli capax,* and could discern between good and evil, he may be convicted and suffer death." That this understanding of the common law was generally adopted in the United States may be illustrated by a case involving a twelve-year-old Negro boy in New Jersey in 1828. The boy had been found guilty of the murder of a sixty-year-old woman by a lower court, and the case had been appealed to the New Jersey Supreme Court on the grounds that the boy was too young to be found guilty of such an offense. The Supreme Court upheld the verdict of the lower court, finding that the judge had correctly charged the jury with the relevant points of law in the case. The lower court judge had told the jury that "with respect to the ability of persons of his age, to commit crimes of this nature, the law is, that under the age of seven, they are deemed incapable of it. Between seven and fourteen, if there be no proof of capacity, arising out of this case, or by testimony of witnesses, the presumption is in their favor; a presumption, however, growing weaker and more easily overcome, the nearer they approach to fourteen." The judge went on to explain that a twelve-year-old boy in New Jersey at that time probably possessed "sufficient capacity" to commit murder. Finally, he told the jury: "You will call to mind the evidence on this subject; and if you are satisfied that he was able, in a good degree, to distinguish between right and wrong; to know the nature of the crime with which he is charged; and that it was *deserving* of *severe* punishment, his infancy will furnish no obstacle, on the score of incapacity, to his conviction."

None of the statutes which established the houses of refuge in New York, Boston, and Philadelphia changed the basic premises of the common law, but in effect they raised the age below which a child could expect to receive some kind of preferential treatment from the law. The sentiment behind the creation of the new institutions for juvenile delinquents recognized that children — even children over fourteen — required different treatment from adults. The new laws, although they did not mention any ages except those for the end of minority, created institutions which would provide that treatment. The laws also provided a legal definition of juvenile delinquency. A juvenile delinquent was a child who broke the law, or who was in danger of breaking the law, and the community hoped to keep him from becoming an adult criminal by providing reformatory treatment in a house of refuge.

. . . The house of refuge was a legal institution with certain well-defined powers. Primarily, it was an institution designed to reform youthful criminals, but it also functioned to prevent crime by accepting young vagrants who were potential juvenile criminals. Once a house of refuge received a child, the managers had a wide latitude of authority over him. In effect, they had the same powers over their charges that a natural parent had over his own children. Thus the state, by chartering a private or municipal association to take the place of inadequate or missing parents, had taken a bold step in the direction of providing for the welfare of its children. In addition, such a step appeared almost too attractive to resist. When houses of refuge first appeared, they seemed to have a good chance of preventing or drastically reducing the rate of adult crime. They not only gave the community something to do with juvenile offenders and vagrant children, they promised to cut future welfare and prison costs. When they insisted that the inmates of houses of refuge be taught a useful trade, the managers shrewdly responded to a community prejudice which not only condemned idleness as a sin but also linked it with serious crime. By teaching juvenile offenders how to work, then, houses of refuge were exorcising sin and providing for the future security of life and property. The creation of the New York House of Refuge and similar institutions in Boston and Philadelphia marked the beginning of nineteenth-century America's concern for wayward children. It also marked the beginning of the process of separating juvenile delinquents from adult criminals — a process that would not be complete until the creation of the juvenile court in 1899. But the house of refuge had one essential weakness as an institution — it was a charity, which, although chartered by the state, private citizens operated. The involvement of private citizens had been necessary to launch the first institutions for juvenile delinquents, but once their worth had been proved, many philanthropists felt that the reformation of juvenile offenders was a duty for which the state should take full responsibility.

STUDY GUIDE

1. A good many children and young people were placed in institutions not because they had committed a crime, but because of something in their character, circumstances, or behavior. Describe some of these factors.

2. What do you see as the views of the supporters and administrators of these institutions with respect to (a) the nature of children; (b) religion and an ethical code; and (c) the goals of institutionalizing children?

3. Certain of the practices in these institutions might be criticized today, but both the institutions and the theories by which they were operated were seen as great reforms. What practices do you see in the 1820s and 1830s that might be considered advances over earlier practices? What influences from that period do you see in our modern juvenile court system?

4. Many of the reforms of the Jacksonian period were undertaken by private societies with private funds. What factors in our time have caused most social welfare work to be carried out by government agencies with public funds? What private agencies still operate in such fields?

5. Cities like New York may have extremely high welfare costs because so many people migrate there from other states, which are thus relieved of such a burden. What would be the advantages and disadvantages of having all social problems handled by the federal government, since such problems cross state lines?

BIBLIOGRAPHY

The subject of the treatment of juvenile delinquents and orphans is but a part of such broader topics as the society's view of deviance, the development of state institutions in the modern world, and the spirit of reform in Jacksonian America. Three studies that deal very broadly with change in nineteenth-century America are Robert E. Riegel, *Young America, 1830–1840* (1949); Alice F. Tyler, *Freedom's Ferment: Phases of American Social History to 1860* (1944); and Glyndon G. Van Deusen, *The Jacksonian Era, 1828–1848* (1959). The following three books on pre–Civil War reform are of special interest here: David B. Davis, ed., *Ante-Bellum Reform* (1967); Clifford S. Griffin, *Their Brothers' Keeper: Moral Stewardship in the United States, 1800–1865* (1960); and Ronald G. Walters, *American Reformers, 1815–1860* (1978).

The bibliography following the reading by Lyle Koehler (Reading No. 3) has a section concerning the history of childhood. Two works especially pertinent to the early nineteenth century are Bernard Wishy, *The Child and the Republic: The Dawn of Modern American Child Nurture* (1968) and Robert M. Mennel, *Thorns and Thistles: Juvenile Delinquency in the U.S., 1825–1940* (1973). Anyone interested either in social welfare as a profession or in American social values would do well to read some of the histories of American treatment of the criminal, the mentally ill, and the poor. Blake McKelvey, *American Prisons: A Study in Social History Prior to 1915* (1936) is an older study, while W. David Lewis, *From Newgate to Dannemora: The Rise of the Penitentiary in New York, 1796–1848* (1965) is more modern. Albert Deutsch, *The Mentally Ill in America: A History of Their Care and Treatment from Colonial Times*, 2nd ed. (1949) is a good survey. Two other books go into greater depth on mental institutions and views of insanity: Norman Dain, *Concepts of Insanity in the United States, 1789–1865* (1964) and Gerald N. Grob, *Mental Institutions in America: Social Policy to 1875* (1973). David J. Rothman, *The Discovery of the Asylum: Social Order and Disorder in the New Republic* (1971) deals with nearly all of the social institutions, including orphanages and houses of refuge, in the period studied by Hawes. Raymond A. Mohl, *Poverty in New York, 1783–1825* (1971) and Paul S. Boyer, *Urban Masses and Moral Order in America, 1820–1920* (1978) are other books for somewhat advanced students, while Robert H. Bremner, *American Philanthropy* (1960) is a brief introduction of general interest.

Shaker Village, Inc., Canterbury, N.H.

These New Hampshire women (c. 1914) reflect the continuity of nineteenth century Shaker values of simple dress and segregation of the sexes.

13

EDWARD D. ANDREWS

Utopian Communes

One of the most unusual developments of the counterculture of the 1960s was the establishment of hundreds of communes across the United States. Ranging from a few people buying a farm they planned to work together to much larger groups with a distinctive philosophy of life, these experiments in living revealed a disenchantment with the larger, competitive society and emphasized the sharing of an "extended family."

This was by no means the first movement of this sort in American history. The first settlers of several of the colonies had been members of small, tightly knit groups that stressed a strong sense of mutual responsibility among the members. The same spirit had sometimes characterized new communities on the frontier as Americans moved west. Such religious sects as the Mormons and Moravians had displayed a similar unity of spirit and purpose. The clearest parallel to the communes of the 1960s can be found in the many groups in the 1830s that established small settlements in the Northeast and Midwest in an attempt to create a perfect community as an example for society as a whole.

Some of the communities were formed by European immigrants, such as the Rappites of western Pennsylvania, and some were based on social philosophies of European origin. Others were natively American, such as the Brook Farm community in Massachusetts. Some were religiously oriented; others were socialistic. They embodied a wide range of beliefs including vegetarianism, free love, celibacy, and the abolition of money. So varied were they that there was no such thing as a typical community that would give one an idea of life in any of the others.

Yet there were common impulses and common beliefs be-

hind the founding of most of them. One, of course, was a dis-
satisfaction with the state of society. There was also a widespread
belief that it was possible to establish a perfect social order among
a small group of people. Ideas about what constituted perfection differed from one group to another; some thought it was
to be found in the common ownership of property, while others
believed it would only be achieved by coming into a perfect
kingdom ordained by Christ. Finally, most of these groups believed that if a perfect community could be created on a small
scale, with thirty or one hundred people, it would serve as a
model that could be extended to the entire society.

The Shakers, founded by Mother Ann Lee, were one of several religious groups that adhered to the rule of celibacy in their
communities and thus died out for lack of new recruits. Like
many of the religious minorities of the early nineteenth century,
the Shakers were millennialists, who believed in the second coming of Christ as the answer to the world's problems. In their case,
they felt that Mother Ann was the female embodiment of the
second coming, and that the millenium was already here — in
the small Shaker communities in which they lived. In his book
The People Called Shakers: A Search for the Perfect Society,
Edward D. Andrews explains the theology and worship of the
Shakers and also describes the daily life and human relations
in a celibate, religious community that hoped to create a perfect
order for American society.

Chief among the factors affecting all Shaker life was the unique relationship
existing between brethren and sisters. The application, under the same roof,
of the seemingly irreconcilable theories of equality and separation set the
movement apart from other communal-religious institutions and aroused,
more than any other characteristic of the church, skeptical comment and
barbed abuse. Every reliable source, however, indicates that the dividing line
was held. One sex was always conscious of the presence and support of the
other. But to pass that invisible boundary was to invite both bondage of soul
and communal disfavor.

Convictions concerning a fundamental tenet of the order, of course, aided
the adjustment: for the rule of celibacy was a selective agent, attracting not
only those who believed in the principle on doctrinal grounds, but those

From *The People Called Shakers* by Edward Deming Andrews. Copyright 1953 by Oxford
University Press, Inc. Reprinted by permission of Mrs. Faith Andrews.

others, chiefly women, who were drawn in because of their desire to escape from marital difficulties and broken homes. For persons oppressed by poverty and economic ills the Shaker community, like the cloister, offered the opportunity for a renewal of life in useful service, in which case the rule was accepted as a condition of security. Once the rule was accepted, the Shakers underwent a thorough course of instruction. The work of God, they were told, proceeded by a spiritual union and relation between male and female. If, in the course of the period of probation, the cross seemed repellent, they were free to withdraw or remain in an "out family." On the other hand, should they wish to travel on to the junior and senior order, they did so in full realization of what it entailed. If husband and wife entered together, they were usually assigned to separate families. . . .

. . . [Joseph] Meacham's basic law — that "no male or female shall support, or have a private union or correspondence together, neither shall they touch each other unnecessarily" — was also supported, in time, by detailed "separation acts" and ordinances for the "purity of the mind." It was "contrary to the gift," for instance, for a brother to pass a sister on the stairs, for a brother to go into a sister's room without knocking, for a sister to go to a brother's shop alone, for brethren to shake hands with the sisters and give them presents, and so on.

Surveillance was facilitated by the smallness of the family and the lack of privacy. From two to six individuals shared each sleeping or retiring room, the day's routine was organized, and most of the work was done in groups. In meeting, . . . the ministry could supervise proceedings through shuttered apertures; and at Pleasant Hill, two watchtowers on the roof of the dwelling served a similar purpose during the day. The Millennial Laws stated that if anyone knew of any transgression, he or she was morally obligated to reveal it to the elders, "otherwise they participate in the guilt." Under such conditions an atmosphere of mutual suspicion was almost inevitable; the feeling that one was being spied upon during every hour of the day and night was bound to deprive the individual of dignity and self-respect.

The most noteworthy device for regulating sex relations, however, was a constructive one. As the church was being organized, Meacham realized that "correspondence" was unavoidable, that brethren and sisters must consult on temporalities, that social solidarity could not rest on negative grounds. Since they "*would* have a union together," he testified, "if they had not a spiritual union, they would have a carnal." His corrective was the "union meeting," which for over seventy years, from 1793 on, played an important role in Shaker domestic life. These gatherings usually took place two evenings a week and twice on Sundays. A group of four to ten members of each sex met in a brethren's retiring room, where they sat facing each other in rows about five feet apart. (If girls and boys were present, they were placed beside their elders or by themselves in ranks in the rear.) Then, for a stated period, one hour on week nights and one or two on the Sabbath, each member of the group conversed freely and openly with the person opposite him on some familiar or suitable subject; or the occasion might be turned into a singing meeting. The pairs had been carefully matched, on the basis of age and "condition of travel," by the elders. No one was worthy to attend if he or she harbored any ill-feeling toward another.

The conversation — "simple, sometimes facetious, rarely profound" — was limited, for sacred, literary, and certain secular topics were all prohibited. Some visitors, like [A. J.] Macdonald, found the meetings dull. Nevertheless the time seemed to have been agreeably passed; the company had their own world to talk about, with zest and unrestraint if they wished; "gentle laughter and mild amusement" were not unknown; and in the early years smoking was customary. The union meetings, in fact, belied the common assumption that the Shakers were an austere folk, though discipline varied with the family or community and was likely to be more strict in the Church Order. Self-restraint and sobriety, however, never excluded simple joys. One observer comments on "the amenity of their intercourse [which was] much less restricted than is generally supposed." Another noticed that they were "disposed to be merry and enjoy a joke." Mary Dyer attended meetings at Enfield (N.H.) where there were pipes to smoke, cider to drink, and melons, apples, and nuts to eat; and where the participants sang such "merry love songs" as

> I love the brethren the brethren love me
> Oh! how happy, how happy I be,
> I love the sisters, the sisters love me,
> Oh! how happy, how happy I be.
> How pretty they look, how clever they feel,
> And this we will sing when we love a good deal.

A former member of a Niskeyuna family recalled that two aged brethren, one a Whig and the other a Democrat before they joined the order, used to argue their political principles in these meetings; and that a young sister, on one occasion, raised the issue whether members would not be better Shakers if they were allowed to study instrumental music, languages, and fine literature. The aristocratic Mrs. Hall found the Believers at this community "a very conversible set of people" — a verdict later shared by Howells, who felt that the renunciation of marriage was "the sum of Shaker asceticism."

These social gatherings were nevertheless misinterpreted by the world: as Isaac Youngs put it, "advantage was taken by some apostates and evil minded persons . . . to construe this sacred order of union, [especially the placing of certain brethren with certain sisters] into a particular union or connection, as savoring of husband and wife." Eunice Chapman, for one, testified to seeing "the spiritual husbands, each with their spiritual wife," withdraw after meeting to their different apartments — observing to one of the sisters that there must be "general courtship throughout the house." Furnishing further grounds for detraction was a custom connected with the meeting, namely, that of assigning to each sister general "oversight over the habits and temporal needs" of the brother sitting opposite her — taking care of his clothes, looking after his washing and mending, providing new garments when they were needed, and so forth — in return for which the brethren "did needful favors for the sisters." Visitors sometimes noticed the tender solicitude of a brother toward a certain sister, or vice versa. Though such attention was a violation of the letter of the Separation Acts, it seems to have been accepted, quite naturally, as a justifiable expression of spiritual union.

A combination of factors — the system of orders and surveillance, communal opinion, the rites of confession and atonement, the force of principle, the union meeting, the freedom to withdraw from the society — fostered and enforced a relationship between the two sexes which one enthusiast called "more harmonic than anyone seriously believes attainable for the human race." As to its effectiveness, we have the empirical judgment of the student Macdonald:

> I have always found that those who spoke ill of the Shakers on this subject, to be ignorant, and low minded persons, who probably judged others by themselves, and who founded their opinion upon mere supposition. Those who have been most among them, and consequently the best Judges, have been compelled to believe, that the Shakers are generally speaking, sincere, both in the Belief and practice of abstinence from sexual coition. I have heard Individuals who have lived with them, for periods varying from thirty years, to a few months, all declare, that there was no such immorality among the Shakers, as had been attributed to them. In the vicinity of Union Village, O. I heard suspicions and suppositions, in abundance, and have no doubt the same surmises may be heard in the vicinity of any of their settlements. But I have never met with one individual who was a Witness to or could prove a Case of immoral conduct between the Sexes in any of the Shaker Communities. . . .
>
> It is quite true that sometimes, young Shakers in whom the tender passion is not entirely subdued, fall in love with each other, but these generally contrive to leave the Sect, and go to the "World" to get married and reside.

The "order of the day" left little room, indeed, for vain or idle thoughts. At the sounding of the bell or "shell," the Shakers arose early in the morning, between four o'clock and five in summer, between five and five-thirty in the winter. After kneeling together for a moment of quiet prayer, the occupants of each retiring room stripped the sheets and blankets from their narrow cots, laying them neatly over two chairs at the foot, on which the pillows had previously been placed. Fifteen minutes after rising, the rooms had been vacated, the brethren had gone to their morning chores, and the sisters were entering to close the windows, make the beds, and put the room in order. At breakfast time, six, six-thirty, or seven, the chamber work was finished, fires had been started in the dwelling rooms and shops, the cattle fed, the cows milked, and arrangements for the day's industry were all complete.

Before all meals — the early breakfast, the noon dinner, the six o'clock supper — brethren and sisters would assemble, each group by themselves, in appointed rooms, where for a ten or fifteen minute pause which was a kind of "broad grace," they quietly awaited the bell. Then, in two columns led by the elders and eldresses, respectively, and in the order in which they were to be seated, they proceeded to the dining hall. Taking their places behind their chairs or benches, the sexes at separate tables, they knelt in prayer at a sign from the lead, and after a meal eaten in monastic silence, knelt again before departing directly to their labors. . . .

A series of table monitors, emphasizing economy and good manners at meals, testifies to the concern with standards of behavior. An early monitor (undated manuscript) illustrates how detailed was the instruction:

First, All should sit upright at the table.

2d The Elder should begin first, after which all may take hold regularly.

3d When you take a piece of bread, take a whole piece (if not too large) and when you cut meat, cut it square & equal, fat & lean, & take an equal proportion of bones — take it on your plate together with the sauce, whether it be cabbage, herbs, potatoes or turnips; and not be cutting small pieces in the platter and putting directly into your mouth.

4th When you have tea or coffee, and any kind of minced victuals or meat cut into mouthfuls, it may be proper with a knife or fork to eat it directly from the platter. . . .

8th Eat what you need before you rise from table, and not be picking & eating afterwards.

9th When you have done eating, clean your plate, knife & fork — lay your bones in a snug heap by the side of your plate — scrape up your crumbs — cross your knife & fork on your plate with the edge towards you.

10th When you reach a mug or pitcher to a person give the handle; and when you take hold of bread, biscuit, pies, etc. to cut or break, take hold of that part which you intend to eat yourself, and cut it square & equal — then you will not leave the print of your fingers for others to eat. . . .

12th If you are obliged to sneeze or cough, don't bespatter the victuals, make use of your handkerchief.

13th Clean your knife on your bread before you cut butter, & after cutting butter before you put it into apple sauce, etc. but never clean it on the edge of the platter etc.

14th Scratching the head, picking the nose or ears, belching, snifing the nose, drinking with the mouth full of victuals, or picking the teeth, are accounted ill manners at a table & must be left off.

15th And lastly, when you drink, never extend your under lip so far down that one would think the cup was agoing to be swallowed whole. Always wipe your mouth before & after you drink your bear (beer) or water at the table.

Note — Children under the age of 12 or 14 years must have their pie cut for them & laid by their dishes — Also, when they have bread & butter, suitable pieces must be properly spread & laid by their dishes. . . .

After the evening chores were done, at seven-thirty in summer and eight o'clock in winter, all repaired to their apartments for half an hour, known as "retiring-time," when, on the evenings devoted to family worship, the Shakers disposed themselves in ranks, sitting erect with hands folded "to labor for a true sense of their privilege in the Zion of God." If perchance one should drowse, it was the order to rise and bow four times, or shake, and then resume one's seat. At the end of the period, announced by the ringing of a small bell, brethren and sisters formed separate columns in the corridors, marched two abreast to the meeting-room, and, after bowing as they entered, formed ranks for worship.

Assemblies varied with the time and place. In the early years of the order, and often during revivals, "labouring" meetings were held nightly, and sometimes during the day. As the society expanded, however, evenings not devoted to union meetings or the regular religious service were given over to the practice of songs and exercises. Thus, at New Lebanon in the 'seventies, singing meetings were held on Tuesday and Friday, union meetings on Sunday and Wednesday, and "labouring" meetings on Thursday and Saturday. On Mondays, during this more liberal period, there was a general assembly in the dining hall, where the elder read letters from other communities, selections from the news of the week, or some appropriate book. At the conclusion of such gatherings, to which strangers were admitted on occasion, the family retired quietly to rest. The occupants of each room, after kneeling again in silent prayer, went to bed at a uniform hour — nine o'clock in winter and ten in summer.

Anyone watching such temperate people in the intervals between work and worship would have been impressed, above all else, by the tranquillity of their movements and behavior, as though the daily round was itself a service. No sign of tension or aggressiveness was apparent; speech was subdued; doors were opened and closed with care; all "walked softly." The dwelling, whose orderly, neatly furnished rooms were seldom occupied during the day, was also, in a true sense, a sanctuary. Many a visitor, like Hester Pool, was sensitive to that "indescribable air of purity" which pervaded everything, feeling with her "that this purity is a portion of the mental and moral as well as the physical atmosphere of the Shakerian home." Though all comings and goings followed the pattern of plainness, in the simplicity of domestic life there was an element of freedom, grace, and the contentment, or perhaps resignation, of those who had made peace with themselves and with the world.

The Children's Order was also carefully regulated. Boys and girls lived apart from each other and the rest of the family under "caretakers" responsible to the elders or eldresses. In the indenture agreements the trustees bound the society to provide them with "comfortable food and clothing," the common branches of learning, and training in such manual occupation or branch of business as shall be found best adapted to the "minor's genius and capacity." In return, the parent or guardian relinquished all rights over the child's upbringing. At maturity the youth was free to leave or remain.

In education emphasis was placed on character building and the useful arts. Though the early Believers, "being chiefly of the laboring classes and generally in low circumstances of life," were not in a condition to pay much attention to letter learning, Mother Ann strongly recommended religious and "literary" studies. Meacham advocated the kind of learning that would lead to order, union, peace, and good work — "works that are truly virtuous and useful to man, in this life." The idea that instruction should concentrate on developing good habits and useful talents was subsequently expanded by Seth Wells, the superintendent of the Shaker schools. Self-government, Wells believed, was the prerequisite of both moral and literary education. "When a man is able to govern himself, and subdue his evil propensities . . . he is then in a fair way to be benefitted by moral and religious instructions. . . ."

Nor was innocent recreation considered superfluous. The girls at Canterbury had gymnastic exercises and a flower garden; the boys played ball and marbles, went fishing, and had a small farm of their own. Picnics, sleigh rides, and nutting and berrying parties lent diversion to the ordinary routine. Elkins' frank account of his boyhood at Enfield is the record of a not uncolorful life, with interesting companions, mild paternal control, and normal healthful experiences in a beautiful countryside. Elder Briggs recalls that wood-chopping and maple-sugaring were gala times, like picnics, and mentions the diversions of fishing, swimming, and playing ball, the half-holidays once a week during warm weather, the refreshments during haying, which consisted of sweet buttermilk; lemon, peppermint, checkerberry, raspberry, and currant shrub; cake, cheese, and smoked herring. One who had been a young Shakeress at Niskeyuna remembers many happy days in the Children's Order there:

> Hiding beneath an arcade of the bridge which spanned the dear old creek, we would pull off shoes and stockings, and wade knee-deep in the cool, bright water. Then, loading our long palm-leaf Shaker bonnets with dandelions, which, grown to seed, looked like little white-capped Shakeresses, we would float them down the stream in a race, the boat which won being decorated with buttercups and violets. What mud-pies we made and baked in the sun! What fun we had secreting golden kernels of corn in clam-shells, and peeping from our hiding-place to see the chickens find them and peck them up, firmly believing that they "gave thanks" when they turned their bills up to heaven after sipping water. . . . We had no world's toys, but were just as contented

with our corn-cob dolls, clam-shell plates, acorn-top cups, and chicken-coops for baby houses.

From sources such as the above we suspect that Shaker life was not always as austere as its principles would have had it be; that the Believers, in their effort to extinguish natural affections, tried to do the impossible — particularly where children were concerned. We read of candy-making parties, culinary favors tendered by the "kitchen-sisters," humorous tolerance when children behaved "contrary to order," the attachments for favorite children, close friendships within the Children's Order. Human nature was constantly breaking up the artificial restrictions designed to subdue "carnal desire." It seems that the lot of Shaker youth compared favorably with that of the sons and daughters of farmers in the rural America of the period. . . .

The belief in progress, or "travel," found expression in the field of medicine as in education. Ann Lee's bias against physicians was shared by Joseph Meacham, who assured a doubter that "they that have my spirit have no occasion to go to world's doctors." In the early years Shakers were healed by faith or the laying on of hands. The "gift" against professionals was still held in 1813, when Mother Lucy's attitude to that effect was recorded; but Father Job Bishop, speaking "beautifully" on the same subject, qualified his stand by asserting that a surgeon might be called "in case of a broken bone or any very bad wound." About this time greater reliance was placed on regimen and simple medicines, with resort to shocking, bleeding, sweating, poulticing, and blistering. With the development of the herb industry in the 1820's, the Thomsonian medical practice, which relied on steam baths and herbal remedies and required little academic knowledge, came into increasing favor. Another step was taken in 1840, when messages prohibiting the use of strong drink, swine's flesh, and tobacco ushered in a reform which was more than temporary. In mid-century, largely through the influence of Elder Frederick Evans of New Lebanon, Grahamism and vegetarianism won converts in certain families. Proper diet, supplemented by the water treatment, simple massage, and hot herbal drinks in case of sickness, was the prevalent prescription late in the century. Faith in the "healing gift," however, persisted all this time, with many a cure allegedly effected by spirit touch and mental control.

As interpreted by Elder Evans, the science of health had a theological basis. To provide better food, clothing, and housing, a better distribution of heat, improved lighting, ventilation, and sanitation was the proper field of science. In the "new earth" the human body should be "the central object of influence and attraction," whose "salvation" was no less important than the "health" of the soul. Evans suggested eight main principles of dietetics:

1. Supply the family with at least one kind of course grain flour. Avoid cathartics.
2. Have the "sickly and weakly" cease using animal food, especially fats.
3. Keep the skin clean by regular bathing, with the water at such a temperature as to cause a warm, glowing reaction.
4. Keep room at a temperature not exceeding 60°.
5. Clothing — "regulated on the same principles as water and fire" — should be light, "a little less than you could possibly bear." The young should dispense with underclothes. "Sleep under as little clothing as possible."
6. Breathe pure air. Every room of the home should be of equal temperature. Ventilation of bedrooms important.
7. Thorough ventilation of beds and bedding.
8. "Be comfortable in mind and body."

While these views were the opinion of one person, a natural reformer, they were not unrepresentative of Shaker practice. The vent pipes over the lamps, the slots placed between the two sashes of every window, and the holes in the baseboards in the halls and under the radiators in the gathering rooms were additional evidences of a concern for fresh air. Baths, sinks, and water closets were well ventilated. Pure spring water was ingeniously piped for refrigeration. Temperate outdoor labor, regular hours, wholesome food, good clothing, comfort of mind, and the utmost cleanliness everywhere combined to promote the health of all. On the latter characteristic in particular, often contrasting favorably with conditions elsewhere, strangers were wont to remark from the earliest times. "Great importance is attached to cleanliness," *Blackwood's* correspondent reported in 1823; "this luxury they appear to enjoy in a truly enviable degree." "Visit them upon any day in the week," the historian of the town of Shirley wrote, "at any hour of the day, and when they are engaged in almost any employment, and you will scarcely ever find them in dirty dishabille. The shirts and pants and frocks of the men are rarely soiled, and the plain linen caps and kerchiefs of the women never." "Everything is . . . kept so delicately clean," remarked an English visitor in 1884, "that an air of refinement, not to say luxury, seems to pervade [the] bedchambers, in spite of their absolute simplicity."

Testimonies on the health of the Shakers are nevertheless conflicting. . . . With allowances made for prejudice, it is a matter of wonder, from the phrases used about the sisters, whether they were in health or out. They were called "a wretched-looking lot of creatures" (Fountain); "their pale faces . . . and flabby condition indicated . . . a low state of health" (George Combe); "the females and sedentary people . . . were occasionally indisposed" (*Blackwood's* correspondent); "the females . . . look remarkably pale and sallow" (Silliman); the women were "pallid, thin and withered" (Martineau); the sisters, with few exceptions, were "old, wizened, ascetic — perfect specimens of old maids" (Colonel A. M. Maxwell). The difference in the physical appearance of males and females was due, according to one mid-century author, to the "unaspiring, earthly" quality of the former, and the effect on such natures of a comfortable life, outdoor work, plenty of food, and an absence of anxieties. "The Shaker woman, by contrast, has a more melancholy lot. Love — 'the first necessity of woman's nature' — is dwarfed, in her case, to most unnatural ugliness. She must renounce the natural affections." On the other hand, Finch was struck with "the cheerfulness and contented looks" of the people in all the communities; Dixon remarked on "the rosy flesh" of the people of New Lebanon — "a tint but rarely seen in the United States"; and the usually reliable Nordhoff spoke of the "fresh fine complexion [which] most of the Shaker men and women have — particularly the latter."

If the Shaker way of life was detrimental in any way to physical well-being, certainly life was not shortened. The longevity of members of the sect has often been reported. In 1875 Nordhoff, making the first fact-finding tour of the communities, was impressed by the low rate of mortality: at Harvard, where the average age at death for a number of years was 60 to 68; at Union Village, where a large proportion of the members were over 70, and many over 90; at North Union, where many were past 80; at Pleasant Hill, where a considerable number lived past 90; and at Enfield (N.H.), Watervliet (N.Y.), and South Union, where the brethren and sisters often lived well over 75 years. . . .

When death occurred, complete simplicity marked the funeral. The coffin was pine, plainly lined, unpainted and unadorned. In the mind of the Believer, the life of the spirit was so real that death was but a way-mark in "travel," and the "trappings of grief" superfluous. Following the Quaker custom, the Shakers, led by the elders and eldresses of the family, devoted the main part of the service to personal tributes and memories. Songs were sung, and during one period of Shaker history, messages from the spirit were communicated by the instruments. The procession to the grave was not unlike the heavenly march of worship. Throughout the ritual the tone was one of reverence, strength, and inspiration.

Since followers of Mother Ann did not believe in physical resurrection, they thought of the living soul and not of the dead body. "He is not here," they testified at the burial service. Appropriate, therefore, were the simple slabs of stone, all alike and engraved only with initials, age, and date, which marked the resting place. Many advocated that even these be replaced by a mound of earth, or perhaps a shrub or tree, not as a memorial but rather as a contribution to earth's fertility and beauty.

Comparison of the living conditions of the early Shaker colonists with those prevailing a century or so later furnishes an index to the temporal progress of the society. In 1780 its possessions were limited to a few unpromising acres, a single cabin, the slim resources of John Hocknell.

Eight years later the Believers at Niskeyuna were still poor. Money was scarce, and the community was not allowed to run into debt. According to the account of Jonathan Clark of Hancock:

> Our principle food was rice and milk, sometimes we went to the river to procure fish. . . . We had little, and sometimes no bread, butter or cheese, but upon this simple fare, we all subsisted during the Spring and Summer. . . . All our work was very laborious, and at the end, we looked more like skeletons, than working men. . . . Our breakfast consisted of a small bowl of porridge. Supper the same. Dinner, a small bit of cake about 2½ inches square which Aaron Wood cut up, and gave to us. One day Joseph Preston and another brother went to the River to catch Herring; and Joseph stated that he was so hungry, that he ate two *raw*, as soon as they came out of the water. . . . We had but little house room, and of course were obliged to lie upon the floor. . . . Fifteen of us lay upon the floor in one room; some had one blanket to cover them, while others had none. . . .

The "manner of dress and building" was in the same inferior state. "Those who first believed, in America," Youngs wrote, "adopted such dress as seemed the most suitable, of the common plain forms that prevailed among people at the time they lived in England"; and the form, fashion, and quality of garments were "extremely various." In form and manner of construction, buildings also were of poor quality and ill-adapted to the purpose for which they were needed.

In all departments, however, the Shakers, by the will to make everything uniform with the best, steadily raised their standard of living. During the nineteenth century the preparation of wholesome food was considered more and more important, and as a result the Shakers achieved a considerable reputation for their recipes and public meals. As for clothing, painstaking care came to be paid to the needs of age groups and occasions, to uniformity of color and material, to the marking and laundering of garments. Buildings, too, were constantly improved and their numbers increased to meet the expanding needs of the colony. In New Lebanon, for instance, from the few small farmhouses which the Shakers took over in the 1780's, the community grew until it had 125 buildings in 1839, and property, including 2,292 acres of land, valued at $68,225. Within the same period the original colony at Watervliet had grown to a community of over 2,500 acres, valued, with buildings, at $46,900. When Nordhoff made his survey in 1875, the home farms of the eighteen societies, taken by themselves, amounted to nearly 50,000 acres, to which figure must be added extensive outside holdings in mills, wood lots, and "outfarms" — one in Kentucky, owned by the Watervliet (N.Y.) society, as large as 30,000 acres — which were often operated by tenants.

Following the eight immigrants from England some seventeen thousand persons, at one time or another, were gathered into the society. To the

Shakers this was a "great harvest" — the "blessed binders" had followed closely on the reapers, "severing all the worthless cockle till the work was done complete."

STUDY GUIDE

1. Explain the techniques the Shakers used in order to maintain celibacy. What explanation can you give for the skepticism about celibacy and the rumors of sexual excesses that often develop in the outside world with respect to convents, monasteries, and other celibate communities?

2. Describe the "order of the day" in a Shaker community and the religious life of the Shakers. Aside from separation of the sexes and the religious doctrines, what values and attitudes do you see among the Shakers that were not substantially different from those of many other farm folks in the period?

3. Though some might consider the Shaker life as barren and harsh, Andrews suggests that most of the Shakers felt a sense of freedom, contentment, and peace. What evidence is there in the selection that Shakers really felt this way, and how can one explain such a disciplined, plain, celibate life bringing happiness? What parallels are there between the Shaker philosophy and other experiments in alternative lifestyles that you know of (such as Henry Thoreau's experiment at Walden Pond)?

4. In terms of permanence and long-range influence upon American society, none of the other communitarian groups were any more successful than were the Shakers. What forces in American life and in the development of the American nation made it unlikely that these small-group experiments could successfully serve as a pattern for all of American society?

5. What do you see as the explanation for the development of so many communal groups in our own time? What evidence is there that such groups continue to have — on a reduced scale — the same problems that exist in the larger society?

BIBLIOGRAPHY

The historical literature on the Shakers and on other communitarian groups that flourished in the pre–Civil War years is both ample and interesting. A number of volumes can serve to introduce you to the entire range of communitarianism. You might begin with Arthur Bestor, Jr.'s prize-winning work, *Backwoods Utopias: The Sectarian and the Owenite Phases of Communitarian Socialism in America: 1663–1829* (1950), or with the same author's essay on "Patent-Office Models of the Good Society: Some Relationships Between Social Reform and Westward Expansion," *American Historical Review*, Vol.

LVIII (1953), pp. 505–526. Additional surveys of the topic will be found in the following: Alice Felt Tyler, *Freedom's Ferment: Phases of American Social History to 1860* (1944), a description of almost all of the reform movements, communitarian and otherwise, of the period; Charles Nordhoff's older but still valuable volume, *The Communistic Societies of the United States* (1875; reprinted, 1960); Mark Holloway, *Heavens on Earth: Utopian Communities in America, 1680–1880* (1951); and Everett Webber, *Escape to Utopia: The Communal Movement in America* (1959). More specific in focus is the volume from which the preceding selection was taken, Edward D. Andrews, *The People Called Shakers: A Search for the Perfect Society* (1953). Andrews also wrote volumes on Shaker furniture and on their music and dance. Other works on the Shakers have been written by Marguerite Melcher, Francis D. Nichol, and Clara E. Sears.

There are biographies of Owen, Fourier, and many other communitarian leaders, and studies of most of the communities of the pre–Civil War period. Jane and William Pease describe communities founded to aid recently freed Negroes in their book *Black Utopia: Negro Communal Experiments in America* (1963). Other works of merit include Herbert W. Schneider and George Lawton, *A Prophet and a Pilgrim* (1942); Maren L. Carden, *Oneida: Utopian Community to Modern Corporation* (1969); and Lindsay Swift, *Brook Farm: Its Members, Scholars, and Visitors* (1961). It is not possible here to list the many works dealing with the post–Civil War period of utopianism or the broader aspects of utopian thought in American life. Three works that are essential in understanding these subjects are Donald Egbert and Stow Persons, eds., *Socialism and American Life*, 2 vols. (1952); H. Richard Niebuhr, *The Kingdom of God in America* (1937); and Robert S. Fogarty, *American Utopianism* (1972). The last of these is a collection of source material on utopian communities.

IV INDUSTRIAL NORTH
AND PLANTER SOUTH

In our time, more than in any earlier period, the American people are a single people. They drive the same cars, use the same products, eat much the same food, and dress alike — whether they live in California or New England. With slight differences, their values and their popular culture — on the screen, on the airwaves, and in national magazines — are identical in Atlanta, Georgia, and Minneapolis, Minnesota. The homogeneity of modern American society tends to obscure the fact that differences among classes, nationalities, and sections played a prominent role in earlier American history.

The strong nationalistic sentiments of the first three decades of the nineteenth century faded rapidly after 1830. Always somewhat distinct in language, politics, and social life, North and South saw their respective economic interests as being in conflict. Both hoped for the support of what was rapidly emerging as a third distinct section, the trans-Appalachian West. Industrialization and urbanization were making the Northeast a region of constant change. In mining fields and factory towns, on canal and railroad projects, the strange tongues of several European nationalities could be heard. In contrast, the South was largely untouched by industrialism and the urban growth that would eventually characterize the entire country. Few immigrants went South, and slavery, with all its social as well as economic implications, swept westward from the South Atlantic states into Mississippi, Alabama, and other newly opened cotton lands.

The West was less clearly defined than the North or South; indeed, what was West was ever-changing as the line of settlement passed from western New York to Ohio, Iowa, and beyond. What we now call the Midwest was a region of non-slave-holding farmers, many of them Scandinavians and Germans who had come directly west from the port of entry. On the slavery issue, they were frequently in conflict with their border-state neighbors in Kentucky and Missouri, but on such questions as government support of internal improvements and banking, they found they had much in common.

The first reading in this section provides a graphic picture of slavery, the institution that was more important than any other in setting the South apart. The second selection tells the story of the massive migration of peoples from Europe to the United States in the nineteenth century, which contributed to the extraordinary population growth of the country. Though the vast majority of Americans lived in rural areas, many of the immigrants settled in eastern cities such as New York, whose population numbered 813,000 by 1860. The rapid urban growth required more efficient city government to provide such services as water, sanitation, and police and fire protection. The cities were struck by repeated riots and violence as different ethnic, religious, and racial groups came into conflict. The third reading describes the patterns of rioting. The last article is on labor conditions during the early years of the Industrial Revolution, especially among the new immigrants and women who entered the factory work force.

The opening of new cotton lands in the West made the slave auction a striking feature of southern life.

14

LESLIE H. OWENS

The Black Family

By 1800 slavery had been eliminated in the North, and in 1808 Congress banned the further importation of slaves from Africa. Although some illegal importation continued, other factors primarily accounted for the extraordinary elaboration and expansion of slavery in the nineteenth century. One such factor was the invention of the cotton gin, described in the essay by Joseph and Frances Gies (Reading No. 7), which allowed the quick cleaning of as much cotton as slaves could pick. A second contributing cause was the acquisition of vast new territories beyond the Mississippi River, which created a market for slaves and gave rise to the domestic slave trade within the United States. Between 1820 and 1860, the slave population of the state of Mississippi alone increased from fewer than 35,000 to more than 435,000. In short, southern planters found slavery to be economically profitable. There was also a high birth rate among American blacks, and by the eve of the Civil War nearly four million black people lived as permanent, hereditary slaves. Forming the chief labor force from the tobacco fields of Virginia to the cotton fields of Alabama, blacks were crucial to southern agriculture and to several other parts of the southern economy. As chattels, bought and sold like livestock, they were an easily marketable property that could bring ready cash to the slaveowner.

But slavery was more than a key feature of southern economic life. Its influence was all-pervasive, affecting law, education, social class, sexual mores, and other aspects of life. No one in the South entirely escaped the influence of slavery and racism, whether he or she was slave or slave-owner, free Negro or non-slave-holding white. Wilbur J. Cash has written, "Negro entered into white man as profoundly as white man entered into Negro —

subtly influencing every gesture, every word, every emotion and idea, every attitude."

Few things were influenced more radically than the black family. Today, much is made of the growing instability or breakdown of the American family. The daily press has become a record of divorce, juvenile delinquency, alcohol and drug abuse, wife-beating, and parent-child hostilities so extreme that murder is sometimes the outcome. Imagine, then, what might happen to a family under these conditions: a mother and her children might have to watch the father being whipped; a mother-wife might be forced to have sexual relations with a stranger who invades the family cabin; the children might be sold at the age of ten or twelve to a distant owner, never to see their parents again. Such were the possibilities for the black family under slavery, and some people have suggested that such experiences scarred the black family to the present day.

A full understanding of the black, or any other, family can be gained only by comparisons with families in other periods and societies. Recently, historians have devoted considerable energy to studying the family as a social institution in periods ranging from ancient China to medieval France to contemporary America. They have come to new conclusions as to the role of the Industrial Revolution in affecting the family, how pervasive single-parent households were in earlier periods, and whether or not the "nuclear" family — consisting of parents and children only, rather than broadly extended kin relationships — is a typically modern form. Leslie H. Owens's book *This Species of Property* is an excellent study of slave life and culture, and his chapter on the black family is especially poignant. Despite their enslavement and the breakup of families owing to the slave trade, blacks had a strong sense of family ties and family affection. Many slaves who attempted to escape seem to have been trying to get back to their families, and after the Civil War, thousands of ex-slaves solidified their informal alliances with marriage licenses and wedding ceremonies.

Few aspects of the slave's bondage have come in for as much speculative writing as the impact of slavery upon the slave family. Researchers in many

From *This Species of Property: Slave Life and Culture in the Old South* by Leslie Howard Owens. Copyright © 1976 by Oxford University Press, Inc. Reprinted by permission.

disciplines have argued that bondage rent asunder this most basic of American institutions, injured black identity, and left scars to haunt black Americans down to our day. But all this needs further examination.

Planters usually evidenced concern and not a little ambivalence, as several historians have preferred to put it, when reaching the decision to split up a black household. The practice was in sharp contrast to what many felt to be right, though planters consistently overcame nagging doubts. An agent representing John McDonogh of Louisiana complained to him that a slave trader "refused to give me a little negro boy and girl belonging to the Mulattresses, claiming that he could not separate the families." He added bluntly, "It was a poor reason." It cannot be denied that the slave family took a tremendous beating; its members were sold to satisfy creditors and purchased to increase personal wealth. . . .

To avoid the public disapproval that increasingly attached to putting slaves on the auction block, some masters sold their bondsmen privately. For the slave, however, the impact remained the same, and scenes of mothers crying because they would never see their children again are more than products of historical imagination. George Tucker, a nineteenth-century Virginia novelist, offended many of his southern readers by writing, "One not accustomed to this spectacle [an auction] is extremely shocked to see beings, of the same species with himself, set up for sale to the highest bidder, like horses or cattle; and even to those who have become accustomed to it, it is disagreeable."

Historically, the auction block has both real and symbolic importance. The lyrics from a slave melody, "No more auction block! No more, no more," capture both meanings. For slaves it meant a parting — often final — from relatives and friends. Unable to face such doubtful futures some ran off or mutilated or killed themselves. To curb such occurrences planters sometimes gave only a day's or even just a few hours' notice to bondsmen selected for selling and then guarded them closely or locked them up. One master, no doubt guilty of understatement, conceded that his "Negroes will probably be somewhat distressed at being sold." He therefore advised his son, "You must say what you can to reconcile them."

Slave traders held auctions, advertised well in advance, several times during each year in local towns and cities. A great throng of slaveholders or potential slaveholders attended each session, accompanied sometimes by their wives, who might be clad in stylish dresses. It was, at the larger slave auctions, a time of gala social functions running through the day into late evening. The traders sponsored most of these events and invited planters up to their hotel rooms for pre-auction drinks and casual conversation. There was much imbibing and not a little carousing. Gangs of youths roamed the streets shouting names at free blacks, perhaps indicating a desire to see them returned to bondage. All had a good time except members of the black community — slave and free.

Of course the bondsman's participation in the auction began much earlier than these social functions. His psychological preparation started at the moment his master told him that he was to be put on the market. Parents gathered children too young to understand their fate around them and told stories of going on a long trip and not seeing one another for a great while. It could easily be the infants and adolescents who were being put up for sale, for nearly "all traders dealt in those from 10 or 12 years of age and many advertised for those from 6, 7, 8, and 9." A Virginia agent wrote to a prospective buyer in 1850, "Boys and Girls are selling *best*." For this reason Harriet Tubman, the underground railroad heroine, recalled that while she was in bondage, "every time I saw a white man I was afraid of being carried away." The domestic trade, few would deny, was a basic reason for some bondsmen having only faint memories of their parents and of children growing up under the adoptive care of childless slaves and other foster parents. Frederick Douglass's well-known confession is emblematic: "I never saw my mother to know her as such, more than four or five times in my life. . . . I received the tidings of her death with much the same emotions I should have probably felt at the death of a stranger." . . .

To soothe those slaves intended for auction planters sometimes explained their reasons for selling them, hoping to win their confidence. Dr. James Marion Sims of Alabama wrote to his wife about an impending sale: "Let them understand that it is impossible for us to keep them . . . already are there mortgages on some of them and there is no telling when they may be foreclosed. . . . Let them know too that it lacerates our hearts as much as it does theirs to be compelled to the course we suggest." Masters also promised not to allow reputedly cruel planters to purchase aggrieved bondsmen. Was this merely deception? In many cases it undoubtedly was. Yet there was not always cause to view a master's promises suspiciously, for some tried to keep their word. . . .

The time finally came for slaves to travel to the auction. In preparation, masters plucked out some of the older slaves' gray hairs or painted them over with a blacking brush. This was an illegal practice, but nonetheless widely engaged in, and traders delighted in outsmarting one another and uncovering the hucksters' deceptions. Masters also had some slaves grease their bodies to make their muscles or a smiling face shine, but also to cover up recent or old marks of abuse. At the larger slave markets such as Richmond, Natchez, New Orleans, and Wilmington, North Carolina, bondsmen were placed in slave pens to await the arrival of auction day. The abolitionist James Redpath visited the one in Wilmington in the 1850's and reported it filled with slaves of both sexes. . . .

The sale began as the auctioneer's voice boomed out over the crowd's noise: "Now gentlemen, who bids for Tom? . . . His only fault is that he has a great idea of his own reserved rights, to the neglect of those of his master." Several slaves were on the platform. The auctioneer commented on each one's relative value and merits, "and when the hammer at length falls, protests, in the usual phrase, that poor Sambo has been absolutely thrown away."

An historian has written that many slaves were apparently unaffected by the auction experience "and were proud of the high prices that they brought." This would seem to be an oversimplification of how slaves actually felt. Many, though colorfully dressed, wore somber expressions on their faces. At the Charleston market Captain Basil Hall noted a puzzling air of indifference in the slaves' manner. And another observer, on a different occasion, remarked that "the poor victims did not seem to think hard of this matter, but regarded it as a matter of course." In reality, some slaves had simply resigned themselves to being sold, and saw little need for a display of emotion that might later bring them punishment.

But it seems that many slaves determined ahead of time to take an active part in the direction of the bargaining. They looked over the buyers, as the buyers did them, and selected several preferable ones. Often their decision hinged upon a knowledge of the planter's wealth and the living conditions and work load he would subject them to. They learned the needed information by keeping alert, quizzing other slaves, and sometimes confronting purchasers directly with rather blunt questions. Some were deliberately offensive to small planters, believing that slaves owned by them lacked social status and also life's necessities. The slave John Parker explained: "I made up my mind I was going to select my owner so when any one came to inspect me I did not like, I answered all questions with a 'yes' and made myself disagreeable. So far as I was concerned the game was on, and I began to play it." William Hayden claimed that because of his "utter indifference and apparent independence" to the events around him when he was on sale at an auction in Natchez, Mississippi, many prospective "purchasers were at a loss to know if, in reality, I were a slave, and subject to the hammer." Slaves not as well attuned as Parker or Hayden to fine points of bargaining were less subtle. They might even kick or spit on buyers they did not like, and, according to the traveler E. S. Abdy, even shouted, "You may buy me . . . but I will never work for you." Such threats turned many buyers away, but others were willing to accept the risk, confident in their ability to handle any bondsman.

Another method employed by slaves was simply to complain of imaginary ailments to every buyer except the desired one. Prospective purchasers often believed these stories because of those real instances of doctored-up slaves whose masters sought to dupe the unsuspecting buyer. Female slaves acted the coquette, offending planters and the sensibilities of accompanying wives. They bickered and nagged at masters, convincing many that they would be a disruptive force in any work gang. They also made threats not to bear any children while owned by an undesirable master, and even to put infants that might be born to death. Only planters somewhat unfamiliar with slave management took these warnings lightly. For most, there was always a faint memory of a time on one's plantation or on a neighbor's when a slave had carried out an unheeded threat. . . .

But before a buyer sealed his purchase of a slave, he usually wanted to examine him physically. He looked at his teeth, limbs, and back, felt and poked muscles. Often buyers touched female slaves in most familiar ways, and the auctioneer and members of the crowd told obscene jokes. An English observer at Richmond noted, "I beheld with my own eyes a man . . . go and examine a poor African girl . . . grasping her arms and placing his course [sic] hand on her bosom!" Many domestic slaves were unprepared emotionally for such examinations, and when they occurred many broke into tears, almost as if for the first time the full weight of their bondage pressed down upon them.

For more intimate examinations, a small yard was set aside. Slaves carried back there, according to the ex-slave Solomon Northup, were "stripped and inspected more minutely." Buyers looked for scars or signs of syphilitic ailments, for example, and examined the pelvic areas of females for purposes of speculation on their future as childbearers. The ordeal was especially difficult for husbands who were powerless to assist weeping wives. Yet bondsmen submitted reluctantly to such examinations if they provided the chance of being purchased by a preferred owner. Prospective buyers also compelled slaves to jump and dance as further proof that their limbs were operative. . . .

Because of the frequency of auction block scenes, the composition and stability of the slave family has been the subject of much confusion. Was the family in a state of constant disruption? And if this was commonly so, what impact did such disruption have upon the development of its members' identities and general mode of being?

The primacy of one's family relationships in shaping one's character is axiomatic among today's social theorists. Family members gain personal strength from being loved and trusted by one another, and the family unit serves as a shield against outside attacks and the feeling of emptiness that often comes from being alone. The principles are easy to understand, but the elusive nature of the slave family makes them difficult to apply. Even the concept "family" as it applies to slaves needs reconsideration. With regard to them we might view it as several overlapping concepts. Slavery made it essential that the slave family be a great deal more inclusive than its white counterpart. Its ranks included not only blood relatives but also "adopted" relatives. Few slaves seemed lacking in aunts or uncles, real or otherwise.

The odds against survival of the slave family intact were formidable. To begin with, marriage was not legally binding between slaves in any of the southern states. As late as 1855 there was a petition before the North Carolina Legislature requesting "that the parental relation . . . be acknowledged and protected by law; and that the separation of parents from their young children, say of twelve years and under, be strictly forbidden, under heavy pains and penalties." Though such memorials were frequent, legislators never heeded them, for their implementation would merely have served to increase the moral questions that bothered many slaveholders, as well as greatly restrict the domestic slave trade. In the main, masters dictated the rules governing slave unions. What they were not able to dictate, however, was the seriousness with which bondsmen took their vows. These a sizable majority stood by steadfastly. . . .

Once married, separations were usually not a matter of impulse on the slave's part. The domestic trade annulled an inestimable number of unions, but in the instance of voluntary separations some planters wanted to know the causes for the disunion and, in the case of James Henry Hammond of South Carolina, believed in disciplining the offenders. Slaves, nevertheless, have gained a reputation for licentiousness and immorality that is out of proportion, considering the circumstances under which they lived. There were, of course, slaves who had several wives or husbands. But ulterior motives of both slave and master often spawned these arrangements. One planter thus discouraged his slave Peter from marrying a woman on another plantation because of "temptations to get into the rascality or meanness." He perhaps suspected that such a marriage would lead to eventual disobedience by Peter should their judgments differ on when Peter might visit his proposed wife. And he probably feared Peter's performing some unauthorized errands. Yet other slaveholders sometimes reasoned that preventing a slave from taking a wife of his choice could lead to serious managerial problems with him. At any rate, slaves whose spouses died often remarried as soon as they could. The practice was not uncommon among planters and overseers as well. It was "very common among slaves themselves to talk of" marriage, wrote ex-slave William Wells Brown. What bothered him was that after marriage, "some masters, when they have sold the husband from the wife, compel her to take another" almost immediately, ignoring her personal feelings. . . .

Many past and present researchers have assumed that the slave family was a very loosely organized group whose primary cohesion was provided by women. The black sociologist E. Franklin Frazier capsulized this interpretation in his 1939 study when he characterized the slave mother "as the mistress of the cabin and as the head of the family." Frazier also mentioned that the mother had a "more fundamental interest in her children" and was able to develop "a spirit of independence and a keen sense of her personal rights." His canonization of slave women catapulted them to the forefront of modern discussions about the slave family. Was he correct in his conclusion about the matriarchal structure of the family? His picture seems somehow too inflexible, for the slave family developed in ways which Frazier seems not to have imagined.

Under some conditions — when slave children were infants — southern laws provided that masters could not divide slave families. What these laws sought primarily to prevent was the separation of child from mother; the father might still be sold. Indeed, when planters spoke of slave families they often referred to husbandless women and their children. The logic rings familiar even today, in that when a husband and wife legally separate the wife normally obtains custody of the children. We seldom assume, however, that the husband has been a passive agent in the family. Why then should we assume this to be so in the case of the slave, when there is no significant precedent for such an assumption in the slave's African past or in many of his American associations? Of course, this is not to deny that a slave father was a great deal more helpless than a free father today.

A variety of circumstances determined the position of the slave mother as well as the father. If women were the heads of the households, they rarely gained that dominant status among slaves at large. Women worked side by side with men at nearly every task on the plantation, but there were certain duties considered women's work that men declined to do. Some male slaves refused to do washing for this reason. Cooking was usually the task of women, as was sewing and some forms of child care. Sometimes masters punished males by forcing them to work with women labor gangs in the fields or compelling them to wash the family's clothes and attend to housecleaning. So great was their shame before their fellows that many ran off and suffered the lash on their backs rather than submit to the discipline. Men clearly viewed certain chores as women's tasks, and female slaves largely respected the distinction. . . .

The often peculiar marriage and dating relations of bondsmen have caused many scholars to doubt their morality. Females have borne the brunt of unfavorable conjectures. Scores of mulatto children fathered by masters have been used to support arguments that bondswomen were indiscriminate in their selection of male sex partners. Added to this was the fact that in the "southern states the prostitutes of the communities are usually slaves, unless they are imported from the free states."

Motherhood in bondage provided extremely difficult tests of a slave's energies and identity. The slave had to play the role of wife and mother under circumstances that marred her effectiveness at each. Her plantation duties eroded the time she had to spend with husband and children. Distractions were infinite. This was akin to the condition that some planters' wives found themselves in, trapped in a continuous cycle of chores.

Slavery struck most directly at bonds of affection joining husband and wife. The slave trade occasionally separated slaves married only a few weeks. We may suppose that some slaves were reluctant to love anyone deeply under these circumstances. Yet most spent several years with one owner and one husband or wife, and came to know their fellow bondsmen well. Thus when slaves married it was often the consequence of courtship extending over some time. The resultant marriage was steeped in emotional attachment. "Our affection for each other was strong," wrote a slave of his marriage, "and this made us always apprehensive of a cruel parting." The slave Sam, like so many others, ran away from his Virginia master because he thought "it a hard case to be separated from his wife."

Planters understood such affections. "You have a woman hired in the neighborhood whose husband we own," began a letter to Colonel Barksdale of Virginia. His "name is Israel, he is our Blacksmith, and he seems to be so much attached to her we [would] like very much for her to be hired near him . . . would you sell the woman?" A sound marriage meant a better worker for the planter and often a sense of purpose for the slave.

But slavery compelled an uneven husband-wife relationship. A master could physically discipline either while the other stood by helpless, at least for the moment. Slaveowners worked both hard, and they often had little time left to enjoy each other's company in the evening. The relationship nonetheless had many interesting potentials. "A slave possessing nothing . . . except a wife and children, has all his affections concentrated upon them," wrote Francis Fedric. Occasionally, the marriage partners focused so much attention on each other that the slightest change in the routine of one tended to disrupt the other's habits. Sickness is a good example. Wives and husbands often insisted that they nurse each other back to health, fighting bitterly against efforts to force them into the fields when the possibility of a loved one dying existed. Slaveholders severely punished many and accused them of merely trying to escape duties — but discipline was seldom an effective deterrent. A planter could, of course, make arrangements for such times; expecting that wives and husbands might be off work briefly or difficult to manage during days when important personal matters came up. Sometimes a sick husband would prolong his sickness by refusing to take medicine from any but the hands of his wife, whom he could also trust to find out if someone had "hexed" him. . . .

The arrival of children served in large measure to solidify the slave marriage. Yet some parents feared that slaveholders would mistreat offspring or sell them away. A few adults also refused to assume parental responsibilities. They married and had children, but declined or allowed others to take care of them, and were occasionally abusive parents. Still, most assumed parental ties eagerly and were, according to a Mississippi mistress, "all so proud of showing their children." While discussing the possible sale of a slave to an Annapolis slaveholder, Charles Ridgely wrote that she "is married in the neighborhood and has a family of young children, and would I think now be extremely unwilling to be separated from them."

In Africa "tribal customs and taboos tended to fix the mother's attitude toward her child before it was born," making children greatly appreciated,

and such tendencies were not absent in American slaves. Few women probably did not want children, though they were aware they might not be
able to devote the attention to them that would be required. The emotional outbursts of mothers following the deaths of infants, and their resistance to being parted from offspring, indicate that female slave attitudes
in this regard were not markedly distinct from those of mothers worldwide.

In fact, many disruptions of the workday stemmed from slave parents' requests to tend their children. Masters set aside a period during the day for
the nursing of babies, but there was also frequent disciplining of bondswomen when they failed to return to their duties on schedule. Yet mothers
repeatedly risked the lash in order to allow their body temperatures to cool
down enough for effective milk nourishment. Still, Moses Grandy observed
that overseers forced many to work in the field carrying full breasts of milk.
"They therefore could not keep up with the other hands," and when this
happened overseers whipped them "so that blood and milk flew mingled
from their breasts." It does not appear that he was merely trying to achieve
literary effect with this dramatic statement. But often mothers got their way,
for it was difficult for a master to justify, either to his conscience or his hands,
children found dead from want of care. The slave's human increase was also
an owner's most valuable form of property. On many plantations masters
periodically assigned one or two slaves to furnish the nursing needs of all
infants. They also hired slaves to nurse their own offspring. . . .

In bondage, the varieties of adult family behavior served as the most significant models after which slave children patterned their own actions. We
know that "where a variety of behavior or models is available, selection can
be influenced either by affection and rewards, by punishment, or by awareness
of what is appropriate." All these factors operated with peculiar force within
and upon the slave family. J. W. C. Pennington, the fugitive blacksmith, experienced what he called a "want of parental care and attention." By way
of explanation he added, "My parents were not able to give any attention to
their children during the day." While this was not unusual, many parents
did devote their evenings and weekends to family affairs — a first duty of
which was to teach children the limits placed on their conduct. This was no
simple task. . . .

For the young slave, family life was vastly important. His early years
somehow slipped past with the idea probably seldom if ever occurring to
him that he was but a piece of property. His main worries related to minor
chores assigned to him at about age five or six by parents and master; and
adult slaves at times bore much of the burden of these. Children also escaped
much of the stigma of racial inferiority that whites attached to the personalities of their mothers and fathers. Concerning his childhood one slave remi-
nisced, "let me say to you that my case were different from a great many of my
colore so I never knew what the yoke of oppression was in the early part of

my life." He was relatively carefree and innocent, he explained, until "the white boy . . . began to Raise his feathers and boast of the superiority which he had over me." . . .

It was not true that when black children learned to walk and then play with the master's children their "first lesson is to obey everything that has a white skin," as one bondsman claimed. Some masters' children learned this lesson the hard way when they tried to boss the little "niggers" about: "Every time they crossed me I jumped them," recalled one ex-slave about his white playmates.

Frequently the tendency among black and white children was towards a general equality. They played marbles together, and the slave children themselves spent many hours at this game: "My favorite game was marbles." They also played sheepmeat, a game of tag played with a ball of yarn that was thrown by one child at others running about the grounds. They enjoyed a great variety of childhood sports. Sir Charles Lyell, the English geologist, witnessed slave and white children playing, "evidently all associating on terms of equality." One slave narrator remembered too that he was very close to a son of his Virginia master: "I was his playmate and constant associate in childhood." He learned the alphabet and some of the elements of reading from him. "We were very fond of each other, and frequently slept together."

On large plantations communities of children were largely autonomous. Slave narratives relate that often one of the bondsman's earliest recollections of slavery was the sight of his mother or father being whipped or his brothers and sisters standing on the auction block. But this side of childhood can be overplayed. Fear did not perpetually pervade the environment. There are accounts of seeming childhood contentment which, though occasionally overdrawn by some interpreters, are to some measure accurate. The slaveholder did not constantly try to shape the character of slave children. There was little time for that. "The master, I think, does not often trouble himself with the government of these juvenile communities," observed a doctor from Kentucky. "He is not, therefore, an object of dread among them."

To a great extent, children learned to shape their behavior to the expectations of other slaves. A beginning lesson was to respect slave elders, particularly the aged. Tradition shaped this differential treatment. The child was, moreover, at the bottom of the hierarchy of both blacks and whites, while old slaves were in a manner the domestics of the slave quarters. Their functions were not unlike those of the slaves who ordered the master's children about and instructed them in etiquette. . . .

Some parents also saw initial work responsibilities, if properly performed, as an opportunity for their sons and daughters to escape the rigors of field labor. They encouraged their children to learn a trade if possible. A skill meant an opportunity to obtain preferred duties in later life. Masters wanted at least a few trained hands, chiefly as carpenters, for they increased the efficiency of the plantation as well as their own monetary value. John McDonogh of New Orleans hired a slave brickmason and later recommended him to a neighbor, suggesting that he might teach bricklaying to "two or three of your black boys" and "with two boys of 10 or 12 years of age to work with him in laying brick he will do all your buildings."

Occasionally, children's jobs required that they go through a prolonged or permanent separation from their families; but a determined parent was willing to accept this if it promised ultimately to provide an easier life for a son or daughter. The slave Julianna, age twelve, was the subject of a contract that engaged her services for six years. Her contractual master guaranteed "to teach her to sew, & bring her up to be a good seamstress, and a useful servant." The arrangement continued on a partially personal note: "In addition to the above I agree to allow the said girl Julianna to go to Shirley [Plantation] . . . once each year to see her relations, & remain with them one week each year."

Bondsman Henry Bibb was especially aware of the shortened childhood of the slave. "I was taken away from my mother," he wrote, "and hired out to labor for various persons, eight or ten years in succession." Other hired-out children were more fortunate than Bibb. Employed as families, as were "Great Jenny & her 3 youngest children," they partially escaped the emotional turmoil that accompanied separations. . . .

When the terms of bondage necessitated the division of families, parents often sought the aid of masters to reunite them. Lucinda, who served as a washwoman for a planter "nearly twelve years," asked him to hire her daughter Mary Jane from a nearby planter. "To oblige her," wrote her owner to Mary Jane's master, "I will become responsible for the amount, if you will let her have her daughter for the sum of Thirty dollars," which Lucinda was apparently willing to repay by her earnings during the remainder of the year. In another case, the slave George approached his master R. Carter about his daughter Betty — "7 years old, motherless, now at Colespoint-plantation —." In a letter to his overseer, Carter noted that "George wishes Betty live at Aires, with his Wife who lives there." As if not to appear overly accommodating to George's wishes, Carter continued, "If Betty is not useful where She now lives — I desire to indulge George . . . you will accordingly permit him to take his daughter." At other times, slaves acted on their own to reunite themselves with loved ones. One runaway was persistent in this way: "She has a husband, I think, at his [a neighbor's] house & tho' taken up by him the first time came straight back to his house."

When a master abused or humiliated one member of a family, the rebuff reverberated throughout the slave household and beyond. An example appears in the opening pages of the fugitive blacksmith's narrative. Following the whipping of his father, J. W. C. Pennington remembered, "an open rupture" developed in his family [against their master]. Each member felt deeply offended by the deed, for they had always believed their conduct and faithfulness was exemplary. They talked of their humiliation in the "nightly gatherings, and showed it in . . . daily melancholy aspect."

Planters' ill-handling of slaves was only one of many factors that brought out family consciousness. Bondsmen's misdeeds against other bondsmen sometimes marked families for harassment and shame. A serious offense, such as stealing another's hunting catches, might lead to brief periods of social isolation, with members of the offending family finding themselves excluded from slave gatherings or nightly ramblings. Bondsmen saw themselves as having their primary identification with a distinct family unit to which they had responsibility and which had responsibility to them.

However, the slave family was a unit with extensions. Quite frequently it seems to have consisted of more than just parents and their natural children. It could include a number of blood or adopted relations — uncles, aunts, and cousins — who lived on the same plantation or on nearby estates. Adults "claimed" parentless children, and the slave community seldom neglected old slaves. Local bondsmen usually absorbed new arrivals on a plantation into a family setting and expected them to make a full contribution immediately. But can such a group really be called a family? Slaves considered it as such and treated adopted relatives with real affection.

The extended slave family frequently arose to augment or replace the regular family unit split up by slavery's misfortunes. There were deaths resulting from disease, accidents, and natural causes that left wives husbandless and children without parents. Then there were the family breakups caused by the slave trade. In an important, though not typical, exception, however, Robert Carter of Virginia agreed to sell his slaves to the Baltimore Company only "if the Company will purchase men their wives & children [ten families]." . . .

In slave families wives seldom possessed greater financial stability than husbands, a circumstance that often gives rise to psychological problems in men of minority households in our day. Both worked at tasks that the slave culture did not stigmatize as menial, so there was no need for the male to feel a lack of importance in his family on that score. The power of masters to disrupt families at any time weakened male slaves' sense of responsibility and dignity, but they did not invariably see this as a slight to their manhood. Yet for the slave who experienced the breakup of his household there remained that indelible hurt, as perhaps exemplified by Charles Ball's father, who "never recovered from the effects of the shock" of losing a portion of his family and became "gloomy and morose." Whenever the slave family — natural or extended — was intact, however, and slave males were reliably performing their duties, they most likely did symbolize authority within the family structure.

Except for sales of its members, much of the time slaveholders left the slave family to its own devices. And though the slave trade drove blood rela-tives apart, bondsmen's common persecution brought many of them back together in extended family groupings which provided for many of the emo-tional needs whose satisfaction the regular family, had it remained un-touched, might have rendered less vexatious. Under these conditions the personalities of bondsmen were certain to gain much strength.

STUDY GUIDE

1. How would the following factors affect a slave's price on the auction block: age, sex, health, and attitude? What techniques were used by sellers to try to make a slave appear more valuable?

2. Summarize Owens's view of the role and attitudes of male and female parents in the black family under slavery. What kind of evidence does he use to argue that slaves made clear distinctions in the roles of men and women, though both did the same kind of field labor?

3. What generalizations can be made about the attitudes of masters toward selling slaves, toward slave marriages, and toward breaking up families?

4. Many European and American white families were "nuclear" — consisting only of parents and children without grandparents or uncles and aunts living in the same household. Owens suggests that the black family was more "extended," with considerable respect for age and the care of parent-less children by others. Why would you expect such features to have de-veloped in southern slavery?

5. What factors in modern society have somewhat modified the differences among families with varied backgrounds? Think, for example, of a southern rural and a northern urban black family; a second-generation Slavic fam-ily; a Chinese-American family; an Italian Catholic family. Compare the differences you see today in such groups with those that existed several decades ago.

BIBLIOGRAPHY

The book by Leslie H. Owens from which the preceding selection is taken is a fine study of life and culture under slavery. While it reveals much about slave conditions and the slaves' reactions to their enslavement, there are many other studies of slavery in the period just before the American Civil War. An older southern historian, who had a patronizing view of the Negro and a rather rosy view of slavery, was Ulrich B. Phillips. Despite the limitations of his work, he was one of the first scholars to study slavery as a total system, rather than as only an economic or a racial system. The most important of his works are *American Negro Slavery* (1918) and *Life and Labor in the Old South* (1929). The most interesting works of a general nature written since Phillips' books are Kenneth Stampp, *The Peculiar Institution: Slavery in the Ante-Bellum South* (1956) and John W. Blassingame, *The Slave Community: Plantation Life in the Ante-Bellum South* (1972). Virtually every major conclusion of earlier historians on the social and economic aspects of American slavery has been challenged in the highly controversial study by Robert William Fogel and Stanley L. Engerman, *Time on the Cross*, 2 vols. (1974).

An issue of great interest is the influence of slavery upon the personality of American blacks and their reactions to slavery. In his work *Slavery: A Problem in American Institutional and Intellectual Life*, 3rd ed. (1976), Stanley M. Elkins compares the American slavery system with the Nazi concentration camp. Elkins believes that the slaves identified with their oppressors, and he empasizes the "Sambo" personality of the American black in studying the effects of slavery upon the black's psychology. Other scholars have argued that the Sambo role was merely a survival technique in a white world, and Mullin and Blassingame suggest that there were different personality types.

Equally interesting is the question of the influence of slavery upon the black family. A number of writers, including Daniel Patrick Moynihan in a very controversial book, have suggested that the black family was characterized by strong mothers, irresponsible fathers, sexual promiscuity, and a general lack of stability. In an important book entitled *The Black Family in Slavery and Freedom, 1750–1925* (1975), Herbert Gutman disputed such conclusions, argued that there was a strong sense of family and kin among blacks, and provided the best study to date of the black family over an extended period. On this and other subjects, one can get the slave's own perspective from the collection of reminiscences of ex-slaves edited by Benjamin A. Botkin, *Lay My Burden Down: A Folk History of Slavery* (1945). Eugene Genovese, who previously had written about southern slaveholders, used such reminiscences as well as other sources to get at the daily life of southern slaves in *Roll, Jordan, Roll: The World the Slaves Made* (1974). Frank Owsley, *Plain Folk of the Old South* (1949) gives a fair picture of the life of poor whites, but the studies of slave life are generally better. Richard C. Wade, *Slavery in the Cities: The South, 1820–1860* (1964) is a study of the sizable number of slaves who do not fit the plantation stereotype. John Hope Franklin, *From Slavery to Freedom: A History of American Negroes*, 3rd ed. (1967) is a general history of black Americans.

*An immigrant transfer barge docked at Castle Garden
offers transportation to the Erie Railroad, 1874.*

15

CARL WITTKE

Nation of Immigrants

The extraordinary flow of people from Europe, Asia, and Africa to the New World for more than three centuries constitutes the largest human migration ever experienced on this planet. All of us here are descendants of immigrants — of Indians who crossed the Bering land bridge from Asia, of early black and white migrants who settled the British colonies, of German, French, Italian, Russian, Hungarian, Chinese, or other immigrant ancestors who poured into the United States in the nineteenth century. By 1930 the tide had waned, but by then the country's history could not be understood without taking into account the impact upon American civilization of the many races and nationalities that had immigrated to the United States.

The most obvious question involved in the study of immigration history is why particular groups left their homelands to come to a strange country. As Carl Wittke indicates in the following selection, there were some factors common to most groups of Europeans, but in each country there were special influences that promoted emigration at a particular time. A second question is why certain nationalities settled in the areas they did and tended to enter particular trades and occupations. Some remained largely in eastern cities as unskilled manual laborers, while others went on to Minnesota or Wisconsin to enter farming. One of the striking characteristics of early nineteenth-century population movements was the extensive immigration to the North and the very small number of immigrants who were attracted to the southern states. This pattern was determined by a number of factors, including the greater industrialization taking place in the North, the slave labor system of the Old South, and the different social attitudes in the two regions.

Many immigrant groups, even in the colonial period, faced substantial hardship and considerable animosity in establishing their roots in this land. In many ways, the difficulties increased during the nineteenth century, and even English-speaking groups such as the Irish found that adapting to the new culture posed serious problems. Most nationalities developed one or another sort of agency to assist them in preserving their heritage while adjusting to their new society; churches, schools, recreational associations, and other institutions served such purposes. Wittke describes the special problems faced by one such group, the Irish, a group that one might expect to have had fewer difficulties than some others.

Attitudes of immigrants toward their heritage have varied, as have attitudes of older Americans toward immigration policy and assimilation of new nationalities. For many years, much of our thought was dominated by the "melting pot" metaphor, which implied that the distinctive characteristics of each group should disappear into a new American nationality. In our time, there has been a resurgent interest in preserving the cultural heritage of various nationalities, and a suggestion that the melting pot theory should be replaced by a cultural pluralism that recognizes the integrity and contribution of different ethnic groups.

In the nineteenth century, and with increasing volume after 1830, the tide of emigration set in again from Europe. Wave after wave rolled over the cities and prairies of the New America. The Irish, the Germans, and the Scandinavians, in more or less sharply defined but overlapping streams, poured into the United States; and these major groups, together with several minor ones, constitute the "old emigration" from western and northern Europe, in contradistinction to the newer groups that came in the last quarter of the century from the south and east. Each deserves detailed treatment. In each case, specific causes, . . . operated to start the emigrant tide on its way across the Atlantic and to keep it flowing steadily for decades. Aside from the universal desire for adventure and greater opportunity, there were certain causes for emigration common to all these groups; and

Reprinted by permission from *We Who Built America* by Carl Wittke. Copyright 1964, 1967 by The Press of Case Western Reserve University.

it must be remembered that much of the European emigration was arti-
ficially stimulated and encouraged by interests in America desirous, for
one reason or another, of bringing in a larger population.

First of all, . . . the earlier population movements were influenced by the
"America letters," "the literature of the unlettered" written home by those
who had ventured out first and whose accounts of the New Canaan were
eagerly awaited and devoured by those who had remained behind. Christopher Saur's "America letters" praising "the goodness .I have heard and
seen" were printed and reprinted many times in Germany during the latter
half of the eighteenth century, in order to induce people to come to
Pennsylvania. What the United States after 1776 symbolized to the liberty-
loving, thwarted, and exploited Irishman can readily be imagined, especially
when the glowing accounts that reached the Irish countryside assured
the readers that "there is a great many ill conveniences here, but no empty
bellies." In 1818, an enthusiastic reporter described the region around
Wheeling in extravagant terms that must have been irresistible. He wrote:

> I believe I saw more peaches and apples rotting on the ground than would
> sink the British fleet. I was at many plantations in Ohio where they no more
> knew the number of their hogs than myself . . . . The poorest family has a
> cow or two and some sheep . . . good rye whiskey; apple and peach brandy,
> at 40 cents a gallon . . . . The poorest families adorn the table three times
> a day like a wedding dinner—tea, coffee, beef, fowls, pies, eggs, pickles, good
> bread; and their favorite beverage is whiskey or peach brandy. Say, is it so in
> England? . . .

. . . "There are no large estates," wrote one Swedish-American, "whose
owners can take the last sheaf from their dependents and then turn them
out to beg." Ministers and churches were said to be less worldly in America,
and "there is ceaseless striving to spread the healing salvation of the
Gospel." Hired men and maids ate at the same table with their employers
and wore clothes of the same style. "Neither is my cap worn out," added
another, "from lifting it in the presence of gentlemen." Small wonder
that enthusiastic newcomers wrote: "We see things here that we could
never describe, and you would never believe them if we did. I would not
go back to Sweden if the whole country were presented to me." "It is no
disgrace to work here," wrote a Swede in 1841. "Both the gentleman and
the day laborer work. No epithets of degradation are applied to men of
humble toil . . . . I do not agree . . . that in order to appreciate the blessings
of monarchy, one must live in a democracy." . . .

Ship companies and organizations interested in land speculation did
their part to keep the America fever burning at the proper temperature.
Advertisements in American newspapers reveal a veritable flock of emigration agents; immigrant bankers dealing in remittances, steamship, and railroad tickets; and dealers in foreign exchange, each of whom had his special

reasons for keeping the immigrant tide flowing in a steady, unbroken stream to the United States. Land agencies, with acreage for sale in Texas, Missouri, Wisconsin, and other parts of the West, advertised their bargains in newspapers published at the Eastern ports of arrival. . . .

In the middle of the last century, the Middle West needed population above everything else. To attract desirable immigrants was the overpowering ambition of practically every new state in this region. State after state began to enact legislation to encourage and stimulate migration to its borders. The attractions offered by favorable legislation and the persuasiveness of the agents of state immigration commissions were important factors in directing the immigrant tide into the Mississippi Valley.

By its constitution of 1850, Michigan gave the franchise to all newcomers who had declared their intention to become naturalized and who had resided in the state for two and a half years. Its immigration agency, established in 1848 and not abolished until 1885, issued attractive pamphlets in German, and its first immigration commissioner was instructed to spend half his time in New York and half in Stuttgart, Germany. Wisconsin had a special commissioner as early as 1851, and its board of immigration, created by legislative act in 1867, published pamphlets in seven different languages. From 1871 to 1875, 35,000 copies were printed for distribution in Europe. Other material was distributed in New York, in taverns and at the docks; and advertisements lauding Wisconsin's attractions were published in eight foreign newspapers, such as the London *Times*, the Tipperary *Free Press*, the *Baseler Zeitung*, and the *Leipziger Allgemeine Zeitung*. In 1880, Wisconsin issued 10,000 pocket maps of that state, with legends in English, Norwegian, and German. The Wisconsin Constitutional Convention of 1846 gave the franchise to immigrants after a declaration of their intention to become naturalized and one year's residence in the state. . . .

From 1860 to 1862, Iowa had a state commissioner of immigration, the German-born lieutenant governor, Nicholas J. Rusch, who maintained offices at 10 Battery Place, New York City. Later, an immigration board, similar to those in other states, was created. A handbook, *Iowa: The Home for Immigrants*, was prepared in English, German, Dutch, Danish, and Swedish; and agents were sent to Holland, England, and Germany to make propaganda for the state.

Steamship and railway companies [also] had a special interest in stimulating the immigrant traffic, for obvious reasons, but the latter had an additional objective in promoting the disposal of their railroad lands to actual settlers. In 1870, Jay Cooke, as the financial promoter of the Northern Pacific Railroad, employed Hans Mattson, who resigned his position as secretary of state of Minnesota to undertake the assignment, to go to Sweden to advertise the resources of the road and to draw up a plan for the disposal of its lands. J. J. Hill may have saved his road from financial disaster by promoting the settlement of Minnesota by Norwegian and

Swedish farmers, whose bumper crops quickly tripled the earnings of the railroad. Hill, in order to make the Red River Valley district more attractive to settlers, described it as an area "where the depth of the humus was equal to the height of a man." The Northern Pacific at St. Paul gave special passes to ministers of the Gospel, so that they might more frequently visit outlying immigrant settlements where no church had as yet been organized. When a trainload of Dunkards moved from Indiana to North Dakota, they went by special train, with streamers on the railroad cars advertising "the bread basket of America." The Atchison, Topeka, and Santa Fe Railroad, through its foreign immigration department, extended its activities to the Ural Mountains, bringing over 15,000 Russian-German Mennonites to Kansas. By 1883, they had settled along the route of the railroad in Kansas, with branch settlements in Oklahoma and Colorado. The Burlingame and Missouri Railroad also was active in attracting Mennonite settlers to the American West.

The sea voyage safely passed, the immigrant was likely to run afoul of the beasts of prey in human form who waited to pounce upon him on his arrival in New York, to exploit his ignorance of the English language, and his "greenness" about American conditions generally. New York was infested with "runners," who were paid by trucking firms, railroad ticket offices, and immigrant hotels and boarding houses for no other purpose than to compete with other runners and lead the unsuspecting immigrant into the clutches of the hotelkeeper or baggage agent. Runners were paid from $10 to $30 a week, or a certain percentage of the business they secured. Competition became extremely keen and, on many occasions, violent; for, in order to hold his job, a runner had to be a good "shoulder hitter" as well as a persuasive talker.

When a ship arrived, runners rushed to the gangplank and began fighting with other bullies over the immigrant's luggage, in order to get him to stop at a particular boarding house. These immigrant hotels and boarding houses were generally operated, not by native Americans, but by foreigners who congregated like vultures in the seaport towns to prey upon their own countrymen. In the worst of these houses, the immigrant was overcharged for everything, particularly for the storage of his baggage, which was then held as security until all bills had been paid. Occasionally, but not often, an immigrant runner's license was revoked for fraud. Usually, the law was indifferent to the plight of the stranger in a strange land. Occasionally, too, charges were lodged against runners and steamship, baggage, or railroad agents who had cheated unsuspecting immigrants out of hundreds of dollars or had collected sums of money as commissions for securing jobs that never materialized. The newspapers usually recorded that the culprit had "left for parts unknown," and that ended the case. An article in *The New York Times* for June 23, 1853, accurately described the arrival of an emigrant ship as follows:

Every one in the great City, who can make a living from the freshly arrived immigrants, is here. Runners, sharpers, pedlars, agents of boarding-houses, of forwarding offices, and worst of all, of the houses where many a simple emigrant girl, far from friends and home, comes to a sad end . . . .

Some immigrants hung around the German boarding houses in Greenwich Street, each day losing more of their savings. Others, Irish and Germans, settled down in the Eleventh Ward, to become peddlers and ragpickers and to succumb to the vice of intemperance. . . .

The ordinary prices by steamer and canal from New York to Albany and thence inland were reasonable enough, and the railroads tried to stop the selling of bogus tickets by swindlers in New York, but forwarding houses were hard to regulate and generally charged the immigrants higher rates, on one pretext or another, in order to divide the profits with their agents and runners. In the 1840's, the "official" table of prices was as follows:

New York to Albany	$ .75
New York to Buffalo	4.50
New York to Cleveland	7.00
New York to Detroit	8.00
New York to Milwaukee	14.50
New York to Chicago	14.50

Baggage up to 50 pounds was supposed to be transported free. Children under twelve paid half fare; those under two were carried free. A Norwegian immigrant, in 1847, was able to go from New York to Albany, up the Hudson, for $.50. To go by rail from Albany to Buffalo cost $12, but by way of the Erie Canal the rate was only $7.50, including meals, with a special price of $2 if immigrants brought their own food.

There apparently was little uniformity in the charges made. In 1844, a Norwegian immigrant went by steamer from New York to Albany, on a boat 290 feet long and with cabins on three decks, for $1.50. Nine hours were required to make the trip. The next year, a traveller who went by train from New York to Buffalo, in "wonderful closed wagons with windows," paid $3.50. The journey took several days, because in the dark nights "we stood still." To go from Albany to Buffalo in 1847 by canal boat required a day longer than by train, and the fare was $7.50, including meals. Some canal boats took longer to make the trip, furnished no food, and charged only two dollars.

Immigrant travel over this route, across New York and then into the West by way of the Great Lakes, was heavy. Immigrant trains were not distinguished for their accommodations and comforts. Often the cars marked "Immigrant Cars" were springless boxcars, with hard benches and no drinking water, and the immigrant passenger was expected to bring or buy his own food. Sometimes the coaches had absolutely no conveniences, not even seats, except for long boards running lengthwise along both sides of the cars, so that many had to sit or lie on the floor. Newspapers recorded the passage of long immigrant trains through Albany and Buffalo, trains with extra locomotives and long lines of cars, filled with Germans, Dutch, Swiss, or Scandinavians. In Chicago and other terminal points, runners for land companies, railroads, and state immigration commissioners met the incoming trains. In 1853, a resident of Chicago wrote: "One fourth of the persons you meet in Chicago cannot speak a word of English, and a good part of the remainder cannot speak it well. Germans, Irish and Norwegians seem to be as plenty as natives." The immigrants were so numerous in Milwaukee in 1842 that they were forced to lodge in the streets, while in Racine and Southport all tavern facilities were exhausted. In the 1850's, emigrant trains passed over the New York and Erie road at regular intervals, attracting much attention with their car windows trimmed with green vegetation and their passengers smoking long German pipes and singing German songs. . . .

The figures for the period of the Irish famine immigration mounted to startling totals: 92,484 in 1846, 196,224 in 1847, 173,744 in 1848, 204,771 in 1849, and 206,041 in 1850. The Census of 1850 reported 961,719 Irish in the United States; by 1860, the total had reached 1,611,304. These were to be found in greatest numbers in New York, Pennsylvania, Massachusetts, Illinois, Ohio, and New Jersey. The character of Irish immigration changed under the pressure of intolerable suffering and famine. The poor, small farmer, who had constituted the bulk of the migration up to 1835, who knew English, had sufficient energy to be proud of his independence, and was determined to rise, gave way to a new type — namely, the laborer, with little background aside from his potato patch, who was ignorant of the English language, and who was of a mercurial temperament, and likely to find life and progress in the United States very difficult.

Early in 1847, the roads to Irish ports were literally thronged with immigrant families. Sometimes strong men actually battled with each other at the ports of embarkation to secure passage on ships entirely inadequate to provide transportation for all who wished to go to America. The description of the ravages of the Irish famine tax the reader's imagination. Children and women were described as too weak to stand; the livestock had perished, people were eating carrion, and "the weekly returns of the dead were like the bulletin of a fierce campaign." Beggars crowded the roads and the city streets. People huddled half-naked in fireless and foodless hovels. Thousands crossed to Liverpool and demanded transportation to the United States on crowded and filthy emigrant ships whose resources were taxed to the utmost. . . .

The Irish temperament is noted for buoyancy, and hope sustained the voyagers across the Atlantic, but for many it vanished like the rainbow when the actual conditions of life in America had to be faced. Almost all Irish immigrants had to begin in the United States as unskilled laborers, and many got no farther. Year after year, the Irish Emigrant Society of New York advised immigrants to shun the cities of the Atlantic seaboard and to scatter throughout the United States, particularly into the West. "Thousands continually land entirely penniless and are at once in a state of destitution," the warning continued, "whereas such person should have at least five pounds on his arrival to enable him to prosecute his journey to the interior." The advice was sound, but thousands found it impossible to follow, for all their earthly possessions had been used up during the voyage. They arrived in the New Canaan with their pockets empty. The almshouses and hospitals were filled to overflowing, and beggars wandered aimlessly through the streets. Men and women accustomed to no other existence than eking out a living from the soil were suddenly left stranded in congested cities. They had no trade and no particular skills; some did not even know the language. They were destined to become the unskilled, marginal workers of the America of the middle nineteenth century, with all that that implies. Many lurid accounts of Irish "shanty towns" are available to the historian of the Irish immigration. Some are descriptions obviously colored by a deep hatred for the newcomer, but there is enough in the comments of friendly critics to indicate that conditions were deplorable, to say the least. Indeed, one who is familiar only with the Irish-Americans of the twentieth century may find it hard to credit the tales told about their ancestors of several generations ago.

The Irish, as a class, came to America with less means than many other immigrant groups. The majority were poverty-stricken. Having no money to proceed westward on their own account, they usually got out of the cities only when contractors for internal improvement projects recruited them in the labor markets of the East and transported them to the West and South. On their arrival in the port towns and larger cities, the Irish crowded the tenements, sometimes twenty or more families living in one house. These Irish tenements were hardly more than "human rookeries." What a difference it might have made, and what an excellent investment it might have turned out to be, had the government used its funds to transport the Irish into the West and helped them to become established as farmers on the public lands! There are many unnamed graves of Irishmen along the canal and railroad routes which they helped to build. In South Boston in 1850, the Irish slums were buildings from three to six stories high, with whole families living in one room, without light or ventilation, and even the cellars crowded with families. Saloons were the curse of the neighborhood, and police records abundantly reflected this unhealthy condition. The death rate among the children of the Irish poor was alarmingly high. Disease, particularly during cholera epidemics, always ravaged the immigrants living in hovels in the western and eastern sections of New York City worse than in other communities. Secret societies arose in the Irish shantytowns among Irish laborers with such names as "the Corkonians," "the Connaughtmen," and "the Far Downs," who engaged in bloody brawls and riots, which even the repeated denunciations of the Church authorities seemed powerless to stop. In some of the "better-class" tenement houses in New York, Negroes were preferred as tenants to the poor Irish and Germans. . . .

The Irish laborer in the middle nineteenth century frequently found himself in difficulties because of shameless exploitation and bad working conditions and because of the resentment harbored against him by native Americans who feared his competition, although apparently few Americans had any wish to do the heavy, dirty, unskilled labor that fell to the lot of the Irishman with his pick and shovel. Newspapers friendly to the Irish immigrant warned him to stay away from the canal and railroad construction projects, for "these railroads have been the ruin of thousands of our poor people" and their workers are treated "like slaves" by railroad contractors. Wages were low, usually $1 a day but often less; they were not clearly fixed and were paid partly in whiskey and "store pay," or merchandise, sold at high prices. Friends of the Irish urged them to form protective associations, with objectives somewhat like the trade unions, in order to stop competition, rivalries, and fights between warring gangs which drove wages down in their competition for the available jobs. Above all, the Irish were advised to go to the country to work on farms or squat upon government land in the West, to "do anything, in fact, in preference to railroading."

Irish longshoremen were employed at the docks in all the leading sea and lake ports. They bitterly resented the invasion of Negroes, who were often brought in expressly to depress the wage scale. Riots between Irish and Negro dock workers were not infrequent. It is this economic competition that helps to explain the strong hostility of the Irish toward the abolitionist movement and the New York draft riots during the Civil War. Workers on the Chesapeake Railroad and Ohio Canal were known as the Longfords and Corkonians. On some of the Ohio canals, Irish and German pick-and-shovel workers received only $.30 a day, with board, lodging, and a "jigger-full" of whiskey. Everywhere the Irish were doing the hard work, even in the South, where they were so badly treated at one time that Bishop England found it necessary to publish a warning in Irish newspapers advising Irish workers to avoid the South. Accidents, deaths, and injuries were numerous in road building and canal digging, and cave-ins occurred frequently in excavations for tunnels. Little tumble-down markers in tiny Catholic burying grounds along the route of these internal improvements still bear mute testimony to the hazards of pick-and-shovel work.

In the 1840's and 1850's, little "Dublins" sprang up in the factory towns of New England and in the Middle Atlantic states, for the Irish were invading the mill centers. The Irish population of Boston trebled in a decade. Often the mill population was the residue from the labor supply that had dug the canals or constructed the mill race. In Rhode Island, for example, the first Irish millworkers were recruited from those who had built the railroad between Providence and Boston, and the Woonsocket Irish Catholic settlement was due entirely to the construction of the Blackstone Canal. Irishmen went into the mill towns of Pawtucket and the "coal pits" between Fall River and Newport. At first, the competition of Irish labor was resented by other workers. Towns tried to restrict the sale of lots so as to keep out Catholic purchasers, and the sign "No Irish Need Apply" was posted in some of the factories. The children of the Irish were twitted and abused on the playground and in the school-yards much as some Irish children later joined in making life uncomfortable for "dagos," "wops," and "kikes." But the economic urge was irresistible; and the Irish captured the mill towns, only to be in turn dispossessed in a later generation by Poles, Italians, French-Canadians, and Greeks, the products of the "new" immigration.

Irish workers had a bad reputation for rioting and brawling, and the newspapers of the middle of the last century are full of graphic accounts of their bloody battles. In 1853, for example, the eviction of an Irishman from a circus performance at Somerset, Ohio, for smoking a pipe, started a battle in which Irish railroad workers fought all night and into the next day. A company of militia had to be called from Zanesville to restore order. Feuds between groups of Irishmen hailing from different counties in Ireland led to frequent riots. On one occasion, in Indiana, 400 militia had to be called out to stop an impending assault by several hundred belligerent Irishmen from County Cork. A riot that broke out along the line of a projected Pacific railroad, in 1853, over the election of a foreman of a labor gang, would have had serious consequences but for the timely intervention of a Roman Catholic priest, who served as peace-maker.

After reading the many accounts of brawling and fighting among Irish workingmen that appear in the American newspapers, one becomes aware of the fact that not all the trouble was due to the Irishman's belligerent temperament, his love of the bottle, or his belief that contentiousness is the spice of life. Much of this rioting was the result of intolerable labor conditions. The brawls were often efforts, however misguided and unwise, to achieve an improvement in labor standards at a time when the labor movement had hardly begun. There were strikes for higher wages on internal improvement projects, many of which led to a display of force, particularly when contractors refused later to respect the agreements they had been forced to accept. In 1840, a serious riot broke out when the wages of Irish laborers on an aqueduct in New York City were cut from $1 to $.75 a day. There were similar disturbances, caused by wage reductions, on the Illinois Central, the Buffalo and State Railroad, the Steubenville and Indiana, and other lines.

The reign of terror instituted by the "Molly Maguires" in the anthracite coal regions of Pennsylvania is well known to students of American history and is usually described as one of the worst examples of mob rule and blackmail in the whole history of labor relations, for which Irish coal miners are held primarily responsible. Viewed from a longer perspective, the incident is but another illustration of the battle for better working conditions in the coal-producing areas, although the movement fell under the control of criminals and ended in a number of executions. The anthracite coal regions of Pennsylvania had a mushroom growth in the 1830's, with immigrant labor, poor housing facilities, and all the evils of company towns and company stores as natural concomitants of this rapid expansion. The region suffered from the evils of overdevelopment and frequent business slumps, which weighed especially heavily upon the Irish coal miners. Working conditions in the mines were terrible, with no safety requirements, inspection, or proper ventilation. From 1839 to 1848, wages were $1 or $1.25 a day for miners and $.82 for ordinary laborers. In 1869, a peak of $18.20 a week was reached, but by 1877 the wage had declined again to $9.80. "Breaker boys," aged 7 to 16, worked like slaves in the mines under mine bosses whose character left much to be desired. An editorial in *The Boston Pilot* exposed conditions in the coal mines — the inadequate pay, the "murderous neglect" of ventilation, the "rancid provisions" available at high prices in company stores, the explosions in the firedamp caverns in which Irish and Welsh miners were blown to pieces, and the "scandalous ungenerosity" subsequently shown by the operators toward their mutilated workmen — and concluded by denouncing some of the owners as men with "the conscience neither of Christian nor of Pagan."

Irish benevolent societies were formed to deal with some of these problems. The Ancient Order of Hibernians, a semisecret organization, became the backbone of the miners' unions. In a very long story of real class war, the responsibility for violence in the Pennsylvania coal fields seems to be pretty well divided. By 1860, the Molly Maguires terrorized the whole anthracite region, elected sheriffs and constables, and resorted to arson, blackmail, and murder. The organization was not finally broken up until 1875, when, because of the detective work of James McParlan, 19 were hanged after trials held in an atmosphere of great excitement and prejudice. The incident for a long time blackened the record of Irish-Americans, and many refused to see the industrial conditions which had provoked such criminal action. . . .

The United States has been known and ridiculed as a nation of "joiners." One reason may be the large immigrant element, which has had its special incentives in a new land to form benevolent, patriotic, and social organizations to keep alive the memories of a common origin. The Irish were no exception, and Irish societies of many kinds — such as the Hibernians, athletic clubs, and sodalities — exist in large numbers, generally closely connected with the Church and the Catholic hierarchy. . . .

For many years, fire fighting in the United States was in the hands of volunteer companies. The opportunity to become a "fire laddy" was irresistible for many Irishmen. These companies performed superhuman feats of strength and heroism. Each firehouse, especially in large cities like New York, also attracted a group that ran along to every fire, so that "running with the machine" eventually degenerated into a sport which attracted the hoodlums and gangs of the Bowery districts. The volunteer firemen of the 1840's and later decades appeared in brilliant uniforms and ponderous equipment of the comic opera variety. Much feasting and drinking seemed to be part of the routine of these organizations, and until the temperance movement made its inroads upon the profession, companies frequently had a steward, whose business it was to ladle out liquor to exhausted firemen from a barrel hauled along with the engine to each fire. . . .

How the Irish established themselves on the police force of the larger American cities needs no discussion. A study of the New York force in 1933 revealed that, out of a total of approximately 20,000 policemen, 2,309 were themselves foreign-born and 11,014 were of foreign-born parentage, representing 42 countries in all. Ireland led the list of foreign-born policemen with 1,533, and also the list of those of foreign-born parentage with 5,671.

Nearly all that has been said hitherto has concerned the Irish immigrant as a city dweller. It has been shown that most Irishmen began as unskilled laborers, working in construction gangs on the docks, in livery stables, in the streets, or, with the rise of industrial towns like Lowell and Paterson, in the mills — wherever brawn and not skill was the chief requirement. Many ended their days as unskilled workers in the cities and towns. But although it is true that the Irish immigrant is primarily a phenomenon of urban civilization in the United States, some did go into agriculture. Students of immigration have speculated on the reasons why a predominantly rural people should have shunned the land in their new home. Poverty, of course, made it impossible for large numbers to leave the port towns in which the immigrant ships happened to land them. Ignorance of improved American methods of farming was another reason, along with memories of bitter experiences on the land in Ireland. Irish gregariousness and the incentive of cash wages in the city were other factors. In some cases, the demoralizing effects of the saloon and political clubs in the cities operated to keep Irishmen from moving West. . . .

The importance of the Irish in the history of the Roman Catholic Church in the United States and the role of the Church in the life of Irish-

Americans are so generally recognized that the statement that the Catholic Church in America became essentially an immigrant church in the 1840's, and continued for decades to receive its strongest additions from abroad, will hardly be challenged by anyone familiar with the facts. There were Roman Catholics in America at the time of the Revolution, but they were under special disabilities in a number of the American colonies. The first great accession of Roman Catholics came from the purchase of Louisiana, which brought into the American Church about 100,000 communicants. Others came in with the annexations following the Mexican War, but none of these additions can be remotely compared in importance with the great flood of Irish who came across the Atlantic in the 1840's and later decades.

To the poor Irish immigrant, his Church was a part of home. It had always brought him consolation in time of trouble. In a new land it gave him a measure of dignity at a time when he was often made to feel that he was of a lower breed of humanity. It became the role of the Catholic Church to make law-abiding citizens from the hordes of newcomers, to provide parochial schools for the nurture of their religion, to dispense charity in many forms and to provide the counsel of priests for the crises an immigrant had to face in a new and strange environment.

Lay and clerical leaders have testified to the special mission of the Irish to preserve and spread Roman Catholicism in the United States. "What Ireland has done for the American Church, every Bishop, every priest can tell," wrote Maguire in 1867, in his book on *The Irish in America*. "There is scarcely an ecclesiastical seminary for English-speaking students," he added, "in which the great majority of those now preparing for the service of the sanctuary do not belong, if not by birth, at least by blood, to that historic land to which the grateful Church of past ages accorded the proud title — Insula Sanctorum." . . .

It has been estimated that there were 30,000 adherents of the Roman Catholic faith in the United States in 1790. By 1830, the Church claimed 600,000 and, by 1860, 4,500,000 members. Both figures are probably too large. The Metropolitan Catholic Almanac of 1852 listed 1,980,000 Catholics in the United States. By that time, there were Catholic newspapers in nine of the leading cities and Catholic publishing houses in Baltimore, Philadelphia, New York, and Boston. . . .

Devout Irishmen, of course, followed their clerical leaders in matters of religion and religious education. In politics, they learned to follow the ward boss. The latter's affiliations generally were more intimate with the saloon than with the Church, and saloons and fire houses were the centers from which ward-heelers carried on their activities. To an Irishman, politics proved to be the salt and breath of life, and Irishmen in America found it hard to resist the temptation to plunge at once, and deeply, into the American political stream. They learned the tricks of the political game from native American leaders, and then rapidly improved on their instruction. From the first, Irish allegiance was to the Democrats. The name itself had its allure. "Federalist" and "Whig" were names that had little significance for an immigrant who had come to the United States to enjoy freedom and democracy. Moreover, both Federalists and Whigs were suspected, with much truth, of a nativism that frowned upon the newcomer, seeking to protect American institutions from the inundations from abroad and opposed to the easy and quick naturalization of foreigners. Irishmen had little in common with the "Anglomen and monocrats" who supported Federalists and Whigs. Posing as friends of the poor, the Democrats, in the tradition of Jefferson and Jackson, opened their hearts to the immigrants and sought to win and hold their support by admitting them at once to the inner sanctuary and to the minor spoils of the American political system. Irishmen generally had an ingrained hatred for aristocracy and long-standing reasons to be "agin the government." By the year 1820, Tammany Hall was Irish. Tammany celebrations toasted Ireland's sons and their patron saint, St. Patrick, and Tammany used its charities to win and to hold the immigrant vote.

A regiment of well-drilled Irish voters, once organized in any of the larger port towns, was able to enlist new arrivals among the immigrants as soon as they landed. The Irish usually were more interested in local political issues than in national questions, but thorough organization in the local communities led to party solidarity on any issue that might arise. Needless to add, immigrants favored universal manhood suffrage, and the Democratic leaders championed what their supporters wanted. A deliberately cultivated Anglophobia helped to preserve Irish unity. Irish wit and adaptibility, a gift for oratory, a certain vivacity, and a warm, human quality that made them the best of good fellows at all times — especially in election campaigns — enabled the Irish to rise rapidly from ward heelers to city bosses, and to municipal, state and federal officials of high distinction.

The Irish added turbulence and excitement to political campaigns. They also contributed a new picturesqueness and dramatic quality to the methods of political campaigning and canvassing the vote of large masses of people. By building up strong political machines in the cities, they became, along with the Solid South, the one stable element that kept the Democratic party — then a minority group — alive after the Civil War and gave it its occasional chance for victory. Reformers have often overlooked the fact that the same political boss who bought votes, stuffed ballot boxes, and brazenly perpetrated naturalization frauds was also the warmhearted leader who got the immigrant his pushcart license, "fixed" arrests for petty violations of the law, and sent the poor their Christmas turkeys and coal in winter, paid their rent when the landlord threatened eviction, and sent flowers to their funerals. Indeed, some political bosses contended that they were public benefactors, for they took money out of the public till to help bring about a fairer distribution of the world's pleasures among the underprivileged. . . .

The Americanization of the Irish proceeded so rapidly, in spite of the alarmists of the 1850's and 1860's, that no detailed discussion of this process is necessary here. The Irish have become so much a part of present-day Americanism that it seems curious indeed to review the characteristics they brought with them several generations ago and to describe the reception they received from their American contemporaries. The Irishman is now so thoroughly Americanized that he is not averse to joining in denunciations of later immigrants whose ideas he considers dangerous to American institutions, apparently completely forgetful of the treatment his ancestors received 100 years ago. . . .

STUDY GUIDE

1. In this selection, Wittke mentions only a few of the common factors that operated in most countries to lead people to emigrate. Which ones does he mention, and what other common factors can you think of?

2. The selection is concerned only with pre–Civil War migration, which was mostly from northern and western Europe. Based on your own knowledge, indicate in what areas each of the following settled and what occupations they tended to enter: Germans, Scandinavians, Hungarians, Jews, Poles, Italians.

3. What special factors operated in Ireland to promote emigration? How do you explain the poor economic and social condition of the Irish once they arrived here?

4. In the final paragraph, Wittke suggests that there is not necessarily a positive relation between attitudes of tolerance toward other groups and a history of having been persecuted or discriminated against oneself. How can you explain this irony, which we know to be characteristic of many minority groups?

5. What factors in modern American economic life and in new social attitudes might make a cultural pluralism, in which various nationalities and races live in mutual respect and appreciation of their differences, more feasible in the United States today than in the early nineteenth century?

BIBLIOGRAPHY

The study of immigration as a significant theme in the American experience is a relatively recent phenomenon. In addition to the volume from which the preceding selection is taken, two older studies by Marcus Lee Hansen are well worth reading: *The Immigrant in American History* (edited with a foreword by Arthur Schlesinger, Sr., 1940) and *The Atlantic Migration 1607–1860* (edited with a foreword by Arthur Schlesinger, Sr., 1945). More recent publications on this theme include a number of volumes by Oscar Handlin: his Pulitzer Prize–winning book, *The Uprooted: The Epic Story of the Great Migrations That Made the American People* (1951, revised 1973); *Race and Nationality in American Life* (1957), a series of essays on immigration; and *Immigration as a Factor in American History* (1969), a collection of documents relating to immigration with an introduction by Handlin.

A good, short survey of immigration as an aspect of American life is Maldwyn Jones, *American Immigration* (1960). Another general work by Jones is *Destination America* (1976), which has a great many illustrations of the immigrant experience. Several of the major immigrant groups have been the subject of studies; others have not yet been seriously studied by professional historians. Three very good studies of different groups that migrated to the United States are Rowland T. Berthoff, *British Immigrants in Industrial America, 1790–1950* (1953); Theodore Saloutos, *The Greeks in the United States* (1964); and Terry Coleman, *Passage to America: A History of Emigrants from Great Britain and Ireland to America in the Mid-Nineteenth Century* (1972). Other specialized works treat the adjustment of different nationalities in America and the role of such traditional institutions as the church in the lives of the immigrants. Three works of this sort are Oscar Handlin, *Boston's Immigrants, 1790–1880: A Study in Acculturation* (1941, revised 1959); Louis Wirth, *The Ghetto* (1928), a classic study of Eastern European Jewish response to Chicago; and a more recent study by Jay P. Dolan, *The Immigrant Church: New York's Irish and German Catholics, 1815–1865* (1975). Ray A. Billington, *The Protestant Crusade, 1800–1860* (1938) is a study of nativism. An article on religious prejudice and anti-immigrant feeling is David B. Davis, "Some Themes of Counter-Subversion: An Analysis of Anti-Masonic, Anti-Catholic, and Anti-Mormon Literature," *Mississippi Valley Historical Review*, Vol. XLVII (1960), pp. 205–224.

Philadelphia's 1844 anti-Catholic riot, which required calling in the state militia, suggests the crime and violence that plagued early nineteenth-century cities.

16

MICHAEL FELDBERG

Urban Problems

Today a vast majority of the United States population lives in sizeable towns and large cities. Along the Atlantic seaboard, farmlands near the great urban centers have been turned into housing developments at such a rate that the hundreds of miles between Washington, D.C., and Boston are becoming one great urban corridor. The American people have become so thoroughly an urban people that few are left who know the difference between timothy and alfalfa or who have any idea of what the farm machine known as a harrow does. In recent years, an increasing number of farm museums have developed, where city folks can go on a Sunday afternoon to look at weathered farm equipment and see live sheep and cattle. There is a considerable irony in all this, since during much of American history the country was predominantly rural and the American dream was the acquisition of one or two hundred acres one could farm for oneself.

In the eighteenth century, most centers of settlement were nothing more than tiny farming villages. Boston, the largest city in 1730, had 13,000 people, while Philadelphia was second with 11,500 and New York third with 8,500. As late as 1790, the population of the largest American city, Philadelphia, numbered only 30,000. By 1860, it had risen to an incredible 565,000; New York was home to more than 800,000; and the relatively new, western metropolis of Cincinnati had 160,000 people. The extraordinary growth of cities in the nineteenth century brought new problems and required new policies and institutions for the solving of some of the older problems.

Epidemics of cholera and yellow fever swept American cities

in the early nineteenth century, taking as many as 3,500 lives in a single year in New York. In the same city, hundreds of homeless poor, including orphaned children, roamed the streets begging, and tens of thousands of people lived in dark cellar holes and tenement buildings. Crime and gang violence became critical problems in the larger cities, as did the problem of supplying water, fire protection, and other services to these vast metropolitan areas. Singing the old refrain that the city is "a great place to visit, but I wouldn't want to live there," a visitor to New York in 1828 said that something about it made it "more a gratification to visit, than to abide."

Some of the urban problems were solved by private efforts, some by the development of professional government service departments to replace the earlier private fire-protection clubs. In 1860, for example, 79 private companies and 57 public works supplied water to the cities. Protection against crime and the devastating riots that swept American cities led to the creation of modern, trained police forces. The riots involved many different groups and issues, ranging from religious and ethnic hostilities to political warfare, economic competition for jobs, and abolitionist activity. The following essay by Michael Feldberg depicts crowd violence in Philadelphia in the 1840s.

Americans who remember the urban unrest of the 1960s can readily identify with the crisis of violence that gripped Jacksonian American cities. The 1830s, 1840s, and 1850s produced a constant stream of riots reminiscent of the "long hot summers" of the not-too-distant past. Jacksonian cities were torn by fighting between immigrants and native-born Americans, abolitionists and anti-abolitionists, free blacks and racist whites, volunteer firefighters and street gangs, Mormons and "Gentiles," even rival factions of Whigs and Democrats. And, like the 1960s, Jacksonian collective violence resulted in greatly enlarged and strengthened police forces better able to repress riots and disorders — either with or without death or injury to the rioters.

Yet there are some notable differences between the upheavals of the pre-Civil War decades and those of the 1960s. Compared with the death and devastation in Watts, Newark, or Detroit, Jacksonian rioting seems rather

From *The Turbulent Era: Riot and Disorder in Jacksonian America* by Michael Feldberg. Copyright © 1980 by Oxford University Press, Inc. Reprinted by permission.

tame. Whereas a few major confrontations in the 1840s and 1850s took the lives of at least a dozen persons, deaths in Jacksonian rioting were a relatively rare occurrence. Certainly the property damage to Washington, D.C., after the assassination of Martin Luther King, Jr., or to Harlem during the New York Blackout of 1977, was unequaled by even the most destructive pre-Civil War violence.

In its own way, however, urban rioting posed for Jacksonian society a social and political crisis seemingly equal to that of the 1960s' era of protest. To some contemporaries, violence in the 1830s and 1840s portended the possible destruction of American civilization.... As sober an analyst as Abraham Lincoln warned in 1837 that

> ...there is even now something of an ill omen amongst us.... Accounts of outrages committed by mobs form the every-day news of the times. They have pervaded the country from New England to Louisiana; they are neither peculiar to the eternal snows of the former nor the burning suns of the latter; they are not the creatures of climate, neither are they confined to the slaveholding or the non-slaveholding states. Alike they spring up among the pleasure-hunting master of Southern slaves, and the order-loving citizens of the land of steady habits. Whatever their causes be, it is common to the whole country.

Lincoln was not exaggerating the dimensions of the crisis. Historian Richard Maxwell Brown has counted thirty-five major riots in Baltimore, Philadelphia, New York, and Boston during the three decades from 1830 to 1860. Historian John C. Schneider found that "at least seventy percent of American cities with a population of twenty thousand or more by 1850 experienced some degree of major disorder in the 1830–1865 period." The abolitionist movement, which kept its own count of anti-abolition and racially motivated mobs, reported no less than 209 such incidents for the 1830s and 1840s alone....

The historical significance of rioting in a given period should not be measured solely by its frequency or intensity. Collective violence should be judged in its broader social and political contexts as well; it must be seen as one of several forms of interaction that can occur among groups, or between groups and their government. We must look at the functions Jacksonian rioting served, the kinds of groups that employed it, and the success of those groups in using violence to attain their goals. In the Jacksonian context, collective violence was one means by which various groups attempted to control competition among themselves, or by which they responded to changes in their relative status, power, wealth, or political influence.

... Jacksonian collective violence stemmed from a number of sources: the racial and ethnic tensions of the period; the era's ideological climate; the inability of political systems and legal institutions to resolve group conflict by peaceable means; rapid urbanization and population changes; and economic and technological innovation. What distinguishes Jacksonian rioting from collective violence in other periods of American history is not its sources, however, but the frequency of its occurrence, its effectiveness, and the relative inability of public authorities to control or suppress it. Yet the very success achieved by private groups through rioting called forth forces that, by the 1850s, would change the balance of power between rioters and local peacekeeping officials and impose professional police systems on American cities. The epidemic of collective violence in Jacksonian cities ultimately undermined the American public's traditional resistance to the creation of effective urban police forces. By the time of the Civil War, most of the nation's important cities had established recognizably modern police departments. . . . The creation of urban police departments became the most enduring legacy of Jacksonian collective violence.

The great Philadelphia Native American Riots of 1844 were certainly among the most dramatic and violent episodes in pre-Civil War American history. In both their Kensington and Southwark phases, they present a capsule portrait of the sources, uses, and consequences of Jacksonian collective violence. Although they grew out of cultural and religious conflict between Philadelphia's Protestant nativists and Irish Catholic immigrants, the riots were the immediate result of a political controversy over the use of the Bible in the Philadelphia public schools. The fighting also reflected the social and political disorganization of Philadelphia and the weakness of its peacekeeping system. . . . Above all, the two phases of the Philadelphia Native American Riots of 1844 illustrate the ease with which private groups in Jacksonian America employed collective violence as a tool for conducting social conflict and expressing political protest. The riots also reveal the difficulties public authorities faced when they tried to control group violence in the nation's rapidly changing cities.

By February 1844, Louisa Bedford had finally run out of patience. She was having a difficult enough time teaching elementary school in Kensington, a working-class suburb just north of Philadelphia. Now her job was made even more trying because of hard feelings between the parents of both her immigrant Irish Catholic students and her native-born Protestant students. . . . Two years earlier, in 1842, the Philadelphia County Board of School Controllers had ordered that the King James, or Protestant, version of Holy Scripture be used as a basic reading text in all Philadelphia public-school classes. Upon hearing this, the Catholic Bishop of Philadelphia, the Reverend Francis Patrick Kenrick, asked that Catholic children be allowed to read the Douay, or authorized Catholic, version of Scripture, and that Catholic teachers not be compelled to read from the King James during reading exercises. The controllers denied Kenrick's request.

During the 1840s many American Protestants feared Catholicism because it seemed alien and anti-democratic. . . . Because of this widely held prejudice, the Philadelphia School Controllers were afraid to grant equal status to the Douay Bible by allowing it in the schools. . . . Yet to ease Bishop Kenrick's objections to an obvious injustice, the Board of School Controllers saw fit to offer a compromise solution: Catholic children could leave their classrooms while Bible-reading exercises were conducted, but the Douay version was still not to be admitted into the schools.

This compromise pleased almost no one. Catholics believed that the plan ignored their bishop's plea for justice and equality; evangelical Protestants felt that Catholic children should be compelled to read the King James version as an antidote to their "priestly dictated" and "popish" beliefs. The solution also failed to please teachers like Louisa Bedford, who could not tolerate the disruption caused by her Catholic students waiting noisily outside her door until the Bible-reading session was over. To remedy this situation, Bedford took actions which, in a short time, led to the great Philadelphia riots of 1844.

Louisa Bedford was a Protestant, although not a militant evangelical. Seriously committed to teaching the working-class children of Kensington to read and write, she resented the chaos caused by the controllers' policy. Thus when School Controller and Irish Catholic politician Hugh Clark was making his weekly tour of Kensington's public schools, Bedford asked Clark if she could have a word with him. She explained her unhappiness to the politically astute Clark who, one suspects, was waiting for just such a moment. Clark then sympathetically offered an alternative to sending Catholic students out of her room: She could suspend *all* Bible reading in her class until such time as the School Controllers devised a better method for excusing Catholic students from the exercise. Clark volunteered to assume responsibility should she decide to follow this course. Bedford chose to accept Clark's offer and told her students that, for the time being, they would not have to do their Bible reading. Much to her relief, she turned to teaching other subjects.

. . . Word of Clark's decision to "kick the Bible out of the schools," as his enemies inaccurately described it, spread like wildfire throughout the city. Evangelical Protestants, most of them native-born Americans and the remainder immigrant Irish Protestants, had been organizing in Philadelphia for nearly a decade. The evangelicals were alarmed by what they believed to be the growing political and religious influence of Catholics, particularly Irish Catholic immigrants. Nativists, a name given to those who openly opposed all "alien" elements such as Catholics, immigrants, Mormons, and others who did not conform to the dominant white Protestant religious and cultural values of the era, had especially feared the political activism of the Irish Catholic clergy. . . . Protestants concerned with the increasing influence of Catholics and immigrants in American life joined a new political movement known as the American Republican party, which had branches in Philadelphia, New York, Boston, Baltimore, and New Orleans. The American Republicans held rallies and ran candidates to oppose the influence of immigrants in local politics. . . .

For the most part, American Republican leadership in Philadelphia was composed of "middling" and "respectable" men: lawyers, doctors, clergymen, newspaper editors, shopkeepers, craftsmen, printers, barbers, dentists, and teachers. These individuals were neither numbered in the ranks of the city's traditional upper classes — wealthy merchants, bankers, manufacturers, and gentlemen farmers — nor drawn from the ranks of the struggling poor. Rather, these American Republicans had formerly provided the bulk of middle-class voters for the Whig and Democratic parties. With their wives they filled the pews of Philadelphia's Methodist, Baptist, and Presbyterian churches. By their own description they saw themselves as the "bone and sinew" of society, the hard-working silent majority who, while never independently wealthy and secure like the upper classes, would never allow themselves to fall to the level of the impoverished or degenerate immigrants.

Because they saw themselves as the nation's only "real" Americans, nativists could not stand to see their public schools, or the political system in general, "captured" by persons who spoke with a foreign accent — especially an Irish brogue. The social isolation of America's Irish immigrants and their continued loyalty to their native land particularly worried American nativists. They believed that the typical Irish immigrant would never become a loyal American citizen, freed of his allegiance to Ireland or to the Roman Catholic Church. They did not realize that the experiences of Irish Catholic immigrants with English-speaking Protestants had convinced the Irish to cling to their religion and to their nationalism. . . .

To maintain their solidarity, to resist integration into a Protestant-dominated society such as the one they had fled, the American Irish tended to cluster in self-imposed ghettos, to socialize in their own taverns, to attend mass in their own parish churches, and to meet in their own political and nationalist clubs. Such self-inflicted isolation upset Protestant American nativists, but the apparent political control that the Irish-born Catholic clergy seemed to exercise over their immigrant followers appeared to bother them even more. Nativists convinced one another that the American Irish voted overwhelmingly for the Democratic party, not because the Jacksonian political platform or personal style appealed to the newcomers, but because corrupt Roman Catholic priests "dictated" voting orders from Rome to their sheeplike parishioners. . . .

Philadelphia American Republicanism was closely allied with the most popular reform movement of the era, the temperance crusade. At its inception in the early 1800s, the American temperance movement was dedicated to persuading individuals to consume only moderate amounts of alcoholic beverages. In the 1840s, its national membership may have numbered over

100,000, and most of these members believed that all sales of drinking alcohol should be outlawed. Alcoholism had become closely associated with poverty, unemployment, crime, ill health, and broken families. Somewhat unfairly, it was also closely associated with urban immigrant communities: gin and rum with the Irish, beer with the Germans, and wine with the French and Italians. Since nativists considered immigrant groups, and especially the Irish, responsible for most of the nation's poverty, crime, and prostitution, their interest in temperance reflected their critical attitudes toward the life-styles of America's urban immigrant populations.

It was unfair of nativists and temperance advocates to equate alcohol consumption primarily with immigrants. The nation's upper classes were the chief consumers of good French wines, port, sherry, and Madeira. Many native Protestant workingmen were paid a portion of their wages in a daily allowance of rum, and nearly every workshop and factory employed young boys to run out frequently for buckets of beer. Drinking to excess was a universal problem that crossed ethnic and class boundaries. The vast quantities of alcohol consumed in Jacksonian America convinced many temperance advocates, nativist and non-nativist alike, that an individual's mere verbal pledge to drink moderately was not enough to keep him from abusing alcohol, and temperance crusaders increasingly switched from a voluntarist to a prohibitionist position. They argued that only by outlawing the sale of liquor could its evil effects be controlled.

The conversion of Philadelphia's temperance movement to a prohibitionist stance was tied in important ways to the American Republican and evangelical Protestant movements of the era. Closing bars and rum shops could have important social and political implications for immigrant communities. Taverns were one of the focal points in working-class Irish and German neighborhoods, and they often served as social and political centers. Their patrons did not usually welcome native Protestant — or even other ethnic — outsiders, and many a Philadelphia brawl was started when an unwitting stranger of the wrong ethnic background violated the sanctity of a German or Irish saloon. Particularly in Irish neighborhoods, taverns became symbols of Irish-Catholic separatism and Irish immigrant rejection of integration into wider American culture.

But nativists had political as well as cultural objections to the immigrants' fondness for alcoholic beverages. They argued that just as priests could control the consciences of immigrant Catholics through the religious doctrine of papal infallibility, so could tavern owners manipulate the political loyalties of immigrants by trading liquor for votes. Nativist temperance advocates feared an unholy alliance between Catholic priests and ambitious tavern-owning politicians that would maintain the immigrants' dependence on the Church and the bottle. The battle against liquor, then, was in part a battle to preserve American political freedom from Catholic-sponsored conspiracies.

One person's reform, though, is another person's oppression, especially when the targets of the reform movement saw nothing wrong in their style of life or religious values. Catholic and Irish community leaders believed strongly that the Constitution entitled community members to liberty of conscience in their religion, freedom of association in their social contacts, freedom of thought in their political beliefs, and freedom of choice in their use of alcohol. The Catholic Archdiocese of Philadelphia organized its own voluntary temperance societies, but it strongly opposed any attempt to legislate away the individual's right to indulge in alcohol. And while it urged its parishioners to attend mass on Sunday, the Archdiocese resisted efforts to suppress popular amusements on the Sabbath. Most important, Bishop Kenrick personally resented the efforts of Protestant activists to "save" Catholic children by forcing them to read the King James Bible in the public schools.

Unfortunately for Bishop Kenrick and the rest of Philadelphia's Catholics, the school Bible issue stirred intense hatred in the "City of Brotherly Love." The city's nativists chose (deliberately or otherwise) to interpret Kenrick's request to grant equality to the Douay Bible as a demand that the King James Bible be *removed* from the public schools. . . .

Thus it is clear why Hugh Clark's suggestion to Louisa Bedford that she suspend Bible reading in her Kensington classroom caused such upheaval throughout Philadelphia. It was as if the bishop's alleged conspiracy had finally come out in the open. The first word of Clark's actions was carried by Henry Moore, a Methodist minister who burst into a prayer meeting at his Kensington church to inform the congregation that Clark had forced Miss Bedford against her will to "kick the Bible out of her classroom." Word spread rapidly throughout the city's nativist network, and Philadelphia's American Republican leaders and evangelical Protestant clergymen convened a series of mass rallies in mid-March to protest Catholic attempts to "trample our free Protestant institutions in the dust." At one rally more than 3,000 protestors gathered to hear an American Republican spokesman remind those who would "remove the Bible from the public schools" that, "when we remember that our Pilgrim Fathers landed on Plymouth Rock to establish the Protestant religion, free from persecution, we must contend that this was and always will be a Protestant country."

Their enthusiastic reception at the city-wide rallies encouraged the American Republicans to carry their crusade right to the lair of the beast, the very neighborhood that symbolized Irish Catholic solidarity in Philadelphia: Third Ward, Kensington. The community was long and widely recognized as immigrant Irish "turf." It was dominated by Irish handloom weavers, dock laborers, teamsters, and other semiskilled workers who held little love for their native Protestant neighbors in adjoining wards. The neighborhood had been the scene of several riots in recent years, including a series of attacks on railroad construction workers trying to lay tracks down Front Street and some violent attacks on nonunion weavers who were failing to honor a strike by their fellow "brothers of the loom." Perhaps the most notorious incident had occurred a few months earlier, when the striking weavers attacked and dispersed a sheriff's posse, beat the sheriff soundly, and had to be quelled by the state militia troops. It was in this neighborhood of militant and aggressive Irish immigrants that the American Republicans chose to hold a rally on Friday afternoon, May 3, 1844, and invite the general public to attend.

That Friday meeting might well have been calculated to provoke a fateful confrontation with Kensington's immigrant Irish. The American Republicans chose to hold their rally in a schoolyard at Second and Master streets. When the American Republican spokesmen began their speeches, they were heckled, booed, and pelted with rocks and garbage by a crowd of several hundred, and eventually driven from the speaker's platform they had erected earlier in the afternoon. Undaunted (and quite self-righteously), the party decided to reconvene the meeting in the schoolyard on Monday, May 6, and placarded the city with notices urging every American Republican loyalist to attend. This time a large crowd of 3,000 turned out. Around 3:00 P.M., while noted temperance lecturer and political nativist Lewis C. Levin was arousing the crowd's interest, a sudden rainstorm erupted and the crowd moved spontaneously in search of shelter toward the Nanny Goat Market.

Relocating the rally in the market proved catastrophic. The Nanny Goat Market was the hub of the Third Ward Irish community. An open-sided, block-long covered shed at Third and Master streets, the market house served as a shopping center, a meeting place, and a social center for local residents. When the noisy but peaceable nativists arrived, a group of thirty or so Irish locals was waiting there to greet them. One Irishman was heard to proclaim, "Keep the damned natives out of our market house; this ground don't belong to them, it's ours!" Lewis Levin tried to continue his speech from a vendor's stand but hecklers drowned him out. Pushing and shoving began, someone pulled a pistol, a rival dared him to shoot, he did, and panic erupted under the shed. The Irish residents fled to their nearby homes, but the nativists were trapped in the open-sided shed with few places to hide. A rain of gunfire poured down on them from surrounding buildings, most of it from the Hibernia Hose House, the headquarters of an Irish volunteer fire company. The first nativist killed in the shooting, nineteen-year-old George Schiffler, became a martyr to the cause. His name was soon immortalized when a nativist militia company, a volunteer fire company, and a fighting street gang each took his name as their own. In subsequent years the street gang known as the Schifflers would fight many battles with Philadelphia's Irish and Democratic street gangs and volunteer fire companies.

The initial advantage possessed by the Irish snipers was soon balanced by the arrival of approximately eighteen nativist reinforcements who brought rifles and shotguns with them. Protected by the fire of their own sharpshooters, nativists began making forays out of the Nanny Goat Market, breaking windows and doors of the houses from which gunfire had been coming and scattering the inhabitants. Several Irishmen were badly beaten and left for dead as others saw their homes and furniture wrecked by the furious nativists. Finally, after two hours of heavy fighting, Sheriff Morton McMichael and a posse of two hundred deputies arrived and the fighting subsided.

That night, when darkness descended on Kensington, nativists from every corner of Philadelphia found their way to the neighborhood around the Nanny Goat Market. Around 10:00 P.M. a crowd "collected in the vicinity of Franklin and Second streets," marched toward the Nanny Goat Market, and on the way "commenced breaking into the houses on both sides of the street, destroying the furniture, demolishing the windows, and rendering the houses completely uninhabitable." The crowd then arrived at the gates of the seminary of the Catholic Sisters of Charity and were threatening to burn it down when a group of Irish defenders "advanced from above and fired a volley of ball and buckshot into the crowd." One nativist attacker died instantly, a second lingered for a month before dying of a chest wound, and several others were injured. On this note, Monday night's fighting in Kensington drew to a close.

Philadelphians awakened Tuesday morning, May 7, to find their city plastered with printed calls to a rally protesting the murder of George Schiffler. The message ended with the inflammatory words, "LET EVERY MAN COME PREPARED TO DEFEND HIMSELF." That morning, the nativist press was filled with militant cries for revenge. The daily *Native American* proclaimed:

Another St. Bartholomew's day has begun in the streets of Philadelphia. The bloody hand of the Pope has stretched forth to our destruction. Now we call on our fellow-citizens, who regard free institutions, whether they be native or adopted, to arm. Our liberties are to be fought for — let us not be slack in our preparation.

By 3:30 P.M. that Tuesday afternoon, more than 3,000 persons had gathered behind Independence Hall to hear speeches condemning Kensington's Irish. . . .

When the speeches were finished and the American Republicans called for the meeting to adjourn, a voice in the crowd shouted, "Adjourn to Kensington right now!" The crowd took up the call, marched in loose military fashion out of the meeting ground, and turned northward to Kensington. When they arrived in the neighborhood of Second and Master, the marchers found that many of Kensington's Irish had fled the neighborhood and taken their belongings with them. Other inhabitants simply waited at home with their loaded guns. This time, the nativist procession did not pause to convene a meeting and hear speeches, but immediately attacked the Hibernia Hose House. Armed defenders there and in some of the houses along the street immediately opened fire, and in the few moments of shooting four nativists lay dead and eleven others fell wounded. The remaining nativists with a stomach for a fight retreated to the Nanny Goat Market for shelter, and it seemed that the pattern of the day before would repeat itself. This time, however, the nativists changed their tactics. Rather than try to shoot it out with the well-concealed Irish, the nativists snuck out of the market building and set fire to each of the houses from which gunfire had been coming. This tactic proved successful as hidden Irish snipers came tumbling out of the flaming buildings. They made easy targets for nativist gunners, and only poor nativist marksmanship explains why no Irishmen were killed. It was not until 5:00 P.M., nearly an hour after the shooting started, that General [George] Cadwalader, previously unprepared, arrived with several militia companies to restore order in the neighborhood.

The use of fire struck panic in the hearts of the remaining Kensington Irish, and by Wednesday morning most of them had packed their possessions and gone elsewhere to stay with friends and relatives, or to camp in the woods on the outskirts of Philadelphia. The militia was left to guard their abandoned homes, but the outnumbered soldiers were inadequate for the task. Roving bands of nativists snuck from house to house in the vicinity of the Nanny Goat Market and set each on fire. The city's volunteer firefighters, mostly native-born Americans, had little enthusiasm for fighting the flames. In addition, after setting up a diversion to draw the militia away, a group of arsonists gained access to St. Michael's Roman Catholic Church, whose priest had been an outspoken foe of nativism, and set it to the torch. Flames rapidly devoured the wooden structure, and as the cross fell from the toppling steeple the crowd cheered loudly. Volunteer firefighters, arriving on the scene, determined that the gathering would never permit them to extinguish the fire, so they contented themselves with hosing down nearby buildings to keep the flames from spreading. Other rioters completed the day's work by ransacking two stores that had been selling ammunition to Irish marksmen, and eventually they invaded the home of Hugh Clark, the man whose decision to suspend Bible reading in Louisa Bedford's class had provided the pretext for the fighting. The invaders threw Clark's valuable books and furniture into the street and used them to start a bonfire. Finally, several hours after the arson had begun in Kensington, General Cadwalader and Sheriff McMichael arrived with reinforcements and brought the wandering rioters under control.

Thus blocked, the angry nativists simply transferred their field of activity to downtown Philadelphia. By 10:30 that Wednesday night, a huge crowd had gathered in front of St. Augustine's Roman Catholic Church in the heart of that city. Although the mayor stood on the building's front steps and pleaded with the crowd to disperse, his appeals went unheard. Someone knocked him down by heaving a stone against his chest, and a young boy managed to sneak past the constables at a rear door and set the church afire.

Within half an hour the $45,000 brick structure was a total loss. As the steeple fell, the crowd cheered as it had done at St. Michael's. Again the volunteer firemen dared only hose down nearby buildings.

The burning of St. Augustine's marked the last major violence in the Kensington phase of the Native American Riots. Governor David R. Porter placed Philadelphia under martial law, and the chief commander of the Pennsylvania militia, General Robert Patterson, took complete command of the city's government. More than 2,000 soldiers from across the state patrolled the streets of Philadelphia, and General Patterson banned all meetings and demonstrations. . . .

Martial law remained in effect for a week without a serious confrontation between troops and civilians, after which civilian government was restored to Philadelphia. Thus ended the Kensington phase of the 1844 Native American Riots.

The Kensington Riots had been the worst in Philadelphia's history. At least six persons had been killed, and as many as fifty had been seriously injured. Property losses in the three days of violence were conservatively estimated at $250,000, not counting the cost of medical bills and lost time from work.

While unusually destructive, the Kensington riots were in other ways typical of collective violence in the Jacksonian period. First, despite the fact that there was gunfire and killing in the first two days of fighting, it appears that only a relatively small portion of combatants on either side was armed. There is no way for us to know how many Philadelphians owned firearms in 1844, although rifles for hunting seem to have been quite common, and ammunition was widely sold in shops around the city. One of the stores set aflame by the crowd in Kensington, Corr's Grocery, was burned because its proprietor had been supplying bullets to his Irish compatriots. Jacksonian cities seem to have had no legal regulations about who could own, sell, or distribute guns or ammunition. Yet the use of guns by rioters was rarely reported in contemporary newspaper accounts. Crowds usually fought by hurling rocks, paving stones, bricks, and garbage, or by wielding clubs, knives, and slingshots. As a result, it was the exception rather than the rule for pre-Civil War rioting to claim the lives of its victims, or for more than one or two persons to be killed in the course of even the most serious fighting. During the three days and nights of the Kensington riots, for example, only one Irishman was killed, and he was an innocent bystander.

Second, the pattern of damage to property in Kensington indicates that, like most Jacksonian crowds, the nativist rioters exercised a good deal of restraint in their attacks. Despite their anger over the school Bible issue, the ambush at the Nanny Goat Market, and the murders of Schiffler and the others, it was not until Wednesday, two days after the outbreak of fighting, that widespread destruction was inflicted on Irish property. Before then only a few houses that had served as shelters for Irish snipers were targeted for burning. Other houses were stoned or damaged, but these two were suspected of harboring Irish marksmen. Even the choice of targets on Wednesday, when widespread arson was employed, was hardly random: Hugh Clark's house, his brother's tavern, Corr's Grocery, and two Catholic churches. Some additional homes may have been deliberately burned, especially in the area around the Nanny Goat Market, but many others fell unintended victim to the spreading flames. Rioters even bypassed the home of one elderly Irishman when they found him inside, too ill to make his escape. However much their anger had been provoked, the nativist rioters never rampaged through Kensington randomly destroying property or retaliating against whoever fell to hand. There was, in short, no orgy of irrational nativist fury. The rioters possessed clearly defined notions of what and who their targets ought to have been and why those targets deserved to suffer violence. While no one would argue that either the nativist or Irish rioters were acting dispassionately during the fighting, neither can one say that the rioters were insane, deranged, animalistic, or totally without sense or reason.

Third, the social composition of both sides in the Kensington riots was characteristic of that in many other Jacksonian riots. Contrary to many current stereotypes of rioters and looters, the Kensington combatants were not drawn from the poorest or most oppressed strata of Jacksonian society. The names of those injured or arrested, when traced to city directories, indicate that the rioters, frequently boys and young men in their twenties, were often employed as apprentice artisans, weavers, or laborers. They were not poverty-stricken outcasts, nor were they without a permanent residence. Many of the older men and women who participated on both sides were established members of their communities. Among the Irish there were property-owners, landlords, and employers who became as caught up in the heat of battle as their less affluent fellow immigrants. On the nativist side there were respectable American Republican lawyers, doctors, and dentists, as well as some constables and other elected officials. They fought alongside the youthful working-class members of nativist street gangs and volunteer fire companies notorious for their rowdy and combative behavior. What motivated rioters on both sides was not alienation, a sense of economic oppression, or a feeling of having "nothing to lose," but rather a deep commitment to their ethnic heritage and their political cause, intensified by their anger over the course of events that unfolded at the Nanny Goat Market. Tellingly, in three days of fighting and destruction, there was only one reported instance of looting. When rioters removed property from an Irish shop or Hugh Clark's home, it was to destroy it, not to keep it.

Fourth, the Kensington riots illustrate the intertwining of Jacksonian era collective violence with other, more peaceable forms of political and social behavior. The competition between immigrant Irish Catholics and native

Protestant American Republicans began as a cultural controversy over the use of the Bible as a reading text in the public schools. It became a political issue when Hugh Clark convinced Louisa Bedford to remove the King James version from her class's daily lesson. After that, American Republicans began campaigning over the issue of "foreign interference" in the public schools, and when they carried this political campaign to Third Ward, Kensington, the debate changed from a clash of words to a clash of arms. . . . [T]he transition from cultural conflict to political conflict to physical conflict was all too frequent in Jacksonian group relations.

That the school Bible controversy shifted from a battle of petitions before the School Controllers to a battle of weapons in the streets of Kensington is stark testimony to the power of ethnic and religious issues to stir the passions of Philadelphians in 1844. It is also indicative, however, of the fifth and final factor common to most Jacksonian riots: the inability of public officials to prevent or suppress riots before they required the intervention of military troops. How strange it would seem today if, like Philadelphians on May 7, 1844, we awoke to find the walls, lampposts, and fences of our city or town plastered with calls for us to arm ourselves and attend a rally in order to seek revenge for the death of one of our fellow citizens. Then, once we arrived, we would find *no police officers* present to control the crowd or disarm its members. The current form of urban policing, in which uniformed officers actively patrol the streets searching out crime and disorder, and in which the police routinely patrol any political or protest rally prepared to disperse the crowd at the first sign of violence, was simply unknown in Jacksonian America.

"Preventive policing," as Jacksonians came to call it, was not introduced in Philadelphia until the 1850s. Like its sister cities Boston and New York, Philadelphia in 1844 still maintained public order through a system of constables, watchmen, and sheriff's posses whose origins dated back to the Middle Ages. . . .

. . . In the pre-Civil War era, city governments suffered from a shortage of manpower to police their citizens effectively. For various reasons, the majority of urban residents was not yet ready to surrender to local governments the tax monies or the authority needed to repress disorder and anti-social behavior. Jacksonian Americans seemed to possess a certain fatalism about the inevitability of periodic rioting — "intestine disorder," as it was known — and so cities and their residents simply learned to live with collective violence.

But neither the fatalistic outlook nor the weakness of public authorities was to survive the 1850s. By the eve of the Civil War, most of the nation's major cities had established preventive peacekeeping systems along lines still recognizable in today's urban police departments. With their introduction, collective disorder declined steadily in the 1850s and 1860s, and the 1870s was marked by a higher standard of urban public order than Jacksonians had ever imagined possible.

However dramatic their introduction, the police were not the only innovation that helped to pacify American cities by the time of the Civil War. By 1860, the northern industrial states had made public-school attendance compulsory for their youth. Public schools were meant to serve as nurseries for moral training and good citizenship. At the same time, the temperance movement stepped up its legal efforts to curb or eliminate liquor sales to the urban masses. In addition, having fought to a stalemate in the street, nativists and immigrants both channeled their competitive efforts into electoral politics, further diminishing the level of collective violence in the 1850s. Finally, other events such as the Mexican War of 1846–47 permitted a significant portion of America's urban street-fighting populations to vent their aggressive feelings on a common foreign foe, rather than each other. When reinforced by determined and street-wise police forces willing and able to carry out a mandate for civic order, these developments helped to make the 1850s a far less violent period than the 1830s and 1840s.

STUDY GUIDE

1. In the colonial period, many crowd demonstrations and riots were to *support* local government, such as the Boston selectmen or colonial legislature, against British policies. In our time, many demonstrations are *against* constituted authority, as in black protests against police arrests or antiwar and antinuclear sit-ins. How would you characterize the Philadelphia riots in this respect?

2. Feldberg mentions several causes of collective violence: religious prejudice; ethnic hostility; job competition; threats to an established group's wealth, power, or status; and a struggle for political power. Which causes seem to you to have been the key factors in the riots he describes? Why was the violence directed against the Irish, but not against the German immigrants?

3. The riots took place largely on "Irish turf" in Kensington and Southwark, and in the relatively good weather of May. What might have been different if the nativists had held their rallies in their own neighborhoods and in January? Were these factors of locale and timing also important in the riots of the 1960s and the Miami riots of the 1980s?

4. Feldberg concludes that "the nativist rioters exercised a good deal of restraint in their attacks." In view of his description of the riots, do you agree with this conclusion? What does he mean by restraint in this context?

5. Do you see any differences between the kinds of people involved in riots in the 1840s and those involved in our time? Can one argue that rioting in the 1840s was provoked by the majority group in society, and that rioting today is more likely to be instigated by minority groups?

BIBLIOGRAPHY

Like many words in our language, the word "urban" is derived from Latin, a fact that suggests the long, influential role of cities in European civilization. Though the colonists were largely farmers, they came from countries where government, culture, and commerce were centered in large cities such as London and Paris. Through much of our history, Americans have had a kind of love-hate relationship with cities, with the pastoral life of the farmer being held up as the ideal by adults and the big-city life being seen as an escape by many farm children. The attitudes of intellectuals are traced in Morton and Lucia White, *The Intellectual Versus the City* (1962). The sizeable towns of the colonial period were mostly seaports, the history of which is traced in books by Carl Bridenbaugh: *Cities in the Wilderness* (1938) and *Cities in Revolt* (1955). The growth of cities has been closely related to the development of transportation, commerce, and manufacturing. David T. Gilchrist, ed., *The Growth of the Seaport Cities, 1790–1825* (1967) examines developments along the Atlantic seaboard in the first decades of the new republic.

The history of particular cities can serve as case studies that illustrate general patterns of urban development. A great many "biographies" of cities have been published; two illustrative works are Bayrd Still, *Milwaukee*, rev. ed. (1965) and Bessie L. Pierce, *A History of Chicago*, 3 vols. (1937–1957). Allen F. Davis and Mark H. Haller, eds., *The Peoples of Philadelphia: A History of Ethnic Groups and Lower-Class Life, 1790–1940* (1973) examines poverty, housing for the poor, violence, and several of the ethnic groups of Philadelphia. In this fourth edition of *The Social Fabric*, the preceding essay by Feldberg replaces one by David R. Johnson, whose book *Policing the Urban Underworld* (1979) is a fuller account of the development of modern policing. The study of some other urban problems can be followed in Charles E. Rosenberg, *The Cholera Years* (1962) and Nelson M. Blake, *Water for the Cities* (1956). Demography, the study of population trends, is used in much research in urban history: a fine example of this type of study is Stephan Thernstrom, *Poverty and Progress: Social Mobility in a Nineteenth Century City* (1964).

There is a growing body of writing on the role of crowds and violence in the different periods of American history, some of which may be cited in the bibliography of your textbook. Much of this writing reflects the influence of the outstanding scholar of the crowd, a student of European history named George Rudé. An excellent introduction to the whole subject is his book *The Crowd in History, 1730–1848* (1964).

Some broader works treat cities of a particular type or of one region, as indicated in the following two titles: Robert R. Dykstra, *The Cattle Towns*

(1968) and Richard C. Wade, *The Urban Frontier: The Rise of Western Cities, 1790–1830* (1959). Two general surveys of urban history are Constance Green, *The Rise of Urban America* (1965) and Charles N. Glaab and Theodore Brown, *A History of Urban America* (1967). Some excellent writing on urban history has been in the form of articles in historical magazines; Alexander B. Callow, Jr., *American Urban History*, 2nd ed. (1973) is one of several collections of such articles.

LOWELL OFFERING

August, 1845.

" Is Saul also among the prophets?"

A REPOSITORY
OF ORIGINAL ARTICLES, WRITTEN BY
"FACTORY GIRLS."

LOWELL: MISSES CURTIS & FARLEY.
BOSTON: JORDAN & WILEY, 121
Washington street.
1845.

This magazine was one of the many projects of the "Improvement Circles" organized by women in the Lowell Mills.

17

NORMAN J. WARE

The Industrial Worker

There are few developments in all of human history as important as the Industrial Revolution. This great movement created wealth, material goods, and services on a scale unimaginable to the people of any earlier society. It created the resources to provide a reasonable standard of living for virtually the entire society, and standards of education, medical care, and nutrition unknown anywhere in the world before. The essay by Joseph and Frances Gies (Reading No. 7) describes the role of new inventions in the industrialization of America. Equally important was the contribution of the millions of men and women who made up the labor force in the new factory system.

Industrialization had some unfortunate social consequences as well as beneficial economic ones, and the history of labor was not necessarily characterized by steady improvement in either wages or conditions. A number of factors determined the condition of workers in a particular period. Among them were the available supply of labor, the skills necessary to a particular job, the type of industry in which one was employed, and the attitudes of courts and other governmental agencies toward labor and business. During much of our industrial history, the economic theory that considered labor a commodity whose value would fluctuate with supply and demand, just as the cost of raw materials or manufactured products might, dominated American thinking.

The first half of the nineteenth century is an especially interesting period in American labor history. During these years, industrialization — with substantial technological innovation and the introduction of the factory system of labor — proceeded quite rapidly. Yet there was a widespread ambivalence about the new machinery and the new spirit of industrial growth. There was also a well-established social philosophy as to the position of classes, the responsibilities of the employer, and the roles of men and women in the labor force and in the home. Such deep social beliefs are not easily discarded; only grudgingly were they modified to meet the demands of the new industrialism. However, one of the interesting facets of labor history during this period is the way in which some of the new capitalists attempted to reconcile the old social philosophy of the paternalistic employer and his responsibility for the worker with the factory system of labor and the introduction of women workers.

In his book *The Industrial Worker: 1840–1860,* Norman Ware studies the period 1840 to 1860, when the controversy over the factory system and the issues of child and female labor were fully developed. He gives a graphic picture of the wages and conditions in the iron industry and the needle trades and describes the two different systems of factory labor that developed. As you read the selection, consider the differences between labor then and labor now with respect to standard of living, type of work, and union organization.

The problem of primary importance for the industrial worker of the forties and fifties is to be found in the changes in his status and standards of living. A rising money wage is no sign of improved standards. Increasing commodity wages constitute a better test, but if accompanied by losses in other respects of greater significance, conclusions drawn therefrom are of little value. Working conditions, hours, speed, or effort must all be taken into account before an approximation can be made to a true estimate of the worker's condition. But in the last analysis the status of the worker is not a physical but a mental one, and is affected as much by comparisons with past conditions and with the status of other groups in the community as by the facts in themselves. In other words, the problem of status is one of satisfactions, and satisfactions are relative.

The depressions of 1837–39 left one-third of the working population of New York City unemployed. [Horace] Greeley estimated that there were not less than ten thousand persons in the city "in utter and hopeless distress with no means of surviving the winter but those provided by charity." The same was true, in a somewhat less pronounced degree, throughout the industrial districts. The New England mills were either closed down or running only part-time and undermanned. Between 1839 and 1843 wages generally fell from thirty to fifty per cent, and the improved business conditions of the latter year were not reflected in the wages of the workers. In 1844 the same amount of labor that had once produced for the mechanic and his family a comfortable subsistence was inadequate to maintain his standards, and his only alternative was increased effort or the reduction of his wants.

Pauperism was increasing. "Thirty years ago," said Evans, "the number of paupers in the whole United States was estimated at 29,166, or one in three hundred. The pauperism of New York City now amounts to 51,600, or one in every seven of the population." In New York State the proportion of the poor was said to be increasing and the wages of labor to be steadily declining.

The labor papers that sprang up in these years constantly complained that the condition of the worker was growing worse; that he was becoming more and more dependent on capital; that his resources were being curtailed and a new uncertainty had entered his life as to wages and employment.

In the iron industry, the wage per ton of ore produced was being constantly reduced. The following are the "prices" for certain kinds of work in the Pittsburgh district from 1837 to 1858:

Year	Boilers	Puddlers	Hammermen
1837	$7.00	$4.25	$1.25
1838	7.00	4.25	1.25
1839	6.50	4.00	—
1840	6.00	3.75	—
1841	5.50	3.75	—
1842	5.00	3.50	1.00
1845	6.00	4.00	—
1850	4.50	3.50	—
1858	3.00 to $4.00	1.90 to $2.50	—

After a steady decline of wages in the iron industry from 1837, a strike of the boilers occurred in February, 1842, as a result of notification of a further cut to five dollars a ton. The strike lasted until July, when the boilers resumed work at the reduced price. This price was continued until May, 1845, when a second strike occurred for the recovery of the one dollar a ton they had lost between 1840 and 1842. This lasted until August and resulted in the advance being granted. The new price, identical with that of 1840, lasted until 1850 when reductions were again proposed:

Puddlers	from $4.00	to $3.50 per ton
Boilers	from $6.00	to $4.50 per ton
Refiners	from $1.00	to $0.80 per ton
Scrappers	from $3.75	to $2.50 per ton
Heaters	from $1.37½	to $1.00 per ton . . .

The strike against these reductions had not been broken by February when some of the mills were started with imported labor. Riots broke out in which the puddlers took possession of one of the mills, in the face of the protest of some of their fellows and the pistol of the mayor. The wives of the workers were said to have been the most violent of the rioters. Some slight damage was done and arrests were made. But by the end of March the mills were fairly well filled with imported help working at the reduced rates. Many of the strikers left the city and those who remained returned to the mills in the summer. Of those who were arrested, three men were acquitted and two men and four women found guilty. The men were sentenced to pay fines of six and one-fourth cents and costs and imprisonment for eighteen months. The women were sentenced to pay fifty dollars each and costs and imprisonment for thirty days. On petition of the jury that convicted them and of a large number of citizens, they were pardoned and the fines remitted in August, 1850. . . .

No class of workers was better paid than those in the building trades. Where shoemakers, printers, hatters, cabinet-makers, and so on were getting $4, $5, and $6 a week, the carpenters, plasterers, and bricklayers were getting $10. But even this latter wage was inadequate to maintain the worker's family at anything like a decent comfort standard. In 1851 the carpenters of Philadelphia struck for an advance of twenty-five cents a day which would give them a wage of $10.50 a week. The [New York] *Tribune* published a week's budget for a family of five, as follows:

Budget for Family of Five for One Week

Barrel of flour, $5.00, will last eight weeks	$0.62½
Sugar, 4 lbs. at 8 cents a pound	.32
Butter, 2 lbs. at 31½ cents a pound	.62½ (*sic*)
Milk, two cents per day	.14
Butcher's meat, 2 lbs. beef per day at 10c per lb.	$1.40
Potatoes, ½ bushel	.50
Coffee and tea	.25
Candle light	.14
Fuel, 3 tons of coal per annum, $15.00; charcoal, chips, matches, etc., $5.00 per annum	.40
Salt, pepper, vinegar, starch, soap, soda, yeast, cheese, eggs	.40
Furniture and utensils, wear and tear	.25
Rent	3.00
Bed clothes	.20
Clothing	2.00
Newspapers	.12
Total	$10.37

"I ask," said Greeley, "have I made the working-man's comforts too high? Where is the money to pay for amusements, for ice-creams, his puddings, his trips on Sunday up or down the river in order to get some fresh air, to pay the doctor or apothecary, to pay for pew rent in the church, to purchase books, musical instruments?" . . .

There was not in [this] period, or probably in any other, a more helpless and degraded class of workers than the needlewomen of the cities. Their condition had earlier enlisted the efforts of Mathew Carey and others, without appreciable result. They were incapable of organizing themselves permanently because of the semi-industrial nature of their trade and the surplus of that sort of labor. What little organization was achieved among them depended rather on the spasmodic efforts of "humane persons" who interested themselves in their behalf.

From 1840 to 1860 a complete revolution occurred in the tailoring industry as a result of the introduction of ready-made clothing in common use. Until 1835 the only clothing kept for sale was "shop clothing" which was sold almost entirely to seamen. The wholesale manufacture of clothes began in New York in 1835, but went under in the panic of 1837. In 1840 the trade revived and offered employment, such as it was, to thousands of women. At first, much of this work was sent into the country to be made up, but it was gradually being brought into the "factories."

The sewing machine made its appearance in the clothing trade in the early fifties. At first the tailor was required to buy his own machine and, as those who had sufficient savings to do this were few, those who had not were compelled to pay the machine tailor for straight stitching. The machine tailor soon discovered that his investment was not a paying one. His earnings were no greater than before and his savings were gone. The profit of the machine went to the bosses; "they got their work quicker and it was done better." . . .

There were at this time four groups of needlewomen corresponding to the classes of work and the stages of advance toward the complete factory system of a later date. The journeymen dressmakers, who were employed by the week, often worked fourteen to sixteen hours a day, and were paid from $1.25 to $2.50 per week. The dressmakers who went into the homes of their customers were better paid, receiving 62½ cents, 75 cents, and $1 a day. Apprentices were usually paid nothing for the first six months and boarded themselves. They were frequently required to pay the employer $10 or $15 for the privilege of "learning," and, if they were unable to pay, they worked for a year without wages and boarded themselves. Instead of being taught the trade, the apprentices were usually kept at plain sewing, and at the end of the apprenticeship two-thirds or three-quarters of them were not trained dressmakers at all. The last group, and the lowest in the scale in every respect, were those who worked in their own homes, calling for their work and returning to the shop with it when finished. There were ten thousand of these women in New York City alone in 1854, and their wages, hours, and conditions of work were inconceivably bad. Widows in Cincinnati were supporting children by making shirts for ten cents each and pants for fifteen and seventeen cents. It was estimated that they could make nine shirts in a week, or ninety cents for a long week's work. In New York, in 1845, some of the needlewomen were being paid ten to eighteen cents a day for twelve to fourteen hours' work, while others, who were more proficient, were paid twenty-five cents a day. Work which had brought 97½ cents in 1844 was paid only 37½ cents in 1845. The average earnings of these women were $1.50 to $2 a week, though many of them could not earn more than $1.

> A great number of females are employed in making men's and boys' caps [said the *Tribune* reporter in 1845]. By constant labor, 15 to 18 hours a day, they can make from 14 to 25 cents. We are told by an old lady who has lived by this kind of work for a long time that when she begins at sunrise and works till midnight, she can earn 14 cents a day. . . .
>
> The manner in which these women live, the squalidness and unhealthy location and nature of their habitations, the impossibility of providing for any of the slightest recreations or moral or intellectual culture or of educating their children, can be easily imagined; but we assure the public that it would require an extremely active imagination to conceive the reality.

When the industrial worker and his friends protested that there was white slavery in the North as evil as the black slavery of the South, they were thinking of conditions of this sort. But the wages, hours, and homes of these women were not their only difficulties. It was a common occurrence for one of the seamstresses to carry back to her employer, after a week's work, a heavy bundle of clothing in her arms and find that it would not pass his examination. Many of the cheap "slop shops" required the women to pay a deposit of the full value of the material before it could be taken out. When work fell off and there was no more to be given out, this deposit was frequently retained by the employer. Needlewomen receiving only five cents for shirts, on which they were required to deposit the full value of the material, were said to have been paid at the rate of ninety-six cents on the dollar. In some cases only a part of the money due was paid, the woman being told to allow the remainder to stand over for later settlement. In this way many of the employers who professed to pay good wages reduced them to the level of the worst. Instances were known where fifty cents was paid on account and the remainder postponed week after week until the claimant became discouraged and gave up trying to collect. In the meantime she had to neglect her chances of getting other employment. One woman after seeking work for two days managed to get something that paid her sixty cents for the first week. When she returned the goods, she was given credit on the books to be settled when the amount was worth while. In another case, the girl delivering her work and asking for payment was kicked into the street and left without money to cross the ferry to her home. . . .

In New York, in 1853, prices were as low as they had been in 1845: summer vests were eighteen cents; pantaloons, twenty cents; light coats, eighteen cents. A twelve-hour day gave a return of about twenty-four cents, "provided [the goods] were not returned upon the hands of the worker." Shirts were made for four, five, seven, and eight cents apiece; three of them were a hard day's labor and brought the worker from twelve to twenty-four cents a day. "The average yearly income of these women at the best of the above prices, all doing full work the year round, amounts to ninety-one dollars!"

The beginnings of the "sweating system" are to be found here. The *Tribune's* reporter described it in 1853 as a "middle system." Near one of the streets running from the Bowery to the East River an old Irish woman was found with four girls working for her. Their pay consisted solely of their food for six days a week. Another woman had hired four "learners," two of whom received only board and lodging, while the other two were paid one dollar a week without their food.

The milliners of New York were [no?] better off than the sewing-women. As apprentices they received no pay or board for a year, and, in the better shops, had frequently to pay a bonus for the privilege of "learning." The hours were from ten to twelve, and at the end of the year they were turned out to find employment, and a new batch of apprentices was taken on. All through the period and in very many trades the apprenticeship system had become little more than a cheap method of getting the greater part of the work done. There was no attempt made to teach the full trade. One or two journeymen were sufficient as overseers to supply all the craft knowledge and skill required for the shop and the routine work was done by so-called "apprentices." The journeymen milliners working from sunrise to 9 P.M. could earn from $2.50 to $3 a week. Their board and washing cost at least $2. . . .

The new industrialism found its completest expression in the textile mills of New England, New York, and Pennsylvania. Here the New Power was most firmly established and the new discipline most intense. In the barracks-like mills by the swift rivers of the northern seaboard the Industrial Revolution reached completion, and the lesser status of the industrial worker was revealed. And there developed in the forties a remarkable controversy over the Factory System, originating, in part, in the political field and involving the tariff question, and, in part, in the feeling that the new industrialism was alien to and destructive of American ideals and standards.

The introduction of the cotton industry in Massachusetts at the beginning of the century was achieved under difficulties that arose, on the one hand, from the want of a labor force and, on the other, from the English control of the new machines and the technical knowledge required to set them in operation. A new labor force was available in the women and girls of New England, once their initial aversion to the factory discipline could be broken down. The degraded condition of the operatives of the English mill towns was notorious, and Americans, including the Boston capitalists intent on cotton manufacture, had no desire to reproduce those conditions here.

"The question . . . arose and was deeply considered," said Nathan Appleton, "whether this degradation was the result of the peculiar occupation or of other and distinct causes. . . ." The matter was decided in favor of the latter hypothesis, and the Boston capitalists who had interested themselves in cotton manufacture proceeded to make such arrangements as seemed good to them to attract the New England women into the mills and guard them from immoral influences as best they could.

This protection involved what is known as the "Waltham System" which was copied in the foundation of Lowell and came to be regarded as the perfection of what an industrial community should be. The basis of the Waltham system was the company boarding-house, where the girls were required to be in at 10 P.M. and generally to live under the somewhat fictitious supervision of the boarding-house keeper. Upon this basis was erected a puritanical paternalism originally intended for the welfare of the girls, but capable — in the hands of agents less high-principled than the early mill-owners — of being turned into a very effective and harmful despotism. In addition to the boarding-houses, the Waltham system involved the payment of wages in cash, the "moral police" or community censorship of morals, the requirement that the girls should attend church, discharge for immoral conduct, and a thorough understanding among the corporations as to wages, hours, and the "blacklist."

> I visited the corporate factory establishment of Waltham within a few miles of Boston [said Harriet Martineau in 1834]. The establishment is for spinning and weaving of cotton alone and the construction of the requisite machinery. Five hundred girls were employed at the time of my visit. The girls can earn two and sometimes three dollars a week besides their board. The little children earn one dollar a week. Most of the girls live in houses provided by the corporation. . . . When sisters come to the mill it is a common practice for them to bring their mother to keep house for them and some other companions, in a dwelling built by their own earnings. In this case they save enough out of their board to clothe themselves and have two or three dollars to spare. Some have thus cleared off mortgages from their fathers' farms; others have educated the hope of the family at college; and many are rapidly accumulating an independence. I saw a whole street of houses built with the earnings of the girls; some with piazzas and green venetian blinds, and all neat and sufficiently spacious.
>
> The factory people built the church which stands conspicuous on the green in the midst of the place. The minister's salary, eight hundred dollars last year, is raised by a tax on the pews. The corporation gave them a building for a Lyceum which they have furnished with a good library and where they have lectures every winter, the best that money can procure. The girls have, in many instances, private libraries of some value.
>
> The managers of the various factory establishments keep the wages as nearly equal as possible and then let the girls freely shift from one to another. . . . The people work about seventy hours a week on an average. . . . All look like well-dressed young ladies. The health is good, or rather it is no worse than elsewhere.

This picture is somewhat *couleur de rose* and naïve in its treatment of the compulsory tax for the upkeep of the church and the uniform wage and freedom of movement of the operatives. The only fault Miss Martineau found with the mills was the overcrowding of the boarding-houses where girls sometimes slept three in a bed and six or more in a room. She must have been misinformed as to the hours of labor which were nearer seventy-five than seventy a week. . . .

In sharp contrast with the Waltham system there was found in the Middle States, and especially in Rhode Island, what can be called the English system of *laissez-faire*. This was the original method of cotton manufacture in New England, having been established by Samuel Slater at Pawtucket before the beginning of the century. The Rhode Island system, to be found also at Fall River, Massachusetts, was not a conscious method at all, but simply a growth along English lines with the material at hand. Instead of employing adults almost exclusively, as in Massachusetts, whole families were employed, and it is in this district that child labor was chiefly found. There was no attempt made by Slater and those who followed him to guard the morals of the operatives or to do anything for them within or without the mills. There were no company boarding-houses, the operatives being allowed to find what homes they could, and instead of cash wages being paid, factory stores were established and store orders issued. The first mill opened by Slater was operated by seven boys and two girls between the ages of seven and eleven, and some of the early mills recruited children from the almshouses and overseers of the poor.

The contrast of the two systems is interesting because the scarcity of factory labor was probably as great in Rhode Island as in Massachusetts, which suggests that the Waltham system was the result of the Puritan traditions of the Boston capitalists, rather than the real necessities of the case, while the presence of the company store in Rhode Island reveals it as less a convenience for the operatives than a means of exploitation by the companies. For if the company store had been a real convenience to the operatives, as is often assumed, it would probably have been found in Lowell rather than Pawtucket, though the large percentage of single women at Lowell would have reduced its trade. . . .

But the essential difference between Lowell and Rhode Island or Fall River was the psychological one between paternalism and *laissez-faire*. General Oliver, who had been an agent at Lowell, visited Fall River in 1855 and was greatly shocked by the attitude of the agents at the latter place.

> I inquired of the agent of a principal factory whether it was the custom of the manufacturers to do anything for the physical, intellectual, and moral welfare of their work-people. . . . "We never do," he said. "As for myself, I regard my work-people just as I regard my machinery. So long as they can do my work for what I choose to pay them, I keep them, getting out of them all I can. What they do or how they fare outside my walls I don't know, nor do I consider it my business to know. They must look out for themselves as I do for myself. When my machines get old and useless, I reject them and get new, and these people are part of my machinery."

A Holyoke manager found his hands "languorous" in the early morning because they had breakfasted. He tried working them without breakfast and got three thousand more yards of cloth a week made.

It would appear at first glance that there could be no comparison, from the standpoint of the operatives, between the two systems; that the puritanical paternalism of Lowell was infinitely superior to the callous indifference of Fall River. Nevertheless, two rather unexpected facts emerge to modify this opinion: the attack on the factory system by the intellectuals centered not on the evil conditions of Fall River, but on the relatively admirable conditions of Lowell; and the operatives' revolt began at the former rather than at the latter place. This would suggest, at least, that there were elements in the Lowell situation that were regarded as even more harmful than bad conditions, and that the Fall River system left the operatives greater initiative. It would be unwise to press these deductions too far because it is equally possible to say that the Fall River revolt was the result of exceptionally bad conditions and the attack on Lowell, the result of its proximity to Boston.

The Lowell factory system was being attacked in our period from two directions. The Battle of Books represented the opposition of the intellectuals and was directed chiefly against the alleged tendency to degrade the morals and health of the operative, while the attack of the operatives themselves was chiefly against the "tyranny" and "despotism" of the system, its increasing discipline and antirepublican nature.

> That the factory system contains in itself the elements of slavery, we think no sound reasoning can deny, and every day continues to add power to its incorporate sovereignty, while the sovereignty of the working people decreases in the same ratio.

Like other workers of the period, the factory operatives — men and women — felt that they were losing something of their dignity and independence, so that, from the point of view of the workers, much of the heated argument over factory conditions missed the point. The worker objected to his cage, whether it was gilded, as in Lowell, or rusty and unkempt, as in Fall River.

In the matter of discipline the Fall River system had advantages over that of Lowell. Once out of the Fall River mills, the worker was free, while in Lowell there was hardly an hour of the day or a relationship of any sort that was not covered by the regulations, written or understood, of the corporations. . . .

The factory controversy began with an editoral in the Boston *Daily Times* (Democrat) for Saturday, July 13, 1839, entitled "A Manufacturing Population." The interest of the *Times* in the matter was partly political. The Whigs had always contended that the factories gave easy, pleasurable, and remunerative employment to women and girls who would otherwise have been idle, and that the fears of the opponents of the system were unfounded. The *Times* undertook to show that the young girls are compelled to work in unhealthy confinement for too many hours every day; that their food is both unhealthy and scanty; that they are not allowed sufficient time to eat: . . . that they are crowded together in ill-ventilated apartments in the boarding-houses of the corporations, and that in consequence they become pale, feeble, and finally broken in constitution . . . and that hundreds of the vilest of the female sex throng to the manufactories with corruption in their manners and upon their tongues to breathe out the pestilence of the brothel in the boarding-places.

The *Times* objected to the fact that the girls were made to board at the company houses except when they had friends or relatives in Lowell; that they had to be in their rooms at ten o'clock; and that the price of their board was fixed by the corporations at $1.50 a week and deducted from their wages. It was claimed that the price of board was too low, that a decent table could not be maintained at the price when potatoes were selling for 75 cents to $1 a peck, flour was $9 to $12 a barrel, and beef 10 to 16 cents a pound. The girls were underfed and unhealthy-looking, except the newcomers from the country.

In the early days, the *Times* contended, conditions had been better. When the Merrimack Mill was started, besides the workmen employed from Europe the proprietors had to rely on such girls as they could obtain to attend the looms and spindles. These girls came in gradually from the surrounding country — daughters of farmers and mechanics, "generally poor, but of unblemished reputation." Provisions were cheap, the food sufficient, and the girls seemed happy and healthy. They dressed well and preferred the mills as their own mistresses to being servants. Many of them saved money and went home, but others squandered their earnings and found themselves tied to the mills. But the supply was still inadequate and the corporations had to send men out to scour the country through New Hampshire, Vermont, and Canada. Thus the permanent mill population increased and their dependence upon the corporations. The labor turnover was tremendous, one hundred girls arriving and leaving every day for several weeks in the spring and fall, but always some remained behind to swell the factory population, unfitted to be wives and mothers, in slavish dependence on the mills.

When the corporations began to realize, said the *Times,* that this permanent factory population was increasing, they reduced wages by agreement. On the first occasion the girls "turned out," but new hands were found, and "there has been created and there is now growing up in Lowell a manufacturing population whose tendency in the scale of civilization, health, morals, and intellectuality, is manifestly downwards."

As to the morals of the girls, the *Times* quoted a Lowell physician to the effect that

there used to be in Lowell an association of young men called "The Old Line" who had an understanding with a great many of the factory girls and who used to introduce young men of their acquaintance, visitors to the place, to the girls for immoral purposes. Balls were held at various places attended mostly by these young men and girls, with some others who did not know the object of the association, and after the dancing was over the girls were taken to infamous places of resort in Lowell and the vicinity and were not returned to their homes until daylight.

Another medical practitioner in Lowell stated that, in one week, he had more than seventy persons apply to him for remedies for venereal diseases, most of whom were girls. Occupants of brothels in New York and Boston who had become diseased were also said to have entered the mills. The late deputy sheriff of Lowell had stated that he had found three houses to which these professional prostitutes were in the habit of bringing factory girls.

Dr. Elisha Bartlett of Lowell replied to the *Times* articles in the Lowell *Courier*, and this was later published as a pamphlet under the title "A Vindication of the Character and Condition of the Females Employed in the Lowell Mills against the charges contained in the Boston Times and Boston Quarterly Review." The editor of the *Courier* also replied, as did Harriet Farley, editor of the *Lowell Offering*.

As is frequently the case in controversies of this sort, the opponents were not talking about the same thing and never really came to grips. Bartlett insisted that the morals and health of the factory operatives were good, while the *Times* claimed that their morals and health were getting bad. Bartlett was thinking of a condition, often of a past condition, and the *Times* of a tendency. Neither was concerned with the problem that bothered the worker, the problem of social status and freedom. The mill girls had been, and the majority perhaps still were, what Bartlett claimed, but at the same time they were becoming more or less what the *Times* insisted they were: "a permanent factory population" of a more degraded sort than the New England mill girls of the twenties and thirties.

Dr. Bartlett dealt chiefly with health, morals, chances of marriage and wages, and his argument was followed quite closely by Miles and Scoresby in 1845. He made a statistical comparison between Lowell and Portsmouth, New Hampshire, . . . and declared that "the manufacturing population of this city is the healthiest portion of the population." He defended the morals of the factory girls, claiming that the mill overseers, the "moral police" of the corporations, and the censorship of the girls themselves kept the tone of the community high. He insisted even that the morals of the girls improved on coming from the country where all was not as pure as it looked.

As to wages, the average, clear of board, amounted to about two dollars per week. The number of depositors in the Lowell Savings Institution was 1976 and the amount of deposits $305,796.75. Of these depositors, 978 were factory girls. The amount of their deposits is not given, but it is estimated at not less than $100,000, while it was a common thing for a girl to have $500 in the bank. Bartlett claimed that the girls' chances of marriage were good and the boarding-house keepers quite able to make a living and supply satisfactory food if they managed properly.

The controversy was continued by a reply to Dr. Bartlett which appeared in the *Vox Populi* of Lowell in 1841. This was written by "A Citizen of Lowell" and was later published under the title "Corporations and Operatives: Being an exposition of the condition of factory operatives and a review of the 'Vindication' by Elisha Bartlett, M.D." The reply was an able discussion that left nothing of Bartlett's mortality and marriage statistics, but began in a demogogic vein that tended to obscure the value of the later argument. The Lowell "Citizen" charged the defenders of the factories with being paid "servants of interested aristocracies," a "pensioned press" and "bought priesthood." The question of the hours of employment, that later supplanted all others, was here first emphasized. It was claimed that the operatives had only fifteen minutes in which to eat their meals when time was deducted for going to and from the boarding-houses. The price allowed for board had been $1.25 until 1836, when it had been raised to $1.37½ because the boarding-house keepers had been unable to live. There it remained until 1841, when it was again reduced to $1.25. The boarding-houses were overrun with vermin. The hours in the mills were nearly thirteen a day and not less than twelve and one-half of actual toil. But this was to reckon only the time actually in the mills, and even this was not correct because some corporations cheated the operatives by starting before the ringing of the bell. Reckoning the time stolen and the time occupied in preparing for meals, eating, and going to and fro, the operatives were engaged fifteen hours out of the twenty-four.

Not only were the hours long, but they were getting longer. The corporations were adding to them "year after year, week after week, minute by minute," until they ran fifteen minutes a day longer in 1841 than twelve years before. "I do not believe," said the "Citizen of Lowell," "that there is upon the face of the earth any large class of persons who labor incessantly for so many hours each day as do the factory operatives of New England." . . .

STUDY GUIDE

1. How did each of the following contribute to the debased condition of labor described by Ware: technological changes such as new, heavier machinery; machinery that required less skill to operate; a labor surplus; social attitudes toward labor?

2. In terms of potential labor force and the type of labor involved, why were the needle trades more susceptible to exploitative labor conditions than some other industries?

3. What were the differences between the Waltham and the Fall River or Rhode Island systems of factory labor? Which of them seems more exploitative and which more paternalistic? In what ways did the less paternalistic system have advantages from the worker's point of view?

4. In another country or another period, the expansion of the available labor force by the introduction of women, children, and immigrants might not have resulted in a general degradation of the position of all labor. What, in the position of labor in the early nineteenth century or in the general state of the Industrial Revolution at that time, might account for the fact that such degradation did happen in the United States?

5. What similarities and differences are there in the lot of workers in the early nineteenth century and in the present with respect to: their ability to bargain to improve their positions; the training necessary for their jobs; their mobility; their relationship to their employers; their security?

BIBLIOGRAPHY

While Ware's book is one of the best specialized works ever published on American factory labor, it is limited to the two decades before the Civil War. Also, there are many other aspects of the Industrial Revolution in the United States that merit attention, which were not within the scope of Ware's study. A number of books on technology and other subjects are listed in the bibliography following the selection by Joseph and Frances Gies (Reading No. 7). Carl Bridenbaugh, *The Colonial Craftsman* (1950) is an interesting study of labor in the preindustrial period. Two works that elaborate on the topics of which Ware writes are Caroline F. Ware, *The Early New England Cotton Manufacture: A Study in Industrial Beginnings* (1931) and Hannah Josephson, *Golden Threads: New England's Mill Girls and Magnates* (1949). The writings of factory women themselves are published in Philip Foner, ed., *The Factory Girls* (1977), while Steve Dunwell, *The Run of the Mill* (1978) is a marvelous collection of photographs of the factories, with an accompanying text. Indicating an extraordinary versatility, Anthony F. C. Wallace turned from studying the Seneca Indians to examining the social and economic life of small factory towns in his book *Rockdale: The Growth of an American Village in the Early Industrial Revolution* (1978). Two other recent works that study particular towns are Alan Dawley, *Class and Community: The Industrial Revolution in Lynn* (1976) and Thomas Dublin, *Women at Work: The Transformation of Work and Community in Lowell Massachusetts, 1826–1860* (1979).

There are a number of one-volume surveys of American labor history that carry the story beyond the Civil War. Henry Pelling, *American Labor* (1960) is a very brief introduction. Foster R. Dulles, *Labor in America: A History* (1949) and Joseph G. Rayback, *A History of American Labor* (1959) are longer works. Barbara M. Wertheimer, *We Were There: The Story of Working Women in America* (1977) is a popular study of the subject.

V WESTERN EXPANSION AND CIVIL WAR

At the time of the Treaty of Paris of 1783, the boundaries of the United States had been set at the Mississippi River on the west and along the 31st parallel on the south. By 1853, the country had added the huge territory of the Louisiana Purchase, acquired Florida from Spain, and swept westward over Texas, California, and Oregon into every square mile of territory that was to make up the continental United States. This breathtaking acquisition of territory had involved American intrigue in Florida, revolution in Texas, a blustering threat of force in Oregon, and full-scale war against Mexico. Generally, however, the American people were in advance of their government. Rather than gold, land — to settle on or to speculate in — was the chief lure that drew Americans westward into lands beyond the borders of their own country.

The acquisition of millions of acres of land beyond the Mississippi was one of the crucial factors in accentuating the sectional conflict that had begun in the 1830s. During the 1850s, the morality of slavery was the overriding issue in the minds of abolitionists. But for most people of both the North and the South, a matter of more immediate concern was whether or not slavery would expand into the western territories. The slogan of the Free Soil party of the North embodied the several aspects of sectional conflict: "Free Soil, Free Speech, Free Labor, and Free Men." This party's concern that labor and soil in the West be free points up the economic division of North and South. But the other parts of the slogan — free speech and free men — suggest that the country was also divided by psychological and social differences.

By 1861, many national social institutions, including the major religious denominations, had broken apart along sectional lines. And by that time, many thousands of Southerners saw the triumph of the northern Republican party in the 1860 election as not simply a political defeat but a threat to all southern institutions and to the southern way of life.

When we think of the westward movement, we usually imagine small parties struggling, in near starvation and haunting loneliness, across the Great Plains. The first reading describes the crowded conditions on the trails at the height of the migration and the cooperation that eased the hardships. The second and third readings describe the abolitionist movement that led to the Civil War and the astounding costs of that great conflict, both in casualties and in social and psychological destruction. American society had been torn asunder, and the reweaving of the disparate threads into a new social fabric was to prove a long and trying process. Some of the difficulties that were involved are described in the essay on the Reconstruction period that concludes this volume.

This photograph of pioneers on the trail west illustrates their mode of travel and the way they clung to the fashions they were used to back East.

18

JOHN D. UNRUH, JR.

The Way West

Few movements in all of our history have captured the imagination as has the settlement of the great American West. The image of the sturdy pioneer, plodding beside a lumbering covered wagon, fighting off Indian attacks, fording swift streams, and finally looking out upon the blue Pacific, has become enshrined in American folklore and on Hollywood celluloid. There is much in all of this that is sheer myth, but there is also much that is true.

The earliest openings of some American frontiers were accomplished by lone trappers and hunters who, because the game was there or because they weren't comfortable in more settled communities, turned their paths westward. Such men served as guides and added to the scant geographical knowledge of nineteenth-century America. But even in the fur trade, the single hunter was rapidly supplanted by the business organization, and it was John Jacob Astor's Pacific Fur Company that led thousands of other Americans to dream of the Oregon country.

In fact, settlement of the West in large numbers required careful planning, substantial equipment and supplies, organization, and community effort. Whether seeking gold in California, land in Oregon, or a religious Eden in Utah, the pioneers usually went west in a group. Leaders were chosen, supplies carefully assembled, and laws of the trail set down. But the fact that pioneer life primarily involved organized communities rather than lone scouts does not mean that struggle and hardship were any less a part of the frontier experience.

Americans today are still a migratory people, and until very recently California was the chief lodestar. But as we speed on interstate highways alongside the Platte River or fly over the Rocky Mountains in jet comfort, we have little idea of life on the trail in 1848. For this we must turn to the diaries of the men and women who made the long trek, who gave birth to infants on the wooden beds of wagons and pushed on the next day, and who buried children and parents in unmarked graves to which they would never return.

The view of western migration provided in the following selection, from John D. Unruh's book *The Plains Across*, is rather different from that of most writings on the subject. The author indicates how crowded the trails were during the height of the westward movement, and emphasizes the cooperation of the migrants with one another and with the Plains Indians.

[Between 1840 and 1860] approximately a quarter of a million overlanders had worn the trails to Oregon and California so deeply that in places the ruts are still visible. In that same period over 40,000 Latter-Day Saints traveled portions of those same trails to their Salt Lake Valley refuge, and by 1860 thousands of expectant gold seekers were penetrating the Pike's Peak region. . . .

These masses of westering overlanders do not coincide with the popular media image of widely scattered wagon trains traveling in relative isolation. Indeed, particularly between 1849 and 1853, most overlanders longed for privacy instead of the congested trails, crowded campsites, and over-grazed grasses they were experiencing. So many overlanders, for example, set forth from near St. Joseph on the same day in 1852 that teams traveled twelve abreast. Franklin Langworthy reported in 1850, from near South Pass, "The road, from morning till night, is crowded like Pearl Streat or Broadway," noting also that fathers had actually become separated from their sons in the "endless throng" and did not meet again until their arrival in California. Bennett C. Clark's company, in 1849, traveled late into the night near Ash Hollow in a desperate search for a vacant campsite.

Statistically inclined emigrants kept track of trail traffic during noon stops, on rare rest days, early in the mornings, and on particularly dusty days. James B. Persinger reported that their company passed 200 wagons early one 1850 morning, were passed by 100 another noon, and passed at

Reprinted by permission from John D. Unruh, Jr., *The Plains Across: The Overland Emigrants and the Trans-Mississippi West, 1840–1860* (Urbana, Chicago, and London: University of Illinois Press). © 1979 by the Board of Trustees of the University of Illinois.

least 500 more another day. Joseph Price wrote to his wife from Pacific Springs the same year that the 160 wagons which passed that point on June 27 was a smaller number than usual. . . .

Not anticipating this trail congestion, emigrants during the gold rush consciously endeavored to travel in companies, formally or informally organized, just as they had in previous years when the trails had not been so crowded. The emigrant goal was always to insure that sufficient manpower would be available for whatever contingencies might arise: bridging or fording a stream, climbing a mountain, rounding up stampeded stock, resisting Indian attack. This vast armada of overlanders swarming together along the trails, especially during the gold rush, often created friction; tempers periodically flared as drivers jockeyed for position on the dusty main trail, and on occasion one traveling company passed another only after an actual race.

Such frustrations, however, were much overshadowed by the omnipresent emigrant interaction, which contributed so significantly to the success of the overland migrations. It is this cooperative quality of the migrations which scholars have so largely overlooked. Two neglected phases of emigrant interchange revolve around travelers who began the westbound journey only to turn back, and overlanders who traveled the trails eastward from the Pacific Coast to the Missouri and Iowa frontiers. For many westbound emigrants, the significant exchanges deriving from interaction with west-to-east trail travelers proved an unexpected bonus.

Although most of the turn-arounds were products of the gold rush years, a few overlanders had reconsidered the wisdom of their proposed venture ever since the overland movement had begun. In 1841, in fact, nearly 10 percent of the departing caravan of California- and Oregon-bound overlanders, Jesuit missionaries heading for the Flathead Indian territory, and other tourists and trappers made their way back to the Missouri settlements. . . .

. . . Since many of them had gone at least as far as Fort Kearny, and some to Fort Laramie and even beyond, their knowledge and advice were helpful to those pressing on. Indeed, the oncoming hordes so desired information — even if it was slightly exaggerated — that they pestered all returnees they met, unless there was serious sickness among them. . . .

Through information and mail service (one "goback" forty-niner brought back several letters), the turn-arounds provided their major assistance. But numbers of westbound overlanders who had suffered losses or had discovered outfitting errors or omissions were also much aided by this unexpected opportunity to purchase draft animals, wagons, tents, provisions, and other needed materials, since turn-arounds were usually willing to part with much of their outfit which they would not now be needing. On the other hand, a few returnees, having lost their draft animals, were forced to rely completely upon the charity of westbound emigrants in order to return to the frontier settlements. It is difficult to estimate the actual numbers of overlanders who retraced their steps, but in 1849, 1850, and 1852 there were certainly hundreds, and the yearly total probably approached and may even have surpassed 1,000 in 1850 and 1852.

Hasty conversations on the trail or at noon and evening encampments with eastbound overlanders direct from Oregon or California provided the most helpful and reliable sources of information to westbound emigrants. Such returning travelers were able to provide accurate — and sometimes disheartening — data on how far it really was to the mines, rumors notwithstanding, and whether the Indians evidenced hostile or friendly intentions. They also furnished advice regarding the various cutoffs, the availability of supplies at forts and trading posts, the presence of ferries at the various river crossings, the prices being charged there, and the location of buffalo herds. On occasion these eastbound parties also served as escorts for turnarounds. . . .

Because west-to-east travelers were able to answer questions on the two matters of most interest and concern to overland emigrants — conditions on the trail and in California and Oregon — they were plied with questions by oncoming overlanders even more persistently than were the turn-arounds. And since eastbound travelers encountered almost the entire westbound migration this could become extremely frustrating, especially in years when 50,000 overlanders were trailing west. One 1850 party simply kept their mules going at a rapid pace, never stopping to entertain the "hundreds" of queries with which they were peppered, although they did shout back answers until they could no longer be heard. . . .

There was cause for eastbound overlanders being circumspect, especially those coming from California with gold dust in their possession. Enoch Conyers, while riding some distance from the main trail in 1852, encountered a solitary eastbound traveler encamped for the night. Upon first questioning, the man claimed to be a discouraged turn-around. When Conyers recognized him as his uncle, however, the solitary traveler admitted to be returning from California with considerable gold in his possession. He explained that he frequently camped far from the main trail and if seen claimed to be a turn-around. He had adopted this strategy because he feared robbers — especially "white Indians" — although he had barely survived a harrowing attack from real Indians shortly after crossing the Sierra Nevada Mountains.

Conyers's uncle had been more fortunate than a number of eastbound overlanders who fell victim to Indians and "highwaymen." . . . A particularly dangerous year for eastbound travelers was 1856, when the bodies of at least eight returning Californians were found along the Humboldt River after apparent robbery-murders. . . .

Although the impact of turn-arounds and eastbound overland travelers upon the overland emigrations was significant, the most important cooperation and interaction obviously prevailed among the much greater number of westbound overlanders. Because attrition, traveling company splits, combinations, and recombinations were so common to the overland emigrating experience, the matter of conveying advice, progress reports, and other newsworthy information to relatives, friends, and former traveling companions was extremely important. The "roadside telegraph" which the overlanders devised was a crude but surprisingly effective means of communication. Anyone wishing to leave a message would write a short note and place it conspicuously alongside the trail so that those following behind would be certain not to pass it by.... Even human skulls were used. With surfaces which had been smoothed and whitened by the elements, these skulls and bones were strikingly visible, especially when hung on a stick by the side of the trail. The inscriptions, when not purposely rubbed out, lasted a long time. Lodisa Frizzell in 1852 was still able to read penciled messages written in 1849.

Most overlanders were careful not to disturb these precious sources of information. Messages specifically directed to individual emigrants or particular companies were removed, but most others, after having been studiously read, were not otherwise disturbed....

The roadside messages frequently communicated advice and information reflective of the cooperative concern most overlanders had for each other's safety and progress. The advice was often especially helpful to the many greenhorn travelers of the gold rush period. For example, forty-niner James Wilkins's outfit gratefully followed the recommendation on a trailside notice for avoiding a twenty-mile desert. The notice, according to Wilkins, had been posted "by a philanthropic Kentuckian" who had backtracked specifically to share his discovery of the alternate route for the benefit of those behind. Alonzo Delano found a signboard beyond Fort Laramie which read, "Look at this — look at this! The water here is poison, and we have lost six of our cattle. Do not let your cattle drink on this bottom." At a poisonous waterhole the next year James Evans commented, "Happy is the man who can read!" after observing a myriad of signs warning against tasting the water in phrases such as "He drank of this water and died" and "For God's sake do not taste this water." In addition to cautioning against bad water and grass, overlanders erected signs directing their comrades to fresh-water springs some distance off the road, or admonishing that this was the last available water or the last good grass before a desert stretch was to be crossed. So-called "cutoffs" which saved neither time nor energy were forcefully denounced. Harriet Ward spoke for many grateful overlanders after following a signpost's directions to reach a refreshingly cool spring some distance off the road in 1853: "Oh! what a pleasure to meet with such little mementoes of disinterested benevolence from strangers!"

A great many roadside communications dealt with Indian depredations, warning oncoming overlanders that losses of stock and human life had occurred at a particular location. Such announcements probably served the dual purpose of alerting emigrants to potential dangers as well as reporting the loss of animals, so that if any were subsequently found by other over-landers, the initial owner could claim the animal. Forty-niner John Edwin Banks even saw a notice offering a 200-dollar reward for five stolen horses and the persons who had committed the theft. . . .

. . . In 1849 some overlanders who had gone via Salt Lake changed their minds and traveled the southern trail to California in lieu of the usual Humboldt River route, having been influenced by rumors that Missouri packers had coldbloodedly killed three Indians and burned the grass for 200 miles to impede the progress of overlanders. As a result the trails were re-portedly aswarm with revenge-minded Indians and completely unsafe. . . .

Most unplanned route changes, however, stemmed from the favorable accounts about shortcuts and cutoffs which wishful overlanders helped propagate. Emigrant diaries reveal much animated discussion and debate, and occasionally votes, as to whether an unknown cutoff should be attempted. Alonzo Delano, recording the deliberations of his company in 1849 regarding the Lassen Cutoff possibility, noted that emigrants from several traveling companies consulted together and that one man even went out thirty miles on horseback to check the new route. Delano's company, prompted by the urgings of its adventurous young men, took the supposed shortcut. Some of the various cutoff rumors were promulgated by interested parties, but there is ample evidence that many of the stories about how much time and distance cutoffs would save were freely circulated by and among emigrants eager for the trip to end but quite ignorant of any definite facts which would corrobo-rate their roseate assertions. . . .

There were numerous other ways in which westbound overlanders cooper-ated to lessen the demands of the journey, almost always in a cheerful spirit of cooperation without seeking personal gain. Seasoned plains travelers ad-vised novice overlanders of safe places to ford rivers so that expensive tolls could be avoided. Emigrant wagons bogged down in mudholes were pulled out by passing overlanders. Ropes, chains, boats, and bridge-building equip-ment were shared among different traveling groups. Overland companies encamping close together occasionally set out a mutual guard during the night. Following a rainstorm or stampede it was sometimes necessary for sev-eral traveling companies to cooperate in sorting out cattle which had milled together.

Also, emigrants on occasion volunteered to help strangers search for stock which had been stolen by Indians. This was emigrant cooperation at its best, for such errands of mercy could be dangerous. In 1857 one group of forty-two men from seven or eight different trains spent two fruitless days seeking sixty-one head of cattle stolen from an Arkansas train along the Humboldt River. Upon their return a second company was mustered from some of the trains which had come up in the interim, and this second group finally re-covered thirty-six head of cattle and killed one Indian — seventy miles distant from where they had begun their search. Emigrant hunting parties killing more buffalo, deer, or other prairie game than needed often shared surplus meats with fellow overlanders.

A less joyous cooperative task was the burial of deceased overlanders. Passing emigrants were often asked to assist members of other traveling companies in digging graves and constructing coffins and grave markers. Most overlanders also stopped to rebury any deceased overlander whom they discovered, as Heinrich Leinhard's company did along the Humboldt River in 1846, after finding a man whose body had not only been dug up (presumably by wolves) but stripped of clothing and mutilated as well.

One of the most prevalent forms of interaction among westering overlanders was the inadvertent visit paid to another group of emigrants. Most frequently this was for the night, but it often occurred at mealtimes as well. While traveling westward, overlanders persistently rode ahead, lagged behind, or wandered off from their traveling company to hunt, explore, fix a wagon, read, sketch a picture, visit, and sometimes sleep. Often they did not conclude their activity quickly enough to be able to reach their own outfit that same day, and gladly accepted the hospitality and protection their fellow travelers readily extended in such circumstances. Captains and other traveling luminaries were also periodically invited to share a meal with captains of trains they were passing — Edwin Bryant in 1846 and J. Goldsborough Bruff in 1849 were frequent guests at other campfires during the course of their respective overland trips.

There was always considerable visiting among overlanders who had chosen to halt for a day of rest and recuperation and who were encamped in fairly close promixity. When the rest day was on Sunday, as it usually was, emigrants from various companies frequently assembled for a religious service. Gregarious overlanders, of course, needed no excuse to stop, chat, and make new friends. Some occasionally went to great lengths to do so, as with the young 1853 overlander who swam the Platte River to visit a company of emigrants traveling on the other side of that waterway. In addition to the interaction between trains on opposite sides of the Platte, on occasion ladies functioned as nurses among the sick in other trains. And, as proof that the amenities of civilized life were not neglected on the plains, Charlotte Pengra reported in 1853 that she gave her sunbonnet pattern to another lady who had admired it while passing by. . . .

Opportunities for purchasing additional oxen to pull an overloaded wagon, an extra wagon tongue, a new or extra wagon or riding horse regularly presented themselves somewhere along the trail. Numerous trades of cattle, horses, and mules were also recorded in emigrant diaries. Particularly in 1849, when most overlanders took too much along and had to lighten their loads for the sake of their draft animals, fantastic bargains in clothing, revolvers, ammunition, foodstuffs, and almost everything else were available at many encampments. As the trip stretched out, many overlanders chose to sell their cumbersome wagons and most of their supplies in order to pack in to California by mule or horse. Some gold rushers made this change very early in the journey, retaining just as little in the way of provisions and supplies as they calculated would be necessary to complete the trip. This meant that mules and horses came to be increasingly valuable in the buying, selling, and trading among the overlanders, while oxen, wagons, and many other supplies and foodstuffs were sold at ridiculously low prices, if they could be sold at all.

An additional problem loomed toward the end of the journey, when overworked animals gave out or fell victim to Indian theft or arrow. Emigrants thus left with no way to transport their belongings sometimes were able to arrange with more fortunate overlanders to have their baggage carried through to the end of the journey, usually for some monetary or equivalent consideration. A few munificent overlanders asked nothing. These were real acts of compassion, since almost everyone's team was considerably worn down toward the journey's end. Along the Humboldt River in 1850, after traveling with his goods on his back for a day, Hugh Skinner secured accommodations in an Illinois wagon, thanks to a lady whose kindness led Skinner to remark, "I have uniformly found the women on the road more alive to the sufferings of their fellow creatures than the men." The bargain made, the emigrant usually traveled with his benefactor, but on occasion forged ahead on foot or with pack animal, planning to retrieve his goods later in California.

Clothing, blankets, and other personal belongings were important to overlanders, but food was crucial. The most significant assistance overlanders rendered to one another was certainly in sharing and selling provisions. A few gold rushers had even begun the journey with virtually no food supply, frankly planning to "sponge" off their better-prepared colleagues. One such 1849 foot traveler from Maine had reached Fort Kearny by such tactics, and figured that he would continue to find enough "Christians" on the route to supply his needs. . . .

In 1850 food was at a premium, especially on the later portions of the overland route. The rapidly increasing number of packers and other gold rushers running perilously low on rations frantically searched for overlanders well enough supplied to part with some of their provisions. The rapidly diminishing number of overlanders retaining surplus provisions happily watched prices skyrocket. Flour commanded up to $2 per pound; one overlander reported a man going from wagon to wagon unsuccessfully offering $50 for three pounds of flour. Hard bread sold at $1 a pound. One small group of hungry emigrants immediately slaughtered the worn-out ox they had chipped in to purchase for $65 from a passing train. . . .

In such precarious circumstances, desperate overlanders resorted to tactics both clever and violent to induce their fellows to offer up precious provisions. . . . After Oliver Goldsmith had been refused foodstuffs by some southern overlanders, his companion, John Root, who possessed a strong southern accent, managed to get some food from the same group. Root apparently used his accent to good advantage on other occasions.

But ruses seem not to have been as much used as force. Goldsmith and four friends, after being told by one emigrant that they could have all the provisions they wanted, but at the steep price of $2 per pound, "marched up to him and said there were five of us to his one and that we intended to take what we needed at our own price, twenty-five cents a pound, which we did." When 1850 emigrant James Campbell encountered begging overlanders who had eaten nothing but frogs for four days, he prudently began sleeping in his wagon to prevent possible thievery. . . .

Often, too, westering overlanders took up collections to provide unfortunate emigrants with the means to replace stock, wagons, or provisions. Thus, forty-niner Bernard Reid came upon a seventeen-year-old girl all alone save for her younger brother, who lay in their wagon sick with cholera. Both the mother and father had already died of the dread disease. The oxen were gone, and so was the faithless company with which the family had been traveling. Reid and others immediately took up a collection so that oxen might be purchased, two passing doctors prescribed medicine for the boy, and a Missouri group volunteered to take care of the orphans for the rest of the trip. Another 1850 gold seeker had been left by the trail after having been accidentally shot by one of his company. A passing physician attended to him, and westbound overlanders contributed money for his continuing care. When overlanders fording Thomas' Fork of the Bear River witnessed the drowning of one of the two horses an old man was relying on to take his family to California, they immediately took up a collection so the father could purchase another horse. And at the Green River ferry, in 1854, westbound emigrants again contributed funds to forward on to California the widow of a man who had just drowned.

Another common act of compassion was the attempt to ease the ordeal of desert crossings with "water wagons" manned and financed by overlanders having just completed the trip. Thirst-crazed overlanders were known to offer astronomical sums for a single drink of water during desert crossings. In 1850 on the desert beyond the Humboldt Sink, $5 was offered for a drink of water, and five gallons of water sold for $50. Henry Bloom reported that on the Hastings Cutoff desperate 1850 overlanders offered $10, $20, and up to $500 for a single drink of water. Fortunately for Bloom and his friends, the water wagon arrived before thirst elicited similar offers from them. This humane venture was especially prominent in 1850, when a wagonload of water was sent back every day by the emigrants who had crossed the preceding day. Not only water for the men but grass for draft animals was included, the effort being financed by contributions from the emigrants encamped at the spring which marked the welcome end of the treacherous long drive. An 1850 physician noted that their group had sent two relief loads back at a cost of $25 per wagon, the funds having been generously subscribed by passing overlanders. The wagon drivers gave the water free of charge to destitute overlanders, but those with money were charged from $1 to $5 per gallon. . . .

An additional legacy of the gold rush contributing considerably to emigrant interchange, albeit in a strange manner, was the trail of debris the greatest "litterbugs" of American history left in the wake of their transit across the West. Some traces had remained of the westward march of the overlanders of the 1840s, but since almost twice as many overlanders trailed westward in 1849 as in the entire previous decade, it was only natural that their residue would be greater. Further, their leavings were compounded by the overloaded wagons with which they had begun. They soon realized that the basic question was what they could do without, since their draft animals could never survive pulling such heavy loads. . . .

Many forty-niners began disposal operations as soon as they launched out onto the prairies. In the long run theirs was the wisest decision, providing they did not throw away too much. So much was abandoned within fifty miles of St. Joseph in 1849 that one emigrant indicated he would never go to California if he could have all that had been sacrificed that early in the journey. Persons went out from the outfitting points to collect the usable debris and brought back wagonloads of bacon, ham, flour, bread, beans, stoves, tools, medicines, extra wagon wheels and axle-trees, clothing, and similar items, which were presumably resold or used by the scavengers. After viewing the perfectly good food and other materials along the trail, one forty-niner wrote: "If I was going to start again, I would get a light wagon for mules, and gather up the rest of my outfit along the road."

While debris accumulated everywhere, much of the abandoned merchandise was concentrated in the Fort Laramie vicinity. Many overloaded forty-niners had endeavored to persevere as far as the fort, where they anticipated profitable sales of their excess supplies. Upon discovering that the traders there needed none of their surplus commodities — which could be picked up along the trail for nothing in any case — the overlanders had no alternative but to begin dumping. Joseph Berrien reached the fort on May 30, well in the forefront of the 1849 migration, and dubbed the area "Camp Sacrifice" because of all that had already been left there. More than 20,000 pounds of bacon alone had been abandoned near the fort before June 1, and the great masses of overloaded emigrants were still to come. Howard Stansbury, en route to an exploration of the Great Salt Lake Valley, enumerated some of the debris he saw in the Deer Creek area: "The road has been literally strewn with articles that have been thrown away. Bar-iron and steel, large blacksmiths' anvils and bellows, crow-bars, drills, augers, gold-washers, chisels, axes, lead, trunks, spades, ploughs, large grind-stones, baking-ovens, cooking-stoves without number, kegs, barrels, harness, clothing, bacon, and beans, were found along the road in pretty much the order in which they have been here enumerated." Virtually everything imaginable was found at least once somewhere along the overland trail: weapons, ammunition, tobacco, an iron safe, a Gothic bookcase, law and medical books — even a diving bell and accompanying apparatus.

If anything expendable remained in the wagons, it rarely lasted beyond the desert crossing to either the Carson or Truckee rivers. Here not only supplies but wagons and draft animals were left behind in ever-increasing numbers. Estimates of the number of abandoned wagons on the forty-mile desert ranged as high as 2,000 in 1850. Overlanders had already been passing and bemoaning the foul-smelling carcasses of dead animals — the victims of over-work and alkali poisoning — ever since leaving the Upper Platte ferry; what they witnessed on the desert crossings was merely the culmination. Though such tribulations were by no means unique to California gold seekers (Oregon-bound Maria Belshaw counted 190 dead animals along a 321-mile stretch of the Snake River in 1853), the debris, destruction, and stink reached their most astounding proportions on the deserts beyond the Humboldt Sink during the gold rush. . . .

A few gold rushers attempted a count. One 1850 traveler counted 2,381 horses and mules, 433 oxen, and 787 wagons, estimating the value of this and all other property left on the Carson Desert at $100,000. A subsequent tabulation of 4,960 dead horses, 3,750 dead oxen, and 1,061 dead mules led another observer to appraise the value of the abandoned property at $1 million. . . .

"The Dalles at present form a kind of masquerading thoroughfare, where emigrants and Indians meet, it appears, for the purpose of affording mutual aid." Jesuit missionary Pierre-Jean De Smet thus described, in 1846, a scene near the end of the overland route into Oregon's Willamette Valley. He could have written similarly of a multitude of other places along the Oregon-California Trail where overland emigrants and Indians met for purposes of aid and trade. That such beneficial interaction occurred, frequently and with considerable significance, contradicts the widely disseminated myth of in-cessant warfare between brave overlanders and treacherous Indians. The mass media view is not, of course, completely erroneous: Indians did kill hundreds of overlanders on the trails before the Civil War. The preoccupation with Indian depredations, however, has resulted in radical distortion of the his-torical record. Moreover, the depredations which did occur can be under-stood only in the context of the number and nature of Indian-emigrant encounters along the overland trails. . . .

While a relatively small number of overlanders relied upon Indians for route information or trail guidance, many overlanders willingly entrusted their stock, wagons, belongings, and even their families to Indian swimmers and boatmen at dangerous river crossings all along the trail. . . .

. . . [I]t was the Oregon overlanders during the 1840s and the early 1850s who relied most extensively on this form of Indian assistance. In doing so they were presumably following the advice of writers such as J. M. Shively, who had explicitly stated in his 1846 guidebook that "you must hire an Indian to pilot you at the crossings of Snake river, it being dangerous if not perfectly understood." Elizabeth Wood secured an Indian pilot after first attempting to ford the Snake River without one, perceiving, "It is best in fording this river to engage a pilot." Amelia Stewart Knight obviously agreed in 1853, remarking that there were many droves of cattle that could not be gotten across the Snake River without Indian help. Emigrant provisions, personal belongings, and wagons were also often put into Indian canoes to be rowed across raging rivers.

Payment was generally made in articles of clothing or in ammunition. James Longmire discovered on two occasions in 1853 that Indians were by no means devoid of effective bargaining techniques. At the Salmon Falls crossing an Indian, after swimming a few horses over the Snake River, mounted one of the best horses and rode off, while his employers remained helpless on the other side of the river. Later, in crossing horses over the Columbia River, Chinook Indians suddenly halted their exertions in midstream, demanding more money to complete the project. They got it, since any further delay would likely have been disastrous. Usually, however, the bargain, once made, was lived up to by both parties. . . .

Some of the 1843 overlanders who avoided Indian pilots and boats fared disastrously. The Applegate company constructed their own canoes, which they manned themselves with such lack of skill and luck that three in their party drowned and another was crippled for life. Sarah Cummins praised the Indians who helped their party portage around the Cascades in 1845 as "careful and considerate helpers. Not one deserted the ranks." She also stated that not a single dishonest act had been noticed. Mary Jane Long recalled how the Indians taking their party down the Columbia in 1852 had caught fish, built campfires, and brought up spring water while encamped. Once they even went back to a previous encampment to retrieve a gun which her father had inadvertently left behind but had not yet missed. Of course not everyone who took passage in Indian canoes was ecstatic about the experience. David Maynard, for instance, grumped in 1850, "We had a hard time, in consequence of the Indian being so damned lazy." Most emigrants, however, made the trip safely and with considerable respect for the skill of the native boatmen.

Indians aided overlanders in numerous other ways. Always eager to find ways of getting letters back to family and friends in the States, emigrants periodically negotiated with passing natives to transport letters back to the eastern settlements. At least some of these messengers faithfully fulfilled their trust, since many of the letters reached their destination. Forty-niner William Wells, for example, wrote to his wife from along the Kansas River: "This probably is the last chance I shall have to write to you and I do not know that you will even get this one. We have hired an Indian to take our letters to Independence — he may take them and he may not." One 1849 episode revealed both the shrewdness and trustworthiness of some Indian entrepreneurs. Although some of the forty-niners were dubious about the project, Reuben Shaw's company negotiated with three Sioux braves to carry numerous letters back to Council Bluffs. The Indians sagely refused a package deal for all the letters but instead bargained with each individual sender, thereby securing far more clothing, notions, tobacco, and jewelry. Shaw bartered a calico shirt for his letter and wrote, "The Indians got the shirt, and several months later I had the satisfaction of knowing that my wife received the letter." . . .

Even more astonishing to overlanders normally approaching all Indians with considerable suspicion, at least at the beginning of their overland trek, were the occasional acts of kindness and compassion by the Indians. Seeing William Johnston's difficulty in getting his mule-drawn wagons up the steep banks of Wakarusa Creek, a Shawnee Indian brought his pair of oxen to help pull the wagons up. An Indian with an extra horse overtook John Minto, who was walking ahead of his traveling company to Fort Hall, offered him a ride, and even gave Minto a saddle when he had trouble riding bareback. Another Indian brought wood and kindled a fire for John Zeiber's family at the Elkhorn River crossing in 1851 while Zeiber was occupied with fording wagons. . . .

James Evans was involved in a touching encounter on the Humboldt Desert in 1850. Exhausted and struggling on foot toward the Truckee River, Evans met a nearly naked Indian carrying a little tin bucket filled with water for thirsty emigrants — "When we met he offered me the bucket exclaiming, 'Watty, Watty, Oh! white man — watty!' " Evans declined because he was not in as dire straits as some he had passed, and urged the Indian to minister to them instead. "He went on, and I afterwards learned that he came up to the famishing man and after giving him two or 3 drinks of water brought up an Indian poney, put the white man on him and took him on until he came to Trucky River! Oh! such generosoty! and pray, why do not those Emigrants who are ahead have the same feelings of humanity?" Even the much-despised Digger Indians had their moments: Silas Miller reported a daring 1852 rescue of a drowning emigrant by two Digger braves. The Indians were rewarded for their heroics with suits of clothing and a two-month supply of provisions. . . .

. . . [D]uring the course of their trip virtually every overlander met at least a few Indians anxious to "swap." Most encountered a great many. Though some emigrants did manage to purchase certain items outright from native entrepreneurs, almost all the trading was conducted on the barter principle, since specie had little appeal for most prairie or mountain tribes. Many emigrants quickly learned, much to their surprise, that Indians were not easy marks in the bargaining process. Indeed, the traditional stereotype of the easygoing Indian, victimized in his every dealing with the white man, is simply not accurate. Finley McDiarmid, for example, found the Snake Indians to be "very sharp traders not easily cheated"; Cecelia Adams portrayed the Walla Wallas as "pretty shrewd fellows for money"; William Kelly suggested that the crafty Sioux compared favorably with wily British merchants; and Ansel McCall stated that the Sioux "in every case get the best of the bargain." . . .

Trade and aid were extremely significant aspects of the almost infinite variety of emigrant-Indian encounters. But they have been too often bypassed in the usual concentration upon pitched battles, scalps, and massacres. Initially the westbound emigrant wagons were strange curiosities to the natives in the same way that the overlanders were fascinated by the Indian life-style and customs. Accordingly, interaction, trading, and mutual aid prevailed throughout most of these crucial two decades of overland travel.

An analysis of the type and pattern of emigrant-Indian interaction during the antebellum era does suggest, however, that the overland emigrations quickened and perhaps made inevitable the military conquest of the western Indians. Almost from the very first, the perceptive plains Indians had recognized the threat the overland caravans represented to their way of life. Therefore, one of their first responses was to demand tribute of the passing trains. This tactic was employed at least as early as 1843. An 1845 overlander, speculating on the origin of this Indian tax, believed the practice to have begun with frightened emigrants willing to promise almost anything to travel safely. But it seems clear that tribute demands, which were most widely experienced by overlanders during the gold rush period, were grounded in more than simple repetition of a previous chance success. Emigrants continually reported that the Indians who came to demand tribute explained also why they were requesting the payments. The natives explicitly emphasized that the throngs of overlanders were killing and scaring away buffalo and other wild game, overgrazing prairie grasses, exhausting the small quantity of available timber, and depleting water resources.

STUDY GUIDE

1. Consider the preparations for a journey from Independence, Missouri, to Oregon or California. What would be essential in terms of food, clothing, housing, transportation, medicine, and tools? What mistakes in planning seem to have been the most common?

2. Gold was important in the great migration described by Unruh, but millions of people stayed home in the settled communities of the East, and many went to Oregon and other areas rather than responding to the lure of gold in California. In social and psychological terms, rather than in terms of striking it rich, how do you explain the motivation of the people who left their homes and went west?

3. How do the activities and behavior of the migrants along the trail, and the things they brought with them, indicate an attempt to preserve the life and values they had known in the East?

4. Suppose you were a contemporary Hollywood screenwriter-director with a knowledge of Unruh's work and an interest in doing a different kind of motion picture of the migration. How would it differ from the classic Western saga?

5. For some states entry into the Union depended on special circumstances, such as whether or not slavery would be allowed. But, in general, the date of admission indicates that the area had become fairly well populated with a settled society. Explain why California (1850), Oregon (1859), Nevada (1864), and Colorado (1876) were developed to the point of statehood well before the Dakotas, Montana, Washington, Idaho, and Wyoming, which were admitted in 1889–1890.

BIBLIOGRAPHY

As mentioned in the introduction to the preceding selection, the West and the great migration have a special place in the American imagination. A substantial number of diaries were kept by the overlanders, and both amateur and professional historians, as well as novelists and poets, have created a large body of literature on these subjects. Some have been interested in tracing the California and Oregon trails, others in depicting the life of the cowboy on the Plains or the miner in the camp. Some have romanticized the qualities of the pioneers, and some have created distorted pictures of the "savage" Indian. The first historian to call attention to the great significance of the frontier in American history was Frederick Jackson Turner; see especially his book *The Frontier in American History* (1920). Another great historian, Francis Parkman, gave his own account of a trip west in *The Oregon Trail* (1849). In *The Great Plains* (1931), Walter Prescott Webb examined the unique natural environment of the area and how it affected the life of the settlers there.

Various aspects of the "Turner thesis" have been elaborated or subjected to severe criticism in the decades since its publication. A number of essays on the subject have been collected in Ray A. Billington, ed., *The Frontier Thesis: Valid Interpretation of American History?* (1966). Billington, a student of Turner, carried forward his teacher's work in a number of studies, especially *Westward Expansion: A History of the American Frontier*, 3rd ed. (1967). The deep symbolic and psychological significance of the West for Americans is set forth in Henry Nash Smith, *Virgin Land: The American West as Symbol and Myth* (1950).

In his many volumes on the frontier, Everett Dick discussed virtually every aspect of life in the American West; two volumes that are marvelous reading are *Vanguards of the Frontier* (1941) and *Tales of the Frontier from Lewis and Clark to the Last Roundup* (1964). The ultimate peril, being trapped in a mountain blizzard, is described in George R. Stewart, *Ordeal by Hunger: The Story of the Donner Party*, rev. ed. (1960). Recently a large number of excellent studies of the westward movement have been published; John M. Faragher, *Women and Men on the Overland Trail* (1979) ranks with Unruh's book as one of the most important. Faragher's text places much greater emphasis on pioneer women, who are the subject of three other books as well: Julie R. Jeffrey, *Frontier Women: The Trans-Mississippi West, 1840–1880* (1979); Sandra L. Myres, *Westering Women and the Frontier Experience, 1800–1915* (1982); and Glenda Riley, *Frontierswomen: The Iowa Experience* (1981).

There are special studies of the mining frontier, the cattle frontier, and particular groups such as the Mormons. The following books are especially interesting: Rodman W. Paul, *Mining Frontiers of the Far West, 1848–1880* (1963) and Wallace Stegner, *The Gathering of Zion: The Story of the Mormon Trail* (1964). Daniel J. Boorstin, in his book *The Americans: The National Experience* (1965), argues persuasively that community cooperation, rather than individual effort, was the key to western settlement.

Wood engraving after an 1844 daguerreotype of Theodore Dwight Weld (1803–95), abolitionist crusader.

19

ROBERT ABZUG

The Abolitionist Impulse

Studying the American Revolution, the War of 1812, and the Mexican War has made you aware of the difficulties involved in understanding the causes of wars. As is the case with these earlier conflicts, so it is with the American Civil War — different historians have come to different conclusions as to the most important causes of the conflict. The distinguished historian Charles A. Beard, for example, suggested that the Civil War represented an economic conflict between an agricultural South and an industrializing North. Some historians have seen the cause as a breakdown of established political procedures, while others have suggested that the issue of control of the western territories was at the root of the struggle.

Whatever their interpretation might be, most historians would agree that slavery was deeply involved in the development of sectional feelings and the disruption of the Union. The Republican Party platform of 1860 conceded the rights of the states to control domestic institutions, which included slavery, and Lincoln tried to reassure the South that his election was not a threat to black slavery. Yet the South Carolina convention that voted secession from the Union saw the Republican triumph as a clear threat to slavery. In part, this was because many Southerners equated Republicanism with abolitionism.

Actually, abolitionists were highly unpopular in the North until after the passage of the Fugitive Slave Act of 1850. In the first decades of the nineteenth century, Benjamin Lundy had been a very lonely crusader, publishing his newspaper and walking the land to talk about the evils of slavery. With the exciting upsurge of social reform after 1830, people from many different backgrounds joined the antislavery crusade. The radical from New England, William Lloyd Garrison, called for the immediate abolition of slavery; two South Carolina sisters, Angelina and Sarah Grimké, became preachers in the cause; the ex-slaves Frederick Douglass and Harriet Tubman spoke against slavery and worked to help slaves escape; and the southern politician and editor James G. Birney ran for president of the United States on the Liberty Party ticket, which advocated abolition. Many historians consider the midwestern wing of abolitionism to have been the most important, and Theodore Dwight Weld was the most influential of several leaders in Ohio, Indiana, and neighboring states. Working through the churches and other social institutions, rather than denouncing them for their compromises on the slavery question, as others had done, Weld was remarkably successful in persuading people to join the abolition movement in the face of bitter denunciation and physical violence. The following essay from Robert Abzug's study of Weld gives a good picture of the courage of the abolitionists and the strong sense of a Protestant mission and moral reformation that underlay this and other reforms of the period.

Theodore [Weld]'s assignment for the Manual Labor Society included the task of finding the best location for a National Manual Labor Institution, one that would be the model school for training a millennial ministry. Though some in the manual labor camp favored Rochester, New York, voices from over the mountains turned Weld's attention toward Cincinnati. J. L. Tracy, a fellow Oneidan who now taught school in Kentucky, reminded Theodore that the Ohio Valley was "to be the great battlefield between the powers of light and darkness," and asked, "Why not train the soldiers of the Cross within sight of the enemies' camp?" At the same time, F. Y. Vail, a Cincinnati educator, offered his fledgling Lane Seminary as a site for the great experiment.

Tracy's argument was particularly compelling to Weld, who had long stressed the importance of the West. As early as 1827 he had urged [Charles G.] Finney to work in the hinterland rather than in eastern cities. . . . By

From *Passionate Liberator: Theodore Dwight Weld and the Dilemma of Reform* by Robert H. Abzug. Copyright © 1980 by Oxford University Press, Inc. Reprinted by permission.

1832, as Finney preached in New York City, Weld argued ever more urgently that the "battlefield of the world," "Satan's seat," could not be won "by working the lever in Boston, New York, or Philadelphia." Only in the West could Finney "electrify the whole mass."

Weld's advice was well within one important tradition in Christian thought. As the scholar George H. Williams has argued, the wilderness, whether existing in the mind or in the world, symbolized to the Christian a "moral waste but a potential paradise," a ground upon which to fight one's personal battle for salvation or mankind's struggle for the Second Coming. . . .

In the end, Weld chose Lane for the experiment and his backers concurred. Unable to lure Finney from his New York activities, the manual laborites turned to Lyman Beecher as their choice for president of Lane. The peppery minister had moved strongly toward the Finneyite camp in the years after the Oneida revival, and he gladly accepted this position of leadership in the Christian vanguard. "If we gain the West," he wrote to his daughter, "all is safe; if we lose it, all is lost." . . .

Lyman Beecher was the kind of man who felt that the world depended on him for ultimate salvation; his hyperbolic prose spilled over with notions of disaster if his own way were blocked. Beecher's defensive tone — protection of American destiny from ignorant Catholics and infidels — rarely admitted a note of self-questioning. He concentrated on the defense of institutions and the defeat of external enemies. His Truths were embodied in the church and its auxiliaries. Debates over what constituted the true Christian life mattered less than solidarity in the larger battle. Weld and those who followed him from Oneida to Lane held a somewhat different view. To them victory in the millennial cause depended upon discovering the Truth and then acting in accord with its dictates; such an attitude called for scrupulous self-cleansing by both individuals and institutions as the first order of business. Purging oneself of sin was a prerequisite to dealing with Satan's legions. Still, as the Beecher family, Weld and his Oneida boys, and a miscellany of new students and faculty marched toward Lane, implicit differences could be ignored for awhile in the glow of Christian mission. . . .

. . . [T]hough the Oneida boys who followed Weld to Lane were enthusiastic about the prospects, they harbored a vigorous skepticism about the motives and qualifications of those outside their group. Men like Henry B. Stanton, Sereno W. Streeter, Calvin Waterbury, and John Alvord had learned too much about human fallibility at Oneida to allow a more charitable view, especially when the Millennium was at stake. . . . Streeter criticized a Mr. Grant, for instance, because he refused to be an example for the rest: "His influence was not a straw. He walked among the students like a speechless ghost. He gave no compositions nor declamations, lay abed late in the mor[ning], drank tea and coffee stoutly and his manual labor consisted in journeying from his room to the backhouse."

Fearing repetition of such mistakes at Lane, the Oneidans promoted their own nominees for faculty and criticized others whose names had been suggested. They were desperately afraid that antimanual labor men would "crush us by their caresses when they find they can't ever shin us by their kicks." More galling were the rumors that some trustees "were of the opinion that the Oneida boys had conspired to overthrow Lane Seminary." In fact, the image that the Oneidans presented might have inspired such fear. They flaunted their power, referred to Lane as their "ship," and at least one of them nicknamed the group "Illuminati." ...

At the center was Weld. Beecher thought him a genius; he noted that the students considered him "a god." All could admire his hardy but saintlike presence. One story told how most of the students could not decide on room assignments; arguments became heated, and finally a lottery was decided upon. Weld drew second choice, but in a grand gesture said he would wait until the end; the act shamed the rest and they came to an "amicable adjustment" — all except, that is, for finding quarters for a particularly "slovenly and unsavory" fellow. Weld promptly offered part of his own room to him. According to another legend, a deep and dangerous well once had to be cleaned; only Theodore cheerfully volunteered and did the job all by himself. His physical courage, studied selflessness, and willingness to take command made him a model, a leader, a father. ...

Weld took his role as "master-spirit" with full confidence. "I have a fine class," he boasted to his brother, "and have never been placed in circumstances by any means so *imposing*. When I came here matters were getting at loose ends." Presumably matters had been tightened up. Nor was the administration unappreciative; though leader of the students, Weld seemed far more responsible than his fellows. Professor Biggs, later a particular target of the Oneidans' contempt, wrote to Vail on the occasion of Theodore's return to school in July 1833: "Weld is here and we are glad." A year later he would change his mind.

As long as issues between students and administration were not clear, as long as tensions lay in the realm of personal suspicion and fear, of complaints about the lack of exemplary behavior on the part of either students or faculty — as long as the vying concepts of a millennial strategy had not squared off on some important issue — then Lane Seminary could proceed with its educational tasks and keep private resentments private. In fact, it was the strategy of men like Beecher to make sure that disputes between Christians did not obscure the larger shared task of defending against infidelity. Men like Weld, however, once sure of the moral worth and importance of a particular stance, could not help but enter it into the millennial equation and demand the loyalty of all good Christians. It was Lane's and Beecher's bad luck that the issue Weld chose was that of slavery. Slavery and the question of the rights of black freemen had vexed Americans of conscience for years. Yet for Theodore, who pressed the issue of slavery and the condition of free blacks on Lane and Cincinnati, the very intractability of the problem inspired forthrightness. It had to be dealt with if America was to be saved and the Millennium achieved. By introducing the issue, Weld supplied Lane's uneasy populace with a cause over which to battle, a topic around which each side could mold a position against the other. The end result was that faculty and administration, despite their professed admiration for the theological class, asserted a belief in their own absolute authority. The students, for their part, left Lane, renouncing their commitment to an institution in favor of commitment to a set of ideals. Easy compliments faded as one found out the truth about the other.

The story of the Lane rebellion really begins with the saga of Weld's own conversion to abolition. The process was a long and subtle one, far more complex than indicated by Weld's own simple explanation of 1850, when he claimed that on the mnemonics tour he had seen "slavery at home, and became a radical abolitionist." The truth was that he became no instant abolitionist in the early 1820s — hardly an American in those years came close to such a position — but rather that a combination of experiences, coincidences, and personal traits slowly built a web of thought that in late 1832 led to Theodore's conversion to the cause. . . .

. . . Before 1831 the best solution Christians could offer was colonization: the shipping of slaves and free blacks back to Africa.

Colonizationists assumed that the black man was inferior and could not prosper alongside whites in America; he would of necessity sink to the bottom of society, creating problems of crime and saddling white America with an unproductive and undesirable population. In addition, many colonizationists feared retribution from these inferior beings, retribution for slavery and its excesses. If slaves remained enslaved, they would revolt; if freed on American soil, they would use their freedom for revenge. The logical solution was colonization, which would gradually remove the festering sore of black presence without causing undue tumult in white society.

Giving up colonization meant giving up these assumptions. In Weld's case the bases for rejection of black inferiority had been building in the 1820s. In the revival he found and embraced an egalitarian concept of men at odds with hierarchical structures and deferential attitudes. His advocacy of manual labor was, in part, a call for respect between classes and, in part, a romantic, personal urge to bring men of all walks of life together. In fact, Weld's emphasis on the physiological aspects of man focused on the human body all men shared rather than on the distinctions of class, color, or sex that divided them. Although Weld's emerging egalitarian vision did not yet include the black man it was compatible with basic assumptions of abolition thought. . . .

Such influences can only be considered preparatory in Weld's changing consciousness, very important preconditions that sensitized him to the plight of the slave or the free black but that did not immediately suggest the doctrine of abolition. First of all, issues like manual labor and temperance and Theodore's own shaky plans for completing his theological education stood in the forefront of his mind. Second, no one had yet presented him with some concrete argument and plan that might replace colonization as the solution to slavery. As late as September 27, 1832, Weld could write to his new friend James G. Birney, "I am ripe in the conviction that if the Colonization Society does not dissipate the horror of darkness which overhangs the southern country, we are undone. Light breaks *in from no other quarter.*" ...

The first major direct influence turning Theodore toward a new position on slavery probably was Charles Stuart, who had become extremely active in British antislavery and anticolonization efforts. "Pray for me, my beloved Theodore," Stuart wrote from England in March 1831; "I am traversing the country, holding meetings wherever I can, and endeavoring to awaken the conscience of the Nation, that Negro Slavery may be put off." He wrote again in June, "long[ing] to hear of [Theodore] being engaged in the Sacred cause of Negro emancipation"; Stuart enclosed ten copies of his latest pamphlet on the subject. The following spring he sent more material. At the same time, Tappan and his circle in New York began to take a more active interest in the slavery issue. Weld carried the influence of Stuart's probings and antislavery interest among his reform cohorts as he entered the South for manual labor and temperance lectures. In Huntsville, Alabama, he engaged in long discussions with James G. Birney, a slaveholder who had begun to consider taking on an agency with the American Colonization Society. Weld encouraged him in this course and hoped that he would find it in his heart to emancipate his own slaves.

Theodore's increased interest in the slavery question presented a crucial dilemma. Stuart had argued for immediate emancipation without colonization, but, with no slaves on English soil, it was relatively easy for an Englishman to advocate such a position. For an American it was different. Slavery had seeped into every aspect of politics, economics, and social custom in the United States; fear of blacks had pervaded the white consciousness. It was a working assumption among the citizenry that emancipation on American soil would cause a race war unmatched in history. They had before them the examples of Santo Domingo, Nat Turner, and the images of their own irrepressible fantasies. And so it was that a troubled Theodore Weld could endorse Birney's work for colonization, sensing that "light breaks *in from no other quarter.*"

Soon new light shone in the small college town of Hudson, Ohio, where three members of the Western Reserve community — Beriah Green, Elizur Wright, and Charles B. Storrs — were already spreading Garrisonian doctrine. Weld had come to speak on manual labor and temperance; by the time he left he had been converted to immediate emancipation. What exactly transpired is not known, but it is clear from what followed that two key points were stressed upon Weld's agitated conscience. The Hudson Garrisonians must have demonstrated that even by their own standards the colonizationists were doomed to failure, that they could not remove enough free blacks and newly freed slaves to reduce the black population to the point of safety. More important, however, they must have shown Weld that colonization doctrine itself avoided the central moral question of the black man's humanity and that not recognizing his humanity was a sin. Slavery and race discrimination were no mere misfortunes but sinful acts, whether engaged in actively or passively countenanced.

. . . Thus colonization, which sought to avoid rather than foster a change of heart, lulled America into a sleep of self-satisfaction while God's wrath continued to mount. The only answer was to convert slaveholders to immediate recognition of their sin and then to immediate emancipation, and to bring all Americans to a full recognition of the black man as a man. Then there would be no reason to fear freedom for the slave, for the attitudes that might have fostered contempt and rage would have begun to encourage love.

These doctrines cleared Theodore's mind on this most difficult of issues. By December, Elizur Wright was corresponding with Weld as an abolitionist comrade-in-arms. Arthur Tappan, informed of Theodore's conversion to the cause, promptly informed William Lloyd Garrison. Garrison invited Weld to an organizing session for the proposed American Anti-Slavery Society. Theodore declined because of "engagements quite indispensable," but affirmed to Garrison what he had learned at Hudson. Endorsing the "expressive name" of the New England Anti-Slavery Society, he wrote:

> From that I infer that the Society is based upon the great bottom law of human right, that *nothing but crime* can forfeit liberty. That no condition of birth, no shade of color, no mere misfortune of circumstances, can annul that birth-right charter, which God has bequeathed to every being upon whom he has stamped his own image, by making him *a free moral agent,* and that he who robs his fellow man of this tramples upon right, subverts justice, outrages humanity, unsettles the foundations of human safety, and sacrilegiously assumes the prerogative of God.

Thus Theodore conjoined antislavery with the egalitarian principles of the revival, of manual labor, and of the broadest interpretation of the Declaration of Independence, leaving behind the dictates of "expediency or necessity." . . .

"I hardly know how to contain myself," Theodore exclaimed to Wright in January 1833. "If I was not positively pledged for two or three years to come, and if I had finished my education, I would devote myself to the holy work, come life or death." Nonetheless antislavery work edged into his life. He engaged in "many pitched battles" over slavery, sometimes even debating colonization agents. . . .

It was inevitable that Theodore should bring the cause to Lane, though his policy at first was to wait for just the right moment to strike. He could hardly do otherwise. "This Institution stands fiercely committed for Colonization and *against* Abolition," Weld wrote to Amos Phelps. "*Our Theological Professors* are exceedingly anxious to keep us from bringing up the subject for discussion." One reason was geography. "The proximity of Cincinnati and the whole eastern line of Ohio to slaveholding states," explained Theodore, "has thus far muzzled men both in public and private upon the subject of slavery. A universal paralysis pervades — tongues, pens, and presses." He promised Phelps, however, that "in due time you may expect to hear from this Institution — a more favorable Report."

In fact, Theodore had already begun to make plans for open discussion of immediate emancipation and colonization. After meeting with faculty and fellow students of colonization persuasion, he agreed not to "push" a debate for the fall 1833 term so that each side might have time "to prepare for a thorough discussion." Still, he was sure that a public meeting in the winter term might quadruple the small number of abolition advocates at Lane. These original supporters were among "the very first fellows in the Seminary," and included Asa Mahan of the Trustees and Professor John Morgan on the faculty. Other sympathetic hearts in the Cincinnati area included Weld's old Oneida friend, Horace Bushnell, then minister at a nearby town, and Thomas Cole, a Newport, Kentucky pastor. All told, the numbers were paltry; only faith in "changeless eternal right" buoyed their spirits.

It was with this faith that Theodore and his abolitionist fellows planned what were to become known as the Lane Debates. They were scheduled for February 1834, but months earlier preparations commenced in the revival style. "We early began to inculcate our views," Weld remembered, "by conversation, upon our fellow-students. Those of us who sympathized together in our abhorrence of slavery selected each his man to instruct, convince, and enlist in the cause. Thus we carried one after another, and, before ever we came to public debate, knew pretty well where we stood." In other words, the meetings were hardly debates at all. Asking two questions — "Ought the people of the Slaveholding States to abolish Slavery immediately?" and "Are the doctrines, tendencies, and measures of the American Colonization Society, and the influence of its principal supporters, such as render it worthy of the patronage of the Christian public?" — they were conceived of as conversion-oriented educational barrages. Despite doubts about the wisdom of such public meetings, President Beecher agreed not to stand in the way.

The debates lasted eighteen days, each question being discussed two and a half hours each of nine evenings. Weld held forth on the first two days; he introduced the topic of immediate emancipation through "facts ... gathered from various authentic documents" and drew appropriate conclusions. The most dramatic moments of the series came not from Weld, but rather from Southerners who gave firsthand testimony concerning the "peculiar institution." James Bradley, an ex-slave, countered notions that emancipation would be "unsafe to the community" and that "the condition of the emancipated negroes would be worse than it now is." Bradley himself had worked for five years to buy his freedom; having done so, he left Arkansas for a free state and finally enrolled at Lane for an education.

White Southerners, however, made the greatest impact. The audience could witness the sin of slavery as it acted in men's consciences; they could watch the process by which heartfelt recognition of sin would, if allowed to be spread, sweep the South and emancipate both master and slave. None of their speeches was recorded, but James A. Thome, a southern Lane student converted during the debates, described his experience to the first anniversary meeting of the American Anti-Slavery Society in May 1834. As Thome recounted it, he had always harbored uneasy feelings about slavery, but these sentiments had led him to colonization. Colonization's only effect, Thome now conceded, had been to "lessen [his] conviction of the evil of slavery, and to deepen and sanctify [his] prejudice against the colored race."

The debates showed to him that the true evil of slavery lay in the denial of black men's God-given rights and in the cruelty that enforced that denial. He described the burning sense of sin this realization brought: "Sin revived and I died." Thus the debates were something of a special form of revival. Slavery's sin "seize[d] the conscience with an authoritative grasp; it [ran] across every path of the guilty, haunt[ed] him, goad[ed] him, and [rang] in his ear the cry of blood. . . . It [wrote] 'thou art the man,' upon the forehead of every oppressor." But the conviction of sin also brought in the sinner "every susceptibility to compassionate outraged humanity" and found him "pledged to do its work." . . .

With the debates at an end, Theodore took a prominent role in galvanizing excited feeling into an Anti-Slavery Society. Its constitution summarized the meaning of immediate emancipation doctrine — what it was and what it was not. The society's object? "Immediate emancipation of the whole colored race, within the United States" — slave from master and "free colored man from the oppression of public sentiment" — "and the elevation of both to an intellectual, moral, and political equality with the whites." Why? Because the black man was created by God as "a moral agent, the keeper of his own happiness, the executive of his own powers, the accountable arbiter of his own choice." . . .

In acting on such propositions, the society promised to abide by the "law of love." It ruled out instigating slave rebellion as well as forcible intervention by the free states — one meant murder and the other meant war. Nor would it seek congressional interference. Rather the Lane abolitionists hoped to "induce [the slaveholder] to forsake *this*, as every other sin, by speaking the truth in love." They would demonstrate the advantage of emancipation by showing its "pecuniary interest," its safety, and by encouraging religious and secular public sentiment against slavery.

Moreover, the constitution of Lane's Anti-Slavery Society attempted to dispel the terror that the very phrase "immediate emancipation" seemed to provoke. It defined the term first by excluding the intention of "turn[ing] loose [slaves] upon the nation, to roam as vagabonds and aliens," denying that "they would be instantly invested with all political rights and privileges," but also refusing to allow "that they shall be expelled from their native land to foreign clime, as the price and condition of their freedom." In positive terms "immediate emancipation" meant that slaves would receive protection of the law instead of being at the mercy of unbridled passions, that they should be employed as free laborers, "fairly compensated and protected in their earnings," and that "they shall be placed under a benevolent and disinterested supervision, which shall secure them the right to obtain secular and religious knowledge, to worship God according to the dictates of their consciences, and to seek an intellectual and moral equality with the whites." While none of the sentiments expressed at Lane was new — William Lloyd Garrison and his followers had been espousing them since 1831 — those at Lane propounded them as if they had just invented them. Yet it was not so much the doctrines as the wondrous process of conversion that made the Lane Debates a momentous eighteen days.

Forming an Anti-Slavery Society was only one way of working out the millennial mission in relation to blacks. With a zeal typical of Oneida men, Weld, Huntington Lyman, Augustus Wattles, and others began to promote religious and secular schools in Cincinnati's black community. "We believe that faith without *works* is dead," Weld wrote to Lewis Tappan in March 1834. "We have formed a large and efficient organization for elevating the colored people in Cincinnati — have established a Lyceum among them, and lecture three or four evenings a week, on grammar, geography, arithmetic, natural philosophy, etc." Other activities included an evening school for reading skills, a library and a new reading room, three Sabbath schools and a number of Bible classes, all run or participated in by Lane students. Weld also suggested a plan for a "SELECT FEMALE SCHOOL." Two students, Augustus Wattles and Marius Robinson, became so committed to these projects that they dropped out of Lane to devote themselves full time to running a school for blacks. . . .

Theodore's enthusiasm over the Lane Debates and subsequent work in Cincinnati's "Little Africa" was further strengthened by the news of James G. Birney's conversion to abolition. Since Weld's meetings and correspondence with Birney in 1832, the troubled slaveholder had become a star in the colonization galaxy. An exemplary agent, he also had fired well-reasoned salvos at the upstart immediate emancipationists in various newspapers and finally in the Colonization Society's *African Repository*. It must have come as something of a shock to Weld when he received a letter from Birney announcing his turn to abolition and promising an open letter that would explain his position in full. Theodore assured him that the news would be "ringing in the public ears within a few days, from different papers on both sides of the Alleghany, but of course *only as something* REPORTED *not definitely known.*" . . .

Even as Weld welcomed Birney to abolitionism, however, the citizens of Cincinnati were beginning to show their displeasure with antislavery activities at Lane and with the entry of Lane students into the black quarter of town. The confrontation that resulted became a major turning point in the history of abolition in America.

Theodore resolved one major question when he left Lane Seminary. Since early youth he had ostensibly been following a path to the ministry. No matter what the detours — a breakdown at Andover, the mnemonics tour, conversion by Finney, revival and temperance work, and finally the manual labor agency — he had returned to seminary. Yet upon leaving Lane, he gave up school and a career within the church forever. Instead he chose the life of an antislavery orator. Others among the Lane rebels, his closest comrades, had decided to continue their educations. They first set up a school of their own in Cumminsville, Ohio, and later flocked to Oberlin when Finney himself became head of its theological department. In June 1834, however, Weld made his own commitments clear in a letter declining a professorship at Oberlin. "The Providence of God has for some time made it plain to me," he wrote, "that the Abolition of Slavery and the elevation of the free colored race have intrinsic demands upon me superior to every other cause."

Theodore accepted an antislavery agency for Ohio and by late fall was in action. Hearing of Weld's decision, James G. Birney wrote in his diary, "I give him one year to abolitionize Ohio." Lewis Tappan made the same prediction. In the year and eight months that followed, Weld would become an antislavery legend. Theodore began his campaign at Ripley, an Ohio River town across the water from Kentucky. There he lectured eleven times and formed an antislavery society with little fuss. He then moved on to West Union, "one of the most hopeless places for anti-slavery effort," where he thought he had done some good. For the balance of December, he canvassed Hillsborough and Greenfield, and in January penetrated the Ross County towns of Concord and Frankfort. In February and March, Weld concentrated on the Circleville and Bloomingsberg areas. In April he led the planning of the Ohio State Antislavery Society's first meeting, which took place at Putnam on April 22–24. After this convention he continued his tour, moving south to Marietta and on to Pittsburgh, Pennsylvania, for the Presbyterian Church's General Assembly, then back to Ohio and into the Western Reserve — to Cleveland, Ravenna, Elyria, and Oberlin. Late in the year Weld moved back into Pennsylvania; by then the American Anti-Slavery

Society had persuaded him to break new ground in New York State.

In preaching the antislavery cause Theodore followed a routine reminiscent of his prior agencies and illustrative of his ambivalence about authority. As in the past, he chose to work in the West, far from what in his mind were those oppressive centers of authority, the cities of the East. Some years earlier, he had assured Lewis Tappan that God had marked out for him a "diocese" in "the highways and hedges of the West." He dressed simply, in what he termed a "John the Baptist attire," emphasizing again his direct responsibility to God rather than to some earthly church or organization. Normally Weld stayed with a local minister or other sympathetic townsman, sought a hall or church, and then lectured on antislavery anywhere from six to twenty-five times. He then left town, expecting that local supporters would build upon the interest in abolition he had sparked. . . .

Opposition varied from town to town. Sometimes, as at West Union, Weld's enemies displayed no more than "a good deal of squirming and some noise and blustering threats, etc." Other towns, like Circleville, were not quite so hospitable. Mobs pelted him with stones through the open windows; one missile struck Weld on the head and stunned him for a few minutes. In typically heroic fashion, however, he finished the lecture. Theodore remembered another incident when a mob tramped four abreast into the courtroom where he was speaking and pushed his audience out into the night. The meeting reconvened at a schoolhouse, but the mob soon returned, this time bringing sleigh bells, tin pans, tin trumpets, and a dog. As Weld commenced, horns tooted, pans rattled, bells rang, and one man pulled the dog's ears to make it bark.

Despite the mobs, Weld was optimistic. In February 1836, after almost a year and a half of lecturing, he predicted to Tappan that within five years half a million slaves would be free, one million and a half within the decade. Such a view necessitated an extraordinary reading of abolitionist power and public reactions. In all, the world view and strategy of Weld and his comrades require close examination, for they were beliefs that allowed these men and women to struggle against seemingly impossible odds.

Theirs was first of all a religious vision, one based upon the evangelical notion of converting the world to bring on the Millennium. Weld, in fact, described his antislavery efforts in terms reminiscent of a classic revival meeting. First he met "coldness, suspicion, opposition, and threats of personal violence and *thin* attendance." Gradually, interest and "anxious inquiry" increased. Finally, victory came — conversions, contributions, and perhaps a local antislavery society. "In each place the opposition has been strong, in two instances rising to absolute ferocity," Weld reported in February 1835, "but the Lord enabled me to move deliberately onward until the truth triumphed gloriously." A year later he reported the same pattern of triumph from Utica, New York: "I lectured for the eleventh time in the

Bleecker Street Church tonight — great crowd. The Lord is with us — truth *tells*. Mob dead, buried, and rotten." . . .

Thus abolition, with its daring commitment to freedom and coexistence with blacks, engendered ardent support in a way colonization never could with its easily supported doctrine of expatriation. Abolitionism did not appeal to many people, but those most attracted to it were young men and women with the explosive, rebellious energy to get things done. Abolitionists tapped the same vein of discontent that sparked earlier and contemporaneous revivals of religion. Indeed, one colonizationist surmised with dismay, "I find that where New Measures flourish there Abolition (and kindred fanaticisms), flourishes." Colonizationists asked men to contribute time or money to solve what they considered an unfortunate moral, political, and economic problem, one open to solution without a basic change of heart on the part of the white man. Such a lukewarm appeal could only inspire a lukewarm response. But abolition asked men, dared men to confront the sins of slavery and racism as their own and demanded a regenerative commitment to the cause. Such an appeal was bound to infuriate most and inspire zealous devotion in a chosen few.

STUDY GUIDE

1. Weld apparently was a remarkable man who exercised a powerful influence upon acquaintances. One purpose of a biography is to give the reader a sense of the subject's personality. Where in the preceding pages do you get a sense of Weld's motivation, courage, and power as a speaker?

2. Some abolitionists devoted their efforts to assisting fugitive slaves, some to speaking against slavery, others to writing propaganda or working through churches or politics. They also differed in their views on how emancipation would be achieved. In your textbook or in *The Dictionary of American Biography* in your library, find information that will help you understand the differences among Weld, William Lloyd Garrison, Lyman Beecher, and James G. Birney.

3. How did Weld's strong Christian revivalist background influence his decision to take up the abolitionist cause, his crusading techniques, and his break with Beecher and Lane Seminary?

4. Southerners frequently claimed that the abolitionist program would deny slaveholders their constitutional rights. On the other hand, some Northerners came to support the antislavery movement because they felt that the civil rights of abolitionists were being violated. How much truth was there in each of these arguments? How might the following clauses of the Constitution be relevant: Article IV, Section 2; Amendment I; Amendment V, and Amendment X?

BIBLIOGRAPHY

At the time of John Brown's execution, Ralph Waldo Emerson referred to him as a saint who had made the gallows as glorious as the cross. But a good many Americans of the pre–Civil War period thought of abolitionists as the devil incarnate. The attitudes of historians on the abolitionists have varied, as have their views of the relationship of abolitionism to the coming of the Civil War. Dwight L. Dumond provided a sympathetic view of the abolitionists in *Antislavery: The Crusade for Freedom in America* (1961) and argued that the slavery question was an important cause of war in *Antislavery Origins of the Civil War in the United States* (1939). Other historians have denounced the reformers, and agreed with Avery O. Craven, *The Repressible Conflict, 1830–1861* (1939), that it was a needless war.

There has been a great deal of study of abolitionism in the last two decades. An earlier work by Gilbert Barnes, *The Antislavery Impulse, 1830–1844* (1933), first pointed out the great significance of Weld and the midwestern wing of the movement. There are several good studies of blacks in the antislavery movement, including Benjamin Quarles, *Black Abolitionists* (1969) and Jane and William Pease, *They Who Would Be Free: Blacks' Search for Freedom* (1974). In another volume, *Bound with Them in Chains* (1972), the Peases provide biographical sketches of various types of abolitionists. There are also biographies of most of the leading abolitionists, including John L. Thomas, *The Liberator: A Biography of William Lloyd Garrison* (1963) and Benjamin Quarles, *Frederick Douglass* (1948). Women were an extremely important force in most aspects of nineteenth-century reform; their role in abolitionism is studied in Alma Lutz, *Crusade for Freedom: Women of the Antislavery Movement* (1968). Blanche G. Hersh, *The Slavery of Sex: Feminist-Abolitionists in America* (1978) is more recent and innovative.

Rather than approaching the subject through a study of the leaders, some historians have examined a particular phase of the antislavery crusade or the thought of people on the relationship of race and slavery. Larry Gara, *The Liberty Line* (1961) is one of several works on the underground railroad. Lorman Ratner, *Powder Keg: Northern Opposition to the Antislavery Movement, 1831–1840* (1968) is a full study of the animosity toward abolitionists. The attacks upon the abolitionists and upon the rights of free Negroes led to a concern about civil liberties, a subject that is examined in Russel Nye, *Fettered Freedom* (1949). Few free blacks, even those in northern states, were in an enviable position, as Leon Litwack indicates in *North of Slavery: The Negro in the Free States, 1790–1860* (1967). Another theme that has received much less attention than has abolitionism is the defense of slavery in pre-war thought. William Jenkins, *Pro-Slavery Thought in the Old South* (1935) dealt with this subject some years ago. Most writing on the abolitionists follows their activities only to 1860, but recently James McPherson carried their story through the Civil War and Reconstruction period in *The Struggle for Equality* (1964). Martin B. Duberman, *Antislavery Vanguard* (1965) is a collection of essays by several different scholars, as is Lewis Perry and Michael Fellman, eds., *Antislavery Reconsidered: New Perspectives on the Abolitionists* (1979).

These wounded troops near Fredericksburg, some perhaps maimed for life, were at least luckier than the 600,000 people who died in America's bloodiest war.

20

ALLAN NEVINS

The Price of War

The selections in this volume have illustrated the exceptional variety of American life in different parts of the country from the founding of the British settlements to the Civil War. The editors hope that you have received some impression of the actual working conditions in early American factories, of the life of Indians and slaves, of family life and social reform. The two selections on the American Revolution touched upon certain aspects of what has been called the age of limited warfare. The following selection, from Allan Nevins's article "The Glorious and the Terrible," gives a chilling picture of modern war.

In the twentieth century, there is little about war that is glamorous or chivalric. Those who fought in World War II, the Korean War, or the long war in Southeast Asia know the full import of General William T. Sherman's famous phrase, "War is hell." Massive bombings of civilian areas, atomic weaponry, napalm, massacres, and pushbutton slaughter have made a grim mockery of wartime heroism. The American Civil War has been described as the first modern war — partly because of tactical and logistic innovations and partly because of the astounding casualties, the use of scorched-earth policies, and a number of other grim forecasts of the future.

Yet, there are common elements in nearly all wars — elements that connect the Civil War and our modern warfare with the so-called gentlemanly wars of the seventeenth and eighteenth centuries. Death, cruelty, callousness, cowardice, and bravery are a part of the human condition in wartime, and they know no special period. In some wars, the devastation and dehumanization have been borne largely by the armies engaged. But where a civil war is fought in one's own country, the destruction and the psychological scars extend beyond the battlefield. In the sectional split of the United States that led brother to fight brother, wartime life assumed a very special poignancy, and the scars took a very long time to heal.

Every great war has two sides, the glorious and the terrible. The glorious is perpetuated in multitudinous pictures, poems, novels, statues: in Meissonier's canvases of Friedland and Austerlitz, Byron's stanzas on Waterloo and Tennyson's on the Light and Heavy brigades, St. Gaudens's Sherman riding forward victory-crowned, Freeman's "Lee." The terrible is given us in a much slighter body of memorabilia: Jacques Callot's gruesome etchings of the Thirty Years War, Goya's paintings of French atrocities in Spain, Zola's "The Debacle," Walt Whitman's hospital sketches, and the thousand-page novels that drearily emerged from the Second World War.

The two aspects do exist side by side. Every student of war comes upon hundreds of veracious descriptions of its pomp and pageantry, innumerable tales of devotion and heroism. They exalt the spirit. Yet every such student falls back from this exaltation upon a sombre remembrance of the butchery, the bereavement, and the long bequest of poverty, exhaustion, and despair. In observing the centenary of the Civil War, every sensible man should keep in mind that the conflict was a terrible reproach to American civilization and a source of poison and debilities still to be felt. . . .

. . . Who wishes to while away an idle hour by looking at the harrowing pictures in the "Medical and Surgical History" of the war? It is a trick of human memories to forget, little by little, what is painful, and remember what is pleasant, and that tendency appertains to the folk memory as well. One of the finest descriptive pieces of the war was written by the true-hearted Theodore Winthrop, novelist and poet, just after his regiment crossed the Potomac on a spring night in 1861 to encamp on the Virginia side. It is rapturous in its depiction of the golden moon lighting a path over the river, the merry files of soldiers, the white tents being pitched in the dewy dawn. But ere long Winthrop was slain at Big Bethel in an engagement too blundering, shabby, and piteous for any pen. We remember the happy march but forget the death.

From Allan Nevins, "The Glorious and the Terrible," © 1961, Saturday Review Magazine Co. Reprinted by permission.

Or take two contrasting scenes later in the war, of the same day — the day of Malvern Hill, July 1, 1862. That battle of Lee and McClellan reached its climax in the gathering dusk of a lustrous summer evening, no breath of wind stirring the air. The Union army had placed its ranks and its artillery on the slope of a great hill, a natural amphitheatre, which the Southerners assaulted. Participants never forgot the magnificence of the spectacle. From the Confederate and Union guns stately columns of black smoke towered high in the blue sky. The crash of musketry and deeper thud of artillery; the thunder of gunboat mortars from the James River, their shells curving in fiery golden lines; the cavalry on either flank, galloping to attack; the foaming horses flying from point to point with aides carrying dispatches; the steady advance of the Confederate columns and the unyielding resistance of the dense Union lines; then as darkness gathered, the varicolored signal lights flashing back and forth their messages — all this made an unforgettable panorama.

But the sequel! The troops on both sides sank exhausted on their arms. From the field the shrieking and moaning of the wounded were heartrending, yet nothing could be done to succor them. The sky grew overcast; intense darkness shut down; and at dawn came a fierce downpour. "Such rain, and such howling set up by the wounded," wrote one Southern soldier; "such ugly wounds, sickening to the sight even of the most hardened as the rain beat upon them, washing them to a pale purple; such long-fingered corpses, and in piles, too, like cordwood — may I never see the like again!"

Both novelist and poet almost instinctively turn to the heroic aspects and picturesque incidents of war. Lowell's "Commemoration Ode," one of the half-dozen finest pieces of literature born from the conflict, necessarily eulogizes the heroes; Mary Johnston's "The Long Roll," perhaps the best Southern war novel, celebrates the ardors, not the anguishes, of Stonewall Jackson's foot-cavalry; St. Gaudens's monument on Boston Common to Robert Gould Shaw and his black infantry — the men whose dauntless hearts beat a charge right up the red rampart's slippery swell — shows the fighters, not the fallen. The historian assists in falsifying the picture. Cold, objective, he assumes that both the glorious and horrible sides exist, and need no special emphasis. He thus tends to equate the two, although the pains and penalties of war far outweigh its gleams of grandeur.

Then, too, a problem of expression impedes the realistic writer. It is not difficult to describe the pageantry of Pickett's charge. But when we come to the costs, what can we say except that the casualties were 3,000 killed, 5,000 wounded? It is impossible to describe the agony of even one soldier dying of a gangrened wound, or the heartache of one mother losing her first born; what of 10,000 such soldiers and mothers? Moreover, most historians, like the novelists and poets, have an instinctive preference for the bright side of the coin. Henry Steele Commager's otherwise fine introduction to his valuable compilation "The Blue and The Gray" has much to say about gallantry and bravery, but nothing about the squalor, the stench, and the agony.

If we protest against the prettification of the Civil War, the thoughtless glorification of what was essentially a temporary breakdown of American civilization, we must do so with an acknowledgment that it did call forth many manifestations of an admirable spirit. The pomp and circumstance, the parade and pageantry, we may dismiss as essentially empty. The valor of the host of young men who streamed to the colors we may deeply admire, but as valor we may fortunately take it for granted, for most men are brave. The patriotic ardor displayed in the first months of the war may also be taken for granted. What was highly impressive was the serious, sustained conviction, the long-enduring dedication, of countless thousands on both sides for their chosen cause. This went far beyond the transient enthusiasms of Sumter and Bull Run; far beyond ordinary battlefield courage. Lecky was correct in writing: "That which invests war with a certain grandeur is the heroic self-sacrifice which it elicits." All life is in a real sense a conflict between good and evil, in which every man or woman plays a part. A host of young Americans felt that they were enlisted in this large struggle, and regarded their service to the North or South as part of a lifetime service to the right.

Those who seek examples of this dedication can find them scattered throughout the war records. Lincoln specially admired his young friend Elmer Ellsworth, who had endured poverty and hardship with monastic devotion to train himself for service; Lee specially admired John Pelham, the daring artillerist. Both gave their lives. Some fine illustrations of the consecrated spirit can be found in the two volumes of the "Harvard Memorial Biographies" edited by Thomas Wentworth Higginson just after the war. The ninety-eight Harvard dead were no better than the farm lads from Iowa or Alabama, the clerks from New Orleans or New York, but some of them had special gifts of self-expression. Hearken, for example, to Colonel Peter A. Porter, who wrote in his last will and testament:

> I can say, with truth, that I have entered on the course of danger with no ambitious aspirations, nor with the idea that I am fitted, by nature, or experience, to be of any important service to the government; but in obedience to the call of duty, demanding every citizen to contribute what he could, in means, labor, or life, to sustain the government of his country — a sacrifice made the more willingly by me when I consider how singularly benefitted I have been, by the institutions of the land....

As we distinguish between the shining glory of the war — this readiness of countless thousands to die for an enduring moral conviction — and the false or unimportant glories, so we must distinguish between the major and the lesser debits of the conflict. Some evils and mischiefs which seemed tremendous at the time have grown less in the perspective of years; some which at first appeared small now loom large.

It was one of the bloodiest of all wars; the total deaths in the Union and Confederate armies have been computed at about 620,000; and one of the facts which appalls any careful student is the enormous amount of suffering on the field and in the hospitals. The evidence of this, while not within the view of general readers, is incontrovertible. Armies the world over in 1860 were *worse* provided with medical and surgical facilities than in Napoleon's day. The United States, after its long peace, began the war with practically no medical service whatever. Surgical application of the ideas of Pasteur and Lister lay in the future. Almost every abdominal wound meant death. Any severe laceration of a limb entailed amputation, with a good chance of mortal gangrene or erysipelas. The North systematically prevented shipments of drugs and surgical instruments to the South, a measure which did not shorten the conflict by a day, but cost the Southern troops untold agony. Had it not been for the Sanitary Commission, a body privately organized and supported, Northern armies would have duplicated the experience of British forces in the Crimea; yet Secretary of War Stanton at first deliberately impeded the Commission's work.

The story of battle after battle was the same. Night descended on a field ringing with cries of agony: Water! Water! Help! — if in winter, Blankets! Cover! All too frequently no help whatever was forthcoming. After some great conflicts the wounded lay for days, and sometimes a week, without rescue. Shiloh was fought on a Sunday and Monday. Rain set in on Sunday night, and the cold April drizzle continued through Tuesday night. On Tuesday morning nine-tenths of the wounded still lay where they fell; many had been there forty-eight hours without attention; numbers had died of shock or exhaustion; some had even drowned as the rain filled depressions from which they could not crawl. Every house in the area was converted into a hospital, where the floors were covered with wretches heavily wounded, sometimes with arms or legs torn off, who after the first bandages, got no nursing, medical care, or even nourishment. "The first day or two," wrote a newspaper reporter, "the air was filled with groans, sobs, and frenzied curses, but now the sufferers are quiet; not from cessation of pain, but mere exhaustion." Yet at this time the war was a year old.

Still more poignant versions of the same story might be given. Lee and Pope fought Second Manassas on the last Friday and Saturday in August, 1862, so near Washington that groups standing on housetops in the capital heard the rumble of artillery. The battleground, five miles long and three wide, was thickly strewn with dead and wounded. Pope retreated in confusion; many in Washington feared the city might be taken. In these circumstances, as late as the following Wednesday one member of the inadequate body of surgeons estimated that 2,000 wounded had received no attention.

Many had not tasted food for four days; some were dying of hunger and thirst. A reporter for the Washington *Republican* wrote on Thursday that some dying men could yet be saved by prompt help. And on Friday, a week after the battle began, a correspondent of the New York *Tribune* told of heart-rending scenes as the doctors searched among heaps of putrefying dead men for men yet clinging to life — men who, when anyone approached, would cry, "Doctor, come to *me;* you look like a kind man; for God's sake come to *me.*"

Anyone who is tempted to think of Gettysburg only in terms of its heroic episodes, its color and drama, should turn to the pages in "Battles and Leaders" in which General John D. Imboden describes the transport of the Confederate wounded, after their defeat, back into Maryland. He was ordered to ride to the head of the long wagon column as, in darkness and storm, it moved south:

> For four hours I hurried forward on my way to the front, and in all that time I was never out of hearing of the groans and cries of the wounded and dying. Scarcely one in a hundred had received adequate surgical aid, owing to the demands on the hard-working surgeons from still worse cases that had to be left behind. Many of the wounded in their wagons had been without food for thirty-six hours. Their torn and bloody clothing, matted and hardened, was rasping the tender, inflamed, and still oozing wounds. Very few of the wagons had even a layer of straw in them, and all were without springs. The road was rough and rocky from the heavy washings of the preceding day. The jolting was enough to have killed strong men, if long exposed to it. From nearly every wagon as the teams trotted on, urged by whip and shout, came such cries and shrieks as these:
>
> "My God! Why can't I die?"
>
> "My God! Will no one have mercy and kill me?"
>
> "Stop! Oh, for God's sake stop just for one minute; take me out and leave me to die on the roadside."
>
> Occasionally a wagon would be passed from which only low, deep moans could be heard. No help could be rendered to any of the sufferers. No heed could be given to any of their appeals. Mercy and duty to the many forbade the loss of a moment in the vain effort then and there to comply with the prayers of the few. On! On! We must move on. The storm continued and the darkness was appalling. There was no time even to fill a canteen with water for a dying man; for, except the drivers and the guards, all were wounded and utterly helpless in that vast procession of misery. During this one night I realized more of the horrors of war than I had in all the preceding two years. . . .

Yet *this* was far from being the ugliest side of war. Nor was the suffering in the huge prison camps, South and North, part of the worst side of war; the suffering which MacKinlay Kantor describes in his novel and to which Benét briefly adverts in "John Brown's Body":

The triple stockade of Andersonville the damned,
Where men corrupted like flies in their own dung
And the gangrened sick were black with smoke and their filth.

What maims the bodies of men is less significant than what maims their spirit.

One ugly aspect of the Civil War too generally ignored is the devastation, more and more systematic, that accompanied it. For three reasons too little has been said of this devastation; the facts were kept out of official reports, the tale is too painful, and the recital easily becomes monotonous. Yet by 1862 the war in the South had become one of general depredation; by 1863, of wanton destruction; and by 1864, of an organized devastation which in terms of property anticipated the worst chapters of the two world wars. Georgia and the Shenandoah suffered in 1864 almost precisely as Belgium and Serbia suffered in 1914 — the executions omitted. It was barbaric, and the only excuse to be made is that war is barbarism.

The turning point in the attitude of Northern military men was reached when General John Pope on July 18, 1862, issued from Washington headquarters a set of Draconian general orders. Order No. 5 directed that the army should subsist as far as practicable upon the country, giving vouchers for supplies seized. Order No. 7 decreed the summary execution of persons caught firing upon Union troops from houses. Order No. 11 (five days later) required officers to arrest immediately all disloyal males within reach, to make them take the oath of allegiance or go South, and to shoot all who violated their oath or who returned from the Confederacy. The order for living on the country, widely publicized East and West, changed the attitude of troops, and inspired private looting as well as public seizures of property. Pope was soon ousted, but the moral effect of his orders persisted.

Though most of the facts were excluded from official reports, their sum total, insofar as one shrewd observer could arrive at it, may be found in John T. Trowbridge's graphic volume written in 1866, "A Picture of the Desolated States." In his preface Trowbridge speaks of the Union forces not as our heroic armies but our destroying armies. Even this practiced reporter is less graphic, however, than the people who suffered under the onslaught and wrote while their emotions, like their property, still burned. Hear a lady of Louisiana tell what occurred when N. P. Banks's army passed:

I was watching from my window the apparently orderly march of the first Yankees that appeared in view and passed up the road, when, suddenly, as if by magic, the whole plantation was covered with men, like bees from an overthrown hive; and, as far as my vision extended, an inextricable medley of men and animals met my eye. In one place, excited troopers were firing into the flock of sheep; in another, officers and men were in pursuit of the boys' ponies, and in another, a crowd were in excited chase of the work animals. The kitchen was soon filled with some, carrying off the cooking utensils and the provisions of the day; the yard with others, pursuing the poultry....

They penetrated under the house, into the outbuildings, and into the garden, stripping it in a moment of all its vegetables.... This continued during the day... and amid a bewildering sound of oaths and imprecations.... When the army had passed, we were left destitute.

Sherman believed in total war; that is, in waging war not only against the Southern armies, but the Southern people. His theory was that every man, woman, and child was "armed and at war." He wrote his wife in the summer of 1862 that the North might fall into bankruptcy, "but if they can hold on the war will soon assume a turn to extermination, not of soldiers alone, that is the least part of the trouble, but the people." He denied, in effect, that Southerners had a right to resist invasion. When Union steamers were fired on near Randolph, Mississippi, in the fall of 1862, he destroyed Randolph, and a little later had all houses, farms, and cornfields devastated for fifteen miles along the banks.

When he drove his red plowshare across Georgia and the Carolinas, his object was to leave only scorched earth behind. He had already written of his Western operations: "Not a man is to be seen; nothing but women with houses plundered, fields open to the cattle and horses, pickets lounging on every porch, and desolation sown broadcast; servants all gone, and women and children bred in luxury... begging... for soldiers' rations." His aim was that which Phil Sheridan avowed: to leave them nothing but their eyes to weep with.

The final devastation of half the South was horrible to behold, and it was distressing to think that these savage losses had been inflicted by Americans upon fellow Americans. Yet this was far from being the worst aspect of the conflict, or the least easily reparable. Damages on which we can fix the dollar sign are important not in themselves, but as they become translated into cultural and spiritual losses; into the intellectual retardation caused by poverty, for example. The physical recovery of the South was rapid. As it was primarily an agricultural section, a few good crops at fair prices did much to restore it; and the swiftness with which housing, railroads, bridges, and public facilities were rebuilt astonished observers of the 1870s just as the swift postwar recovery of Germany and Poland has astonished observers of our day.

Infinitely worse were the biological losses — the racial hurts — inflicted by the Civil War. The killing of between 600,000 and 700,000 young men in a nation of 33,000,000 and the maiming or permanent debilitation of as many more had evil consequences projected into the far-distant future. We lost not only these men, but their children, and their children's children. Here, indeed, was a loss that proved highly cumulative....

... [T]he multitude of Civil War dead represent hundreds of thousands of homes, and hundreds of thousands of families, that might have been, and never were. They represent millions of people who might have been part of our population today and are not. We have lost the books they might have written, the scientific discoveries they might have made, the inventions they might have perfected. Such a loss defies measurement.

The only noteworthy attempt to measure the biological losses was made by David Starr Jordan and his son Harvey in a volume called "War's Aftermath" (1914). The authors circulated carefully drawn questionnaires in Spottsylvania and Rockbridge Counties in Virginia, and in Cobb County in Georgia, inquiring particularly into the eugenic effects of the conflict. One of their queries brought out evidence that by no means all casualties were among the men; numerous girls and women succumbed to the hardships and anxieties of the conflict in the South. Another question elicited unanimous agreement that "the flower of the people" went into the war at the beginning, and of these a large part died before the end. President Jordan, weighing all the responses, reached two conclusions: first, that the evidence "leaves a decided evidence in favor of grave racial hurt," and second, that "the war has seriously impoverished this country of its best human values."

Even the terrible loss of young, productive lives, the grave biological injury to the nation, however, did not constitute the worst side of the war. One aspect of the conflict was still more serious. It was the aspect to which Lowell referred in lines written a few years after Appomattox:

> I looked to see an ampler atmosphere
> By that electric passion-gust blown clear
> I looked for this; consider what I hear. . . .
>
> Murmur of many voices in the air
> Denounces us degenerate,
> Unfaithful guardians of a noble fate. . . .

The war, as Walt Whitman truly said, had grown out of defects in the American character; of American faults it cured few, accentuated a number, and gave some a violently dangerous trend. Far behind the lines, it added to the already discreditable total of violence in American life. Applying to industry a great forcing-draft, the bellows of huge wartime appropriations, it strengthened the materialistic forces in our civilization. Its state and federal contracts, its bounty system, its innumerable opportunities for battening on the nation's woes, made speculation fashionable, and corruption almost too common for comment. Its inflation bred extravagance and dissipation.

Every month heightened the intolerance of war; it began with mobs in New York threatening newspaper offices, a mob in Philadelphia trying to lynch Senator James A. Bayard, and mobs in the South flogging and exiling Union men; as it went on, freedom of speech almost disappeared over broad areas. The atmosphere of war fostered immorality; Richmond and Washington alike became filled with saloons, brothels, and gambling dens, and such occupied cities as Memphis and Nashville were sinks of iniquity. For every knightly martyr like James Wadsworth or Albert Sidney Johnston there arose two such coarse, aggressive, selfish careerists as Ben Butler and Dan Sickles. Wadsworth and Johnston died in battle, but Butler and Sickles remained to follow postwar political careers. Seen in perspective, the war was a gigantic engine for coarsening and lowering the American character even while it quickened certain of our energies.

Parson Brownlow, a Tennessee Unionist, went from city to city in the North in 1862 demanding "grape for the Rebel masses, and hemp for their leaders"; saying that he himself would tie the rope about the necks of some rebel generals; calling for the confiscation of all Southern property; proclaiming that he would be glad to arm every wolf, bear, catamount, and crocodile, every devil in hell, to defeat the South; and declaring he would put down the rebellion "if it exterminates from God's green earth every man, woman, and child south of Mason and Dixon's Line."

In the South two famous leaders, Robert Toombs and Howell Cobb, united that year in an address to their people just as vitriolic. "The foot of the oppressor is on the soil of Georgia," it began. "He comes with lust in his eye, poverty in his purse, and hell in his heart. How shall you meet him? . . . With death for him or for yourself!" Better the charnel house for every Southerner, they continued, than "loathsome vassalage to a nation already sunk below the contempt of the civilized world." Thaddeus Stevens nursed his hatred until he spoke of "exterminating" or driving into exile *all* Southerners, just as Sherman declared he would "slay millions" to assure the safety of the Mississippi. Women of the South meanwhile expressed the most vindictive detestation of all Yankees. "I hate them," wrote one Mississippi woman after a raid on her community, "more now than I did the evening I saw them sneaking off with all we cared for, and so it will be every day I live."

Hatred was seen in its most naked form in those communities divided against themselves and racked by guerrilla war; in Missouri, Arkansas, parts of Kentucky, and East Tennessee. Writes Charles D. Drake, a distinguished Missouri leader, of his state: "Falsehood, treachery, and perjury pervaded the whole social fabric." He went on: "Could there be written a full account of all the crimes of the rebels of Missouri, and the outrages and wrongs inflicted by them upon her loyal inhabitants, during the four years of the rebellion, the world would shrink aghast from a picture which has no parallel in the previous history of any portion of the Anglo-Saxon race." Confederate sympathizers in Missouri would have said the same of Union irregulars. One atrocity provoked another. These hatreds long survived the conflict, and indeed in some spots the embers still smoulder. Typifying the whole range of spiritual injuries wrought by the war, they justify the poet Blake's cry:

> The soldier, armed with sword and gun,
> Palsied strikes the summer sun.

The historian Mendelssohn Bartholdy, in his volume entitled "War and German Society," written as part of the Carnegie Endowment's huge economic history of World War I, concluded that the moral effects of war are much worse than the material effects. He also concluded that they are radically bad, for they strike at the very heart of a country's character: "modern war, with its robot-like disregard of individual values, is bound to make the peculiar virtue of a nation an object of attack." As respects the Civil War, we can agree. If it was necessary for preserving the Union and extinguishing slavery, it was of course worth more than it cost; but should it have been necessary? Could not better leadership from 1830 to 1860 have averted it? This is a bootless question. But it is certain that the conflict, so much the greatest convulsion in our history, so tremendous in its impact on our national life, so fascinating in its drama, was in spite of all compensating elements, all the heroism, all the high example we find in Lee's character and Lincoln's wisdom, materially a disaster and morally a tragedy.

It is unfortunate that of the flood of books on the war ninety-nine in a hundred are on military topics and leaders, and that a great majority fasten attention on the floating banners, the high-ringing cheers, the humors of the camp, the ardors of the charge; the whole undeniable fascination and romance of the first true *volkskrieg* in history. It is right, within measure, to let them lift our hearts. But the long commemoration will pass essentially unimproved if it does not give us a deeper, sterner, more scientific study of the collision of two creeds and two ways of life as related to an examination of war in general.

We should probe more deeply into its roots, a process that will expose some of the weaknesses of our social fabric and governmental system. We should pay fuller attention to its darker aspects, and examine more honestly such misrepresentations as the statement it was distinguished by its generosity of spirit, the magnanimity with which the combatants treated each other; a statement absurd on its face, for no war which lasts four years and costs 600,000 lives leaves much magnanimity in its later phases. We should above all examine more closely the effects of the great and terrible war not on the nation's politics — we know that; not on its economy — we also know that; but on its character, the vital element of national life.

This examination will lead into unpleasant paths, and bring us to unhappy conclusions; but it will profit us far more than stirring battle canvases. All nations must be schooled in such studies if the world is ever to find an answer to a question uttered just after World War I by William E. Borah, a question that still rings in men's ears: "When shall we escape from war? When shall we loosen the grip of the monster?"

STUDY GUIDE

1. Nevins raises the question as to whether the Civil War was necessary to abolish slavery. Some historians feel that slavery would have died out because it was becoming economically unprofitable; others argue that only

conflict could have eliminated a system so deeply embedded in American life as was slavery. Is this a question that can be answered by historical study? What kind of evidence might be relevant if one attempted to do so?

2. Generally, historians simply study and try to *explain* wars, rather than make moral judgments on them. Do you see any special limitations to historical study or training that makes this sensible; or are historians in a better position than most people to judge, and in failing to do so are they abdicating their responsibility to inform society? How would you approach the question of judging the relative justness of the American Revolution and the Civil War or World War II and the Vietnam War?

3. Consider the following aspects of warfare, and indicate how wars in our time differ from the Civil War in each respect: treatment of civilian populations, individual atrocities, personal confrontations of infantry soldiers in battle and in picket-line duty, ways in which soldiers are killed, and the degree of personal responsibility and concern that higher officers feel for their armies.

4. Compare the feelings described by Nevins with the animosities that are described by Wallace Brown in his essay on the Loyalists during the American Revolution (Reading No. 6). What differences and similarities can you think of in the relations of the two opposing forces during these two wars? Why were the Loyalists in a more difficult position with respect to confiscation of property and such personal abuse as tarring and feathering than were the enemy forces during the Civil War?

BIBLIOGRAPHY

There are more books and articles on the American Civil War than on any other aspect of American history. Much of this material deals with the causes of the war and the military campaigns; to discover some of this literature, you can examine James G. Randall and David Donald, *The Civil War and Reconstruction,* 2nd ed. (1961) and Thomas J. Pressly, *Americans Interpret Their Civil War* (1954). Many aspects of army life are treated in Bell I. Wiley, *Johnny Reb* (1943) and its companion volume by the same author, *The Life of Billy Yank* (1952). The attitudes of contemporaries toward the war are described in Henry S. Commager, ed., *The Blue and the Gray: The Story of the Civil War as Told by Participants,* 2 vols. (1940). Among the many general treatments of the war, the best are Allen Nevins, *The War for the Union,* 3 vols. (1959–1971); Bruce Catton, *This Hallowed Ground: The Story of the Union Side of the Civil War* (1956); and a three-volume series by Catton, of which the best volume is *A Stillness at Appomattox* (1953). George W. Smith and Charles Judah, eds., *Life in the North during the Civil War: A Source History* (1966) is a collection of writings from the period of the Civil War that will give you an idea of life behind the lines. One of the best secondary works on the same subject, but limited to the northern capital, is Margaret Leech, *Reveille in Washington, 1860–1865* (1941). Conditions there, of course, were considerably different from life in the Confederate capital, which is studied in Alfred H. Bill, *The Beleaguered City: Richmond, 1861–1865* (1946).

For a number of reasons, there are more good works on social conditions in the Confederacy than on wartime life in the North. A general work on the Confederacy, with several chapters on economic and social conditions, is E. Merton Coulter, *The Confederate States of America, 1861–1865* (1950). Charles W. Ramsdell, *Behind the Lines in the Southern Confederacy* (1944) is an excellent work more strictly confined to the home front, while Mary E. Massey, *Ersatz in the Confederacy* (1952) is a fascinating study of the substitutes that were used for food, clothing, and other necessities of life.

Bell I. Wiley also has works on southern whites and blacks in the Confederacy: *The Plain People of the Confederacy* (1943) and *Southern Negroes, 1861–1865* (1938). The latter work should be read in conjunction with the study of Negroes in the North by Benjamin Quarles, *The Negro in the Civil War* (1953). Chapters 7 and 8 of Quarles's book give an interesting picture of the reaction of blacks to emancipation. If you would like to supplement Nevins's general essay with a detailed account of the devastation in one campaign, see Burke Davis, *Sherman's March* (1980).

Southern blacks in the post–Civil War South soon learned that emancipation did not bring social equality.

21

JOEL WILLIAMSON

After Slavery

Few dreams in the history of the United States have been so cruelly unrealized as the hope that with the end of the Civil War and the destruction of the institution of slavery, black Americans would be accorded some measure of equality and opportunity in American life. With the end of the war in 1865, reform-minded Republicans, known as Radical Republicans, sought to make this dream a reality. Through their control of Congress they initiated Reconstruction, a program designed to restructure the social and political relations between whites and blacks in the defeated South. In 1865 and 1866, Congress funded the Freedmen's Bureau to feed, clothe, and protect the ex-slaves; civil rights legislation was passed in 1866 and reinforced by the Civil Rights Act of 1875, intended to outlaw varied forms of segregation; and three amendments were added to the Constitution. The Thirteenth Amendment (1865) outlawed slavery, the Fourteenth Amendment (1868) extended federal citizenship to blacks and made illegal many parts of the black codes, and the Fifteenth Amendment (1870) protected the black man's right to vote.

Despite this and other legislation, and despite the ascension to power of Reconstruction governments in the southern states — state governments in which political power was shared by a combination of Southern scalawags, Northern carpetbaggers, and emancipated blacks — the Radical Republican effort to reconstruct the relations between the races in the South ended in failure. The first stage of that failure, what one historian has so aptly called "darkness at noon," came with the end of Reconstruction. Reconstruction was ended by the disputed election of Republican Rutherford B. Hayes over Democrat Samuel J. Tilden in 1876 and by the Compromise of 1877, in which the rights of black Americans were made secondary to the economic opportunities and social privileges of white Americans, both Democrats and Republicans. The second stage in the disfranchisement and segregation of American blacks came between the end of Reconstruction and the American entry into World War I in 1914. The caste system created in these decades paralleled, to a degree, the relations between the races in parts of southern Africa today.

The selection that follows tells us about the origins of the Southern caste system. In his book *After Slavery: The Negro in South Carolina during Reconstruction, 1861–1877*, Joel Williamson finds that patterns of segregation came to South Carolina in the Reconstruction period. Williamson thus refutes a cardinal assumption made by C. Vann Woodward, the dean of Southern historians. Woodward contends that until the 1890s, Southern whites still held open options in their treatment of Southern blacks and that "Jim Crow," the disfranchisement and the segregation of blacks, was a product of decisions made by Southern whites *after* Reconstruction, closer to the turn of the century. Williamson's essay, taken from his study of the Reconstruction in South Carolina, demonstrates that in South Carolina this was not so.

The physical separation of the races was the most revolutionary change in relations between whites and Negroes in South Carolina during Reconstruction.

Separation had, of course, marked the Negro in slavery; yet the very nature of slavery necessitated a constant, physical intimacy between the races. In the peculiar institution, the white man had constantly and closely to oversee the labor of the Negro, preserve order in domestic arrangements within the slave quarters, and minister to the physical, medical, and moral needs of his laborers. In brief, slavery enforced its own special brand of interracial associations; in a sense, it married the interests of white to black at birth and the union followed both to the grave. Slavery watched the great mass of Negroes in South Carolina, but those Negroes who lived outside of the slave system were not exempt from the scrutiny of the whites. Even in Charleston, the free Negro community was never large enough to establish its economic and racial independence. In the mid-nineteenth century, as the bonds of

From *After Slavery: The Negro in South Carolina during Reconstruction, 1861–1877*, by Joel Williamson. Copyright 1965 The University of North Carolina Press. By permission of the publisher.

slavery tightened, the whites were forced to bring free Negroes under ever more stringent controls and to subject their lives to the closest surveillance.

During the spring and summer of 1865, as the centripetal force of slavery melted rapidly away, each race clearly tended to disassociate itself from the other. The trend was evident in every phase of human endeavor: agriculture, business, occupations, schools and churches, in every aspect of social intercourse and politics. As early as July of 1865, a Bostonian in Charleston reported that "the worst sign here . . . is the growth of a bitter and hostile spirit between blacks and whites — a gap opening between the races which, it would seem may at some time result seriously." Well before the end of Reconstruction, separation had crystallized into a comprehensive pattern which, in its essence, remained unaltered until the middle of the twentieth century.

There is no clear, concise answer to the question of why separation occurred. Certainly, it was not simply a response of Negroes to the prejudiced fiat of dominant whites; nor was it a totally rationalized reaction on the part of either race. Actually, articulate whites and Negroes seldom attempted to explain their behavior. Yet, the philosophies and attitudes each race adopted toward the other lend a certain rationality to separation, and, if we are always mindful that this analysis presumes a unity which they never expressed, can be applied to promote an understanding of the phenomenon.

For the native white community, separation was a means of avoiding or minimizing problems which, they felt, would inevitably arise from the inherent inferiority of the Negro, problems which the North, in eradicating slavery and disallowing the Black Code, would not allow them to control by overt political means. In this limited sense, segregation was a substitute for slavery.

Thus, first, total separation was essential to racial purity, and racial purity was necessary to the preservation of a superior civilization which the whites had labored so arduously to construct, and suffered a long and bloody war to defend. After the war, that civilization was embattled, but not necessarily lost. Unguarded association with an inferior caste would obviously endanger white culture. In this view, children were peculiarly susceptible to damage. "Don't imagine that I allow my children to be with negroes out of my presence," wrote the mistress of a lowcountry plantation in 1868, "on one occasion only have they been so with my knowledge." Even the Negro wet nurse, that quintessence of maternalism upon which the slave period paternalist so often turned his case, emerged as the incubus of Southern infancy. "We gave our infants to the black wenches to suckle," lamented an elderly white, "and thus poisoned the blood of our children, and made them *cowards* . . . the Character of the people of the state was ruined by slavery and it will take 500 years, if not longer, by the infusion of new blood to eradicate the hereditary vices imbibed with the blood (milk is blood) of black wet nurses." . . .

Separation also facilitated the subordination of the inferior race by constantly reminding the Negro that he lived in a world in which the white man was dominant, and in which the non-white was steadfastly denied access to the higher caste. Further, the impression of Negro inferiority would be constantly re-enforced by relegating the baser element, whenever possible, to the use of inferior facilities. The sheer totality of the display alone might well serve to convince members of the lower caste that such, indeed, was in the natural order of things.

Many whites had envisioned the early elimination of the freedman from the Southern scene, and many had eagerly anticipated this event. In time, however, it became evident to all that the Negro would be neither dissolved nor transported to Africa. In a sense, separation was a means of securing the quasi elimination of Negroes at home. It was, perhaps, a more satisfactory solution than their demise or emigration, since it might produce many of the benefits of their disappearance without losing an advantageous, indeed, a necessary supply of labor.

Finally, separation was a logical solution to the problem posed by the widespread conviction that the races were inherently incompatible outside of the master-slave relationship. If the white man could not exist in contentment in the proximity of Negroes, then partial satisfaction might be achieved by withdrawal from associations with members of the inferior caste. This spirit was evident among some of the wealthier whites who voluntarily dispensed entirely with the services of Negro domestics. Elderly William Heyward, in 1868 still second to none in the ranks of the rice aristocracy, stopped taking his meals at the Charleston Hotel because, as he said, he found "the negro waiter so defiant and so familiar in their attentions." "A part of the satisfaction is," he explained to a friend, "that I am perfectly independent of having negroes about me; if I cannot have them as they used to be, I have no desire to see them except in the field." Planters were often manifesting precisely the same sentiment when they deserted their land and turned to grain culture, or to the use of immigrant labor. Separation was also a way of avoiding interracial violence. B. O. Duncan and James L. Orr, both native white Republicans, argued against mixing in the public schools because they were convinced that minor irritations between children would generate major altercations between parents of different races. Conceived as a means of avoiding violence, separation, ironically, was subsequently enforced by the use of violence. . . .

Contrary to common belief, the separation of the races was not entirely the work of the whites. Suspicious, resentful, and sometimes hateful toward the whites, chafed by white attitudes of superiority, and irritated by individual contacts with supercilious whites, Negroes, too, sought relief in withdrawal from association with the other race. In many instances, the disassociation was complete — that is, many Negroes left the state. During the war, Corporal Simon Crum of the First South Carolina declared his intention of leaving South Carolina after the capitulation because, as he phrased it, "dese yer Secesh [secessionists] will neber be cibilized in my time." For those who could not or would not leave, alternative forms of withdrawal were possible. A major facet in the new pattern of agriculture was the removal of Negro labor from the immediate supervision of white men. As the Negro agriculturalist moved his labor away from the eye of the white man, so also did he move his family and his home. Plantation villages became increasingly rare as Negro landowners and renters either built new houses on their plots or, in a rather graphic symbolic display, laboriously dragged their cabins away from the "Negro street." Negroes in the trades and in domestic service followed similar trends. Furthermore, Negroes chose to withdraw from white-dominated churches, though they were often urged to stay, and they attended racially separated schools in spite of the legal fact that all schools were open to all races. Negroes also tended to withdraw from political association with members of the white community.

Finally, on those few occasions when Negroes entered into polite social situations with whites, Northern as well as Southern, they were often ill at ease. For instance, while driving along a road near Columbia, a planter and his wife met William, "a fine looking light mulatto" who had been their stableboy as a slave. William was driving a buggy and seated beside him was a young white woman, elegantly attired. The woman was a "Yankee school marm," probably one of the new teachers in Columbia's Negro school. As he passed his late master and mistress, the Negro averted his gaze and did not speak. The following day, he approached the planter and apologized for having been escort to a "white woman." He had met the teacher at a celebration, he explained, and she had insisted on his taking her to see the countryside.

During Reconstruction, the Negro's withdrawal was never a categorical rejection of the white man and his society. In the early days of freedom, it was primarily a reaction against slavery, an attempt to escape the unpleasant associations of his previous condition and the derogatory implications of human bondage. However, as the memory of slavery faded, a more persistent reason for withdrawal emerged. Essentially, it was the Negro's answer to discrimination. Almost invariably, attempts by individual Negroes to establish satisfactory relations across the race line were unsuccessful, and, all too often, the pain of the experience was greater than the reward for having stood for principle. During Reconstruction and afterward, only a few were willing to undergo such pain without the certainty of success. It was much easier, after all, simply to withdraw.

Withdrawal as a solution to the race problem was by no means satisfactory to the Negro leadership. Implicit in the behavior of Negro leaders during Reconstruction was a yearning for complete and unreserved acceptance for members of their race by the white community. However, overtly, and rather politically, they carefully distinguished between "social equality" and what might be appropriately termed "public equality." For themselves, they claimed only the latter. "Our race do not demand social equality," declared W. J. Whipper, a member from Beaufort, on the floor of the house of representatives in Columbia. . . .

What the Negro leadership did insist upon was public equality, that is, absolute civil and political parity with whites and full and free access to most public facilities. These latter included restaurants, bars, saloons, railway and street cars, shipboard accommodations, the theater, and other such places of public amusement. Once they gained political power, Negro leaders hastened to embody this attitude in legislation. Within a week after the first sitting of the Constitutional Convention of 1868, a Negro delegate introduced a resolution which was eventually included in the state's bill of rights: "Distinction on account of race or color, in any case whatever, shall be prohibited, and all classes of citizens shall enjoy equally all common, public, legal and political privileges." Similarly, one of the first bills passed by the Republican legislature prohibited licensed businesses from discriminating "between persons, on account of race, color, or previous condition, who shall make lawful application for the benefit of such business, calling or pursuit." Convicted violators were liable to a fine of not less than $1,000 or imprisonment for not less than a year. During the debate on the measure in the house, not a single Negro member spoke against the bill, and only five of the twenty-four votes registered against it were cast by Negroes, while fifty-three of the sixty-one votes which secured its passage were those of Negro legislators.

Negro Congressmen were no less ardent in championing the same cause in Washington, particularly in 1874, when a federal civil rights bill was up for consideration. ". . . is it pretended anywhere," asked Congressman R. B. Elliott, who had only recently been denied service in the restaurant of a railway station in North Carolina on his journey to the capital, "that the evils of which we complain, our exclusion from the public inn, from the saloon and the table of the steamboat, from the sleeping-coach on the railway, from the right of sepulture in the public burial-ground, are an exercise of the police power of the State? . . . Are the colored people to be assimilated to an unwholesome trade or to combustible materials, to be interdicted, to be shut up within prescribed limits?" Several days later, in the same place, Congressman R. H. Cain declared, "We do not want any discrimination to be made. I do not ask any legislation for the colored people of this country that is not applied to the white people of this country. All that we seek is equal laws, equal legislation, and equal rights throughout the length and breadth of this land."

It was upon this emotional, uneven ground that an essentially new color line was drawn. It was established in a kind of racial warfare, of assaults and withdrawals, of attacks and counterattacks. Nevertheless, well before the end of Reconstruction, both forces had been fully engaged and the line was unmistakably formed.

Even before the Radicals came into power in South Carolina in 1868, native whites had already defined a color line in government-supported institutions, on common carriers, in places of public accommodation and amusement, and, of course, in private social organizations. The degree of separation in each of these areas varied. In many instances, obviously, some compromise between expense and the desire for complete separation had to be made. Usually, the compromise involved the division of available facilities in some manner. If this was thought to be inconvenient, Negroes were totally excluded.

Typical was the treatment of Negro and white prisoners in the state penitentiary under the James L. Orr regime [1865–68; South Carolina]. Criminals of both races were confined in the same institution but were quartered in separate cells. Ironically, the racial concepts of white prison officials sometimes redounded to the benefit of Negro inmates. Minor violations of prison rules were punished every Sunday by the offenders being tied closely together, blindfolded, and forced to work their way over a series of obstacles in the prison yard. The chief guard explained that the white offenders were placed in the most difficult middle positions of the "blind gang" because "they have more intelligence than the colored ones and are better able to understand the rules of the institution."

It is paradoxical that the Negro leadership, once in office, pressed vigorously for an end to separation in privately-owned facilities open to the public but they allowed a very distinct separation to prevail in every major governmental facility. The most obvious instance was the schools, but the distinction also stretched into the furthermost reaches of gubernatorial activity. For example, a visitor to the state insane asylum in Columbia in 1874 found that "The Negro female inmates occupy a separate part of the same building" in which the white women were housed.

On the other side, within a month after they had gained the vote, Negroes in South Carolina opened a frontal attack against racial discrimination on common carriers. Typical was their assault on the Charleston Street Car Company. At the time of its inauguration, the facilities of the company consisted of double tracks running the length of the peninsula with a spur branching off near the mid-point. Horse-drawn cars, each manned by a driver and a conductor, ran along the tracks at regular intervals. The cars contained seats in a compartment, and front and rear platforms. Before the cars began to run in December, 1866, the question of the accommodation of Negro passengers was thoroughly canvassed. "Proper arrangements will in due time be made to allow persons of color to avail themselves of the benefits of the railway," the management assured the Negro community, but it had not then decided between providing "special cars" for the Negroes as was done in New Orleans, or "assigning to them a portion of the ordinary cars as is more usual in other cities." Negro leaders rejected both alternatives. As a Northerner wrote from Charleston in January, 1867, "Every scheme that could be devised that did not contemplate the promiscuous use of the cars by whites and negroes alike, was scouted by the Negro paper here; and the result is that negroes are now debarred the use of the cars altogether, unless they choose to ride upon the platform." . . .

After the Negro gained political power, the battle against discrimination became more intense and assumed a wider front. The so-called antidiscrimination bill, passed in the summer of 1868, on paper was a most formidable weapon. In essence, it imposed severe penalties upon the owners of public accommodations who were convicted of discrimination. Burden of proof of innocence lay on the accused, and state solicitors (public prosecutors) who failed to prosecute suspected violators were themselves threatened with heavy punishments.

The effect of the new legislation on common carriers was immediate. A Northern teacher returning to Beaufort in the fall of 1868, after a few months' absence in the North, observed a portion of the results:

> We took a small steamer from Charleston for Beaufort. Here we found a decided change since we went North. Then no colored person was allowed on the upper deck, now there were no restrictions — there could be none, for a law had been passed in favor of the negroes. They were everywhere, choosing the best staterooms and best seats at the table. Two prominent colored members of the State Legislature were on board with their families. There were also several well-known Southerners, still uncompromising rebels. It was a curious scene and full of significance. An interesting study to watch the exultant faces of the negroes, and the scowling faces of the rebels . . .

The same legislation applied to railway facilities; and, apparently, it was applied without a great amount of dissent. Adjustment was made easier, perhaps, by the acquisition of some of the railroad companies by Radical politicians within the state, or by Northern capitalists, and by the close understanding which usually prevailed between Republican officeholders and those Conservatives who managed to retain control of their railroads. While formal discrimination was not practiced by railway operators, unofficial racial separation did occur on a large scale. On all of the major lines first- and second-class cars were available. Most Negroes apparently deliberately chose to ride in the more economical second-class accommodations, and virtually all of the whites — particularly white women — took passage on the first-class cars. The separation thus achieved was so nearly complete that the first-class car was often referred to as the "ladies' car." It is highly relevant that the first Jim Crow legislation affecting railroads in South Carolina provided for the separation of the races only in the first-class cars, because, of course, this was the only place on the railroads where there was any possibility of a significant degree of mixing. . . .

In the winter of 1869–1870 and through the summer which followed, a concerted attempt was made by the Negro leadership to win the full acceptance of Negroes into all places of public amusement, eating, drinking, and sleeping. Special provisions for the accommodation of Negroes at public entertainments had been made in ante-bellum times, but physical separation of the races was invariably the rule. In December, 1868, Charles Minort, a mulatto restaurateur and lesser political figure, nearly provoked a riot in a Columbia theater by presuming to seat his wife and himself in the front row, a section traditionally reserved for tardy white ladies. Presumably, he should have chosen seats among the other Negroes present who "had taken their seats, as has always been the custom, in the rear." Minort yielded to the clamor of the whites in the audience, but, a year later, the Negroes of Charleston instituted judicial proceedings against the manager of the Academy of Music for refusing to mix the races in the boxes of the theater. The management barely succeeded in winning a postponement but was able to complete the season before the case came to trial.

In the spring of 1870, Negro leaders in Charleston launched an attack against discrimination in restaurants, bars, and saloons. On March 25, for instance, Louis Kenake, accused of violating the antidiscrimination act, was brought before Magistrate T. J. Mackey and put on a bond of one thousand dollars while awaiting trial. Other white restaurant keepers of Charleston united to oppose and test the validity of the act, but, in the week which followed, at least six additional charges were lodged against operators of such businesses. The assault was not confined to Charleston and demonstrations by Radical politicians were frequent during the campaign of 1870. In April, a Laurens woman wrote to her son in Missouri that "On Monday the yankees & some negroes went to Hayne Williams' and asked for drink, which 'Ward' refused them, that is, to drink at the gentlemans bar. They quietly marched him off to jail, & locked the doors, putting the keys in their pockets. The family are all at Spartanburg, we look for H. Williams to night, and I am afraid of a fuss, for he is a great bully." In the same month, during a Radical meeting in Lancaster, a Negro was refused service in a local bar with the comment that no "nigger" could buy a drink there. Lucius Wimbush, a Negro senator, hearing of the incident, went to the bar, ordered a drink, and was refused. He immediately had the barkeeper arrested and placed under bail. . . .

Negroes were also ambitious to open sleeping accommodations to their race. In the summer of 1868, as the first Negro legislators gathered in Columbia, native whites had been extremely apprehensive that they would attempt to occupy rooms in the city's hotels. Even *The Nation*, which had applauded the opening of common carriers to both races, declared that hotels were another and "delicate" matter, where separation was everywhere observed. The white community was vastly relieved to find that no such invasion was attempted, one upcountry newspaper having sent a special correspondent to

Columbia to ascertain the fact. Nevertheless, when Negro legislators debated the antidiscrimination bill early in the session, they made it very clear that hotels were included. William E. Johnson, the African Methodist Minister then representing Sumter County in the statehouse, noting that the management of Nickerson's Hotel was concerned lest Negroes apply for rooms, declared that if he found private accommodations filled he would want to know that this resort was open to him. George Lee, a Negro member from Berkeley, observed that a group of junketing legislators had recently failed to find lodging in Greenville and that this law was desired to prevent that sort of occurrence. "Equal and exact justice to all," he demanded, ". . . it is what we must have." Negroes were subsequently allowed to attend meetings in Columbia hotels, but it is apparent that none were ever given lodging.

Negroes also decried the fact that places of permanent rest occupied by whites, as well as those of a more temporary variety, were denied to their race. For instance, S. G. W. Dill, the native white Radical who was assassinated in Kershaw in the summer of 1868, and Nestor Peavy, his Negro guard who was killed in the same assault, were buried in racially separated cemeteries.

Thus, from 1868 until 1889, when the antidiscrimination law was repealed, Negroes in South Carolina could legally use all public facilities which were open to whites. However, in actual practice, they seldom chose to do so. "The naturally docile negro makes no effort at unnecessary self-assertion," a Northern visitor in Charleston explained in 1870, "unless under the immediate instigation of some dangerous *friends* belonging to the other race, who undertake to manage his destiny." This particular reporter was certainly prejudiced against the race; but four years later another Northern observer congratulated the Negroes of South Carolina on the "moderation and good sense" which they exhibited in their "intercourse with the whites." He concluded, "They seldom intrude themselves into places frequented by the whites, and considering that in South Carolina they have a voting majority of some thirty thousand and control the entire State Government, it is somewhat remarkable that they conduct themselves with so much propriety." Indeed, after 1870, even the Negro leadership hardly seemed inclined to press further their political and legal advantage to end separation. Of the numerous charges lodged under the antidiscrimination law, not a single conviction was ever recorded.

Even when Negroes pressed themselves in upon the prejudice of whites, the latter adjusted by total or partial withdrawal, so that a high degree of separation was always and everywhere maintained.

Some whites responded to the pressure by total withdrawal, that is, by leaving the state entirely. Of course, many of those who left South Carolina did so primarily for economic reasons, but many also departed from purely racial motives. A Winnsboro lawyer and pre-war fire-eater revealed the thinking of many emigrants when he asked William Porcher Miles, in April, 1867, how he could live in a land where "Every 'mulatto' is your Equal & every 'Nigger' is your Superior." Pronouncing the Negro majority "revolting," he advised Miles to go to England. ". . . I have no doubt you could succeed & at any rate w[oul]d not have as many Negro Clients & negro witnesses to offend y[ou]r nostrils as in these USA. I can't conceive of any ones remaining here who can possibly get away — Suppose, it were certain, wh[ich]. it is not, that no U S Congress will ever pass a Law requiring that your Daughter & mine shall either marry Negroes or die unmarried. Still the Negro is already superior to them politically & to their Fathers also, & must ever be so henceforth." . . .

After Negroes were firmly entrenched in official positions in government, native whites evinced a distinct tendency to refrain from associations which recognized the authority of Negro officers over white citizens. For instance, in the heavily Negro county of Abbeville, in 1870, a distressed guardian asked one of the magistrates, who happened to be a Democrat, to dispatch a constable to return an orphan girl stolen away from his house. "When you send for Laura," he begged, "please send a white man, as she is a white girl under my charge, and I would not like to subject her to the mortification of being brought back by a colored man. Besides that I would be censured by the community as they would know nothing of the circumstances of the case." . . .

Withdrawal was also the means by which native whites combatted attempts by Republican officials to end separation in institutions supported by the government. The withdrawal of native whites from the University and the State School for the Deaf and Blind at the prospect of Negro admissions are illustrations of white determination either to maintain separation or to dispense with the services afforded by related state institutions. If the Radicals had attempted to end separation in the common schools, it is virtually certain that the whites would have removed their children from these schools too. As one post-Redemption [post-Reconstruction] proponent of universal education argued, separation was essential to academic progress. Only by this means, he explained to Governor [Wade] Hampton, could it be achieved "without any danger of social equality — *and this is the great bug bear.*" Doubtless, it was the threat of withdrawal by the whites which dissuaded the Radical leadership from further attempts to end separation in institutions over which they had, by political means, absolute control.

Whites also refused to engage in normal civic activities in which the color line was not distinctly drawn. Thus, native whites chose not to join militia companies in which Negroes participated and were reported to be extremely apprehensive of being forced to undergo the "humiliation" of joining a mixed company. Too, whites were reluctant to sit with Negroes in the jury box. An elderly Spartanburg farmer verbalized his feelings on this point in the summer of 1869: "When I go to court & see negroes on the jury & on the stand for witnesses it makes me glad that I am so near the end of my race to sit on a jury with them I dont intend to do it we have a law that exempt a man at 65 & I take the advantage of it." This kind of withdrawal often reached odd extremes. In the spring of 1870, at the peak of the Negro leadership's drive for admission to privately owned public accommodations, the white Democrats of the Charleston Fire Department refused to decorate their engines and join in the annual parade because Negro fire companies were being allowed to march in the procession. . . .

Native whites also tended to withdraw from public places where the color line could not be firmly fixed and the Negro could easily assert his equality. "The whites have, to a great extent — greater than ever before — yielded the streets to the negroes," wrote a Columbian on Christmas Day, 1868. Similarly, in Charleston, in the late spring of 1866, a young aristocrat noted that the battery with its music and strollers had been yielded to the ladies and gentlemen of non-noble lineage on Saturdays, and by all whites to the Negroes on Sundays. On Saturdays, he declared, "the battery is quite full of gentlemen and ladies but it is not much patronized by the elite. . . . On Sunday afternoon the ethiops spread themselves on the Battery."

The same reaction was manifested by the whites wherever the Negro leadership succeeded by legal means in ending separation. For instance, when Negroes won admission to the street cars of Charleston, the whites simply withdrew. "On Sunday I counted five Cars successively near the Battery crowded [with] negroes, with but one white man, the Conductor," wrote a native white in May, 1867. "The ladies are practically excluded." When the Academy of Music was threatened with a discrimination suit in 1870, the white community replied with a counterthreat to withdraw its patronage and thus close the theater. Adjustment which fell short of complete separation remained unsatisfactory to whites. "Even the Theatre is an uncertain pleasure," complained a Charleston lady in 1873, "no matter how attractive the program, for you know that you may have a negro next to you." Probably many of her contemporaries found the exposure too damaging and stayed home.

The social lives of native whites were, of course, absolutely closed to Negroes. Access to the homes of the whites was gained by Negroes only when they clearly acquiesced in the superior-inferior relationship dictated by the owners, and even then entrance was often denied. "I told him I would never allow negroes to go in it while I owned it," wrote a Laurenville woman, incensed that a man who had bought her former home had rented it to Negroes. In spite of the fact that some Negro domestics lived in quarters behind the houses of their employers, whites were already rejecting Negroes as neighbors. A real estate agent in Aiken in 1871 responded to this sentiment when he refused offers from Negroes for city lots at triple prices because, as he explained to the owner, "purchasers among the whites will not settle among the Negroes, and I am afraid to sell to only a few of the latter." Negroes were also not permitted to join any of the numerous social organizations in which native whites participated. The Patrons of Husbandry (the Grange), waxing strong in the state in the early 1870's, was not only exclusively white in membership, but was accused of widening the racial gap by its attitudes and actions toward Negroes. Of course, such separation had been practiced before, but the exclusion of the Negro in freedom from the social organizations of the whites was not so much tradition as it was deliberate decision. . . .

Separation is, of course, a relative term. It was obviously not possible for Negroes and whites to withdraw entirely from association with each other. If intimate contact led to irritation and violence, it also led to warm personal friendships — often with the superior-inferior, paternal bias, but no less real for all of that. Cordiality could and did breach the barrier of race. Yet the fact remained that it was difficult to establish a human bond across the color chasm and, once established, the tie had to be assiduously maintained against the constant erosion induced by a thousand and one external forces of social pressure.

That there was sometimes tenderness between individuals of different races is abundantly evident. On the Elmore plantation near Columbia, in the fall of 1865, the young white master was nightly importuned by the Negro children to get out his fiddle and play. Frequently he did so, the dozen or so Negro boys and girls dancing around the fire, begging for more after the fiddler had exhausted himself in a two-hour concert. The concern of many late masters for their ex-slaves was matched by the interest of individual Negroes in the welfare of their recent owners. A freedman seeking relief for a white family from a Bureau officer explained his motivation: "I used to belong to one branch of that family, and so I takes an interest in 'em." Occasionally, ex-slaveowners retained the friendship and assistance of their erstwhile bondsmen when all others had deserted them. . . .

Sometimes, intimacy became miscegenation. The census reports are uncertain witnesses and contemporaries are typically mute on the point; but scattered references suggest that racial interbreeding was markedly less common after emancipation than before. "Miscegenation between white men and negro women diminished under the new order of things," a Bureau officer later wrote. "Emancipation broke up the close family contact in which slavery held the two races, and, moreover young gentlemen did not want mulatto children sworn to them at a cost of three hundred dollars apiece. In short, the new relations of the two stocks tended to separation rather than to fusion." A Northern traveler visiting the state in 1870 concurred: "From all I could see and learn, there are far fewer half-breed children born now than before the Rebellion. There seems, indeed, a chance that the production of original half-breeds may be almost done away with. . . ."

Legal, moral, and social pressures exercised by the white community upon its members, as well as the physical separation of the races suggest that these were valid observations. The Black Code pointedly declared that "Marriage between a white person and a person of color shall be illegal and void," and when the code was revised in 1866 this portion emphatically remained in force. Children born of Negro mothers and white fathers, so recently especially prized for their pecuniary value, became simply illegimate issue and a liability to the community. In addition, the laws of bastardy came to be applied against the fathers of mulatto children. Perhaps most important was the fact that, in the minds of the native whites, children of mixed blood personified the adulteration of the superior race and embodied in living form the failure of Southern civilization. Many whites, turned to soul-searching by their defeat, fixed upon miscegenation as their great sin. "It does seem strange that so lovely a climate, and country, with a people in every way superior to the Yankees, should be overrun and destroyed by them," wrote a rice aristocrat in 1868. "But I believe that God has ordered it all, and I am firmly of opinion with Ariel that it is the judgement of the Almighty because the human and brute blood have mingled to the degree it has in the slave states. Was it not so in the French and British Islands and see what has become of them."

Just as complete separation of the races was physically impossible, there was little possibility that miscegenation might entirely cease. One does not have to travel far into contemporary sources to discover instances in which white men had children by Negro women. In 1867, a lowcountry planter, accused of fathering the mulatto child of his Negro house servant, wrote plaintively to his mother: "This child was begotten during my absence in Charlotte & Charleston, from the middle of December until nearly the middle of January, & the Father of it was seen night after night in Emma's house, this I heard on my return, but as it was no concern of mine I did not give it a thought. She was *free,* the Mother of 5 Children & could have a dozen lovers if she liked. I had no control over her virtue." In 1874, a planter on the Cooper River in St. John's noted the existence of circumstances on his plantation which might have led to similar results. "Found a white man staying with one of the colored people on the place," ran the laconic note in his journal. "He being engaged in rebuilding Mayrents Bridge." Some of these liaisons were of prolonged duration. In 1870, Maria Middleton, a Negro woman, brought suit against a Pineville physician for failure to support her three children which he had allegedly fathered. Strangely, the defendant's lawyer did not deny the paternity, but sought dismissal on the plea that the plaintiff had no legal grounds for suit.

Once in power, the Radicals hastened to repeal the prohibition against interracial marriage. Thereafter, informal arrangements were sometimes legalized. In the spring of 1869, a reporter stated that three such marriages had occurred within the state — a Massachusetts man had married a Beaufort mulatto woman, and two white women had married Negro men. In 1872, the legislature explicitly recognized interracial unions by declaring that the "children of white fathers and negro mothers may inherit from the father if he did not marry another woman but continued to live with their mother."

There were a surprisingly large number of cases in which white women gave birth to children by Negro fathers. During his stay in Greenville, Bureau officer John De Forest heard of two such births and noted other instances in which white women were supported by Negro men. Such situations, he believed, were largely the result of the loss of husbands and fathers in the war and the destitution of the country generally. In 1866, in neighboring Pickens District, a case came into the courts in which Sally Calhoun, "a white woman of low birth," and a Negro man were brought to trial for the murder of their child. Ironically, the Negro was freed, though obviously implicated, and the woman was convicted and imprisoned. Apparently, some of these liaisons were far from casual as a Spartanburg farmer rather painfully suggested to his brother in Alabama: "My dear Brother as you have made several Enquiries of me and desiring me to answer them I will attempt and endeavor to do So to the best information that I have on the Various Subjects alluded to by you the first Interrogatory is Relative to John H. Lipscomb's daughter haveing Negro Children, I am forced to answer in the affirmative no doubt but she has had two; and no hopes of her Stopping. . . ."

By the end of Reconstruction, Negroes had won the legal right to enjoy, along with whites, accommodations in all public places. In reality, however, they seldom did so. On the opposite side of the racial frontier, the pattern of separation was fixed in the minds of the whites almost simultaneously with the emancipation of the Negro. By 1868, the physical color line had, for the most part, already crystallized. During the Republican regime, it was breached only in minor ways. Once the whites regained political power, there was little need to establish legally a separation which already existed in fact. Moreover, to have done so would have been contrary to federal civil rights legislation and would have given needless offense to influential elements in the North. Finally, retention of the act had a certain propaganda value for use against liberals in the North and against Republican politicians at home. Again and again, the dead letter of the law was held up as exhibit "A" in South Carolina's case that she was being fair to the Negro in the Hampton tradition [a reference to the relatively mild and paternalistic forms of racism practiced by upper-class whites, who, for many years, were led by governor, and later senator, Wade Hampton]. After the federal statute was vitiated in the courts, after racial liberalism had become all but extinct in the North, and as the Negro was totally disfranchised in South Carolina, the white community was ready and able to close the few gaps which did exist in the color line, and to codify a social order which custom had already decreed.

Ultimately, the physical separation of the races is the least important portion of the story. The real separation was not that duo-chromatic order that prevailed on streetcars and trains, or in restaurants, saloons, and cemeteries.

The real color line lived in the minds of individuals of each race, and it had achieved full growth even before freedom for the Negro was born. Physical separation merely symbolized and reinforced mental separation. It is true that vigorous assaults by one side or the other forced the enemy to yield his forward trenches and to alter slightly the precise line of the color front. It is also true that material changes in post-Reconstruction Southern society pushed the trenches into areas which had not existed before. This often gave the illusion of basic change, of a breakthrough by the dominant whites in the war of races, whereas, actually, it merely represented the extension of the old attitudinal conflict onto new ground, only to bring with it the stalemate that marked the struggle elsewhere. Viewed in relation to the total geography of race relations, the frontier hardly changed; and the rigidity of the physical situation, set as it was like a mosaic in black and white, itself suggested the intransigence of spirit which lay behind it. Well before the end of Reconstruction, this mental pattern was fixed; the heartland of racial exclusiveness remained inviolate; and South Carolina had become, in reality, two communities — one white and the other Negro.

STUDY GUIDE

1. What motives, according to the author, led Southern whites to seek segregation from their ex-slaves? Does Williamson consider these motives to be entirely rational?

2. What were the basic demands of the black leadership?

3. List the various institutions of the South in which segregation took place, and explain how.

4. Williamson draws a distinction between separation by segregation and separation by withdrawal. When did Southern whites tend to practice one and when the other?

5. Intimacy between the races does not appear to have ceased after emancipation. What evidence does the author have for this, and how does he account for it?

6. Would you, on the basic of this selection, agree that segregation began in the immediate postwar years? If so, why; if not, why not?

BIBLIOGRAPHY

The Reconstruction experience is dealt with in a number of volumes. James G. Randall and David Donald, *The Civil War and Reconstruction* (1969) is basic. More specialized are the following: Kenneth M. Stampp, *The Era of*

Reconstruction (1965); John Hope Franklin, *Reconstruction: After the Civil War* (1961); and Rembert W. Patrick, *The Reconstruction of the Nation* (1967). Studies of race relations in individual states will be found in Joel Williamson, *After Slavery: The Negro in South Carolina during Reconstruction, 1861–1877* (1965), from which the above selection was taken; Vernon C. Wharton, *The Negro in Mississippi* (1965); Herman Belz, *Emancipation and Equal Rights* (1978); and Howard Rabinowitz, *Race Relations in the Urban South* (1978). White resistance to black freedom and equality is dealt with in Allen W. Trelease, *White Terror: the Ku Klux Klan Conspiracy and Southern Reconstruction* (1971) and in Michael Perman, *Reunion without Compromise: The South and Reconstruction, 1865–1868* (1973). The institutionalization of white racism before the turn of the century is traced in the following: C. Vann Woodward, *The Strange Career of Jim Crow* (1974); Hortense Powdermaker, *After Freedom: A Cultural Study in the Deep South* (1930); John Dollard, *Caste and Class in a Southern Town* (1937); and Allison Davis, Burleigh B. Gardner, and Mary R. Gardner, *Deep South: A Social Anthropological Study of Caste and Class* (1941).